DISCOVERING
GREAT MUSIC

DISCOVERING GREAT MUSIC

A NEW LISTENER'S GUIDE TO THE TOP CLASSICAL COMPOSERS AND THEIR BEST RECORDINGS

ROY HEMMING

SECOND EDITION

NEWMARKET PRESS   NEW YORK

Second edition 1994

Copyright © 1988, 1990, 1991, 1994 by Roy Hemming

This book published simultaneously in the United States of America and in Canada.

94 95 96   10 9 8 7 6 5 4 3 2 1   PB

Library of Congress Cataloging-in-Publication Data

Hemming, Roy.
    Discovering great music : a new listener's guide to the top
classical composers and their masterworks / Roy Hemming.—2nd ed.
        p.   cm.
    Includes index.
    ISBN 1-55704-210-1
    1. Sound recordings—Collectors and collecting.
2. Sound recordings—Reviews.   3. Music—Discography.
4. Music—Bio-bibliography.   I. Title.
ML111.5.H44   1994
016.78026'6—dc20   94-26873
                                                    CIP
                                                    MN

Quantity Purchases

Companies, professional groups, clubs and other organizations may qualify for special terms when ordering quantities of this title. For information contact: Special Sales Dept., Newmarket Press, 18 East 48th Street, New York, New York 10017, or call (212) 832-3575.

Book design by Jaye Zimet/Neuwirth & Associates

Manufactured in the United States of America

This book is dedicated to the memory of my father, who, to my knowledge, attended only one concert in his life, but who encouraged me in thousands of ways to discover things he never knew.

CONTENTS

ACKNOWLEDGMENTS

Parts of this book are adapted and updated from an earlier book by the author, titled *Discovering Music: Where to Start on Records & Tapes*, which was first published in 1974. Parts are also based on scripts written by the author for the radio broadcasts of the New York Philharmonic and the Boston Symphony Orchestra between 1979 and 1991, and on his reviews and articles for *Stereo Review*, *Video Review*, *Gramophone*, *Musical America*, *Keynote*, *Ovation*, *World Week*, and *Senior Scholastic*.

The author wishes to extend deepest thanks to the following people for their invaluable counsel and assistance on various musical and editorial matters: Christie Barter, Sedgwick Clark, Donald Foster, Louise de la Fuente, Lloyd Gelassen, David Hajdu, Richard L. Kaye, Genevieve A. Kazdin, Frank Milburn, Carlos Moseley, Marvin Schofer and Loren Toolajian.

Special appreciation also goes to the following people for verification of background information and recording dates, the providing of needed review materials, and other kinds of important assistance: Alison Ames, Karen Bakst, Martin Bookspan, Mari Beth Bittan, Herbert Breslin, Tony Caronia, Margaret Carson, Peter Clancy, Kevin Copps, Charles Croce, Marilyn Egol, Tom Evered, Mary Lou Falcone, Henry Fogel, Aimee Gautreau, Bob Goldfarb, Jennifer Heinlein, Albert Imperato, Judy Janowski, George Jellinek, Alfred Kaine, Jill Kaufman, Andrew Kazdin, David Levenson, Joe McKaughan, Audrey Michaels, Karen Moody, Linda Moxley, Melanne Mueller, Grace Patti, Sheila Porter, Marilyn Posnick, Gary Reigenborn, Robert Ripps, Ellen Schantz, Constance Shuman, Caroline Smedvig, George Sponhaltz, Edgar Vincent, George Volckening, Jennifer Wada, Stewart Warkow, Robert Woods, Steve Winn, Carole Yaple, and Nancy Zannini.

A deep personal debt of gratitude must go to Eric Berger, who gave me my first professional opportunity as a reviewer, and to Morris Goldberger, who published my original *Discovering Music* book and so generously cleared the way for Newmarket's subsequent editions.

Last, but far from least, very special thanks to Esther Margolis, Theresa Burns, Clifford Crouch, and Keith Hollaman of Newmarket Press, for their crucial and always on-target guidance and nurturing of the book from its planning stages through to its publication and latest update.

INTRODUCTION

This book is *not* written for musicians or music students. It is written in simple, non-technical language for general listeners who like good music and want a guide to the best works now on records and tapes.

The recording catalogs today are filled with hundreds of thousands of listings—offering a tremendous feast to anyone who wants to indulge. But how and what does the non-expert listener choose? This book is designed as a guide for those who want to get started building their own record or tape collections, according to their own tastes.

The book is divided into three sections:

First, a brief overview (a non-technical primer, if you will) of the major formats for listening to classical music—Compact Discs (CDs), Long-Playing Records (LPs), and Cassette Tapes—plus some of the terminology the record companies and music experts like to throw around (digital, analog, etc.). This section also offers opinions, from well-known practicing musicians as well as from the author, on where a newcomer should start—and why.

Second, the book's major section, on composers from the Baroque to today's New Age, with capsule reviews of their major works as available on CDs, LPs, and Cassettes. The 50 major composers who make up the heart of this section are arranged alphabetically, for easy reference.

Third, a "Who's Who" section, providing basic information on the leading conductors, pianists, violinists, singers, and other performers whose work is available on CDs, records, and tapes today—plus a guide to the world's major orchestras.

Although LPs are no longer being manufactured by most record companies, many are still in circulation through public and college lending libraries, as well as in specialty collectors' shops in some cities. Accordingly, we continue to list the best LP editions of works recommended in Part Two. At the end of the book, company addresses are listed for your convenience in inquiring about or locating a particular recording not readily available in local stores or libraries.

At the end of the book, there is also a comprehensive glossary of musical terms.

PART ONE

"WHERE DO I START?"

"Nothing is, in a way, more exciting than a first discovery in music through listening."
—*Pianist Alexis Weissenberg*

People either love rock'n'roll or hate it. They either love country music or hate it. The same goes for various types of jazz, too. But I don't know anyone who really *hates* classical music.

Not everyone will admit that they love or even like it. Some are intimidated by all those foreign names and titles, all those B-flat-minors and F-sharp-majors, all those opus numbers. They have concluded—wrongly—that appreciating classical music requires a couple of degrees in music or musicology. Of course, there *are* some musical elitists who would have you believe that that's the case. Forget them.

One of the reasons the music of Beethoven and Bach and Mozart and Tchaikovsky and Ravel and so many others survives—and can still sell out the seats of our concert halls—is that these composers have something to say that still communicates to those who will listen.

And the means for listening have never been greater than they are today—thanks to the plentiful number of recordings of virtually every major piece composed over the past two or three centuries. Moreover, the quality of the recordings can equal (and in some cases even surpass) what you can hear in many concert halls, even from the best seats.

Through CDs, LPs, and Cassettes it is possible to hear the world's greatest orchestras and soloists at any time you wish, in any work you wish, almost anywhere you wish. But how do you go about choosing those works and performances from the hundreds of thousands that are available? My answer is a simple one: Start with the best. This book is designed to help you do just that.

WHAT IS CLASSICAL MUSIC?

Before going any further, we should consider exactly what "classical music" is. There is, after all, disagreement about that very name. To most musicians, "Classical" (usually with a capital C) refers to a specific historical period and style in Western music—essentially of the 18th century, as represented by the music of Haydn, Mozart, and others of that era. (Within that definition, *Classical* music is a distinctively formal style that is usually more advanced in harmonic content and musical structure than the *Renaissance* and *Ba-*

roque music that preceded it historically, and more emotionally restrained than the *Romantic* music that followed and dominated the 19th century.) But let's get into the specifics of different musical styles a bit later. For now, just keep in mind that the phrase "classical music" can have multiple meanings — just as jazz can mean many things (from Dixieland to swing to bop and so on), or just as "modern art" can refer to many different styles of art from cubism to expressionism to hyperrealism, and so on.

Somehow, the term "classical music" long ago attached itself to music outside the areas of popular, folk, jazz, rock, and other present-day forms. In recent years there has been a trend among some people to call it "serious music" — which I find no improvement, since you can certainly have serious jazz, serious show music, and so on. Some others label it "concert music," ignoring the fact that you can have rock concerts, jazz concerts, and so on. So I guess we are stuck with "classical music" as the most widely used and most widely understood name to describe the vast area of Western music from the 15th to the 20th centuries, written primarily for performance by classically trained musicians. But to simplify its usage in this book, the term "Classical" (with a capital C) will always refer to the 18th-century style or historical period of overall "classical" (with a lower-case "c") music.

GETTING STARTED

One of the great joys of classical music is its enormous scope. There is literally something for everyone. So you can and should seek to discover and build according to your own tastes. You may find you enjoy certain styles, or certain composers within that style, more than others. That's inevitable — and natural.

But where do you actually begin? A dozen or more years ago I conducted a series of interviews with prominent musicians as to where each of them would start a newcomer. My question to some 50 conductors, solo instrumentalists, composers, coaches, and teachers was as follows: If someone should come up to you and say, "I don't know very much about classical music, but I'd like to learn more, and I've got enough money to go out and buy five or six recordings" — what pieces would you recommend they start with? What composers or specific works or performances — and why?

I expected diversity in the answers, but not as much as I got. The basic conclusion was that there is *no* one way or one place to start, and that much depends on the individual listener. Yet most agreed that certain guidelines could be suggested—and proceeded to make their recommendations. Most also, interestingly enough, shied away from naming specific performances (particularly their own), perhaps out of professional politesse towards their colleagues.

Only one conductor flatly refused to answer the question. "You wouldn't start with records," insisted Erich Leinsdorf, former music director of the Boston Symphony and Cleveland Orchestra. "If you want to know music, you have to learn to a certain degree as an active participant. Music cannot be studied passively. You have to study music as a discipline. You must do something with your body and create rhythms. My recommendation is very simply: rhythm first, pitch next, and a recognition of musical notations."

Leinsdorf continued: "You cannot learn about music just by *listening* to compositions. You can acquire a taste or a certain amount of aesthetic sympathy and understanding, but you cannot really learn about music that way. I think music must be more than a spectator sport."

I strongly disagree. I find Leinsdorf's viewpoint much too elitist, despite his earnest and unquestionably sincere concern that new listeners get the most out of music. It is, perhaps, representative of a "clubby" attitude among some musicians that, without their always realizing it, turns many people off to classical music. When I asked Leinsdorf if he honestly expected all the people attending the particular concert he was conducting on the day of our interview to meet his standards of musical knowledge, he simply shrugged.

Fortunately, many other equally prominent musicians feel differently. Among them: pianist-conductor Daniel Barenboim, who told me, "It isn't really necessary to know a great deal about music and the way it is constructed in order to appreciate it. What makes music so universal, and gives it so powerful an impact, is that it is one of the most direct forms of human expression. It addresses itself to different people in different ways. Music can be appreciated intellectually or it can be appreciated emotionally, as when the listener gets carried away by the climaxes of a big symphony. Or perhaps it just grows on you. This is the marvelous thing about music.

"I feel a lot of people avoid concerts or classical records," continued Barenboim, "because they hear musicians talking about 'the dominant chord' or something else that sounds complicated, and they become frightened. It's a pity, because we *need* people to appreciate music in different ways, so that music can have its full impact. Once you understand that, the choice of the specific records or tapes you buy, or the music you listen to in the beginning, is relatively unimportant."

Music *is* legitimately a spectator sport for many—and not just a passively enjoyable one but an actively enlightening and stimulating one. A newcomer to classical music, therefore, should not be ashamed that he or she doesn't know all the musical terminology or all the fine points. Some of that will come from listening over a period of time. Just as you do not have to know the detailed technical workings of television transmission in order to enjoy a TV program, so it is with enjoying great music on CDs, LPs, and Cassettes.

THE CHRONOLOGICAL "SAMPLER" APPROACH

Most of the musicians of whom I asked "Where do you start?" suggested a chronological or historical "sampler" approach. This means choosing an important work from each major period of music history, thereby tracing the development of classical music in chronological sequence.

To understand the specific recommendations made within that context, let's look briefly at the major periods of music history of the past four centuries, keeping in mind that some composers overlap certain of the following periods or musical styles.

BAROQUE   Music from the period of about 1600 to 1750, in which simple instrumental and vocal music became more highly ornamented than before, and in which such written musical forms as the fugue, chaconne, passacaglia, toccata, concerto, sonata, and oratorio were developed. (For further definitions of these forms, see the glossary at the end of this book.) Among the best-known Baroque composers: Bach, Couperin, Handel, Monteverdi, Pachelbel, Scarlatti, Telemann, and Vivaldi.

CLASSICAL   Music of the period from about 1740 to 1820, in which composers developed the symphony, concerto, and other musical forms in a distinctively formal style generally characterized by emotional restraint and structural compactness. Among the best-known Classical composers: Haydn, Mozart, Beethoven, and Schubert (although the later works of the last two are actually a bridge to the next period, the Romantic).

ROMANTIC   Music of the period from about 1820 to 1910, which was characterized by the development of more openly emotional and subjective elements in musical expression, partly akin to the European Romantic movement in literature. Romantic music is often subdivided into three periods: *Early Romantic* — represented by Berlioz, Chopin, Mendelssohn, and Schumann; *Middle Romantic* — represented by Brahms, Bruckner, Dvořák, Liszt, Tchaikovsky, and Wagner; and *Late Romantic* — represented by Mahler, Rachmaninoff, and Richard Strauss.

IMPRESSIONIST   A musical style of the late-19th and early-20th centuries, which was, in effect, a reaction against Romanticism. Primarily, it is music that hints and implies rather than explicitly describes. Impressionism in music took its name from the French graphic arts movement of the same period, particularly the paintings of Manet, Monet, and Renoir. Its best-known musical exponent was France's Debussy, although some of the works of Dukas, Ravel, and Roussel in France, Griffes and Loeffler in America, Respighi in Italy, and Falla in Spain are also strongly Impressionist.

NEO-CLASSICAL Another reaction to 19th-century Romanticism, marking a return to less emotional, more abstract music with an emphasis on traditional forms, symmetry, and aesthetic ideals — but frequently with more complex rhythms and harmonies that are clearly of the 20th century (including the use of jazz rhythms and folk melodies). Among the best-known Neo-Classicists: Bartók, Copland, Hindemith, Ravel, and Stravinsky (although not *all* of their works fit into this category).

EXPRESSIONIST A relatively short-lived style of the early 20th century, principally among German and Austrian composers (notably the early works of Schoenberg, Berg, and the lesser-known Ernst Krenek). A reaction against the refinements of Impressionism, it similarly took its name from the graphic arts, and is marked by fervent emotionalism and self-expression.

SERIAL A style of 20th-century composition, originated by Schoenberg around 1925, in which the composition is based on a tone row (a series of notes) in which the notes are placed in a particular order (the row) determined by the composer as the basis for the work, with no note repeated in the row. Since every row must contain all 12 notes of the chromatic scale, such music is sometimes called *12-tone* (or *dodecaphonic*) *music*. Among the major serial composers who followed Schoenberg: Berg, Webern, Boulez.

NEO-ROMANTIC A style of 20th-century music that turns away from the essentially abstract, intellectual orientation of the Serialists and the Neo-Classicists, toward a new expressiveness or sensuousness. The American composer Jacob Druckman, who prefers to call this the "New Romanticism" (and who organized a series of festivals around it for the New York Philharmonic in 1984 and 1986), defines it as music that "reaches backwards and forward simultaneously" and that emphasizes the "re-emergence of mystery, nostalgia, ecstasy, and transcendency." Among such Neo-Romantic composers: Samuel Barber, John Corigliano, David Del Tredici, Joseph Schwantner, and Joan Tower (again, for some but not all of their works).

MINIMALIST A style that emerged in the 1970s, in which the repetition of rhythmic pulses or simple musical patterns is emphasized throughout the course of a composition — often in steady, undulating phrases that pass through different regions of colors and moods. The style, sometimes also called *Neo-Primitivism*, is a reaction to the often-complex music of Serialism and earlier forms. Among the major minimalists: Steve Reich, Philip Glass, John Adams. Minimalism is sometimes linked, not always accurately, with so-called "New Age" music, which generally combines electronic and acoustic sounds in ways that reflect certain aspects (often ambient) of jazz, rock and classical music.

Sampling a work or two from each of these groups would certainly give an overview of the *breadth* of classical music, if only a taste of the *depth* available within most of them. In endorsing this kind of sampling by a newcomer, one of this century's foremost composer-conductors, Pierre Boulez, told me, "I cannot tell you exactly what works [to start with], because there are so many which are very important. But I would recommend a succession of works which would show the evolution of music. That way you could compare, for example, some 20th-century work with, let's say, a 16th-century work. Ideally, I would try to pick something that's important in each period. I would begin with a Baroque work, perhaps the *Vespers* of Monteverdi, and continue on with Mozart and Beethoven, on through a work by Berg or Stravinsky."

Another composer-conductor, Stanislaw Skrowaczewski (for many years music director of the Minnesota Orchestra), suggests not just sampling a work in each style, but also looking into how different composers changed or grew *within* those individual styles. "I would say, first of all," Skrowaczewski told me, "that you should try to get recordings with historical significance—and *in* historical sequence. That way you can see the style of certain periods, how long it was maintained, and what happened when someone else went beyond this style—and, finally, when it comes down to our own times, where no style is more important than another. For example, within Haydn's lifetime you also have Mozart—and there's such a big change between Mozart's first and last works. Then you have, similarly, important changes between the first and last works of Beethoven. For the Romantics, I would suggest one of Schumann's symphonies and certainly some Wagner. Then I would suggest seeing what happened with Debussy and Stravinsky, to see the different roads composers have taken in our own century. With Stravinsky, here again, there is so much change between his early and later works."

"I'd start with Bach first," says Sheldon Morgenstern, founder and music director for the past 20 years of the Eastern Music Festival and Music Camp in Greensboro, North Carolina. "I think that anyone from the generation that's grown up with rock will find some of the things he or she associates with rock inherent in Bach. Then they can go on to try other styles, such as a Classical symphony by Beethoven, a Romantic symphony or concerto by Tchaikovsky, and, certainly, something by a 20th-century American, either Copland's *Appalachian Spring* suite or his Third Symphony."

"I'd start with some crossover-type recording," says Leonard Slatkin, conductor of the Saint Louis Symphony Orchestra. "Perhaps a popular artist like Bob James playing Rameau or Scarlatti in a quite serious manner. That might get someone excited enough to want to hear the original. Then, from there, I'd try different composers from different periods, for an overview."

In choosing an important work from each period, says the Dutch conductor Bernard Haitink, be forewarned that "you may not like it all at first. But you should try to see what you *do* like and what you *don't* like." Haitink specifically suggests "one of the works of Bach, one of Mozart, one of Beethoven, one of Mahler, one of Debussy, and one of either Bartók or Stravinsky."

This chronological "sampler" approach is neat, logical, and comprehensive. But it is only *one* of the ways to discover classical music.

THE REVERSE CHRONOLOGICAL APPROACH

While agreeing with a "sampler" approach, there are some who prefer not to go in chronological sequence but, rather, just the opposite.

"I would start off with modern music," the Viennese-American pianist Hilde Somer told me. "I think music that has a beat or dissonance or folk roots will be easier for someone weaned on rock and country music. People who don't know too much about music may relate better if there is something else that involves them. So I would suggest starting with something with words, such as Copland's *A Lincoln Portrait*, or with something that has a folk element, like Copland's *El Salon Mexico*. Then I'd suggest Stravinsky's *The Rite of Spring*, for the rhythm, and that wonderful Moog Synthesizer recording called *The Well-Tempered Synthesizer*, which includes works by Bach, Handel, Monteverdi, and others, played on a modern electronic instrument. I think it's fascinating to hear such a combination of the old and the modern. It will introduce younger newcomers, especially, to some great old music in an interesting, contemporary way. Then they can investigate the original versions."

The American pianist Misha Dichter also told me that he believes starting with something contemporary and working backwards to older styles can be effective for younger newcomers. "Judging by the remarks of young people who come backstage after concerts, they seem to single out the 20th-century piece on the program, saying 'I particularly liked the Stravinsky-this or the Bartók-that.' So I feel they *do* relate more to the 20th century." Dichter went on to stress, however, that somewhere on the list there should also be works by Mahler, Beethoven, and Bach.

THE POPULAR PILLARS APPROACH

Completely disagreeing with both of these approaches, however, is Christian Steiner, the Berlin-born pianist and photographer (best-known for his photos of musicians on many CDs, LPs, and Cassettes). "I am in violent disagreement with those people who think you have to have one piece from the Baroque period, one piece from the Classical, one from the Romantic, and so forth," he told me. "A newcomer may get a good view of music overall, but I don't believe that's the way to start to *love* music. And loving music is, actually, what the result should be."

Instead, Steiner suggests, start with music that is "the easiest to understand, the easiest to listen to, and the easiest to like immediately. It should be music that stimulates you to listen to *more* music, that is so compelling that someone who has not listened to classical music before has the urge to go on. Take Orff's *Carmina Burana*, for example. Here's a work that's primitive, powerful, and rhythmic. A new listener might say, 'Oh, so *that* belongs to that so-called highbrow music. Well, then, I'm going to listen to more.' The incentive has to be there. The work has to be appealing. Even if, later on, you decide you can't stand the piece anymore after the tenth hearing, it's still a good work to start with, I think."

Starting with likeable, popular concert works was also the preferred approach of others whom I interviewed. As the pianist Tamas Vasary put it: "I believe in popularity. If a work holds onto its popularity over the years, it means it is something special, something really of genius. I think every composer dreams of writing striking tunes, striking rhythms, or striking moments which will be remembered for years and years by others. Almost anyone can learn how to compose a prelude and fugue or a sonata—but what really makes the difference, what makes people react to it, you cannot always tell. If you asked me *why* do I like my favorite pieces, I could probably talk to you about the structure, or the harmonic progression, or things like that. But that's not why it might appeal to *you*. It's exactly like one's reaction to someone of the opposite sex. A person someone sees as attractive may seem less so to someone else, or less lovable. The difference is that, in music, the whole public falls in love with certain works. And the public is, as a whole, a marvelous critic—a better critic than we, as individual musicians, often are."

An enthusiastic supporter of starting with well-known and popular works is Harry Ellis Dickson, longtime associate conductor of the Boston Pops and the father of Kitty Dukakis, wife of the former Governor of Massachusetts (and presidential candidate). "I'd start with *the* most popular piece of all the symphonic literature: Beethoven's Fifth Symphony," Dickson told me. "Then I'd try Mozart's 'Jupiter' Symphony, because there's a grandeur about the style that foretells what Beethoven is going to do, so there's an interesting connection there. If the newcomer is American, I'd suggest something by Aaron Copland—his *A Lincoln Portrait*, which embodies a great deal of both Copland and Americana, and it's a great example of what a composer can do with words. Then, perhaps, the 'Pathètique' Symphony of Tchaikovsky. How can anyone not like Tchaikovsky?"

Tchaikovsky also headed the list of pianist Van Cliburn. "I believe a newcomer can get a great deal of pleasure, and learn a lot about musical form and different rhythmic patterns, from Tchaikovsky's Sixth Symphony, the 'Pathètique,'" he told me. "It has a great deal of melody. It has rhythmic variation. And it has something that, when you get through listening to it, you will want desperately to hear again. To me, that is the first thing to learn about classical music: that when something is classic, it is enduring—that it stands endless rehearing. There is no such thing as being bored with a great piece of music."

Other long-popular works by Tchaikovsky were also frequently named by other musicians I interviewed. For example, Tchaikovsky's Fourth Symphony was among the works suggested by pianist Vladimir Ashkenazy. His Fifth Symphony was among those named by pianist John Browning, his Piano Concerto No. 1 by pianist Malcolm Frager, and his *Romeo and Juliet* Overture-Fantasy by pianist David Bean. Obviously, Tchaikovsky ranks highly with this cross-section of present-day pianists. But, most significantly, the Tchaikovsky works they chose are all among the most popular in the entire concert repertory—so I'd say it's that popularity, and the accessibility of these works to the average listener, that led to their being chosen by these musicians.

Many other pillars of the repertory were also repeatedly named—including Beethoven's Third (the "Eroica") and Fifth symphonies (conductors Karl Böhm, Dean Dixon, and Joseph Silverstein), Bach's Brandenburg Concertos (pianist Ruth Laredo and singers Evelyn Lear and Thomas Stewart), Beethoven's Fifth Piano Concerto (pianists Vladimir Ashkenazy and Malcolm Frager), Mendelssohn's Violin Concerto (violinist Jaime Laredo), Chopin's *Nocturnes* (pianist Christoph Eschenbach), Debussy's *La Mer* (conductor Charles Mackerras), Stravinsky's *Firebird* (pianist Byron Janis and conductor André Kostelanetz), and Bartók's Concerto for Orchestra (pianist-conductor Christoph Eschenbach). And that's only part of the list. The point is that, time and time again, these prominent musicians turned to established, time-tested masterworks.

That applied to operatic works as much as to the symphonic repertory. For example, soprano Leontyne Price told me, "I'd suggest something by Verdi—and you just can't beat his *Aida*. You can always hum Verdi's tunes, and that's a good start. I would then suggest works that not only make a lasting impression but also leave a desire to hear more. Therefore, I can't leave out Puccini. I really think his *Madame Butterfly* is ideal for someone who has not been exposed to much opera. It's the sort of thing that can whet the appetite."

A relevant digression concerning opera: For a newcomer, which is better—to start with a complete opera or with a highlights album of selected scenes? Sopranos Leontyne Price and Anna Moffo both favor the highlights approach. "If a newcomer hasn't been exposed to anything before, I think highlights will suffice. They provide the main background, and they perhaps whet the appetite for more," says Price. Adds Moffo: "There are, let's admit it, a lot of dead places in a lot of operas, such as *Carmen*. So I'd pick a highlights album—for a beginner, that is."

Another great American soprano, Phyllis Curtin, disagrees. "I'm not a believer in highlights," she told me. "If someone listens just to highlights, he or she is never going to know what an opera is. An opera is living, honest-to-God, hot, breathing theater—which is a point so many Americans forget. They want to listen only to arias, and they forget that opera is connected to real life. Take a work like Puccini's *La Bohème*. It's about people who are not unlike today's younger generation—people who are looking for something, young people beginning life and finding out about its beauties, its futilities, its terrible agonies. A newcomer, I feel, should listen to *all* of it, not just excerpts."

And so, once again, we find widely divergent viewpoints among knowledgeable professionals. I myself favor the highlights approach for most operas, especially *Carmen* and, without question, most of Wagner's—for most newcomers. But there are exceptions, and *La Bohème* is certainly one of them. I'd add Puccini's *Tosca* and *Turandot*, too—in which the music and the drama are so tightly linked that no set of excerpts can ever match the impact of the entire work. Moreover, if you're listening on records or tapes, you can follow along with the libretto (which is included in virtually every CD, LP, and Cassette of an opera today)—and really savor the relationship between the music and words.

THE MOVIE-CONNECTION APPROACH

Over the years, many major motion pictures have appropriated pieces of classical music for their principal background scores. One of the most famous is the 1967 Swedish award-winner *Elvira Madigan*, which catapulted the slow movement of Mozart's Piano Concerto No. 21 in C major into an international hit—and helped turn pianist Geza Anda (whose recording was used on the soundtrack) into a major concert celebrity. There are many more examples—such as Pachelbel's *Kanon* in D major in *Ordinary People* (1980), the Adagietto from Mahler's Fifth Symphony in *Death in Venice*

(1971), the opening "Sunrise" section of Richard Strauss's *Also Sprach Zarathustra* in *2001: A Space Odyssey* (1968), a theme from Delibes' *Lakme* in *The Hunger* (1983), and Puccini arias in *A Room with a View* (1986), *The Witches of Eastwick* (1987), and *Fatal Attraction* (1987).

The practice goes back to the earliest days of film soundtracks. For example, in the 1932 version of Hemingway's *A Farewell to Arms*, Gary Cooper and Helen Hayes play their final scene while the *Liebestod* from Wagner's *Tristan and Isolde* throbs behind them. And it was to the principal theme of Tchaikovsky's Piano Concerto No. 1 that Bette Davis and Mary Astor battled royally, soap-opera style, in *The Great Lie* (1941).

The late 1930s and early 1940s were probably the peak years for movies actually built around the lives of classical composers. Johann Strauss was the subject of *The Great Waltz* (1938), Schubert of *New Wine* (1943), Chopin of *A Song to Remember* (1945), and Schumann of *Song of Love* (1947). They were all highly fictionalized and romanticized, but they did introduce some of each composer's great works to moviegoers of their day — and still do through their television showings. The same applies to Ken Russell's more recent (and often more wildly subjective) film studies of Tchaikovsky in *The Music Lovers* (1970), of *Mahler* (1970), and Liszt in *Lisztomania* (1975), as well as several European-made TV miniseries on Verdi and Wagner which have had PBS showings in the United States. And Mozart and his rival Salieri came to life vividly (if not always accurately) in Milos Forman's 1984 *Amadeus*.

The point is that if you've seen these movies and liked the music in them, then make those pieces the starting points for a home record or tape collection. Some of the soundtracks of these films are available on records and tapes, as are compilations of famous classical themes that have been used in films over the years. Start with them and then investigate other, full-length, works by the same or similar composers.

Unlike people who have grown up with rock music and who tend to be attracted at first to either contemporary classical styles or Baroque music, people who grew up with the movies of the 1930s, 1940s, and 1950s are usually more attuned to Romantic or Impressionist classical music — for those are the styles that were most openly imitated by the composers of Hollywood's background scores in that period. One of the most famous of those Hollywood composers, Dimitri Tiomkin, brought down the house during his Oscar acceptance speech in 1954 for *The High and the Mighty* when he wryly and unabashedly extended his thanks to Brahms, Strauss, Tchaikovsky, Rimsky-Korsakov, Ravel, and many others from whom, he said, he and others had been borrowing for years.

It is a fairly easy jump from the predominantly Romantic movie scores of Tiomkin, Korngold, Steiner, Waxman, Newman, and others to the Romantic symphonies, concertos, and tone poems of Rachmaninoff, Strauss, Grieg, Dvorak, Liszt, and others.

THE FAVORITE PERFORMER APPROACH

One other similar approach for a classical newcomer is collecting the recordings of performers you have seen in the movies, on television, or in concerts. The pianist Alexis Weissenberg put it this way to me: "I would try to get not so much certain composers as the right performers. For example, I think it appropriate to consider the image of certain artists such as Leonard Bernstein or Herbert von Karajan, who have done so much television work. I think whatever symphony you get by Bernstein or Karajan is more important at the beginning than who the composer is. It brings people closer to the music because they have *seen* the performer in action. It's unbelievable how much you can bring music *up* to people if they know something about the artist producing it."

Pianist Malcolm Frager expressed a similar view to me. "The *right* performer is terribly important," he said, "because if the performer isn't able to recreate the mood of the music so that the listener instinctively feels it, the music is going to be dead. It's just as important to get the right performance by the right performer as it is the right work."

GOING YOUR OWN WAY

I hope all these divergent views on just *where* to start have not made you think, wrongly, that getting to know classical music is more complicated than it is — and contradictory. Rather, I hope it has underscored one of my basic beliefs: There is no one right way for a newcomer to get started. Just as everyone doesn't have to like the same books or films or TV shows, so you should decide for yourself just what music you want for your own collection — and build it to please *yourself*, not anyone else.

But, in starting out, I believe it's important — and also fun — to look into and listen to *all* types of classical music, from a wide cross-section of composers. In some parts of the country, that's easy to do by tuning in to classical FM radio stations, and checking over their program guides (if they publish one), perhaps with this book as your "pilot." Or you can investigate the recordings section of your local public or college library. Best of all, of course, is attending live concerts by symphony orchestras in your area — or recitals, chamber music programs, or opera performances. Then buy for your own collection those works you feel you want to get to know better or will most enjoy hearing again and again. You may discover that you particularly enjoy the Baroque music of Bach, Vivaldi, and their contemporaries, and cannot relate as readily to the heavier Romanticism of Brahms or Schumann. Or vice versa. Then, too, you may like one Baroque composer but not another. Or one Romantic and Impressionist composer, but not others.

Just remember that in *trying* all types of music, there's no requirement that you like it all. No one ever does—not even all the professional musicians who play it. After investigating certain works, there's no disgrace in deciding they're not for you. That's one of the greatest joys of classical music—that its scope is so broad it can accommodate individual likes and dislikes. What's important is that you make your music discoveries your own.

WHAT TO LISTEN FOR

I've heard some newcomers to classical music say that they are not sure exactly *what* to listen for when they try a piece of classical music for the first time. The answer, of course, depends on the piece and the tastes of the individual listener.

With some works, for example, you may be immediately drawn to the principal theme or melody—to its innate beauty or expressiveness. With some other works, it may be the arresting rhythm or the colorful orchestration. Of course, it can be a combination of all these. Or it may be the way a composer takes a simple theme and develops it into something more dramatically complex or even epic.

With some pieces, especially a Romantic work, there may be a specific story that the composer has set to music. Usually, a synopsis of the story is included in the liner notes of all recordings of the piece. For example, most of Richard Strauss's tone poems and symphonies (*Don Quixote*, *Till Eulenspiegel's Merry Pranks*, *Alpine* Symphony, etc.), have fairly detailed plots that the music is designed to depict and which the listener can fairly easily follow.

Many other pieces have more subtle (or less specific) tales to relate— pieces for which the composer has provided only an outline and then left it up to the individual listener to fill in the details according to his or her own imagination. Among such works: Berlioz's *Symphonie Fantastique*, Rimsky-Korsakov's *Scheherazade*, Mussorgsky's *A Night on Bald Mountain*, or Smetana's *The Moldau*. There can be almost as many scenarios for each of these works as there are listeners.

Ballet scores also usually have specific stories attached to them, such as Tchaikovsky's *Nutcracker* or Stravinsky's *Firebird*. Again, these stories can vary from production to production (as the annual Christmas-season TV versions of *The Nutcracker* attest). If you've seen a ballet production of the piece you're listening to, you already have a visual image to spur along what you're hearing. If not, let your imagination take over — within the guidelines of the synopsis provided with the recording.

With Impressionistic music, such as Debussy's *Nocturnes* or Respighi's *Pines of Rome*, the music will not paint a specific picture so much as it conveys the mood of a scene, or a general feeling. Once again, the reaction is individual. It's up to your own imagination.

Classical symphonies and concertos and most Baroque works are usually more abstract in their designs. The individual movements of such works are usually set in differing tempos, often from fast and rhythmic to slow and lyrical. Trained musicians may follow the thematic development of such movements and the way in which different themes are utilized or transformed within the formal structure of the work. But untrained listeners can bypass these aspects of the work and enjoy the principal melodies or rhythms for themselves — and can also, without technical expertise, almost always sense the basic spirit or feeling of the work, from joyful to melancholic, from playful to tragic, and so on.

With some Late Romantic or Neo-Classical works, such as the symphonies of Mahler or Shostakovich, it is possible to read into them complex psychological interpretations. In Shostakovich's case, for example, some annotators have sensed the brooding despair of the Soviet Union under Stalin during those years in which Shostakovich composed some of his symphonies. Others see more personal and less political interpretations involving a lonely man battling all kinds of complex forces around him. Both interpretations (and still others) are possible, depending on the orientation of the listener.

In other words, even with a non-programmatic work, it's possible to "hear" whatever you want to hear — from the silly to the profound, from the sublime to the ridiculous. As with just about everything about classical music, it's up to you.

WHICH FORMAT: CD, LP, OR CASSETTE?

Before looking into the major works of the foremost composers, a few words are in order about the different formats in which recordings of those works are available today.

LONG-PLAYING RECORDS (LPs)

Most people know about long-playing records or discs (LPs), which have been around for both classical and popular music since the late 1940s. These circular vinyl platters, usually twelve inches in diameter, contain tiny grooves (sometimes called microgrooves) into which the musical sounds have been electronically "pressed." Each side of the disc usually holds up to a half hour of music. When the disc revolves on a turntable (usually at 33⅓ revolutions per minute, although sometimes at 16 or 45 for certain kinds), a sound pick-up device (most commonly called a needle, but more correctly a stylus) travels through the record grooves and transmits a sound signal to an amplifier and loudspeaker system.

Long-playing records come in either monophonic (frequently abbreviated as mono) or stereophonic (stereo) sound. On a mono disc, a single sound signal is printed on the record, to be reproduced through the phonograph system. On a stereo disc, two sound signals are printed within the channels of the disc, to be reproduced and directed to two different speakers. Stereo discs originated in the mid-1950s. Until that time, all recordings were monaural—including the older shellac discs (which usually played at 78 revolutions per minute, and are thus known to old-time collectors as "78s"). Beginning in the 1960s, some originally monophonic recordings have been doctored electronically to simulate stereo with varying degrees of success. Terms such as "electronically enhanced" or "electronically reprocessed" can usually be found on the labels of such discs. By the late 1960s, monophonic releases of classical recordings had been phased out, except for the reissues of historic old mono recordings.

In 1972, the record industry sought to go a step or two beyond stereo, and quadraphonic releases began to be issued by a few companies. On these, *four* sound signals were printed within the channels of the disc, to be reproduced and directed to four different speakers for a supposedly more lifelike listening ambience. But quadraphonic (or quad, as it was nicknamed) never caught on. Most record buyers considered it merely an attempt by the equipment manufacturers to sell additional speakers, amplifiers, and so on—and said that so long as they only had two ears stereo would continue to suit them just fine.

Over the years, the sound quality ("fidelity") of commercial recordings has continued to improve. Sound engineers talk in terms of cycles per second (cps) and frequency range. Whereas the average mono recording of the 1940s could reproduce a frequency range of up to about 10,000 cps, those made in the mid-1950s could reproduce nearly 20,000—going beyond the range of normal human hearing. This was what was meant at that time as high fidelity, or hi-fi. When stereo LPs appeared in the 1950s, refinements continued to be made in the frequency-range capacity of discs.

But the main advantage of stereo engineering was in "spreading" the sound more realistically between the two channels, and in positioning certain sounds more naturally and distinctly within the total sound fabric (such as violins in relation to cellos in an orchestra, or singers on different parts of the stage in an opera).

As refinements continued to be made in the sound quality of both recordings and playback equipment, the term "sonic showpiece" or "sound-buster" came into wider use for certain classical works as well as for rock and pop music. Works by Stravinsky, Ravel, Mahler, Strauss, Respighi, Tchaikovsky, and others that tested the limits of recording techniques (and one's own stereo playback system) became worldwide bestsellers.

TAPES: FROM REEL-TO-REEL TO CASSETTE

Meanwhile, various tape systems had entered the scene to compete with discs. First, back in the 1950s, came reel-to-reel tape recordings. Essentially, these involved a seven-inch reel of magnetic tape (a quarter of an inch wide) onto which the sounds were magnetically "printed." To play such a tape, the listener threads the tape into a playback machine (a tape deck), so that the reel of tape feeds onto another reel. Reel-to-reel tape recordings are either "half-track stereo" or "quarter-track stereo." "Half-track" means that the tape contains two channels of recorded sound, each one taking up half of the tape's width. Accordingly, the tape may be played only in one direction, and then must be rewound for replaying. "Quarter-track" tapes involve the use of four channels of recorded sound across the surface of the tape, with each channel taking up a quarter of the tape's width. The playback "head" is so arranged that the sounds in channels one and three go in one direction, and the sounds in channels two and four in the other. The tape can thus be played in both directions, merely by turning over the reels, just as one turns over a disc. Since this, in effect, doubles the playing time, quarter-track tapes came into much wider use for home listening in the early 1960s. (Half-track recording continues, however, to be preferred by recording engineers and is still used for the professional taping of most symphony orchestras' broadcast-concerts in the United States.)

Despite claims that reel-to-reel tapes offered superior fidelity and longer wear than discs, reel-to-reel failed to catch on with the public at large or to seriously challenge discs among the buyers of recorded music. Too many people feared they would become hopelessly entangled in yards of loose or broken tape in threading a tape into the player.

What really did make a dent in disc sales, however, was the introduction of tape cartridges in the early 1960s and tape cassettes in the late 1960s, both of them by-products of the miniaturization revolution in electronics. Both formats were significantly easier to handle than reel-to-reel tapes, with no complicated threading necessary. The cartridge or cassette could just be snapped into a playback machine and played.

The cartridge started out as a system for automobiles and caught on to such a degree that, by 1966, dashboard-model cartridge players were being offered as optional equipment on all Detroit-manufactured cars. The cartridge itself was a plastic container about the size of a paperback book. It contained a continuous coil or loop of tape (a quarter of an inch wide) that automatically started to roll when the cartridge was inserted into the playback slot—and repeated the program continuously until the cartridge was removed. One of the drawbacks of the cartridge system, however, was that all the tracks had to be the same length, resulting in automatic track-shifting at unnatural places in the music—a throwback to the old 78-rpm days of shellac discs when side "breaks" frequently came in the middle of symphonic movements or any longer selection. Furthermore, cartridge players were generally not equipped with rewind or fast-forward capabilities. Therefore, if you stopped a piece of music midway through, you had to begin at the same midway spot the next time you played the cartridge.

Such drawbacks eventually doomed the cartridge in relation to the cassette. The cassette system had already made a big impact in Western Europe (where Philips, the giant Dutch electrical and electronic complex, developed it) before it started catching on in the U.S. in the early 1970s. As with quarter-track reel-to-reel tapes, the stereo signal on cassettes is arranged in four miniature channels across the surface of the tape (two channels in each direction), so that the tape can be played in both directions merely by turning over the cassette. Fast-forward and fast-rewind capabilities also make it possible (in combination with the cassette player's index counter) to play or replay selected parts of the tape at will. Like the cartridge, the cassette had its first success in automobiles—where it, too, allowed drivers and their passengers to hear their own choice of music, with the sound output remaining constant, without fading in and out the way car radios do because of atmospheric conditions, geographic range, the interference of bridges, tunnels, and so on. The further compactness of cassettes in relation to cartridges (four cassettes fit into one cartridge box) also made cassettes more popular. By the mid-1970s, cartridges were obsolete.

What really put cassettes over, however, was the introduction of portable, combination transistor radio/cassette players that operated via either an electrical outlet or a battery-pack. Suddenly anyone could have the music he or she wanted virtually anywhere—in the backyard, in the laundry room, on the street, on the beach, anywhere one chose. As antagonism grew to the abuses some people made of transistorized "boom boxes" (usually by blasting disco music or other pop styles in public places to the annoyance of lovers of other kinds of music), so-called "personal stereos" or Walkmans entered the scene—with earphones to keep the musical selections private to the specific listener. Soon lovers of all kinds of music, including classical music, were buying cassettes to play not only in their cars but on buses and trains or on the street. Listening to recordings was no longer limited to the room with the phonograph or audio system.

Significantly, the sound quality of cassettes has grown over the past 20 years to the point where it equals that of most LPs. Much, of course, depends on the quality of the playback equipment through which the cassette itself is heard, and on the quality of the original tape and its formulation. However, cassette tapes are subject to a certain amount of tape hiss and, because of the slow speed (1⅞ inches per second) at which the tape moves, occasional flutter. Such technical improvements as Dolby "noise reduction" have sought to minimize these distractions, and, by and large, have done so satisfactorily for the vast majority of listeners.

ENTER THE CD

But the biggest revolution in home listening since the LP has been the introduction in the 1980s of the Compact Disc, or CD. This is an outgrowth of the advancements made over the past 25 years in computer technology —especially in the use of computer chips to process sound digitally and the storing of digital data on laser-read discs.

Even before CDs made their international debut in 1982, the major recording companies had begun to use digital computer technology for recording. The phrase "Digital Recording" began to appear on the covers and labels of both LPs and Cassettes in the late 1970s. All this meant, however, was that digital equipment was used for the original recording sessions. For the LP or Cassette of that recording, the digital data on the master would be converted to what is called an analog signal (in oversimplified terms, a continuous electrical waveform), which had been the standard audio technology up to then. The only thing that was digital (and therefore arguably superior to earlier recordings, as the ads claimed) was the original recording, *not* the LP or Cassette you bought in the store. But the coming of the CD brought the superior digital technology directly to the recording to be played at home and the equipment on which to play it.

All the major record companies have agreed on a simple code, now printed on their CD packaging, which indicates whether a recording is digital or analog, or a combination of the two. This three-letter code (which uses only two symbols—D for digital and A for analog) identifies the type of equipment used in (1) the original recording session, (2) the editing and/ or "mixing" of the original recording, and (3) the making of the "master" from which the recording has been manufactured. As used in that 1-2-3 sequence, the code translates as follows:

D D D: Digital equipment used for (1) recording, (2) editing and/or mixing, and (3) mastering.

A D D: Analog equipment used for (1) recording, but digital equipment used for (2) editing and/or mixing and (3) mastering.

A A D: Analog equipment used for (1) recording and (2) editing and/or mixing, but digital equipment used for (3) mastering.

As for the CD disc itself, its only similarity to an LP is that it's a circular disc — but much smaller than an LP (about 5 inches in diameter, compared with an LP's 12). The music on a CD is played through a wholly new technology of laser optics and digitally stored information (akin to computer information storage), whereby the musical signal encoded within the CD is converted through a finely focused laser beam into a kind of wave form that can be transmitted electronically to an amplifier and speakers.

Without going into the technical wizardry that achieves all this, what makes CDs so appealing is the clearly superior sound quality that can result and the "push-button" ease of playing them. Whereas LPs can be scratched (and thus permanently damaged) or audibly affected by dust collecting within their grooves, the thin but hardy outer coating on CDs protects the musical data within the disc from most normal forms of wear and tear or mishandling.

Once a CD is inserted into a CD player, there is no need to set a tone arm or stylus as with an LP turntable. That's done automatically by the CD player. What if, let's say, the disc contains several different selections and you don't want to start with the first one, but rather want to hear only the second and fourth? You simply punch in tracks 2 and 4 on the CD player's remote-control panel — and those are the tracks that will play. (Or if you prefer to play them in reverse order, you merely punch in 4 and 2.) On most classical CDs, the individual movements of symphonies, concertos, suites, etc., are coded for easy access and individual playing, so that you can "program" the contents of the disc in any sequence you wish.

The sound of CDs is considerably quieter and "cleaner" than that of either LPs or Cassettes. Especially if the music has been recorded digitally, there is no tape hiss, no surface noise or clicks, none of the slight musical distortion that afflicts the inner grooves of LPs. There is also a greater dynamic range to the sound, which means you will hear louder "louds" and softer "softs," as well as a wider frequency response for higher "highs" and lower "lows." Even with older recordings transferred to CD, you should be able to hear more than you could of the same performance on an LP or Cassette.

However, don't believe the myth that CD discs are indestructible. They aren't. Although the lifespan of a CD under normal circumstances should be much longer than that of LPs or Cassettes (which degrade a bit with each playing), certain kinds of dirt on a CD surface can throw off the laser's beam in reading the musical data within the disc. Intense heat (such as leaving a CD on top of a radiator) can cause warpage and other damage.

By the end of the 1980s, CDs had caught on so extensively that many stores cut back or eliminated their LP sections in order to stock more and more CDs. By 1992 new LPs were no longer being pressed by most record companies. But existing LPs continue to be available in specialty stores in some cities, as well as in public and college lending libraries.

CDs should remain the dominant format in the '90s for home listening of classical music, and will even rival the popularity of Cassettes for automobiles and Walkman-type "personal stereos." That doesn't mean other formats won't come along and be touted as superior by their developers. For a while in the early '90s, Sony's digital audio tape (DAT) promised to bring Cassette recording and playback up to the sonic level of a CD. But DAT has failed to make significant inroads in the U.S. (except in professional recording studios)—partly because its smaller, expensive cassettes require the purchase of a separate player-recorder, and partly because most record companies have refused to license their recordings for DAT unless an anti-copying chip is added, because of fears that DAT's superfidelity would prompt prospective buyers to copy their friends' recordings instead of buying their own, thereby slashing sales and rightful royalties to the creative artists.

Then in 1991, Philips previewed its new Digital Compact Cassette (DCC) format, whose tapes are the same size as conventional Cassettes and whose player-recorder can play both DCC *and* conventional Cassettes. DCC tapes include, however, an anti-copying chip that prevents making more than one digitally perfect copy. Sony, to compete with Philips, then unveiled still another new format: the Mini Disc (MD). About half the size of CDs and therefore not compatible with existing CD players, an MD machine can also record as well as play back—up to about the same 75 minutes as a standard CD. Like DCC, the MD includes an anti-copying chip. But with the unsettled economic conditions of recent years, DDCs and MDs have been slow to catch on, and electronic industry forecasters remain divided on whether either format can eventually dislodge CDs from their present supremacy.

Meanwhile, thousands and thousands of recordings of great music now exist in CD, LP, and Cassette formats, beckoning for listeners to discover them and enjoy them. No generation of music lovers has ever had it so good. Which brings me back to a point I made earlier: that a newcomer should start with *the best*—specifically, the best available recordings of works you already know and like *and* the best available recordings of works you'd like to get to know. The next section of this book is designed to help you do just that.

PART TWO

THE GREAT COMPOSERS AND THEIR MAJOR WORKS ON CDs, LPs, AND CASSETTES

HOW TO USE THIS SECTION

Any basic music list can never hope to please everyone. Musical tastes are quite individual—and *should* be. But for those seeking general guidance about the greatest composers and their works, this section seeks to provide concise, pertinent information in non-technical language.

The composers discussed in this section represent those generally recognized today as major figures, those most often featured on concert programs. They are arranged alphabetically, for easy reference. An introductory chapter on early music is also included, as well as two postscript chapters—the first on an additional "Noteworthy Dozen" and the second on the contemporary scene (including New Age).

For each of the 50 major composers in this section, there is, first, a thumbnail **biographical sketch**, followed by suggestions of several of that composer's **best works to start with**—including a brief descriptive note about each piece.

In contrast to many "basic library" listings in magazines or newspapers, which often list just *one* recommended recording for each work (and don't tell you *why* it has been selected), you'll find in this section recommendations for the **two best CDs, two best LPs, and two best Cassettes** for most works. This not only provides an alternative choice if the first recommendation is out of stock or otherwise unavailable in your area; it also gives you concise critical evaluations as to how the two versions may differ. In all cases, the *first* recording listed is the author's first choice.

In most cases, the author's recommendations favor the *best-sounding* performance as well as the best interpretation of a given work. No recording is recommended, however, unless the quality of the interpretation is worthy. In those instances where an older, less sonically up-to-date version is given preference over a better-sounding later recording, the reasons are stated in the comments that follow the listing.

Each recommendation also includes **the year the recording was made**. This date can be important because orchestras, conductors, and soloists sometimes make more than one recording of the same work. (There is usually only a five-year "statute of limitations" in recording contracts prohibiting re-recording the same work for the same or another company.) Record companies also sometimes re-couple previously released works to improve sales prospects, so knowing the date can be helpful in making sure you get the correct version. (The term "coupling" refers to the combining of the featured work with another work to make full use of the playing time available on a disc or cassette.) Wherever actual recording dates were not confirmable through the record company involved, the year given is the one in which the recording was first released. Classical recordings are usually released within one to two years after the recording session. If a date could not be confirmed, that fact is so stated.

Important **vintage recordings** of some works are also noted among the comments, for the benefit of those listeners willing to tolerate dated recorded sound occasionally for the benefit of an outstanding musical performance. As the English critic Peter Gammond has written about one such vintage recording, "Even the miracle of CD cannot make 30-year-old sound seem modern, so the grey hairs are there, but nothing that really interferes with the excellence of the performance." Such a statement is true of many gems still in the active catalog.

Speaking of the active catalog, recordings are sometimes deleted from a current Schwann catalog or the MUZE computer indexes available in most record stores as new recordings are added or as rights change hands. Such changes occur every year in the record business. If a record store tells you a specific recording that you seek is no longer in the catalog and cannot be ordered, you might wish to check out a specialized collectors' shop in your area. Among the best-known for contacting by mail are: Berkshire Records, RR1, Lee, MA 01238; Princeton Record Exchange, 20 Tulane St., Princeton, NJ. 08542; The Record Collector, 1158 N. Highland, Los Angeles, CA 90038.

On the other hand, if a store tells you it doesn't have, and cannot get, a recording that *is* in the current Schwann catalog, don't give up. Write to the record company and ask who distributes that disc or cassette in your area, or if you can order it directly from the company by mail. A list of recording companies and their addresses is given at the end of this book.

Before taking these steps, however, you may want to check your local public or college library to see if it has that particular recording for you to listen to on the premises or take out for a few days.

Keep in mind, too, that in the past few years all the major American record companies have phased out classical LPs and no longer press new copies (as discussed on page 22). This means that LPs recommended in this section, or still listed in computer and print catalogs, will become harder to find except in specialty stores. They are listed here, however, since many are still available in local libraries and can be checked out in this manner before buying a CD or Cassette of the same performance.

A few stylistic points about this section:

(1) The first name in each listing of purely orchestral works is that of the conductor. For recordings of concertos or other works involving an instrumental soloist, however, the soloist's name is listed *before* that of the conductor. For opera recordings, the first name is that of the conductor, followed by those of the principal singers.

(2) If a recording comprises more than one disc or cassette, the number of discs or cassettes is specified. Please note that this number can vary sometimes among CD, LP, and Cassette formats of the same performance.

(3) All recommended recordings are in stereo unless specifically indicated as monaural or monophonic ("mono").

Now, to the top composers and their masterworks.

A FEW WORDS ABOUT EARLY MUSIC

Trying to narrow down the wealth of good music composed over the centuries to 50 major composers is a difficult and, inevitably, arbitrary process. But deciding on a specific composer with whom to begin is even more difficult.

Until recent years, concert programs rarely featured music composed before the 18th century. But since the 1950s there has been a vast reawakening of interest in music of the Renaissance and Baroque periods—spurred on to a large degree by recordings by instrumental ensembles and vocal groups dedicated to unearthing and preserving works that have long been neglected. Accordingly, some introductory comments about early music are in order—first, to help newcomers discover some of the extraordinary works of these early periods and, second, to provide a brief historical background for understanding the development of music by the later composers discussed in the remainder of this section.

Until the Renaissance, European music was primarily vocal music. It generally took two forms: *church music*, usually hymns or psalms sung to Biblical or other religious texts; and *folk songs* such as lullabies, spinning songs, drinking songs, harvest songs, and so on. Originally, both forms of this music were very simple, consisting at first of a single, unaccompanied melodic line—a form called *monody* or *monophony* (one voice). Very little of this early music was written down, for there was no consistent system of musical notation until the late 10th and early 11th centuries, when

Pope John XIX endorsed the system organized by Guido of Arezzo, a system that still forms the basis of modern musical notation.

As time went on, and particularly as new churches and cathedrals rose throughout Europe, church choirs began to embellish their singing. Like the woodcarvers and goldsmiths of their day, the choirs developed more intricate and ornate patterns. And more and more of this music came to be written down.

The Renaissance witnessed a rich and profuse development of the art of music. Literally thousands of pieces of music were composed by such masters as Jacob Obrecht (c. 1450–1505), Heinrich Isaac (c. 1450–1517), Josquin des Prez (c. 1445–1521), Pierre de la Rue (c. 1460–1518), Giovanni di Palestrina (1524–1594), Roland de Lassus (1532–1594), and William Byrd (1543–1623). Sacred music dominated, in the form of the *Mass* and the *motet* (settings of Latin sacred texts). But secular music also thrived—in the *madrigal* in England and Italy, the *chanson* in France, and the *minnesong* in Germany.

The essential feature of Renaissance vocal music (and of much of the Baroque music that followed) is its polyphonic (many-voiced) texture— that is, simultaneous melodic lines, with all of them having roughly the same degree of activity and importance so that no one of them dominates for any appreciable length of time. (In contrast, later musical styles tend to emphasize one predominant melodic line with everything else subjected to a definite secondary or accompanying function, a form called *homophony*.) Rhythmically, music of the Renaissance is steady and continuous, lacking in extreme contrasts. Its harmony is mild, its melodic lines restrained and carefully balanced. In comparison to later styles, this music is nondramatic, although beautiful in its own terms. A good example of Renaissance sacred polyphony is found in a recording of the *Missa Pange Lingua* and the *Missa "La, sol, fa, re, mi"* by Josquin des Prez, which are coupled on a single CD, LP, or Cassette (Gimell, 1987), as performed by the Tallis Scholars.

Instruments performed a variety of functions during this time. More often than not, they were used in conjunction with vocal music, sometimes doubling a vocal part and sometimes replacing the voice altogether. The instruments of the period were many and varied, but were rarely standardized. They included the lute (a multi-stringed, plucked instrument of varying sizes and shapes), the viol (a multi-stringed, bowed predecessor of the violin), the recorder (a reedless woodwind instrument similar to the flute), various other woodwind and brass instruments, and keyboard instruments of the harpsichord type.

Purely instrumental music began to come into its own during the Renaissance, although it occupied a secondary position to choral music. Music for the courtly dance was important, and the Renaissance dance suite was a notable forerunner of the more elaborately worked out and sophisticated instrumental music of the Baroque and later periods. A good example of this type of early dance piece is found in Dances from *Terpsichore* by the German composer Michael Praetorius (1571–1621), available on CD, LP, and Cassette in a recording by the New London Consort conducted by Philip Picket (L'Oiseau-Lyre, 1985).

During the 16th century, kings, princes, counts, dukes, and other nobles increasingly sought out musicians to compose and perform for their courts. They also began to train more and more instrumental players as well as singers. And the development of music printing made possible the increasingly wide distribution of musical works.

The early 17th century ushered in vast changes in musical style—changes so great that the course of music history was profoundly affected. This period of music history, known as the Baroque, was born in Italy, and grew out of the work of a group of Florentine scholars and musicians known as the Camerata. This group, rejecting the tenets of the vocal polyphony of Renaissance sacred music, developed what they called the "new music." Its basic feature was the prominence of a solo singer, with a single instrumental accompaniment (the *continuo*) which supplied an unobtrusive harmonic support for the voice. Moreover, the new music of the Camerata was secular rather than sacred, dramatic and passionate rather than ceremonial. Its rhythms were generally lively, its harmonies expressive, its melodies designed to reflect the meaning and spirit of the words. The work of the members of the Camerata resulted in new techniques of composition which eventually culminated in the great vocal forms that characterize the Baroque: the *cantata*, the *oratorio*, and the *opera*.

Among the first composers to employ these new techniques was Claudio Monteverdi (1567–1643). He was also among the first to write out scores in which he not only used a large number of instruments but also specified exactly which instruments were to play which notes. In 1607 his experiments led him to compose what is generally accepted as the first successful opera, *Orfeo*. (It was by no means the first opera; a 1594 work by two Florentines, Jacopo Peri and Giulio Caccini, is usually accorded that distinction.) *Orfeo* was such a success that Monteverdi's patron, the Duke of Mantua, commissioned a second opera, *Arianna*, which became one of the most popular works of its time. Six thousand people are reported to have seen its first performance in 1608, in an immense theater built especially by the duke to celebrate his son's wedding.

When the duke died, Monteverdi went to Venice to become choirmaster at Saint Mark's Cathedral, then one of the most prestigious posts in all Italy. He raised its standards of performance to the highest in Europe, and remained in the post until his death. For Saint Mark's, Monteverdi composed his finest sacred work: *Vespro della Beata Vergine* (Vespers of the Blessed Virgin), a marvelous combination of Renaissance and Baroque techniques and stylistic elements rolled into a new kind of musical expression. There has long been disagreement over whether Monteverdi intended the Vespers' 14 large and varied movements to constitute a unified work or simply a collection from which individual parts are to be chosen on different occasions. The total performance time of the Vespers is nearly two hours; accordingly, it is not uncommon for an abridged version of the work to be performed as "Selections from *Vespro della Beata Vergine.*" *Recommended CD, LP, and Cassette*: Parrott, Taverner Consort & Choir (Angel, 1983–84), two discs or two cassettes—a first-rate complete performance, recorded with an appropriately spacious, churchlike sound.

The Baroque stands as the era in which instrumental music came into its own, achieving a status at least equal to that of vocal music. The instruments themselves underwent considerable improvement in design and construction, and composers began to write for the individual quality and distinctive characteristics of each instrument. The pipe organ and harpsichord became basic keyboard instruments, and violins fashioned by such craftsmen as Nicolo Amati (1569–1684), Giuseppe Guarneri (1681–1742), and Antonio Stradivari (1644–1737) became world famous.

With these advances appeared new forms of instrumental composition: the *suite*, the *sonata*, the *concerto grosso*, and the *solo concerto*. The Baroque suite was actually not a new form but an expansion of the dance suite of the Renaissance—a set of contrasting dance movements imbued with the new Baroque style and adapted to either the keyboard or an instrumental ensemble.

The Baroque *concerto grosso* provides one of the richest genres that has come down to us from the early periods of music. It is a work in several movements for a group of solo instruments (the *concertino*) and a larger, contrasting group (the *ripieno*).

Among the earliest known and finest concerti grossi are those of the Italian composer Arcangelo Corelli (1653–1731). In his Twelve Concerti Grossi (Op. 6), written in 1682, the solo group consists of two violins and a cello, contrasted with a string orchestra with continuo (making up the ripieno). The contrast involved can be described primarily in terms of soft vs. loud, light vs. heavy, or thin vs. thick. The best-known of the twelve is No. 8 in G minor, titled "Christmas." *Recommended CD and Cassette*: I Musici (Philips, 1962), a performance of style and verve, coupled with Christmas Concertos by three other Baroque composers: Locatelli, Torelli, and Manfredini. *Recommended LP:* Karajan, Berlin Philharmonic (Deutsche Grammophon, 1970), a larger-scaled but still sensitively played performance, similarly coupled with Locatelli, Torelli, and Manfredini.

One short Baroque piece that has won unusual popularity throughout the U.S. in recent years is the Kanon in D major by Johann Pachelbel (1653–1706), with no fewer than 31 different recordings listed in the 1991 Schwann catalog. Its placid, dignified theme was used in the Academy Award-winning film *Ordinary People* (1980), and has also been the signature theme for a number of classical music radio programs. Pachelbel (pronounced *pock*-el-bel) was an organist and organ composer, and was the teacher of Johann Sebastian Bach's elder brother, Johann Christoph, who in turn was one of Bach's first teachers. *Recommended CD, LP, and Cassette*: Paillard, Paillard Chamber Orchestra (RCA, 1984), an irresistibly appealing performance. The same performance is also included in an unusual RCA/BMG set of varying arrangements of the Kanon in D major by the Canadian Brass, flutist James Galway, and the Concord String Quartet.

Today, the three most famous Baroque composers are Bach, Vivaldi, and Handel. Each is discussed individually among the 50 major composers that follow, alphabetically.

JOHANN SEBASTIAN BACH

Pronounced: *bahkh*. Born March 21, 1685, in Eisenach, Saxe-Weimar (Germany). Died July 28, 1750, in Leipzig, at age 65.

SIGNIFICANCE   German organist and composer, an unsurpassed master of counterpoint and other stylistic principles of Baroque music. He brought to his works a maturity, a depth of expression, and a grand design unequaled by his predecessors.

BACKGROUND   Although widely known in his lifetime as an organ virtuoso, Bach did not win world renown as a great composer until the early 19th century. One of his first important champions was the composer Felix Mendelssohn who, at the age of 20, discovered the manuscript of the *Passion According to St. Matthew* (unheard since Bach's own time) and created a sensation when he conducted it in Leipzig in 1829. Over the following decade, other works were uncovered, but it was not until 1850 — one hundred years after Bach's death — that a society was formed to publish Bach's complete works. How incredible that now seems to those of us born in the 20th century who have invariably heard Bach described as one of the greatest composers — if not *the* greatest — of all time.

Bach came from a long line of musicians (seven preceding generations of Bachs had included town musicians and organists). Orphaned at the age of ten, he went to live with an elder brother, an organist who gave him his first organ lessons. At 15 he won a scholarship to become a chorister in St. Michael's Church at Lüneburg. At St. Michael's, he studied, copied, arranged, and reworked the styles and techniques of as many different composers as he could. He also damaged his eyes permanently — copying by moonlight manuscripts of forbidden "radical" composers.

In his adult years, as his reputation as an organist spread, Bach held church or court posts as organist at Weimar, Arnstadt, Mühlhausen, Cöthen, and Leipzig. He composed many works as part of his official duties. They include nearly 300 church (Lutheran) cantatas; the Christmas and Easter oratorios; the *St. John, St. Luke,* and *St. Matthew Passions*; many preludes, fugues, and other works for organ; and the *Goldberg Variations, The Well-Tempered Clavier*, and other works for harpsichord and clavichord.

Aside from his reputation for an irascible temper, Bach was known as a relatively simple, hard-working organist whose home and children meant much to him. His first wife bore him seven children. After she died, he remarried, and his second wife bore him 13 more. Two of his children became well-known composers in their own right: Carl Philipp Emanuel Bach (1714–1788) and Johann Christian Bach (1735–1782). In 1749 Bach underwent an operation to help restore his increasingly troubled sight. It left him totally blind. The following year he died of a paralytic stroke.

BRANDENBURG CONCERTO No. 5

The Fifth Brandenburg Concerto is the best-known and most frequently performed of Bach's six Brandenburg Concertos—and a good introduction to the Baroque concerto grosso, in which musical ideas are developed by pitting a small group of instruments (concertino) against a larger group (ripieno). Each of the Brandenburg concertos is scored for a different combination of instruments, and performances today vary from those using "authentic" instruments of the period (recorders, violas da gamba, baroque oboes, etc.) to those choosing more contemporary ones (including a saxophone used in a Casals performance at Marlboro in the 1960s).

The Concerto No. 5 is perhaps the most ambitious of the six Brandenburgs in its keyboard writing. It is scored for a concertino of harpsichord, flute, and violin—with the harpsichord having probably its most significant solo use to that time in a concerto. Author-broadcaster Martin Bookspan has referred to "the long, tension-laden cadenza for the harpsichord in the first movement" as "one of the most breathtaking moments in all music."

In one of the more curious ironies of music history, Bach's Brandenburg Concertos were probably never performed *in* Brandenburg during the composer's lifetime—nor were they actually written *for* Brandenburg. At the time (1717–1721), Bach, in his early 30s, was in the service of Prince Leopold of Anhalt-Cöthen. Unfortunately for Bach, the prince (in 1721) married a particularly unmusical wife, whom Bach felt jeopardized his position in the court. So he took six of the concertos he had written over the preceding years and sent them to the Margrave of Brandenburg as a sort of job application. Apparently the six concertos were merely filed away in the Margrave's library and forgotten. Bach went on, instead, to new employment in Leipzig, where he remained for nearly 30 years. It was not until after Bach's death that the six concertos he had sent to Brandenburg were rediscovered in the Brandenburg archives—and became known thereafter as the Brandenburg Concertos.

RECOMMENDED CDs————————

Pinnock, The English Concert (Deutsche Grammophon/Archiv, 1982)

Harnoncourt, Vienna Concentus Musicus (Teldec, 1965)

RECOMMENDED LPs————————

Pinnock, The English Concert (Deutsche Grammophon/Archiv, 1982)

Ristenpart, Saar Chamber Orchestra (Nonesuch)

RECOMMENDED CASSETTES———

Pinnock, The English Concert (Deutsche Grammophon/Archiv, 1982)

Ristenpart, Saar Chamber Orchestra (Nonesuch)

COMMENTS————————————

Pinnock's Brandenburg No. 5 is available on a single CD, LP, or Cassette (together with Brandenburgs Nos. 4 and 6), or in a complete set of all six Brandenburgs on two CDs and LPs or four Cassettes.

Harnoncourt's No. 5 is available on a single CD (together with Nos. 3 and 6). On LP or Cassette, it is available only as part of complete sets of all six Brandenburgs.

Pinnock, Harnoncourt, and Ristenpart all conduct the standard version of No. 5, based on the manuscript Bach sent to the Margrave of Brandenburg. Another excellent performance, conducted by Hogwood with the Academy of Ancient Music for L'Oiseau-Lyre (and available in all formats), uses an earlier, so-called "original version" which differs occasionally in content and instrumentation—and deserves looking into after familiarity with the standard version.

An offbeat but interesting jazz version of the Brandenburg No. 5 is part of Jacques Loussier's *Play Bach* series on London (LP and Cassette only). Loussier's trio (piano, bass, drums) replaces the traditional concertino—playing jazz variations on Bach's themes while members of the Royal Philharmonic play them straight. This late 1960s album is filled out with similar treatments of Bach's "Air for the G-String" and the Prelude No. 2 from *The Well-Tempered Clavier*.

Another offbeat version is found in Wendy Carlos' *Switched-On Brandenburgs* series on CBS Masterworks (CD and LP only, in two volumes, available individually), as "recomposed" by Carlos for synthesizer. Carlos' new perspectives on Bach are most interesting after some familiarity with Bach's original versions.

CONCERTO IN D MINOR FOR TWO VIOLINS AND ORCHESTRA

This so-called "Double Concerto" stands out among Bach's works for its rhythmic vitality and its melodic lines. The two soloists constantly cross parts, questioning and answering each other, copying and contradicting each other. Like the Brandenburg Concertos, this work dates from the years 1717–1721, when Bach was in his early 30s and in the service of Prince Leopold of Anhalt-Cöthen. The concerto is well-known among ballet fans today as the score for George Balanchine's *Concerto Barocco*, in the repertory of the New York City Ballet.

RECOMMENDED CDs————
Mutter, Acardo, English Chamber Orchestra (Angel, 1983)
Schroeder, Hirons, Hogwood, Academy of Ancient Music (L'Oiseau-Lyre, 1981)

RECOMMENDED LPs————
Mutter, Acardo, English Chamber Orchestra (Angel, 1983)
Schroeder, Hirons, Hogwood, Academy of Ancient Music (L'Oiseau-Lyre, 1981)

RECOMMENDED CASSETTES————
Mutter, Acardo, English Chamber Orchestra (Angel, 1983)

Schroeder, Hirons, Hogwood, Academy of Ancient Music (L'Oiseau-Lyre, 1981)

COMMENTS————
The two recommended performances above are diametrically opposite to each other in style. Mutter and Acardo (Acardo is both the second violinist and conductor) are luxuriantly warm and eloquent, whereas Schroeder, Hirons and Hogwood are coolly unaffected in a vivid, no-nonsense way. Both approaches have their champions and detractors, so let your own taste be the guide.

SUITE No. 3 FOR ORCHESTRA

The simple, tenderly beautiful "Air," popularly called "Air for the G-String," from this suite remains one of Bach's most widely loved compositions. The rest of the suite is made up of four lively dances (two gavottes, a bourrée, and a gigue) preceded by an extended overture. Of Bach's suites, Albert Schweitzer once said, "Their charm resides in the perfection of their blending of strength and grace."

RECOMMENDED CDs————
Gardiner, English Baroque Soloists (Erato, 1980s)
Pommer, Leipzig New Bach Collegium Musicum (Capriccio, 1980–81)

RECOMMENDED LPs————
Pinnock, The English Concert (Deutsche Grammophon/Archiv, 1979)
Paillard, Chamber Orchestra (Erato, 1964)

RECOMMENDED CASSETTES————
Richter, Munich Bach Orchestra (Deutsche Grammophon/Archiv, 1979)
Ansermet, Suisse Romande Orchestra (London, early 1960s)

COMMENTS————
Pinnock's ingratiating performance is also available on CD, but only in a 4-CD set with other Bach works, including the Brandenburg Concertos. The LP edition is part of a 2-LP set of the complete Bach Suites for Orchestra.

The elegant Gardner performance is available in a 2-CD set of the complete suites, or on a separate CD together with Suite No. 4.

Ansermet, in one of his rare recordings of a Baroque work, avoids the overblown symphonic approach of most other "name" conductors (such as Karajan), for a fresh, spirited performance.

MODERN TRANSCRIPTIONS
OF BACH WORKS

Earlier in this century there was a rash of orchestrated versions of some of Bach's organ works by Ottorino Respighi, Leopold Stokowski, and others. These transcriptions have always been controversial. Their critics say they distort or vulgarize Bach's music. Defenders argue that they have added new dimensions of modern orchestral colors to the works and have helped introduce Bach to listeners accustomed to the sound of the large modern orchestra.

The best-known and most sonically fascinating examples of orchestrated Bach are by Leopold Stokowski. Some are now available in CD reissues on RCA/BMG, London, Pearl, and other labels, in performances with various London, Czech, and other orchestras.

Guitar transcriptions of Bach works popularized by the great Spanish guitarist Andrés Segovia have been released on CD and Cassette on the MCA label. The American guitarist Christopher Parkening also has recorded Bach transcriptions for Angel, available on CD, LP, and Cassette.

One of the best-sellers of the 1970s, Wendy Carlos' *Switched-On Bach* synthesizer series, is still available in various CD, LP, and Cassette versions on CBS Masterworks. These electronic performances have been denounced by some as "the last straw" in the computerization of man and his culture. I side with those others who find them exciting, enjoyable examples of electronic music-making—an occasional substitute but certainly no replacement for Bach's originals.

FOR FOLLOW-UP CONSIDERATION

THE PASSION OF OUR LORD ACCORDING TO ST. MATTHEW
This large-scale setting of the Biblical text for solo voices, chorus, and orchestra is considered by many critics to be Bach's most eloquent and deeply moving choral masterpiece.

RECOMMENDED CD, LP, AND CASSETTE
Richter, Mathis, Schreier, Fischer-Dieskau, Salminen, Munich Bach Orchestra and Chorus. (Deutsche Grammophon/Archiv, 1980), complete on three CDs, four LPs, or three Cassettes. The performance is sung in the original German.

SAMUEL BARBER

Pronounced: *bar*-ber. Born March 9, 1910, in West Chester, Pa. Died
January 23, 1981, in Mt. Kisco, New York, at age 70.

SIGNIFICANCE Twentieth-century American composer, who emphasized fluent melodic writing and expressive Neo-Romantic feeling.

BACKGROUND The nephew of famous contralto Louise Homer (1871–
1947), Barber began to study the piano at the age of six, and a year later
attempted his first composition. At 12 he was organist for a local church. At
14 he entered the Curtis Institute of Music in Philadelphia, later studying
also in Rome. In 1932, when Barber was 22, Koussevitzky and the Boston
Symphony Orchestra introduced his first orchestral work, *The School for
Scandal* overture. Within four years Barber had won two Pulitzer Prizes —
the first composer ever to do so. He also won the American Prix de Rome,
and had his First Symphony (1936) honored as the first American work ever
performed at the Salzburg Festival in Austria. In America, his works were
thereafter played regularly on programs conducted by Arturo Toscanini,
Bruno Walter, Leopold Stokowski, and other major conductors.

Although some critics considered Barber ultra-conservative in relation
to the musical trends of his lifetime, his music conveys a distinctively expressive warmth and humanity that ensures its durability.

Over the years, Barber composed several ballet scores (*Medea, Souvenirs*), a violin concerto, a piano concerto, numerous works for voice and
orchestra, and two operas: *Vanessa* (1958) and *Antony and Cleopatra* (1966).
He long shared his studios near New York City with the composer Gian-
Carlo Menotti, who wrote the libretto for *Vanessa*. The failure of *Antony
and Cleopatra* with both the critics and the public, following considerable
hoopla over its being commissioned for the opening of the new Metropolitan Opera House at Lincoln Center in 1966, deeply upset Barber — and
is believed by many to have caused creative blocks that made it impossible
for him to complete other planned works before his death.

ADAGIO FOR STRINGS

One of Barber's earliest works, this is among his finest and most frequently
performed. It is an orchestrated version of the adagio movement of Barber's
String Quartet No. 1, written in 1936. The lyrical adagio begins quietly,
builds to a grippingly intense climax, then subsides tenderly to its original
mood. Its principal theme was used prominently in the score for the 1986
Academy Award-winning film, *Platoon*.

RECOMMENDED CDs _____
Bernstein, Los Angeles Philharmonic
   (Deutsche Grammophon, 1983)
Slatkin, Saint Louis (Angel, 1989)

RECOMMENDED LPs _____
Bernstein, Los Angeles Philharmonic
   (Deutsche Grammophon, 1983)
Schippers, New York Philharmonic (CBS/
   Odyssey, 1966)

RECOMMENDED CASSETTES _____
Bernstein, Los Angeles Philharmonic
   (Deutsche Grammophon, 1983)
Schippers, New York Philharmonic (CBS/
   Odyssey, 1966)

COMMENTS _____
Bernstein is the most intense, but Slatkin
and Schippers are also both tremendously moving and well-played.

KNOXVILLE: SUMMER OF 1915

Based on a poem fragment by James Agee (used as the prologue of Agee's
Pulitzer Prize-winning novel _A Death in the Family_), this is a deeply moving,
lyrical, and warmly homespun work for soprano and orchestra. Composed
in 1947, it is a nostalgically Romantic look at a bygone era of American life.

RECOMMENDED CDs _____
Steber, Strickland, Dumbarton Oaks
   Chamber Orchestra (CBS/Sony Por-
   trait series, 1950, mono)
Upshaw, Zinman, St. Luke's Orchestra
   (Elektra/Nonesuch, 1989)

RECOMMENDED LP _____
L. Price, Schippers, New Philharmonia
   of London (RCA, 1968)

RECOMMENDED CASSETTE _____
Upshaw, Zinman, St. Luke's (Elektra/
   Nonesuch, 1989)

COMMENTS _____
All three performances are outstanding,
with Steber's perhaps the most memorable despite dated sound.

FOR FOLLOW-UP CONSIDERATION

SYMPHONY No. 1   One of Barber's first international successes (1936)
and still a warmly appealing example of his lyrically surging writing.

RECOMMENDED CD _____
Slatkin, Saint Louis (BMG, 1991)

RECOMMENDED LP _____
Hanson, Eastman-Rochester Orchestra
   (Mercury, 1961).

RECOMMENDED CASSETTE _____
Schermerhorn, Milwaukee Symphony
   Orchestra (Turnabout, 1975). Slatkin
   leads an intense, full-blooded performance, beautifully played. Both Hanson and Schermerhorn are almost as
   vivid.

PIANO CONCERTO   The 1963 Pulitzer Prize-winner in music and one
of the most widely performed contemporary concertos. It is by turns splashy
and technically complex, then disarmingly touching and songful.

Browning, Slatkin, Saint Louis (BMG, 1990). Browning gave the world premiere and has virtually "owned" the concerto ever since—deservedly, for he plays it for all its rhythmic and dramatic worth.

BELA BARTÓK

Pronounced: *bay*-lah *bar*-tock. Born March 25, 1881, in Nagyszentmiklos, Hungary. Died September 26, 1945, in New York City, at age 64.

SIGNIFICANCE Hungarian composer and pianist, whose music varies from darkly full-blooded to austerely folk-like, sometimes with irregular rhythms and harsh harmonies.

BACKGROUND Bartók made his debut as a pianist in Hungary at the age of ten. As a teenager he studied at the Royal Academy of Music in Budapest, later becoming a professor there. A pioneer collector of authentic Hungarian folk songs (he proved that the "Hungarian Rhapsodies" of Liszt were based on gypsy songs), he spent more than eight years collecting, writing down, and making phonograph recordings of them. His own original orchestral music, operas, and ballet scores (*The Miraculous Mandarin*, *The Wooden Prince*, *Bluebeard's Castle*, etc.) met with generally hostile receptions at first.

Bartók lived most of his life in or near poverty, and spent his last years in the U.S., after fleeing the Nazi takeover of Hungary. He worked for a time in Columbia University's music library, until leukemia prevented him from working regularly. Although it was once believed that he died because of neglect, ASCAP (the American Society of Composers, Authors & Publishers) had assured him medical care, which Bartók agreed to accept only as an advance against future royalties. Moreover, the Hungarian-born conductor Fritz Reiner and a few others had helped secure him major commissions, on which he continued to work until his death. Ironically, within a few years of his death Bartók was internationally recognized as one of this century's half-dozen greatest composers.

CONCERTO FOR ORCHESTRA

In 1943, while Bartók was hospitalized in New York with leukemia, two Hungarian compatriots, violinist Joseph Szigeti and conductor Fritz Reiner, set in motion an effort to help him. The effort resulted in a commission from Serge Koussevitzky, then conductor of the Boston Symphony Orchestra, for $1,000 for an orchestral work. The commission so buoyed Bartók's spirits that he was able to leave the hospital and start work on the Concerto for Orchestra. On December 1, 1944, Bartók went to Boston for the premiere, of which he wrote: "The performance was excellent. Koussevitzky is very enthusiastic about the piece, and says it is 'the best orchestral piece of the last twenty-five years.' " Koussevitzky's judgment has long since been confirmed. In fact, few works introduced since 1940 have been admired more enthusiastically by both critics and audiences.

Bartók treats the instruments in a colorful, soloistic manner, contrasting groups of instruments against the full body of the orchestra. Bartók provided this broad outline for the premiere: "The general mood of the work represents, apart from the jesting second movement, a gradual transition from the sternness of the first movement and the lugubrious death song of the third to the life-assertion of the last one." The fourth movement, "Interrupted Intermezzo," is a gentle interlude interrupted by raucous references to themes from Lehár's operetta *The Merry Widow* and from Shostakovich's Seventh (*Leningrad*) Symphony, the latter of which Bartók had heard on its premiere radio broadcast (by Toscanini and the NBC Symphony) while working on the Concerto for Orchestra.

RECOMMENDED CDs————
Reiner, Chicago Symphony Orchestra (RCA, 1956)
Dorati, Amsterdam Concertgebouw Orchestra (Philips, 1983)

RECOMMENDED LPs————
Reiner, Chicago Symphony Orchestra (RCA, 1956)
Dorati, Amsterdam Concertgebouw Orchestra (Philips, 1983)

RECOMMENDED CASSETTES———
Dorati, Amsterdam Concertgebouw Orchestra (Philips, 1983)
Ormandy, Philadelphia Orchestra (RCA, 1970s)

COMMENTS————
Since Bartók's Concerto for Orchestra tests the mettle of any virtuoso ensemble, performances by orchestras such as the Chicago Symphony, the Amsterdam Concertgebouw, and the Philadelphia Orchestra have a distinct edge over performances by lesser orchestras. Moreover, the special affinity for and insight into Bartók's music by the Hungarian-born conductors listed here make their versions preferable to those recorded by other conductors with such otherwise outstanding orchestras as the Boston Symphony, the New York Philharmonic, and the Berlin Philharmonic.

MUSIC FOR STRINGS, PERCUSSION AND CELESTA

Considered by many to be the greatest of Bartók's works and one of his most original, this 1936 composition is scored for double string orchestra —one group on each side of the stage—with piano, celesta, harp, xylophone, timpani, and various percussion instruments between them.

Bartók uses the instruments in unusual ways to explore new sonorities—sometimes for mysterious effects, sometimes for aggressive, sharp accents. The first movement has been described by Pierre Boulez as "a fugue unfolding fanwise to a maximum intensity and then folding back to its initial mystery." The second movement is rhythmically vibrant and jocose, with some of the most arresting combinations of percussive and pizzicato sounds in any orchestral work. The third is a quiet and eerie example of what Boulez calls Bartók's "night music." The finale is violent and dancelike in its rhythmic urgency.

RECOMMENDED CDs————————
Boulez, BBC Symphony (CBS/Sony, 1968)
Bernstein, New York Philharmonic (CBS/Sony, 1962)

RECOMMENDED LPs————————
Rolla, Liszt Chamber Orchestra of Budapest (Hungaroton)
Bernstein, New York Philharmonic (CBS 1962)

RECOMMENDED CASSETTES——————
Ormandy, Philadelphia Orchestra (Angel, 1979)

Skrowaczewski, Minnesota Orchestra (Vox Cum Laude, 1978)

COMMENTS————————
Bernstein's newer (1980s) recording of this work with the Bavarian Radio Symphony lacks some of the thrust and tension of his earlier New York Philharmonic recording listed. Boulez and the BBC Symphony remains marginally better than any of the others, with striking rhythms and exceptional vitality.

FOR FOLLOW-UP CONSIDERATION

PIANO CONCERTO No. 3   Bartók's last work, and one of his most unashamedly Neo-Romantic in mood. He worked on it virtually to the day he died, leaving only the final 17 bars unfinished. They were completed from Bartók's sketches by his friend and pupil, Tibor Serly.

RECOMMENDED CD————————
Ashkenazy, Solti, Chicago Symphony Orchestra (London, 1979)

RECOMMENDED LP AND
CASSETTE————————
Ranki, Ferencsik, Hungarian State Or-

chestra (Hungaroton). Ashkenazy is more introspective, Ranki more outgoing—but both approaches work for this concerto.

BLUEBEARD'S CASTLE   Bartók's only opera, dating from 1911, is a short, two-character work based on the legend of the much-married Bluebeard, but recast as a symbolic rather than a literal horror story. It is not an "easy" work on first hearing, but it has many fascinating scenes and remains one of Bartók's most volcanically powerful scores.

remains superior to several later recordings. Sung in the original Hungarian.

LUDWIG VAN BEETHOVEN

Pronounced: bay-toh-ven. Born December 16, 1770, in Bonn, Germany.
Died March 26, 1827, in Vienna, at age 56.

SIGNIFICANCE   German composer and pianist who has long ranked as the titan of Western music, and is generally regarded today as the most widely popular of all composers for the concert hall. In creating a new "heroic" style he raised instrumental music in the early 19th century to previously unimagined heights of grandeur, marked by a new expressiveness, yet still maintaining basically Classical structures.

BACKGROUND   The son and grandson of musicians, Beethoven had started to play both the piano and violin by the age of four. His father, a minor singer in the court of the Archbishop of Cologne, pushed his son in hopes he would become a child prodigy like Mozart. But Beethoven's talent was slow to ripen, and he showed none of the personal charm of the young Mozart. To supplement the family's meager income, Beethoven, at 11, began to play in a theater orchestra. At 13 he became assistant to the organist at the court chapel.

As his musical talents developed during his late teens, Beethoven won the favor of the archbishop, who finally aided him in going to Vienna to continue his studies. At first Beethoven studied with Haydn, but according to some reports of the time, they did not get along too well. Over the years, the growing fame of Beethoven's piano improvisations made him a performer much sought after by Viennese aristocrats — despite (and sometimes perhaps because of) his reputation as a "country bumpkin." Although most of his first successful works were for the piano, Beethoven earnestly expanded his creative activities to symphonies, trios, and quartets during his first ten years in Vienna.

He composed slowly and with great effort. And in 1799 he became aware of one of the worst calamities that can strike a performing musician: he was going deaf. At one point he seriously considered suicide. But then he vowed in a letter, "I will take Fate by the throat." He continued to compose — and there are some who believe that it was because of his growing deafness that Beethoven poured so much emotion and intensity into his music, thus expanding the Classical forms of his predecessors and paving the way for the Romantics who followed him. By 1822 — after the completion of the Ninth Symphony but before the last three string quartets — Beethoven was completely deaf. Though he never married, Beethoven was known throughout Vienna for many love affairs (his popular "Moonlight" Sonata, for example, is dedicated to Giulietta Guicciardi).

SYMPHONY No. 5 IN C MINOR

The Olympian grandeur and driving power of this symphony (composed in 1805) have kept it one of the most popular of all orchestral works. During World War II its opening theme was used as a symbol of the Allied forces fighting the Nazis (a use reflected in many of the films of that period). Beethoven himself suggested, many years after the first performance, that the opening theme signified the summons of Fate. In more recent years, that theme has endured many non-symphonic adaptations, variations, and plain vulgarizations — including a "Top 40" pop version that was called, not inappropriately, "A Fifth of Beethoven." But the high-voltage energy and dramatic pulse of the original symphony in a top-notch performance can still make more of an impact than almost any other work in the symphonic repertory.

RECOMMENDED CDs⸺
Carlos Kleiber, Vienna Philharmonic (Deutsche Grammophon, 1974)
Karajan, Berlin Philharmonic (Deutsche Grammophon, 1984)

RECOMMENDED LPs⸺
Carlos Kleiber, Vienna Philharmonic (Deutsche Grammophon, 1974)
Karajan, Berlin Philharmonic (Deutsche Grammophon, 1984)

RECOMMENDED CASSETTES⸺
Carlos Kleiber, Vienna Philharmonic (Deutsche Grammophon, 1974)

Karajan, Berlin Philharmonic (Deutsche Grammophon, 1984)

COMMENTS⸺
Although the Kleiber and Karajan recordings are clearly at the top of the list of more than 35 performances now in the Schwann catalog in terms of *both* performance and sound quality, several older, monophonic recordings still deserve recommendation: Toscanini and the NBC Symphony (RCA, 1952) on both CD and Cassette; and Erich Kleiber (Carlos' father) and the Amsterdam Concertgebouw Orchestra (London, 1952), on CD.

SYMPHONY No. 7 IN A MAJOR

Various annotators have linked this symphony (written in 1811 and 1812) to descriptions of a rustic wedding, a royal hunt, a knightly battle, a masquerade party, a sweeping political revolution, and even "the love-dream of a sumptuous odalisque." Beethoven himself disowned all such attempts to attach a program to his Seventh. Yet Wagner's reference to it as an "apotheosis of the dance" has stuck through the years. Rhythmic energy does indeed dominate the symphony, with each of the four movements built around a different rhythmic pattern. The entire symphony bristles with vim and vigor, and occasionally with a gruff kind of humor.

RECOMMENDED CDs————————
Karajan, Berlin Philharmonic (Deutsche Grammophon, 1983)
Suitner, Berlin State Orchestra (Denon, 1981)

RECOMMENDED LPs————————
Karajan, Berlin Philharmonic (Deutsche Grammophon, 1983)
Reiner, Chicago Symphony (RCA, 1981)

RECOMMENDED CASSETTES————
Karajan, Berlin Philharmonic (Deutsche Grammophon, 1983)
Bernstein, Vienna Philharmonic (Deutsche Grammophon, 1980)

COMMENTS————————————
Karajan has recorded Beethoven's Seventh at least four times, and his 1962

and 1977 editions (also with the Berlin Philharmonic), plus an earlier one with the Vienna Philharmonic, are all still in the LP and Cassette catalogs. While the 1983 recording is the best of the lot, the others with the Berliners are only marginally less kinetic. (His Vienna recording is not in the same league.)

Toscanini's 1951 performance remains the most exciting of all, but its monophonic sound is dated. Still, its recent release by RCA on CD is to be recommended to those who are willing to make allowances for limited sonics. The Toscanini performance is also available on an RCA Victrola Cassette, and as part of an eight-LP set of all the Beethoven symphonies with the NBC Symphony.

SYMPHONY No. 3 IN E FLAT ("EROICA")

As a child, Beethoven had been fascinated by stories about the American and French Revolutions. Later, even though he had many friends in the aristocracy, he became a vigorous champion of some of the revolutionary movements of his day. This is reflected musically in two of his major works—the "Eroica" Symphony and his only opera, *Fidelio*. Beethoven so admired Napoleon at first, as a revolutionary leader and liberator, that he originally inscribed his Third Symphony to Napoleon in 1804. But when Napoleon took the title of Emperor, a disillusioned Beethoven changed the inscription to: "Heroic Symphony composed to celebrate the memory of a great man."

The "Eroica" is a symphony on a grand scale, and twice the length of the average Haydn or Mozart symphony. Berlioz said it "is so mighty in conception and execution, its style so terse and constantly exalted, its form so poetic, that it is equal to the greatest works of its great creator."

RECOMMENDED CDs————————
Karajan, Berlin Philharmonic (Deutsche Grammophon, 1984)

Bernstein, Vienna Philharmonic (Deutsche Grammophon, 1981)

Karajan, Berlin Philharmonic (Deutsche
Grammophon, 1984)
Bernstein, Vienna Philharmonic (Deut-
sche Grammophon, 1981)

RECOMMENDED CASSETTES
Karajan, Berlin Philharmonic (Deutsche
Grammophon, 1984)
Bernstein, Vienna Philharmonic (Deut-
sche Grammophon, 1981)

COMMENTS
Karajan's is more eloquent and majestic,
Bernstein's more dramatic and stirring.
Among vintage recordings, Erich Kleiber's 1955 mono performance with the
Vienna Philharmonic, on London CD, LP,
and Cassette, is still dynamic and powerful despite its dated sound. Furtwangler's early 1950 mono performance, also
with the Vienna Philharmonic in an Angel CD edition, is expansive yet gripping, though with similarly dated sound.

SYMPHONY No. 9 IN D MINOR (CHORAL)

This Promethean symphony was the first symphony to combine a huge
choral part with purely orchestral movements. The text of the choral section
is based on the "Ode to Joy" by the German poet Schiller. Beethoven had
read Schiller's poem as a youth and apparently wanted to set it to music
from the start. Its appeal to youth has continued strongly into our own days,
and in the early 1970s a pop version of the Ninth's finale made its way to
the top of the pop charts as "The Song of Joy." (Since then some record
shops have even advertised the "original version" as a way to sell various
complete versions of the Beethoven Ninth.)

The late Lawrence Gilman, for many years program annotator of the
New York Philharmonic, fittingly described the special qualities of the Ninth
as "its strange blend of fatefulness and transport, wild humor and super-
terrestrial beauty, its mystery and exaltation, its tragical despair and its
shouting among the stars."

RECOMMENDED CDs
Bernstein, Jones, Schwarz, Kollo, Moll,
Vienna Philharmonic & Singverein
(Deutsche Grammophon, 1980)
Dohnanyi, Vaness, Taylor, Jerusalem,
Lloyd, Cleveland Orchestra & Chorus
(Telarc, 1985)

RECOMMENDED LPs
Bernstein, Jones, Schwarz, Kollo, Moll,
Vienna Philharmonic & Singverein (2-
LP Deutsche Grammophon set, 1980)
Colin Davis, Donath, Schmidt, König,
Estes, Bavarian Radio Orchestra &
Chorus (Philips, 1985)

RECOMMENDED CASSETTES
Bernstein, Jones, Schwarz, Kollo, Moll,

Vienna Philharmonic & Singverein
(Deutsche Grammophon, 1980)
Colin Davis, Donath, Schmidt, König,
Estes, Bavarian Radio Orchestra &
Chorus (Philips, 1985)

COMMENTS
Among vintage performances still in the
catalog with sonic qualities not up to
the choices above, the most outstanding
is Furtwangler's from 1951, recorded live
at a Bayreuth Festival performance with
Schwarzkopf, Hongen, Hopf, and Edel-
mann as soloists (Angel CD and LP). Another Bernstein recording, made live in
Berlin soon after the 1989 fall of the
Wall, is emotionally supercharged despite technical blemishes (Deutsche
Grammophon, 1989).

PIANO CONCERTO No. 5
IN E FLAT ("EMPEROR")

From its majestic opening theme to its spirited, dramatic finale, this is the Classical concerto at its noblest. It tests not only the technical ability but also the emotional depth of any pianist. The nickname "Emperor" was not Beethoven's, but is reported to have come from a prominent piano-maker who called it "an Emperor among concertos."

Before he composed the "Emperor," Beethoven had always performed his own piano concertos, but because of his growing deafness he chose not to perform this one. He insisted that the pianist follow his intricate score exactly, and instead of allowing him to improvise the cadenza—then a traditional procedure—he wrote his down. What was probably meant only to protect the integrity of one composition soon set a trend, as subsequent composers continued to write out cadenzas for their concertos, too.

RECOMMENDED CDs_____
Arrau, Colin Davis, Dresden Philharmonic (Philips, 1984)
Gilels, Szell, Cleveland Orchestra (Angel, 1969)

RECOMMENDED LPs_____
Gilels, Szell, Cleveland Orchestra (Angel, 1969)
Brendel, Haitink, London Philharmonic (Philips)

RECOMMENDED CASSETTES_____
Serkin, Bernstein, New York Philharmonic (CBS, 1962)

Gilels, Szell, Cleveland Orchestra (Angel, 1969)

COMMENTS_____
Arrau, Gilels, and Brendel find more poetry in the "Emperor" than most other pianists, without sacrificing any of the work's strength and grandeur. Serkin is the most bold and dramatically forthright; his performance with Bernstein is also available on CD and LP but only in multiple (two- or four-LP) sets together with other Beethoven works.

VIOLIN CONCERTO IN D MAJOR

Although almost perfectly Classical in structure, the mood of this concerto is more Romantic than most of Beethoven's works. Some of its special character may be due to the violinist Beethoven wrote it for. Franz Clement was a violinist who used to play as an encore a work of his own while holding his violin upside down—a feat about which author-broadcaster Martin Bookspan has quipped: "Were he alive today [he] would be a natural for television shows."

Tricks or no tricks, violin concertos were not as popular in Beethoven's day as piano concertos, and Beethoven even recast this violin concerto as a piano concerto. The piano version occasionally turns up on concert programs and recordings even today. However, over the past century the original version has become one of the most popular of all violin concertos.

RECOMMENDED CDs———————
Heifetz, Munch, Boston Symphony (RCA, 1958)
Mutter, Karajan, Berlin Philharmonic (Deutsche Grammophon, 1980)

RECOMMENDED LPs———————
Heifetz, Munch, Boston Symphony (RCA, 1958)
Stern, Bernstein, New York Philharmonic (CBS Masterworks, 1960)

RECOMMENDED CASSETTES———
Heifetz, Munch, Boston Symphony (RCA, 1958)
Mutter, Karajan, Berlin Philharmonic (Deutsche Grammophon, 1980)

COMMENTS———————
Preferences among recordings of this concerto depend to a large extent on whether a listener prefers an approach that emphasizes the concerto's noble, Classical line, or a warmer, more Romantic approach. Heifetz is in the first category, Mutter and Stern in the latter.

A recommended recording of the piano version of the Violin Concerto (as mentioned above) is that of Barenboim with the English Chamber Orchestra, on Deutsche Grammophon (LP only).

FOR FOLLOW-UP CONSIDERATION

SYMPHONY No. 6 IN F MAJOR ("PASTORAL") Beethoven's only programmatic symphony describes a day in the Viennese countryside. Its movements are titled "Awakening of Pleasant Feelings Upon Arriving in the Country," "Scene at the Brook," "Peasants' Merry-Making," "The Storm," and "Shepherd's Hymn of Thanksgiving After the Storm." But these titles are meant to be "more an expression of feeling than a painting in sound" (to quote Beethoven himself).

RECOMMENDED CD, LP, AND CASSETTE———————
Karajan, Berlin Philharmonic (Deutsche

Grammophon, 1984), a marvelously flowing performance with a real grabber of a thunderstorm.

SYMPHONY No. 4 IN B-FLAT MAJOR Sometimes called Beethoven's "Romantic" Symphony, the Fourth is more graceful, tender, and sunny than most of Beethoven's other symphonies. Schumann likened the Fourth to "a slender Greek maiden between two Norse giants" (those giants, of course, being the Third and Fifth Symphonies). The Fourth was composed mostly during a summer stay in Hungary in 1806, during which Beethoven was linked romantically, in sequence, with two sisters of his host, the Count of Brunswick. In his diaries for 1806, Beethoven makes several references to an "Immortal Beloved," but no conclusive identification has ever been made, adding to the mysterious romantic aura surrounding the Fourth Symphony.

RECOMMENDED CD, LP, AND CASSETTE———————————
Karajan, Berlin Philharmonic (Deutsche

Grammophon, 1983), a beautiful, warm, and joyous performance.

PIANO CONCERTO No. 4 IN G MAJOR   Like the Fourth Symphony, this concerto is more poetically Romantic in feeling than Beethoven's other piano concertos. Next to the "Emperor," it has become his most popular concerto. Composed between 1804 and 1806, it is generally regarded as the first completely "Beethovenian" concerto, shedding the spirit of Mozart that permeates Beethoven's First and Second Piano Concertos and part of the Third.

RECOMMENDED CD, LP, AND CASSETTE———————————
Perahia, Haitink, Amsterdam Concert-gebouw Orchestra (CBS, 1986), as

perfect a combination of poetry and drama as this concerto has yet had on records.

TRIPLE CONCERTO IN C MAJOR FOR PIANO, VIOLIN, CELLO AND ORCHESTRA   Composed during the same period as the "Eroica" and the Violin Concerto, the Triple Concerto has never achieved their popularity, perhaps because it is less flashy and more traditional in style. Yet it has some of Beethoven's most appealing and melodious concerto writing.

RECOMMENDED CD, LP, AND CASSETTE———————————
Mutter, Ma, Zeltser, Karajan, Berlin Phil-harmonic (Deutsche Grammophon,

1980), with three young but excep-tional soloists and one of the most masterful Beethoven veterans around.

A SPECIAL NOTE ON COMPLETE RECORDINGS OF ALL NINE BEETHOVEN SYMPHONIES

In 1952 Columbia Records issued an historic "first"—an album combining all of its previously, separately released recordings of the nine Beethoven symphonies as conducted by the late Felix Weingartner. Several years later RCA issued a similar "special package" featuring Toscanini's interpretations. Since then it has become something of a status symbol among conductors to record *all* of the Beethoven symphonies and to have them released in "deluxe albums." As a result, there are now many complete Beethoven symphony sets—by Ansermet, Bernstein, Böhm, Haitink, Jochum, Karajan, Klemperer, Krips, Leinsdorf, Maazel, Masur, Ormandy, Steinberg, Szell, Walter, and a few others.

Except for the most loyal fans of the individual conductors involved, most of these sets are not recommended for a beginning collector. A conductor who may be at his best in, say, the Fifth or Seventh Symphonies may not be as good in the very different Second or Sixth—or vice-versa, of course. But for those interested in such a complete set, the following are recommended as offering a conductor with something especially worthwhile to say about each of the symphonies, although each of these conductors, too, is better in certain of the symphonies than in others.

RECOMMENDED CD AND CASSETTE (IN THE BEST CONTEMPORARY SOUND)
Karajan, Berlin Philharmonic (Deutsche Grammophon, 1981–83)

RECOMMENDED ON CASSETTE ONLY
Toscanini, NBC Symphony (RCA Victrola, early 1950s), vintage in sound but still outstanding in musical values.

RECOMMENDED ON LP ONLY
Szell, Cleveland Orchestra (CBS, 1960s)

ALBAN BERG

Pronounced: *bairg*. Born February 7, 1885, in Vienna, Austria. Died December 24, 1935, in Vienna, at age 50.

SIGNIFICANCE Austrian composer, a pioneer in the development of serial music with a deeply expressive and dramatic character.

BACKGROUND Although Berg pursued musical interests as a youth in Vienna, he had no formal musical training until he was 19. After meeting Schoenberg, he gave up his position as a minor government official to study with him in Vienna and Berlin. He became one of Schoenberg's chief disciples in developing the principles of 12-tone (dodecaphonic) composition.

Berg's opera *Wozzeck*, written between 1914 and 1922 (partly while Berg, despite poor health, served in the Austrian army), is a modern milestone—a powerfully dramatic, atonal opera blending realism, irony, and sentimentality in a strikingly original way. Because he was an exacting craftsman, Berg's output was small, and he died (of blood poisoning following a bee sting) before finishing his second opera, *Lulu*. The latter is nonetheless widely considered another modern masterpiece, although for many years it had to be performed in fragmented form because Berg's widow refused to grant permission to anyone other than Berg's mentor Schoenberg to prepare a performing edition from Berg's virtually complete sketches — and Schoenberg declined. But following Schoenberg's death, Berg's publisher, without the widow's knowledge, quietly engaged composer-conductor-musicologist Friedrich Cerha to do the job — and, following the widow's death in 1976, that version has been successfully performed by major opera houses in the U.S. and Europe, and recorded.

THREE PIECES FOR ORCHESTRA

In comparing the music of Schoenberg, Webern, and Berg, some commentators have described Berg as the most openly dramatic and accessible. And the *Three Pieces* of 1914–15 certainly qualify in that respect for the average listener. Dedicated to Schoenberg, they were intended for his fortieth birthday, but were not completed until the following year — and then not given a complete performance for another 15 years. Today they are widely recognized among this century's finest works.

Scored for large orchestra, the *Three Pieces* are basically dark in color — Berg was partial to low sonorities, rarely using instruments in their upper registers. Their mood varies from brooding to violently explosive. The first movement, "Präludium" ("Prelude") is murkily mysterious; the second, "Reigen" ("Round Dances"), plays gloomily with faded waltz rhythms; the third, "Marsch" ("March"), is a big, dramatic, violently anguished processional which is almost harrowing in its intensity. This music, particularly the third movement, is recommended as an introduction to Berg's operatic masterpiece, *Wozzeck* — whose dramatic force has much in common with the *Three Pieces*.

RECOMMENDED CD_____
Colin Davis, Bavarian Radio Symphony
  (Philips, 1983)
Abbado, London Symphony (Deutsche
  Grammophon, 1971)

RECOMMENDED LPs_____
Boulez, BBC Symphony (CBS, 1969)
Abbado, London Symphony (Deutsche
  Grammophon, 1971)

RECOMMENDED CASSETTE_____
Boulez, BBC Symphony (CBS, 1969)

COMMENTS_____
The Boulez performance is dramatically forceful and remarkably clear in texture, bringing out all sorts of subtleties other performances don't even hint at. Both Davis and Abbado are intensely dramatic and sonically impressive.

VIOLIN CONCERTO

Berg's only solo concerto turned out to be his last completed work. Berg was in the midst of composing the opera *Lulu* when he was approached by the American violinist Louis Krasner about writing a concerto. Berg at first declined, saying he could not undertake such a project until he had completed *Lulu*, on which much remained to be done. But three months later, Berg had a change of heart. He was deeply saddened by the death from polio of 18-year-old Manon Gropius, daughter of Alma Mahler (the composer's widow) and her second husband, the architect Walter Gropius. Berg decided to compose a violin concerto as a memorial to her—and he set aside *Lulu* to do so. Then, shortly before Krasner's premiere of the concerto in Barcelona in 1936, Berg himself died.

Although the deeply lyrical concerto is constructed with serial techniques, the basic "row" is made up of clearly tonal intervals. Berg also integrates into the score symbolic quotations from traditional music, including part of a Carinthian folk song and a Lutheran chorale, "Es ist genug" ("It is enough"). One Berg authority, Hans Redlich, has suggested that the concerto's first movement is a musical portrait of Manon Gropius, while the second movement represents her struggle against death and her transfiguration in heaven.

RECOMMENDED CDs————————
Kremer, Colin Davis, Bavarian Radio Symphony (Philips, 1984)
Perlman, Ozawa, Boston Symphony (Deutsche Grammophon, 1979)

RECOMMENDED LPs————————
Zukerman, Boulez, London Symphony (CBS, 1984)
Perlman, Ozawa, Boston Symphony (Deutsche Grammophon, 1979)

RECOMMENDED CASSETTES———
Zukerman, Boulez, London Symphony (CBS, 1984)

Perlman, Ozawa, Boston Symphony (Deutsche Grammophon, 1979)

COMMENTS————————————
Zukerman's performance is high-voltage in both its dramatic ardor and its technical command. Kremer is also most impressive, if less intense. Perlman's performance is tonally splendid and dramatically committed, but Ozawa's accompaniment lacks the depth of either Boulez or Davis.

FOR FOLLOW-UP CONSIDERATION

WOZZECK   To some critics, this is the most important opera of the 20th century, and it is the first primarily atonal opera to win a place in the repertory of the world's great opera houses. Its acceptance was slow, however. The first Metropolitan Opera performance, for example, took place in 1965, 33 years after Berg completed it. The libretto is based on Georg Büchner's early-19th century play about a desperately poor, persecuted soldier and the events that lead him to murder his mistress. Large sections of *Wozzeck*'s three acts are written in a chamber-music style, with Berg using full orchestral resources sparingly to heighten specific points.

LULU SUITE Berg arranged this orchestral suite of five movements from his opera-in-progress, *Lulu*, in 1934—partly to stir public anticipation for the opera, which he hoped to finish soon but was unable to do. This is complex, atonal, but intensely dramatic music.

HECTOR BERLIOZ

Pronounced: *bare-lee-ohz*. Born December 11, 1803, in La Côte-St. André, near Grenoble, France. Died March 8, 1869, in Paris, at age 65.

SIGNIFICANCE French composer, conductor, and critic, sometimes called the "father of modern orchestration." He was one of the first composers to give an orchestral work a "program" (a plot or sequence of events), and an early Romantic who favored super-scaled works scored for bigger and bigger orchestras.

BACKGROUND Although he was sent to Paris to study medicine (his father's profession), Berlioz decided to accept disinheritance in order to take up music instead. Twice Berlioz was denied admission to the Paris Conservatory because he did not meet their standards for previous formal musical training (he could play only guitar and flute). Finally, after he borrowed the money to pay for a successful performance of a Mass he had written (the *Messe Solonelle*), he was accepted by the Conservatory. There he immediately established a reputation as a rebel, expounding what his teachers considered subversive ideas about harmony and structure.

Stories about his fiery behavior abound. The most famous concerns his stormy wooing of the English Shakespearean actress Harriet Smithson, commemorated in his *Symphonie Fantastique*. Later he married her, but the romance soon cooled and they ended up living apart. His personal and professional life was a series of such ups and downs. He constantly charged ahead romantically with some grandiose idea or other, never quite sure where he was heading yet trusting it would all turn out right. Sometimes it did. Mussorgsky, the Russian composer, said soon after Berlioz's death: "There are two giants in music, the thinker Beethoven and the super-thinker Berlioz."

SYMPHONIE FANTASTIQUE
(FANTASTIC SYMPHONY)

In one of his popular TV broadcasts, Leonard Bernstein called this work "the first psychedelic symphony in history, the first musical description ever made of a [drug] trip"—a narcotics trip that ends up taking its hero through hell, "screaming at his own funeral."

Berlioz's symphony, one of the first to have a specific "program," depicts a young man's opium dream after an unhappy love affair with a famous actress—with the real and the imagined intertwined, particularly in the frenzy of the final "Witches' Sabbath" movement. The symphony's five movements are unified by a recurring theme—the *idée fixe*—representing the hero's beloved. The movements have the following titles: "Reveries, Passions"; "A Ball"; "Country Scenes"; "March to the Scaffold"; "Dream of a Witches' Sabbath."

RECOMMENDED CDs
Muti, Philadelphia Orchestra (Angel, 1985)
Munch, Boston Symphony (RCA/BMG, 1962)

RECOMMENDED LPs
Muti, Philadelphia Orchestra (Angel, 1985)
Munch, Boston Symphony (RCA Victrola, 1962)

RECOMMENDED CASSETTES
Muti, Philadelphia Orchestra (Angel, 1985)
Munch, Boston Symphony (RCA Victrola, 1962)

COMMENTS
Muti's performance is supercharged and the virtuosic playing of his Philadelphians is *fantastique* indeed. For many years Munch was the most exciting and passionate conductor of this score, and his 1962 Boston recording remains the best of three versions he recorded, although its sound is not up to later recordings by others.

HAROLD IN ITALY

Though called a symphony, this is in some ways a program concerto for viola and orchestra. It was written on a commission from the great 19th-century violin and viola virtuoso Paganini. Based loosely on Byron's *Childe Harolde*, the work depicts a series of scenes that pass before the wandering Harold's eyes ("Harold in the Mountains," "March of the Pilgrims," "Serenade of a Mountaineer to His Sweetheart," and "Orgy of the Brigands").

The symphony is richly lyrical and expressive, with its chief theme recurring throughout the work. Unlike the recurring *idée fixe* of Berlioz's earlier *Symphonie Fantastique*, however, this theme interposes itself on other themes, modifying them or being modified in the process.

RECOMMENDED CDs
Zukerman, Dutoit, Montreal Symphony (London, 1988)
W. Christ, Maazel, Berlin Philharmonic (Deutsche Grammophon, 1985)

RECOMMENDED LPs
W. Christ, Maazel, Berlin Philharmonic (Deutsche Grammophon, 1985)
Menuhin, Colin Davis, Philharmonia Orchestra of London (Angel, 1968)

RECOMMENDED CASSETTE
W. Christ, Maazel, Berlin Philharmonic (Deutsche Grammophon, 1985)

COMMENTS
Zukerman and Dutoit are the most fervent and colorful.

Christ and Maazel are a bit more dramatic than Menuhin and Davis, who are, however, most eloquent.

NUITS D'ÉTÉ (SUMMER NIGHTS)

One of Berlioz's most intimate and least grandiose works, this is a graceful, sensitive, lyrical setting, for soprano and orchestra, of six poems by the arch-Romantic Théophile Gautier. The texts are primarily lamentations of lost love, with the best-known song, "Absence," a plea for the return of a beloved from a voyage. Berlioz composed the songs in 1841 for voice and piano, and over the next 15 years he orchestrated them — creating the first enduring song-cycle with orchestra.

RECOMMENDED CDs
Norman, Colin Davis, London Symphony (Philips)
Te Kanawa, Barenboim, Orchestre de Paris (Deutsche Grammophon, 1982)

RECOMMENDED LPs
Crespin, Ansermet, Suisse Romande Orchestra (London, 1963)

Te Kanawa, Barenboim, Orchestre de Paris (Deutsche Grammophon, 1982)

RECOMMENDED CASSETTES
Crespin, Ansermet, Suisse Romande Orchestra (London, 1963)
Te Kanawa, Barenboim, Orchestre de Paris (Deutsche Grammophon, 1982)

COMMENTS

Norman and Crespin sing the songs with individuality, character, and insight. Te Kanawa is blander in dramatic terms, but lyrically beautiful.

FOR FOLLOW-UP CONSIDERATION

OVERTURES The overtures Berlioz composed for his various operas have won more popularity in the concert hall and on recordings than the works they introduce have won in the opera house. They remain uniquely colorful, often fiery, orchestral showpieces.

RECOMMENDED CD, LP, AND CASSETTE

Munch, Boston Symphony (RCA Gold Seal/BMG, 1957–61) Sizzlingly exciting yet also elegant and richly virtuosic performances of *The Roman Carnival, Beatrice and Benedict, Benvenuto Cellini*, and *Le Corsair* Overtures. The 1993 CD edition also includes the "Royal Hunt and Storm" from Berlioz's *The Trojans* and the "Queen Mab Scherzo" from his *Romeo et Juliette*, plus Saint-Saens' shimmering *Omphale's Spinning Wheel*, all beautifully performed by Munch and the Bostonians at the peak of their form.

ROMEO AND JULIET Composed in 1839, Berlioz's "dramatic symphony," based on scenes from Shakespeare's play, preceded Gounod's opera by 28 years, Tchaikovsky's "overture-fantasia" by 30, and Prokofiev's ballet by nearly a century. Berlioz's work remains, however, the most penetrating musical approach to Shakespeare's romantic tragedy. The complete score calls for three vocal soloists (a mezzo-soprano, a tenor, and a bass-baritone) plus a chorus in addition to full orchestra. Frequently the orchestral sections are performed alone in concert programs and on recordings, and most critics agree that they are the greatest parts, especially the technically difficult, gossamer-like "Queen Mab Scherzo."

RECOMMENDED CD, LP, AND CASSETTE OF THE COMPLETE WORK

Muti, Norman, Aler, Estes, Philadelphia Orchestra (Angel, 1986). Sung in the original French.

Giulini, Chicago Symphony (Angel, 1970). Muti's version is fervent and well-paced, and Norman is positively glowing. Giulini's instrumental excerpts are among the best of his American recordings.

RECOMMENDED LP AND CASSETTE OF THE ORCHESTRAL EXCERPTS

GEORGES BIZET

Pronounced: bee-zay. Born October 25, 1838, in Paris. Died June 3, 1875,
in Bougival, France, at age 36.

SIGNIFICANCE   French composer who helped create a more naturalistic
form of opera.

BACKGROUND   Bizet's father, a singing teacher, recognized his son's
musical interests early and entered him in the Paris conservatory when the
boy was ten years old. Later Bizet studied with the French composer Halévy,
whose daughter he married and whose last opera, *Noë*, he completed.
Bizet's own works met with little success during his short lifetime, and he
generally lived under financial strain. Just a few months after the premiere
of his opera *Carmen*, he died of heart disease. Although *Carmen* initially
had a mixed reception, it later became one of the world's most popular
operas, and set the pattern for a new kind of realistic opera in the late 19th
and early 20th centuries.

CARMEN SUITES

Bizet himself arranged two orchestral suites of music from his opera *Carmen*. Over the years they have become probably the most popular orchestral
arrangement of music from any opera. In order to create a more dramatic
and cohesive orchestral work, Bizet not only changed the orchestration of
some parts, but also the sequence in which the arias and musical interludes
occur. Suite No. 1 includes the "March of the Toreadors," the Prelude to
Act One, the Intermezzo from Act Three, "Aragonaise," and "Seguidilla."
Suite No. 2 includes the "March of the Smugglers," "Habañera," "Toreador
Song," the Children's Chorus, and "Bohemian Dance."

Another (and more controversial) arrangement of music from *Carmen*
was made during the 1960s by the Soviet composer Rodion Shchedrin for
a ballet starring his wife, the Bolshoi Ballet's Maya Plisetskaya. Shchedrin's
version, for strings and 47 percussion instruments, is a wildly unorthodox
view of Bizet's score which some criticize as too distorted but others find
great fun.

RECOMMENDED CD————————
Slatkin, Saint Louis Symphony (Telarc,
1979)

RECOMMENDED LPs————————
Slatkin, Saint Louis Symphony (Telarc,
1979)

Ormandy, Philadelphia Orchestra (RCA,
1976)

RECOMMENDED CASSETTES————
Munch, New Philharmonia of London
(London, 1967)
Ormandy, Philadelphia Orchestra (RCA,
1976)

COMMENTS ——————————
The best CD edition of the Shchedrin
Suite is by Rozhdestvensky, Bolshoi

Theater Orchestra (Eurodisc, 1968); the
best cassette version is by Fiedler, Boston Pops (RCA Victrola, 1969).

CARMEN

Based loosely on the novel by Prosper Merimée, the opera *Carmen* tells the story of a tempestuous gypsy girl's tragic romance with a young Spanish corporal in 19th-century Seville. Despite the frequently lively, colorful music (for the Changing of the Guard, a bullfight sequence, etc.), there is an underlying sense of foreboding and doom that grows in intensity until the final curtain. The mezzo-soprano title role has become perhaps the most sought-after in that operatic category. However, a number of famous sopranos have also found the role comfortable for their voices and have sung (and recorded) it with success.

Bizet's original version of the opera included spoken dialogue in many scenes, but after Bizet's death, Ernest Guiraud, an American-born French composer (1837–1892), composed recitatives (a form of vocal declamation with orchestral accompaniment) to replace the dialogue. It is Guiraud's version that is used in most opera houses and in most recordings. If performed uncut, Bizet's *Carmen* can challenge some of Wagner's music-dramas for length.

RECOMMENDED CDs —————————
Maazel, Migenes-Johnson, Esham, Domingo, Raimondi, French National Orchestra & Radio-France Chorus (Erato, 1984), *complete (three discs)*; also single highlights disc

Pretre, Callas, Guiot, Gedda, Massard, Paris Opera Orchestra & Chorus (Angel, mid-1960s), *complete (three discs)*

RECOMMENDED LPs —————————
Maazel, Migenes-Johnson, Esham, Domingo, Raimondi, French National Orchestra & Radio-France Chorus (Erato, 1984), *complete (three discs)*; also single highlights disc

Pretre, Callas, Guiot, Gedda, Massard, Paris Opera Orchestra & Chorus (Angel, 1966), *complete (three discs)*

RECOMMENDED CASSETTES ——————
Maazel, Migenes-Johnson, Esham, Domingo, Raimondi, French National Orchestra & Radio-France Chorus (Erato, 1984), *complete (three cassettes)*

Karajan, L. Price, Freni, Corelli, Merrill, Vienna Philharmonic & Chorus (RCA, mid-1960s), *complete (three cassettes)*; also single highlights cassette

COMMENTS —————————
Migenes-Johnson proves here that she is the best Carmen around today. Neither Callas nor Price ever sang the role on stage, but their recordings are superbly compelling. Dramatically Callas is incomparable, even when she sacrifices musical sound for dramatic effect. With Price the excitement is more musical, often breathtakingly so, and her Carmen is more warm-hearted than Migenes-Johnson or Callas. Callas and Price use the Guiraud recitatives, Migenes-Johnson the original version with spoken dialogue. All are sung in the original French.

SYMPHONY IN C

Written when Bizet was 17, this symphony was not "discovered" until 1933, 62 years after his death. It has since become part of the standard concert repertory, and also the score for one of George Balanchine's most popular ballets, titled *Symphony in C* in the U.S. and *Palais de Cristal* (*Crystal Palace*) in Paris. Much the way Prokofiev's *Classical Symphony* looks back to Mozart and Haydn from a 20th-century viewpoint, so Bizet's symphony looks back on the Classical style from a 19th-century viewpoint. It is exuberantly melodic, rhythmically vibrant, and spontaneously likable.

RECOMMENDED CDs

Mata, National Arts Centre Orchestra of Canada (RCA, 1986)

Beecham, French National Radio Orchestra (Angel, 1959)

RECOMMENDED LPs AND CASSETTES

Mata, National Arts Centre Orchestra of Canada (RCA, 1986)

Bernstein, New York Philharmonic (CBS, 1963)

COMMENTS

Mata's performance is wonderfully jaunty yet elegant, with crisply clean sound. Bernstein's has a bit more zip and lyrical breadth, but also more dated sound. Beecham was over 80 when he recorded his version, but the spirit of his performance is as youthful as that of any conductor a quarter his age, though here again the sound is not up to Mata's.

FOR FOLLOW-UP CONSIDERATION

ROMA   A vivacious, brightly melodic work, sometimes listed as Bizet's Symphony No. 2 and sometimes as his Concert Suite No. 3. Begun while Bizet was studying in Rome in 1860 but then put aside and not completed until eight years after his return to Paris. It did not receive a complete performance until after Bizet's death, and then was called *Souvenirs de Rome* (source of the suite designation, although Bizet had always referred to it as a symphony). George Balanchine helped give it some currency as a '50s ballet for the New York City Ballet.

RECOMMENDED CD

J-C Casadesus, Orchestre National de Lille (MusiFrance/Erato, 1990)

RECOMMENDED CASSETTE

Gardelli, Munich Radio Orchestra (Orfeo, 1986)

COMMENTS

Both are good performances if not as scintillating as they might be. The liveliest performance is on an out-of-print 1955 Vox LP by Barzin and New York City Ballet Orchestra, but the sound is now dated and a sizable part of the first movement is cut (as in Balanchine's ballet).

PIERRE BOULEZ

Pronounced: boo-*lezz*. Born March 26, 1925, in Montbrison, France. Now living in Paris.

SIGNIFICANCE French composer and conductor whose tightly constructed, rhythmically mobile works reflect his fascination with music as "layers of sound."

BACKGROUND Boulez was born in the south of France, and went to Paris to study in 1943, primarily with Olivier Messiaen at the Paris Conservatory. In 1948 he began a decade as music director of the famous Jean-Louis Barrault–Madeleine Renaud theater company. In 1954, Barrault let him use his theater on off-days to organize concerts of new music, and the resulting "Domaine Musicale" (Musical Domain) concerts became the center of new music in Paris for many years. During this period Boulez had a series of stormy encounters with French government officials, who kept his music off French radio.

In the 1960s, Boulez turned increasingly to conducting, feeling that symphony orchestras were too rooted in 19th-century styles and traditions, and that if his own music were ever to have a chance it must come from orchestras better trained in a wider repertory, especially in the 12-tone music of Webern, Berg, and Schoenberg as the major classics of our century. Following posts in Baden-Baden and Cleveland, Boulez in 1971 became conductor of the BBC Symphony in London (succeeding Colin Davis) and music director of the New York Philharmonic (succeeding Leonard Bernstein). His tenure in New York was a controversial one, but he is credited with attracting a new audience of younger music lovers.

Boulez left New York in 1977 to concentrate again on composing and to become director of the Institute for Research and Acoustical and Musical Coordination in Paris (known internationally by the acronym for its name in French, IRCAM).

LE MARTEAU SANS MAÎTRE (THE HAMMER WITHOUT A MASTER)

Stravinsky, when asked in 1957 which work of the younger generation most impressed him, cited Boulez's *Marteau* as the "only important work of this new age of search." He added, "It will be a considerable time before the value of *Le Marteau sans Maître* is recognized. Meanwhile, I shall not explain my admiration for it but adapt Gertrude Stein's answer when asked why she liked Picasso's paintings: 'I like to look at them'—I like to listen to Boulez."

Le Marteau, written in 1954 and revised in 1957, is a complex work in nine movements (lasting about 28 minutes altogether), based on three short Surrealistic poems by René Char. Four of the movements are set for contralto and an instrumental group, and five for the instruments alone. Only six instruments are used: guitar, vibraphone, alto flute, viola, xylorimba (which combines the qualities of a xylophone and marimba), and percussion. Words and music are placed in an extremely involved mutual relationship, with related vocal and instrumental sections not necessarily succeeding one another, but instead being woven crisscross into the work's overall fabric. The voice is used especially daringly, with many wide vocal leaps, sometimes on the same syllable. The overall listening effect of the music is not unlike a stream-of-consciousness exploration of a huge underground cavern.

RECOMMENDED CD

Deroubaix, Boulez, six instrumentalists (Adès, mid-1960s)

RECOMMENDED LP

Minton, Boulez, Ensemble Musique Vivante (CBS, 1973)

RECOMMENDED CASSETTE

None presently available.

COMMENTS

Boulez's own two recordings reveal how even composers can change their minds about interpreting the same composition. His 1973 performance is slower than the mid-1960s one, and a number of instrumental details are accented differently. Beyond that, it's a toss-up, although the CBS sound engineering is superior. Minton's voice is more attractive, though not necessarily more convincing than Deroubaix's.

PLI SELON PLI (FOLD ON FOLD)

If *Le Marteau sans Maître* established Boulez's international reputation as a significant composer, then *Pli selon Pli* (premiered in 1960) solidified that reputation. It is a complex but fascinating hour-long set of five pieces for soprano and orchestra, inspired by the work of the French poet Stéphane Mallarmé (1842–1898).

According to Boulez: "The title is taken from a Mallarmé poem not used in my musical transposition; it [instead] indicates the meaning and direction of the work. In this poem the author describes the way in which the dissolving mist gradually reveals the stones of the city of Bruges. In the same way, as the five pieces unfold, they reveal, fold by fold, a portrait of Mallarmé." The "folds" are basically layers of delicate, sensuous sounds—making unusually subtle use of a wide range of percussion instruments (xylophones, vibraphones, several kinds of bells, etc.). The first and fifth pieces — "Don" (Gift) and "Tombeau" (Tomb) — are primarily instrumental, with lines from the Mallarmé poems of their titles intervening only as brief vocal quotations. The three central pieces, titled "Improvisations on Mallarmé I, II, and III," use three longer Mallarmé sonnets — with the vocal line more central to the musical development, and with more modest instrumental forces than the opening and closing pieces.

RECOMMENDED CD _____

Milhály, Sziklay, Budapest Chamber Orchestra (Hungaraton, 1960s; *two parts only*)

RECOMMENDED LP _____

Boulez, Lukomska, BBC Symphony (CBS, 1969)

RECOMMENDED CASSETTE _____

None presently available.

COMMENTS _____

The composer's own 1969 recording is, so far, the only complete one and is available only on LP at present. It is exceptionally clear in the way it delineates the subtlest colors and shifting timbres of the instrumental parts. The excellent Milhály recording includes only the "Improvisations on Mallarmé I and II."

JOHANNES BRAHMS

Pronounced: *brahmz*. Born May 7, 1833, in Hamburg, Germany. Died April 3, 1897, in Vienna, at age 63.

SIGNIFICANCE   German composer and pianist, considered by many in his time as the heir to Beethoven in writing "absolute music" that needed no program or story. Working in Classical forms, but with a freer, more Romantic spirit, Brahms composed works generally marked by deep lyric beauty and emotional gravity.

BACKGROUND   Brahms grew up in a disreputable waterfront district of Hamburg, where his father was a part-time double bass player in the Hamburg City Theater and his mother a seamstress. From his earliest years, Brahms learned everything he could about music, and by the age of 13 he was playing the piano in waterfront cafés to entertain the patrons. By 15 he was giving serious piano recitals. At one of them he was heard by the Hungarian violinist Eduard Reményi, who offered Brahms a job as his accompanist on a tour featuring both serious works and gypsy music. Along the route, Brahms managed to meet some of the leading musicians of the day — including Liszt, Joachim, and Robert and Clara Schumann. He became particularly close lifelong friends with the Schumanns, who enthusiastically championed his piano compositions.

In his 20s Brahms took many jobs briefly—among them, conducting and teaching in Lippe-Detmold and Vienna. But he gave them up and declined others, believing that he composed best when there were no entangling alliances to hamper him. Perhaps for the same reason he never married. "It is as hard to marry as to write an opera," he once said, and he never did either. A painstaking composer, Brahms worked over and over on his pieces before publishing them (his first symphony took him nearly 20 years to complete). He wrote four symphonies, two piano concertos, one violin concerto, one double concerto for violin and cello, a Requiem, plus a number of songs, piano pieces, and chamber works—most of which have become part of the standard concert repertory. He died of an ailment aggravated when he caught cold after an arduous 40-hour journey to attend the funeral of Clara Schumann.

SYMPHONY No. 1 IN C MINOR

The majesty and expressive lyricism of Brahms' themes, and particularly the way they ebb and flow in surging waves of sound, make this one of the most powerful of all symphonies. Brahms, though a well-known composer of piano and chamber works, delayed writing his first symphony until he was in his 40s—declaring at one point: "I shall never finish a symphony. You have no idea how it feels to hear behind you the tramp of a giant like Beethoven." When this symphony was finally completed and performed, one prominent admirer promptly hailed it as "the Tenth Symphony"—linking its Classical form, its grandeur, its dramatic tensions, and its depth of emotional feeling to Beethoven's nine symphonies. The work has long been one of the cornerstones of the concert repertory.

RECOMMENDED CDs
Bernstein, Vienna Philharmonic (Deutsche Grammophon, 1983)
Tennstedt, London Philharmonic (Angel, 1984)

RECOMMENDED LPs
Bernstein, Vienna Philharmonic (Deutsche Grammophon, 1983)
Szell, Cleveland Orchestra (CBS, 1967)

RECOMMENDED CASSETTES
Bernstein, Vienna Philharmonic (Deutsche Grammophon, 1983)
Karajan, Berlin Philharmonic (Deutsche Grammophon, 1963)

COMMENTS
Bernstein's performance has both grandeur and humanity, as well as inner tension. Both Tennstedt and Szell project strong rhythmic urgency and compelling power. Karajan's more spacious performance probes the symphony's depths with both poetry and nobility. Among vintage performances transferred to CD and also available on LP and Cassette, Toscanini's continues to remain justifiably famous. In Toscanini's hands, Brahms' First indeed becomes Beethoven's Tenth—even though the 1951 monophonic recording sounds strident by today's standards.

VIOLIN CONCERTO IN D

A prominent critic in Brahms' time called this not a concerto *for* but a concerto *against* the violin. Indeed, its technical complexities—especially in the final movement—test the mettle of any virtuoso. But over the years the popularity of the concerto has come to rest more on the sunny warmth of its lyricism, on its tender and caressing melodies, and on the symphonic sweep of its interweaving solo and orchestral parts.

RECOMMENDED CDs————————
Heifetz, Reiner, Chicago Symphony (RCA, 1955)
Mutter, Karajan, Berlin Philharmonic (Deutsche Grammophon, 1982)

RECOMMENDED LPs————————
Heifetz, Reiner, Chicago Symphony (RCA, 1955)
Perlman, Giulini, Chicago Symphony (Angel, 1977)

RECOMMENDED CASSETTES———
Heifetz, Reiner, Chicago Symphony (RCA, 1955)

Perlman, Giulini, Chicago Symphony (Angel, 1977)

COMMENTS————————————
Despite its aging sonics, the Heifetz performance remains in a class by itself; he made few recordings as beautiful as this one. It soars lyrically, and the finale is a virtuoso's field-day. Mutter gives a warmer performance that's also superb technically. Perlman also plays with tremendous flair and expressive warmth.

PIANO CONCERTO No. 2 IN B FLAT

Starting quietly with a haunting horn theme, this concerto evolves into one of the most massive and powerful of all piano concertos in the Classical form. One 19th-century critic called it more like "a symphony with piano obbligato." Instead of the customary three movements of a concerto, this one has four—with the additional movement (a stormy "allegro appassionato," a scherzo) inserted between the dramatic first movement and the usual slow (andante) middle movement. Sir Donald Francis Tovey, the British musicologist, justified this as a master stroke, assuring that the slow movement's "emotion is a reaction after a storm, not after a triumph." Throughout, the concerto is filled with subtle poetry and dramatic force, forthright melody and imposing eloquence.

RECOMMENDED CDs————————
Ashkenazy, Haitink, Vienna Philharmonic (London, 1982)
Zimerman, Bernstein, Vienna Philharmonic (Deutsche Grammophon, 1985)

RECOMMENDED LPs————————
Ashkenazy, Haitink, Vienna Philharmonic (London, 1982)
Zimerman, Bernstein, Vienna Philharmonic (Deutsche Grammophon, 1985)

Ashkenazy, Haitink, Vienna Philhar-
   monic (London, 1982)
Richter, Leinsdorf, Chicago Symphony
   (RCA, 1960)

COMMENTS_____
The Ashkenazy-Haitink performance is
full of grace, poetry, and sensitivity. Zi-
merman-Bernstein is more intense and
propulsive, and Richter-Leinsdorf the
most expressively reflective.

FOR FOLLOW-UP CONSIDERATION

SYMPHONY No. 2 IN D MAJOR   Much has been written about how
long it took Brahms to compose his First Symphony, with Beethoven's
shadow inhibiting his efforts to compose *any* symphony for years. What is
often overlooked, however, is that once Brahms had become confident of
his ability (a confidence reinforced by the First Symphony's success), his
Second was composed relatively swiftly—just a year later, in fact. Composed
in part in the Alpine village of Pörtschach, it seems to reflect the sunlight
and peaceful relaxation of that place and time in Brahms' life.

RECOMMENDED CD, LP AND
CASSETTE_____
Bernstein, Vienna Philharmonic
   (Deutsche Grammophon, 1983), an

alternately tender and vivacious performance of enormous Bernstein
warmth.

SYMPHONY No. 3 IN F MAJOR   Toscanini once called this the hardest
to get a "fix" on of all Brahms' symphonies. Viennese critic Eduard Hanslick
dubbed it Brahms' "Eroica," but Clara Schumann saw it instead as a "forest
idyll" and British composer Sir Arnold Bax as "the Four Seasons." Whatever
the interpretation, Brahms' Third is a work of drama, majesty, and intense
lyrical beauty.

RECOMMENDED CD, LP, AND
CASSETTE_____
Bernstein, Vienna Philharmonic (Deut-
   sche Grammophon, 1983), in which

Bernstein keeps all the interweaving
themes moving more dynamically and
dramatically than most other conductors.

SYMPHONY No. 4 IN E MINOR   This most elegaic of Brahms' symphonies was likened by German critic Friedrich Herzfeld to "a heavy-hearted
ballad [that] leads to fierce outbursts, whose impulsive power sets the scene
for ... monumental tragedy." The final movement was considered most
unorthodox in its time for its use of such then-archaic classical forms as the
passacaglia, previously unheard-of in a symphony.

RECOMMENDED CD, LP, AND
CASSETTE_____
Carlos Kleiber, Vienna Philharmonic

(Deutsche Grammophon, 1981), a
surgingly powerful, penetrating account.

PIANO CONCERTO No. 1 IN D MINOR Very different in mood and structure from Brahms' Second Piano Concerto, this one is more restlessly searching, introspective, yet noble. Of its second movement, Brahms wrote to Clara Schumann: "I am making a gentle portrait of you in the form of an adagio."

RECOMMENDED CD, LP, AND CASSETTE
Ashkenazy, Haitink, Amsterdam Concertgebouw Orchestra (London, 1982), a compelling performance that beautifully blends the work's surging drama and poetic lyricism.

DOUBLE CONCERTO FOR VIOLIN AND CELLO Brahms' last concerto (1887) is a broadly lyrical one—and unusual in its combination of two solo instruments performing against orchestral textures. Its nearest relative is perhaps Beethoven's Triple Concerto (for Violin, Cello, Piano, and Orchestra).

RECOMMENDED CD AND LP
Kremer, Maisky, Bernstein, Vienna Philharmonic (Deutsche Grammophon, 1984), a warmly soaring performance.

RECOMMENDED CASSETTE
Perlman, Rostropovich, Haitink, Amsterdam Concertgebouw Orchestra (Angel, 1980), a vivid, compelling performance.

ANTON BRUCKNER

Pronounced: *brook*-ner. Born September 4, 1824, in Ausfelden, Austria. Died October 11, 1896, in Vienna, at age 72.

SIGNIFICANCE Austrian composer and organist, until recently the most neglected of the major 19th-century Romantic symphonists.

BACKGROUND After the death of his father (a poor village schoolteacher), Bruckner was sent as a very young boy to an Augustine monastery to become a chorister. The deep religious feelings he acquired during this period remained with him for the rest of his life. He was first a schoolteacher and then court organist in Linz and Vienna. A performance of Wagner's *Tannhäuser* in 1863 turned him into an enthusiastic Wagnerite, and he sought to adapt some of Wagner's theories and harmonic language to the symphonic form.

But his lengthy, discursive, elaborately scored symphonies met considerable opposition from the leading Vienna critics, who idolized Brahms. This, coupled with Bruckner's lack of self-confidence and unsophisticated country ways, led to numerous revisions and modifications of his original scores — sometimes executed by well-meaning colleagues, conductors, and publishers hoping to make his music more palatable to the general public. As a result, there has long been confusion and debate over various editions of Bruckner's symphonies. In recent years, the Bruckner Society has sought to eliminate the discrepancies in different published editions, and to encourage the use of Bruckner's original scores as the most faithful to his intentions and his true individuality.

SYMPHONY No. 4 IN E FLAT ("ROMANTIC")

Bruckner himself named this his *Romantic* symphony, in contrast to the more Classical forms of the symphonies of Brahms and others of his time. But he was reluctant to give it a program in the manner of the Wagnerians, who considered the programmatic symphonic poems of Liszt and Berlioz's *Symphonie Fantastique* models for Romantic orchestral music. Bruckner did, however, consent to calling the third movement, with its many horn calls, "The Hunting of the Hare." The basic mood of the symphony is assertive. Bruckner builds his themes dramatically and often grandly, with frequent outbursts and ebbs. The complex last movement adds new themes as well as reworking themes from other movements.

RECOMMENDED CDs
Haitink, Vienna Philharmonic (Philips, 1987)
Bohm, Vienna Philharmonic (London, 1974)

RECOMMENDED LPs
Tennstedt, Berlin Philharmonic (Angel, 1982)
Haitink, Amsterdam Concertgebouw (Philips, 1965)

RECOMMENDED CASSETTES
Haitink, Vienna Philharmonic (Philips, 1987)
Tennstedt, Berlin Philharmonic (Angel, 1982)

COMMENTS
Haitink conveys warmth and majesty, spaciousness and strength in the most satisfying combinations. The newer Vienna performance is marginally superior in both performance and recording to the Amsterdam one.

Bohm is more dramatic in his emphases and more intense overall, for one of his all-time great recordings.

With Tennstedt, another outstanding Brucknerian, there is an overpowering feeling of rugged grandeur as well as dramatic intensity.

SYMPHONY No. 9 IN D MINOR

Although this symphony was left unfinished at Bruckner's death, its three completed movements are considered by some critics to be a whole "as is" (like Schubert's Eighth). Perhaps it is even appropriate for a symphony dedicated to "my dear God" to end quietly, at the conclusion of an adagio (the third movement), in a mood of peace and tranquility. It is more advanced than most works of its time in its explorations of harmony. The English musicologist Deryck Cooke has written: "Into the vast cathedral-like architecture of Bruckner's symphonic form there intruded [in the Ninth Symphony] at last something of the disturbing emotionalism of the late Romantics. There is turmoil, perplexity, and pain in this music, but at its heart stands the unshaken faith of a deeply religious man which eventually finds the peace it is seeking in the final bars of the adagio...."

RECOMMENDED CDs
Haitink, Amsterdam Concertgebouw (Philips, 1981)
Walter, Columbia Symphony (CBS, 1959)

RECOMMENDED LPs
Haitink, Amsterdam Concertgebouw (Philips, 1981)
Walter, Columbia Symphony (CBS, 1959)

RECOMMENDED CASSETTES
Haitink, Amsterdam Concertgebouw (Philips, 1981)
Walter, Columbia Symphony (CBS, 1959)

COMMENTS
Haitink's second (1981) recording is profoundly moving, noble and dramatic by turns. Walter, in one of his last recordings, is also deeply moving and eloquent.

FOR FOLLOW-UP CONSIDERATION

SYMPHONY No. 7   One of the first Bruckner symphonies to win widespread acceptance in Europe and the U.S., partly because of the dedication of its dirgelike second movement (an adagio) as an "In Memoriam" to Wagner.

RECOMMENDED CD, LP, AND CASSETTE
Chailly, Berlin Radio Symphony (London, 1985), a vivid, full-bodied, dramatic performance.

SYMPHONY No. 8   One of Bruckner's longest and most grandiloquent scores, with one of the most heartrendingly melancholy and beautifully lyrical movements (an adagio) in any symphony.

RECOMMENDED CD, LP, AND CASSETTE
Haitink, Amsterdam Concertgebouw (Philips, 1981), a beautifully majestic, sensitive, persuasive performance.

FREDERIC CHOPIN

Pronounced: *show*-pan. Born February 22, 1810, in Zelazowa Wola, near
Warsaw. Died October 17, 1849, in Paris, France, at age 39.

SIGNIFICANCE Polish composer and pianist, the great Romantic poet of
the piano. He composed almost exclusively for the piano and was one of
the first to introduce Slavic elements into Classical forms.

BACKGROUND The son of a French father and a Polish mother, Chopin
grew up in Poland but spent most of his adult life in Paris. His musical
studies began at his father's private school for young noblemen in Warsaw,
and he gave his first piano recital at the age of nine. From then on, the
piano was to be his life. By the age of 19 he had written two piano concertos,
some of his most famous polonaises, waltzes, and mazurkas.

At 21 he visited Paris and met with such success with his first concerts
that he stayed there permanently. He never married, but he had a long,
stormy affair with the French authoress Aurore Dudevant, who wrote under
the name George Sand. Chopin never revisited Poland after 1831 (it was
then under Russian occupation), but he was widely known in Paris as a
Polish patriot and an expert on Polish literature. Tuberculosis, aggravated
by his social high-life, led to his death at a young age.

WALTZES

Chopin wrote his first three waltzes when he was nineteen, after his first
visit to Vienna—at a time when the waltzes of Johann Strauss Sr. were the
rage of that city. Yet Chopin's waltzes are of a completely different sort.
Instead of invoking the atmosphere of the ballroom, they are poems in
music more closely akin to his etudes and other solo piano works. They
are often deeply romantic, sometimes melancholy, sometimes gay, and filled
with elegance and wit.

Pianist Artur Rubinstein, one of this century's great Chopin interpreters,
had this to say about Chopin's waltzes: "The point is not to try to define
them all in a word or phrase, or to make them all sound 'like Chopin
waltzes,' but to consider each of them as a unique event and listen very
attentively to what each has to say."

Chopin wrote several sets of waltzes between 1829 and 1847, the most
famous bearing the publisher's opus numbers 18, 34, 42, 64, and 70. Pianists
rarely play them in compositional sequence, preferring to group the various
waltzes according to their own tastes for mood, color, or dramatic effect.
Some of the waltzes have acquired descriptive titles—such as the "Minute
Waltz" (Op. 64, No. 1, in D flat), "Farewell Waltz" (Op. 69, No. 1, in A flat,

written as a farewell gift to Marya Vodzhinska, a Polish girl Chopin almost married), and several "Valses brillantes" (Op. 34, Nos. 1, 2, 3, in A flat, A minor, and F major respectively).

RECOMMENDED CDs————————
Rubinstein (RCA, 1963), *14 waltzes*
Lipatti (Angel, 1950), *13 waltzes, mono*

RECOMMENDED LPs————————
Rubinstein (RCA, 1963), *14 waltzes*
Lipatti (CBS/Odyssey, 1949), *14 waltzes, mono*

RECOMMENDED CASSETTES———
Rubinstein (RCA, 1963), *14 waltzes*
Lipatti (CBS/Odyssey, *14 waltzes, mono*)

COMMENTS————————————
Rubinstein brings a unique elegance and grace to the waltzes, as well as tonal color and rhythmic vibrancy. His recording *is* in compositional sequence.

Lipatti's two recordings remain among the century's most memorable, by a pianist capable of exceptional light and lightness, caressing lyricism, and rhythmic subtlety. The Odyssey set is late 1940s' "low fidelity," but not enough to detract from the beauty of the playing. The similar Angel set is taken from a live recital, actually Lipatti's last — and the waltzes are all beautifully played despite the physical pain Lipatti endured during the recital (from the leukemia which claimed his life just a few months later, at age 33), and which made it impossible for him to play the scheduled fourteenth waltz.

POLONAISES

A *polonaise* is a formal Polish dance in ¾ time that dates back to at least the 16th century. Chopin composed more than 15 polonaises for solo piano. The first one was written when he was a mere eight years old and was his first published composition. The last one, the "Fantaisie Polonaise," was his last large composition. All of Chopin's polonaises blend the stately rhythms of a Polish folk dance with a more martial, patriotic fervor.

RECOMMENDED CDs————————
Pollini (Deutsche Grammophon, 1985), *Nos. 1–7*
Rubinstein (RCA, 1964), *Nos. 1–7*

RECOMMENDED LPs————————
Pollini (Deutsche Grammophon, 1985), *Nos. 1–7*
Rubinstein (RCA, 1964), *Nos. 1–7*

RECOMMENDED CASSETTES———
Pollini (Deutsche Grammophon, 1985), *Nos. 1–7*
Rubinstein (RCA, 1964), *Nos. 1–7*

COMMENTS————————————
Both Pollini and Rubinstein play their sets with fervor as well as tonal sensitivity, with Pollini having more up-to-date sound engineering. Both performances are available on single CDs, but Rubinstein's LP and Cassette versions are part of a two-disc or two-cassette album with other Chopin works. Pollini's LP edition is part of a three-disc album with Chopin preludes and etudes; the cassette edition, however, is a single cassette.

PIANO CONCERTO No. 1 IN E MINOR

Chopin wrote only two piano concertos, both during his late teens. Actually the concerto published as No. 2 (in F minor) was written first, the one published as No. 1 (in E minor) coming within the following year. Some critics maintain that the concertos are not as cohesive as Chopin's solo works, that Chopin was essentially a miniaturist who did not handle the larger forms as well.

There are others, however, who find the concertos a remarkably original pair—particularly considering Chopin's remoteness (in his teen years in Poland) from the musical centers of his day. Both concertos stand out for their grace and elegance, and for their early Romantic expressiveness. The E minor concerto, in spite of its episodic structure, is colorful, charming, richly melodic, and technically demanding.

RECOMMENDED CDs_____
Rubinstein, Skrowaczewski, New Symphony of London (RCA, 1961)
Ax, Ormandy, Philadelphia (RCA, 1978)

RECOMMENDED LPs_____
Rubinstein, Skrowaczewski, New Symphony of London (RCA, 1961)
Ax, Ormandy, Philadelphia (RCA, 1978)

RECOMMENDED CASSETTES_____
Rubinstein, Skrowaczewski, New Symphony of London (RCA, 1961)
Ax, Ormandy, Philadelphia (RCA, 1978)

COMMENTS_____
Rubinstein recorded this concerto at least three times. His last ('61) is superb in every respect—deeply expressive yet always elegant and sensitive, and with an accompaniment by Skrowaczewski that is rich in detail and nuance. Ax, with marginally better sound, brings fresh poetic insights and sparkle to his performance, though Ormandy's accompaniment is a bit heavy-handed. Both performances are coupled with Chopin's Piano Concerto No. 2.

FOR FOLLOW-UP CONSIDERATION

NOCTURNES   Chopin's nocturnes were the most popular of all his works during his lifetime, and he composed 21 of them. A series of atmospheric piano pieces with something of the poetic feeling traditionally linked to the idea of nightfall, they range in mood from calm, moonlit reveries to moments full of clouds and turbulence.

RECOMMENDED CD, LP, AND CASSETTE_____
Arrau (Philips, 1977–78), complete on two discs or cassettes, and performed with enormous feeling and technical clarity.

PRELUDES   A set of 24 short, atmospheric piano pieces that Chopin composed mostly during the winter of 1838–39 while trying to recover from a lung ailment on the island of Majorca.

RECOMMENDED CD, LP, AND CASSETTE————————
Pollini (Deutsche Grammophon, 1986),
performed with character, insight, and masterful technical command.

AARON COPLAND

Pronounced: kope-land. Born November 14, 1900, in Brooklyn, N.Y. Died December 2, 1990, in North Tarrington, New York.

SIGNIFICANCE American composer, conductor, teacher, and writer— generally considered the dean of 20th-century American composers. His best-known works evoke an American folk spirit; much of his music is also abstract, austere, and complex.

BACKGROUND Copland once wrote that he was born in Brooklyn, New York, "on a street that can only be described as drab, that had none of the garish color of the ghetto, none of the charm of an old New England thoroughfare, or even the rawness of a pioneer street.... I mention it because it was there that I spent the first twenty years of my life. Also, because I am filled with wonder each time I realize that a musician was born on that street." He became serious about music at the age of 15, studying first in New York and then in Paris, where he became the first American composition student of the noted teacher and organist Nadia Boulanger.

In 1929 Copland won a competition sponsored by RCA Victor for a symphonic work—his winning entry being a jazz-influenced Dance Symphony. Three ballet scores written between 1938 and 1944 (*Billy the Kid, Rodeo*, and *Appalachian Spring*) established his reputation. In addition to such works, in what Copland has called his "populist" style, he also wrote more abstract, non-programmatic works, some of them employing 12-tone principles. He was also the author of several highly praised books on music (*What to Listen for in Music, Our New Music*), and for many years he headed the composition department at the Berkshire Music Center in Tanglewood, Massachusetts. In the 1970s he was also involved in a series of nationally syndicated educational TV and radio programs about music.

BILLY THE KID

Written in 1938 for the American Ballet Caravan (a forerunner of the New York City Ballet) on commission from Lincoln Kirstein, *Billy* is a musical evocation of the old American West. Actually, the Eastern-born and city-bred

Copland had little interest in "cowboy music" until commissioned to do the ballet. References to such songs as "The Old Chisholm Trail," "Old Paint," and "Git Along, Little Dogies" are worked into the essentially light, catchy score.

The action of the ballet involves key moments in the life of Billy the Kid—from his childhood to the family murder that made him an outlaw and then his capture and death in a shoot-out. About two-thirds of the ballet score has been adapted by Copland into a concert suite, whose section titles describe the musical mood: "The Open Prairie," "Street in a Frontier Town," "The Card Game," "Gun Fight," and "Celebration after Billy's Capture."

RECOMMENDED CD _____
Slatkin, Saint Louis Symphony (Angel, 1986), *complete ballet*

RECOMMENDED LPs _____
Slatkin, Saint Louis Symphony (Angel, 1986), *complete ballet*
Bernstein, New York Philharmonic (CBS, 1968), *suite*

RECOMMENDED CASSETTES _____
Slatkin, Saint Louis Symphony (Angel, 1986), *complete ballet*

Bernstein, New York Philharmonic (CBS, 1968), *suite*

COMMENTS _____
Slatkin conducts the entire ballet score on a single disc, in a vivid, evocative performance. Bernstein conducts only the suite, but with great verve and color.

A fine performance conducted by Copland himself, with the London Symphony Orchestra (CBS, 1970), is presently available only as part of multiple sets of CDs, LPs or Cassettes.

APPALACHIAN SPRING

Copland composed his most sensitively austere and mature ballet score for the great dancer and choreographer Martha Graham in 1942 and 1943—at a time during World War II when a number of major American artists sought to depict through theatrical works the sunny, clean, wholesomely innocent pioneer spirit that has been traditionally linked to American roots. (Another example of the time: Rodgers and Hammerstein's *Oklahoma!*.) Graham provided the scenario for the ballet, which tells about a pioneer celebration of spring in a newly built Pennsylvania farmhouse in the early 1800s.

Copland's original score was for a small ensemble of only 13 instruments. After the success of the Graham ballet, Copland arranged a suite for full symphony orchestra—retaining all the essential scenes and eliminating only a few sections that served merely choreographic purposes. In 1945 Copland's music for *Appalachian Spring* won both the Pulitzer Prize and the New York Music Critics' Circle Award. As Copland later told composer-annotator Phillip Ramey, "I had been lambasted so many times over the years by the critics that getting an award seemed a little odd."

RECOMMENDED CDs

Bernstein, Los Angeles Philharmonic (Deutsche Grammophon, 1984), *suite*

Davies, St. Paul Chamber Orchestra (Pro Arte, 1979), *original chamber version*

RECOMMENDED LPs

Bernstein, Los Angeles Philharmonic (Deutsche Grammophon, 1984), *suite*

Davies, St. Paul Chamber Orchestra (Pro Arte, 1979), *original chamber version*

RECOMMENDED CASSETTES

Bernstein, Los Angeles Philharmonic (Deutsche Grammophon, 1984), *suite*

Davies, St. Paul Chamber Orchestra (Pro Arte, 1979), *original chamber version*

COMMENTS

Bernstein conducts the suite with intensity and eloquence. Davies' performance is smaller-scaled and more relaxed but very well done.

Two worthy, Copland-led performances are also still in the catalog. The earlier one (from the late 1950s) has more idiomatic and colorful playing by the Boston Symphony Orchestra (RCA, LP only). The later one (from 1970), with the London Symphony Orchestra, is sonically superior if interpretively stiffer (CBS, LP and Cassette).

A LINCOLN PORTRAIT

This short, eloquent tribute in words and music to Abraham Lincoln was commissioned in 1942 by conductor André Kostelanetz for his CBS radio series. Says Copland of the work, "No composer could possibly hope to match in musical terms the stature of so eminent a figure as Lincoln. Secretly I hoped to avoid the difficulty by doing a portrait in which the sitter himself might speak. The letters and speeches of Lincoln supplied the text. I avoided the temptation to use only well-known passages, permitting myself the luxury of quoting only once from a world-famous speech [the Gettysburg Address]. The order and arrangement of the selections are my own."

The work is divided into three connected sections. The somber opening, according to Copland, is meant "to suggest something of the mysterious sense of fatality that surrounds Lincoln's personality . . . [and] also something of his gentleness and simplicity of spirit." The lively middle section gives a flavor of the time in which he lived, and quotes from two songs of the period, "Camptown Races" and "Springfield Mountain" (also known as "The Pesky Sarpent"). The concluding section uses a speaker quoting Lincoln's words, building to a simple, forceful conclusion.

RECOMMENDED CD

Henry Fonda (narrator), Copland, London Symphony (CBS, 1970)

RECOMMENDED LPs

Henry Fonda (narrator), Copland, London Symphony (CBS, 1970)

Adlai Stevenson (narrator), Ormandy, Philadelphia Orchestra (CBS, 1965)

RECOMMENDED CASSETTES

Henry Fonda (narrator), Copland, London Symphony (CBS, 1970)

Gregory Peck (narrator), Mehta, Los Angeles Philharmonic (London, 1969)

COMMENTS

Fonda, who played Lincoln in the 1939 John Ford film *Young Mr. Lincoln*, reads the text with dignity and appropriate understatement, and Copland himself conducts an excellent performance. Stevenson, former Illinois Governor, two-time Presidential candidate, and United Nations Ambassador, reads Lincoln's words simply, untheatrically, and movingly. Peck's reading is quietly forceful.

One of the most moving and historically appropriate performances is no longer in the active catalog but may still be found in collectors' shops or libraries: with the late Carl Sandburg (perhaps the nation's foremost authority on Lincoln) reading Lincoln's words eloquently, and Kostelanetz (who commissioned the work) conducting. It was originally on the CBS label (CSP 91A-02007).

FOR FOLLOW-UP CONSIDERATION

SYMPHONY NO. 3 Composed at the end of World War II, this symphony reflects the optimism for the future that permeated the U.S. in that period. But this is no chest-thumping "victory symphony," but a more reflective example of Copland's homespun, affirmative, Americana style. The final movement begins with Copland's *Fanfare for the Common Man*, which had been written as a separate work in 1942 and was slightly reworked by the composer for the symphony.

RECOMMENDED CD AND LP

Bernstein, New York Philharmonic (Deutsche Grammophon, 1986), an intensely expressive performance. (No recommended Cassette presently available.)

EL SALON MEXICO One of Copland's lightest, most attractive scores — a rhythmically catchy tone picture of a Mexican dance hall in the early 1930s.

RECOMMENDED CD, LP, AND CASSETTE

Dorati, Detroit Symphony (London, 1981), a vibrant performance, coupled with three other Copland works: the Dance Symphony, the suite from the ballet *Rodeo*, and *Fanfare for the Common Man*.

PIANO VARIATIONS A complex, partly 12-tone work written in 1930, representative of the composer's more abstract scores, and called by the late composer William Flanagan (writing in *Stereo Review*) "a work of prime significance in the composer's musical development ... [with] stature as a sort of granitic masterwork."

RECOMMENDED CD AND CASSETTE

Tocco (Pro Arte, 1986).

RECOMMENDED LP

Copland (New World, 1945, monaural only)

CLAUDE DEBUSSY

Pronounced: deh-bew-see. Born August 22, 1862, in St. Germain-en-Laye, France. Died March 26, 1918, in Paris, at age 55.

SIGNIFICANCE French composer and critic, father of Impressionistic music, which creates or reflects a mood or image rather than relating a dramatic sequence. Impressionism takes its name from its kinship with Impressionist painting and poetry of the late 19th and early 20th century.

BACKGROUND The poverty of Debussy's parents led them to turn over their children to a well-to-do aunt when things got particularly difficult. And it was she who started Debussy on his musical studies. At the age of 11, he passed the exams for admission to the Paris Conservatory. As a student he experimented with revolutionary harmonies and progressions despite the opposition of his professors. Increasingly, he rebelled against the emotional excesses of German Romanticism, and he sought to develop a more subtle, more original style.

His first significant effort was the sensitive orchestral prelude *Afternoon of the Faun* (1894). It was followed by the *Nocturnes for Orchestra, La Mer* (*The Sea*), *Jeux* (*Games*), *The Martyrdom of St. Sebastian*, and *Images for Orchestra*. In his only opera, *Pelléas and Mélisande* (1902), Debussy completely broke away from 19th-century traditions by supplanting arias with recitatives more closely resembling speech (using the unique sounds of the French language) and by using the orchestra to create an Impressionistic atmosphere. Debussy also wrote many piano pieces, some of which have been orchestrated by others—such as the popular "Clair de Lune" ("Moonlight"). Debussy suffered from cancer during the last ten years of his life, complicated by the harsh living conditions of World War I and financial problems.

PRÉLUDE À L'APRÈS-MIDI D'UN FAUNE (PRELUDE TO THE AFTERNOON OF A FAUN)

Despite its brevity (a performing time of approximately nine and one-half minutes), this sensuously beautiful, perfectly sculptured work laid the foundations of Impressionistic orchestral music. Inspired by Malarmé's poem *L'Après-Midi d'un Faune* (*The Afternoon of a Faun*), the piece evokes the delicate atmosphere of the dreams of a faun on a hot summer afternoon. Its premiere in 1894, when Debussy was 32, was an instant success. Says composer-conductor Pierre Boulez, "Just as modern poetry is rooted in certain poems of Baudelaire, one is justified in saying that modern music awakens with the premiere of *The Afternoon of a Faun*."

RECOMMENDED CDs————————
Boulez, New Philharmonia of London
  (CBS/Sony Classical, 1966)
Ansermet, Suisse Romande Orchestra
  (London, 1952)

RECOMMENDED LPs————————
Boulez, New Philharmonia of London
  (CBS, 1966)
Karajan, Berlin Philharmonic (Deutsche
  Grammophon, 1965)

RECOMMENDED CASSETTES————
Boulez, New Philharmonia of London
  (CBS, 1966)
Munch, Boston Symphony (RCA, 1962)

COMMENTS————————————
All of these performances are beautifully evocative and poetic, with Boulez the most sensuous, Karajan the lushest. The older Ansermet and Munch recordings still give a good indication of why these two conductors were long considered nonpareil in this repertory.

NOCTURNES FOR ORCHESTRA

Following the success of the *Prelude to the Afternoon of a Faun*, Debussy wrote this longer work evoking the mood or atmosphere of three scenes: (1) "Nuages" ("Clouds"), reflecting the "slow, solemn motion of clouds, fading away in gray tones tinged with white," to quote the composer; (2) "Fêtes" ("Festivals"), with restless, flashing rhythms including those of a passing procession; and (3) "Sirènes" ("Sirens," after the ancient Greek myths), depicting a glistening sea in the moonlight, with waves splashing against the rocks from which the Sirens sing their seductive melody. In the final section, Debussy employs a small women's chorus in addition to the orchestra; because of this the first two sections are frequently performed and recorded independently.

RECOMMENDED CDs————————
Haitink, Amsterdam Concertgebouw
  (Philips, 1979)
Stokowski, London Symphony (Angel,
  1960)

RECOMMENDED LPs————————
Haitink, Amsterdam Concertgebouw
  (Philips, 1979)
Abbado, Boston Symphony (Deutsche
  Grammophon, 1976)

RECOMMENDED CASSETTES————
Stokowski, London Symphony (Angel,
  1960)

Abbado, Boston Symphony (Deutsche
  Grammophon, 1976)

COMMENTS————————————
Haitink's recording is exceptional for its combination of orchestral clarity and interpretive subtleties. Abbado's is sensuous and atmospheric. The older Stokowski is still remarkable for the haunting sonic picture he elicits from the orchestra, especially in the "Sirènes" section.

LA MER (THE SEA)

The late English composer-conductor Constant Lambert described *La Mer* (in his book *Music Ho!*) as "a landscape without figures, or rather a seascape without ships." It is just the sea—with its shimmery surface and restless currents, as one might impressionistically feel it while gazing out alone over open waters.

Some critics have called *La Mer* a symphonic poem or even the first great Impressionist symphony. Debussy called the work merely "three symphonic sketches," and gave subtitles to its three parts: "From Dawn to Noon on the Sea," "Play of the Waves," and "Dialogue between the Wind and the Sea." The subtitles are meant only as clues to the atmosphere of the music, not to describe a specific scene—although the composer Erik Satie once joshingly told Debussy that he particularly liked the passage in the first movement "at about a quarter to twelve."

RECOMMENDED CDs———————
Dutoit, Montreal Symphony (London, 1989)
Slatkin, Saint Louis Symphony (Telarc, 1982)

RECOMMENDED LPs———————
Slatkin, Saint Louis Symphony (Telarc, 1982)
Boulez, New Philharmonia of London (CBS, 1966)

RECOMMENDED CASSETTES———
Boulez, New Philharmonia (CBS, 1966)

Ansermet, Suisse Romande (London, 1964)

COMMENTS———————————
All the above performances are filled with marvelous coloristic details and an appropriate rhythmic pulse. Dutoit has the advantage of the most up-to-date recording, but both Boulez and Ansermet from the '60s hold up uncommonly well.

FOR FOLLOW-UP CONSIDERATION

THE MARTYRDOM OF SAINT SEBASTIAN   The incidental music that Debussy composed for D'Annunzio's mystery play of 1911 was later arranged by the composer in two concert versions: one as an oratorio for orchestra, chorus, and vocal soloists, with a narrator reciting a text taken from the play; the other a symphonic suite of four movements, which Debussy called "fragments symphoniques." The symphonic version is partly the work of conductor-arranger André Caplet, who, with Debussy's permission, made the orchestral transcription by replacing the vocal soloists with brass and strings. In either version, the music is among Debussy's most quietly eloquent and mystical.

RECOMMENDED CD AND LP (ORATORIO VERSION) _____

Munch, Curtin, Kopleff, Akos, Boston Symphony, New England Conservatory Chorus (RCA, 1955), a radiant performance, with Munch's expressive narration (cut on the LP edition) restored for the 1993 CD reissue.

RECOMMENDED CD (SYMPHONIC VERSION) _____

Dutoit, Montreal (London, 1989), a nobly eloquent, poetic performance.

JEUX (GAMES) This is the score for a Diaghilev ballet about a three-cornered flirtation between a boy and two girls on a tennis court. Long neglected, it is increasingly viewed as one of Debussy's most inventive scores.

RECOMMENDED CD, LP, AND CASSETTE _____

Boulez, New Philharmonia of London (CBS/Sony, 1967), a playfully luminous performance of a piece Boulez has long made one of his performance specialties.

PIANO MUSIC Debussy's brand of Impressionism revolutionized piano music at the turn of the century. Among the best examples—

RECOMMENDED ON CD, LP, AND CASSETTE _____

Paul Jacobs (Nonesuch, 1975–78), with etudes on one set, preludes on two others.

RECOMMENDED ON CD ONLY _____

Michelangeli (Deutsche Grammophon, 1978), a set of preludes taped at a live recital.

ANTONIN DVOŘÁK

Pronounced: d'-*vor*-zhahk. Born September 8, 1841, in Mühlhausen, Bohemia. Died May 1, 1904, in Prague, at age 63.

SIGNIFICANCE Bohemian (Czech) composer, violist, and teacher; a strong champion of nationalism in music (basing music on native folk elements).

BACKGROUND The son of an innkeeper, Dvořák earned his livelihood as violist in the Prague National Theater before turning seriously to composing in his 30s. At 32 he submitted two symphonies for a competition, and won a stipend from the Austrian government. Brahms was one of the judges for the stipend's renewal, and became a lifelong friend and champion of Dvořák thereafter. A set of colorful, folkish *Slavonic Dances* won Dvořák his first popular success. He became a professor at the Prague Conservatory in 1891, and a year later he was invited to head the National Conservatory in New York.

His arrival in New York was greeted at the ship's pier by a 300-voice chorus and an orchestra of 87. For the next three years, his New York home became a popular rendezvous for leading musicians. Dvořák provoked controversy, however, by seeking to influence U.S. composers to use Negro folk themes in their works, composing his own *From the New World* Symphony, and his String Quartet No. 6, the "American," in such a manner. After three years in New York, he returned to Prague. On his sixtieth birthday he was made a member of the Austrian House of Lords, the first musician to be so honored.

SYMPHONY No. 9 IN E MINOR— FROM THE NEW WORLD

Though once regarded as the first successful symphony to employ "American" themes, Dvořák's *New World* is now generally regarded as reflecting as much of Dvořák's native Bohemia (today part of Czechoslovakia) as America—or, perhaps more precisely, to have a mixture of both Bohemian and American elements. Although some critics have found a resemblance between the second theme of the first movement and the spiritual "Swing Low, Sweet Chariot," Dvořák denied using any specific black or Indian folk material. He did, however, tell one writer that in composing the *Largo* (the second movement), he had part of Longfellow's *Hiawatha* in mind—although, again, he denied using actual Indian melodies. Later, words were adapted to a portion of the *Largo*, and the song, "Goin' Home," has since become accepted throughout the world as an "American folk classic."

Some critics have found in Dvořák's *New World* Symphony a musical portrait of the tensions and conflicts of American culture and life in the late 19th century—basically European-rooted but with qualities adapted from indigenous New World elements.

RECOMMENDED CDs
Tennstedt, Berlin Philharmonic (Angel, 1984)
Dohnanyi, Cleveland Orchestra (London, 1984)

RECOMMENDED LPs
Tennstedt, Berlin Philharmonic (Angel, 1984)
Dohnanyi, Cleveland Orchestra (London, 1984)

RECOMMENDED CASSETTES
Tennstedt Berlin Philharmonic (Angel, 1984)

Dohnanyi, Cleveland Orchestra (London, 1984)

COMMENTS
Tennstedt (who was born in the region of Germany closest to Dvořák's homeland) leads a warm, vibrant performance that is especially moving in the spaciousness of the famous *Largo*. Dohnanyi is also outstanding in his blend of lyricism and powerful drama.

Of historic interest are two other recordings: One, with Arturo Toscanini and the NBC Symphony Orchestra (RCA

CD, remastered from 1953 sessions), remains one of Toscanini's best recordings, full of vitality and strength, with marvelous rhythmic articulation in the final movements. The other, with Arthur Fiedler and the Boston Symphony Orchestra (RCA, Cassette only), was Fiedler's only recording with the full Boston Symphony Orchestra (in contrast to his usual Boston Pops), and it is a warm, spirited, well-recorded 1970 performance.

CELLO CONCERTO IN B MINOR

This greatest of all cello concertos was composed by Dvořák during the last of his three years in the United States as head of a New York conservatory. But the flavor is clearly Czech, and Dvořák admitted being homesick for his native land during that last year in the U.S. The inspiration for the concerto came partly from a concert Dvořák attended of the New York Philharmonic in 1894, at which Victor Herbert was soloist in his own Second Cello Concerto. (Before he became world-famous as a composer of operettas, Herbert had been a widely acclaimed cellist.) The concerto is filled with eloquent, bittersweet melody—some of it darkly mysterious and melancholy, some of it strong, robust, and energetic. Brahms is reported to have said of it: "Why on earth did I not know that it is possible to write a cello concerto like this?"

RECOMMENDED CDs

Rostropovich, Karajan, Berlin Philharmonic (Deutsche Grammophon, 1969)

Harrell, Ashkenazy, Philharmonia of London (London, 1982)

RECOMMENDED LPs

Rostropovich, Karajan, Berlin Philharmonic (Deutsche Grammophon, 1969)

DuPré, Barenboim, Chicago Symphony (Angel, 1971)

RECOMMENDED CASSETTES

Piatigorsky, Munch, Boston Symphony (RCA, 1960)

Ma, Maazel, Berlin Philharmonic (CBS, 1986)

COMMENTS

Rostropovich remains in a class by himself among present-day cellists. His 1969 version is preferable to a newer one with Seiji Ozawa and the Boston Symphony (on Philips), for its combination of glow, excitement, passion, and poetry.

DuPré's version is exceptionally ardent and electric, and it remains the last concerto recording she made with her husband before multiple sclerosis cut short her career and life.

Harrell and Ma are also outstanding in their expressiveness and technical command, and show why they both rank at the top of the younger generation of cellists today.

FOR FOLLOW-UP CONSIDERATION

SLAVONIC DANCES   These most popular of all orchestral dances were composed in two sets (Op. 46 in 1878, and Op. 72 in 1886–87) and are based on Czech dance forms.

Szell, Cleveland (Angel, 1970).

idly spirited and sparklingly played in both versions.

RECOMMENDED LP AND
CASSETTE ⸻
Szell, Cleveland (CBS, mid-1960s), viv-

SYMPHONY No. 8 Next to the Ninth, Dvořák's most popular symphony —an alternately pensive and spirited but always freshly melodic symphony. It was for a time wrongly known as Dvořák's "English" Symphony, because it was published by an English firm, but the music's roots are clearly Bohemian. The third movement, in particular, has much in common with the style and character of Dvořák's *Slavonic Dances*.

RECOMMENDED CD, LP, AND
CASSETTE ⸻
Dohnanyi, Cleveland Orchestra (Lon-

don, 1984), a warm, lively, and completely winning performance.

CÉSAR FRANCK

Pronounced: *frahnk*. Born December 10, 1822, in Liège, Belgium. Died November 8, 1890, in Paris, France, at age 67.

SIGNIFICANCE Belgian composer, organist, and teacher, who developed the *cyclic form* (in which the same theme is carried over into more than one movement or section of a work). His mystical, symmetrical, often delicate works helped restore French instrumental music to a position of eminence in the 19th century.

BACKGROUND Franck's boyhood, first in Belgium and then in Paris, was spent under the influence of his strong-willed father, a bank clerk, who wanted his son to become a great pianist. And indeed Franck showed promising talent in that direction. He toured the Belgian provinces giving recitals at the age of 12, and was accepted as a student at the Paris Conservatory at the age of 15. Ten years later, Franck rebelled against his father's will—at the very time Paris was going through the upheavals of the ill-fated 1848 revolution. In order to marry the daughter of a Parisian actress, he and his bride had to climb over the revolutionaries' street barricades to get to the church.

Franck then settled down to teaching and serving as a church organist, primarily at Paris' Church of St. Clotilde—although he religiously set aside 5:30 to 7:30 AM every morning for composing. For nearly 40 years he and his wife lived frugally, never leaving Paris, and never hearing any of his music performed except what he himself played on the organ during church services.

Finally, in 1887, a group of his students and friends arranged a concert of his works. Although only a mild success, it was enough to spur other performances of his music and to win him increasing recognition as an important composer. But soon after, while crossing a street, Franck was struck by a bus, and never fully recovered from his injuries.

Through such students as Chausson, Chabrier, d'Indy, Lalo, and Fauré, Franck became the figurehead for a whole school of "Franckists" who dominated late 19th-century French musical life until Debussy.

SYMPHONY IN D MINOR

When Franck's only symphony was given its first performance in 1889, composer Charles Gounod walked out, declaring the work to be "incompetence pushed to dogmatic lengths." Although radical for its time, Franck's symphony went on to become one of the most popular of all symphonies. In it, Franck introduced the cyclic form. Analysts have also suggested various mystical interpretations of the music, and have pointed out the relationship of Franck's orchestral sonorities to those of the organ. But what has appealed to the general public most of all are the symphony's noble and flowing melodies.

RECOMMENDED CDs_____
Bernstein, French National Orchestra (Deutsche Grammophon, 1983)
Chailly, Amsterdam Concertgebouw (London, 1986)

RECOMMENDED LPs_____
Bernstein, French National Orchestra (Deutsche Grammophon, 1983)
Monteux, Chicago Symphony (RCA, 1961)

RECOMMENDED CASSETTES_____
Bernstein, French National Orchestra (Deutsche Grammophon, 1983)

Monteux, Chicago Symphony (RCA, 1961)

COMMENTS_____
Bernstein's performance, recorded during a series of live Paris concerts, is emotionally intense and vibrant. Monteux's older version remains one of the finest recordings the revered French maestro ever made — profoundly moving, forthright, and fervent, if sonically no longer up to the later versions. Chailly has the best sound of all, for a somewhat cooler, more portentous, but gripping performance.

SYMPHONIC VARIATIONS FOR PIANO AND ORCHESTRA

This sometimes pensive, sometimes jaunty, imaginatively conceived and intricately worked-out piece is really the equivalent of an uninterrupted, three-movement piano concerto. But instead of depicting a traditional conflict between the solo piano and orchestral forces, Franck places the conflict between two musical themes (one lyrical, one more energetic), which both the piano and the orchestra continually question, respond to, and transform on their way to a joyous finale.

RECOMMENDED CDs _____
Bolet, Chailly, Amsterdam Concertgebouw (London, 1986)
Collard, Plasson, Toulouse (Angel, 1986)

RECOMMENDED LPs _____
Bolet, Chailly, Amsterdam Concertgebouw (London, 1986)
Fleisher, Szell, Cleveland (CBS, 1956)

RECOMMENDED CASSETTES ___
Bolet, Chailly, Amsterdam Concertgebouw (London, 1986)

Weissenberg, Karajan, Berlin Philharmonic (Angel, 1976)

COMMENTS _____
Bolet and Chailly are alternately fine-grained and sweeping, with splendid sound. The older Fleisher-Szell and Weissenberg-Karajan versions are still memorable for the cleanness of the pianistic detail and the interpretive interplay between soloists and conductors.

FOR FOLLOW-UP CONSIDERATION

PSYCHÉ This seven-movement symphonic poem for large orchestra and chorus was one of Franck's last completed works and, in the view of some, his finest. It is a cyclically structured, sensuously beautiful setting of the ancient Greek legend of Psyché and Eros. The fourth movement, subtitled "Psyché and Eros," is sometimes played independently on orchestral programs and has been recorded as such, but it is much more effective when heard as part of the complete work.

RECOMMENDED CD _____
Ashkenazy, Berlin Radio Symphony and Chorus (London, 1989), a gracefully flowing, expressive performance.

RECOMMENDED LP AND CASSETTE _____
Jordan, Basel Symphony (Erato, 1985), more stately but still an affecting performance.

GEORGE GERSHWIN

Pronounced: *gur*-shwin. Born September 26, 1898, in Brooklyn, New York. Died July 12, 1937, in Hollywood, California, at age 38.

SIGNIFICANCE American composer and pianist, one of the first and most successful in combining American popular melody and jazz elements with symphonic forms.

BACKGROUND Gershwin began studying music as a teenager in his native New York City. Almost from the beginning, he talked of blending American popular music with classical music. He published his first popular song at the age of 18, and soon afterward he began contributing to a long series of successful Broadway shows. In 1922 he wrote a one-act "jazz opera," *Blue Monday*, which was to be incorporated in one of George White's popular *Scandals*. But it was dropped after the first performance because the producer considered it too morbid for a Broadway revue. It was seen, however, by bandleader Paul Whiteman, who commissioned Gershwin to write an extended symphonic jazz work for concert performance. The result was *Rhapsody in Blue* (1924), which was a triumphant success. Gershwin was widely hailed as America's most promising composer.

Gershwin continued to write concert works in a partly jazz vein (Piano Concerto in F, *An American in Paris, Cuban Overture*) while also writing songs for Broadway shows and Hollywood films. In 1931, a Gershwin show, *Of Thee I Sing*, spoofing the Presidential politics of its era, became the first musical comedy to win the Pulitzer Prize. But his most ambitious serious effort, the "Negro folk opera" *Porgy and Bess* (1935), had a mixed reception from both critics and the public, and did not achieve success until revivals after his death.

In 1937, while working in Hollywood, Gershwin developed a brain tumor and died a few months before his thirty-ninth birthday. In the years since then, the popularity of both his theater songs and his concert works has remained undimmed.

RHAPSODY IN BLUE

This first notable (and still the most popular) jazz-oriented concert work was written at the last minute for a 1924 concert of American music — during a period when Gershwin, then 25, was also working on the score for a Broadway show (*Sweet Little Devil*). Paul Whiteman had approached Gershwin the preceding year about writing a jazz concerto. But in the press of all his activities, Gershwin had virtually forgotten about the project until a newspaper ad in January of 1924 announced the concert, five weeks away. Because of the shortness of the time left, Gershwin and Whiteman agreed that Gershwin would provide just the piano score, and that the Whiteman band's chief arranger, Ferde Grofé (who later wrote the popular *Grand Canyon Suite*), would handle the details of the orchestration.

About the *Rhapsody*, Gershwin later said, "I had no set plan, no structure. The *Rhapsody*, you see, began as a purpose, not a plan. I worked out a few themes, but just at this time I had to appear in Boston for the premiere of *Sweet Little Devil*. It was on the train [from New York to Boston], with its steely rhythms, its rattly-bang (I frequently hear music in the very heart of noise) that I suddenly heard—even saw on paper—the complete construction of the *Rhapsody* from beginning to end. . . . I heard it as a sort of musical kaleidoscope of America—of our vast melting-pot, of our incomparable national pep, our blues, our metropolitan madness. By the time I reached Boston I had the definite plot of the piece, as distinguished from its actual substance."

Even so, by the night of the first performance, Gershwin still had not worked out all the piano passages, so he improvised whole sections on the spot. Whiteman took cues from Gershwin in order to bring in the orchestra in the right places. The *Rhapsody* was the sensation of the concert. Gershwin biographer David Ewen has written: "It soon became the most famous piece of serious music by an American, and earned fabulous royalties. It was performed by jazz bands and symphony orchestras, by solo pianists, two-piano teams, and piano ensembles; by solo harmonicas, harmonica bands, and mandolin orchestras; by tap dancers and ballet dancers; by choral groups. It was featured in stage shows and in an early talkie. It lent its principal theme to a novel, and furnished the signature for Paul Whiteman's radio shows."

Today, concert performances of the *Rhapsody* usually use one of two versions: the original 1924 Whiteman band arrangement by Grofé, or an expanded version arranged several years later by Grofé for symphony orchestra (different primarily in the orchestral accompaniment). Because of the frequent use of other abbreviated arrangements by pop and jazz orchestras, the second Grofé arrangement is sometimes advertised as the "uncut" version.

RECOMMENDED CDs

Thomas (pianist and conductor), Los Angeles Philharmonic (CBS, 1985)
Bernstein (pianist and conductor), New York Philharmonic (CBS, 1958)

RECOMMENDED LPs

Thomas (pianist and conductor), Los Angeles Philharmonic (CBS, 1985)
Bernstein (pianist and conductor), New York Philharmonic (CBS, 1958)

RECOMMENDED CASSETTES

Thomas (pianist and conductor), Los Angeles Philharmonic (CBS, 1985)
Bernstein (pianist and conductor), New York Philharmonic (CBS, 1958)

COMMENTS

Both Thomas and Bernstein have an intuitive feeling for the *Rhapsody*'s jazz moods and syncopated rhythms that other concert performers who have recorded the piece cannot match. Thomas performs the original jazz-band version, and plays it with enormous élan if also with some occasionally exaggerated accents. Bernstein uses the expanded, second Grofé arrangement, in a somewhat more relaxed but infectious performance. Bernstein's 1958 recording remains much more colorful and jauntier than his overly mannered 1986 recording with the Los Angeles Philharmonic (on Deutsche Grammophon).

Gershwin's own 1927 recording of the original version, with Paul Whiteman's Orchestra, is still available on RCA (LP and Cassette) and, of course, is of great historic interest, although its ancient sonics can only approximate what can be heard on the Thomas or Bernstein recordings.

PIANO CONCERTO IN F

A year after the success of the *Rhapsody in Blue*, Gershwin sought to blend jazz elements in a larger symphonic form, and the result was this concerto, which many consider his finest "serious" work. Gershwin wrote that the first movement "is in sonata form—but." The second movement is a melodic, bluesy *andante*. The finale is a breezy rondo reusing some of the material from the first two movements.

RECOMMENDED CDs

Wild, Fiedler, Boston Pops Orchestra (RCA/BMG Classics, 1961)

Litton, Royal Philharmonic (Virgin Classics, 1991)

RECOMMENDED LPs

Wild, Fiedler, Boston Pops Orchestra (RCA, 1961)

Siegel, Slatkin, Saint Louis Symphony (Vox Cum Laude, 1974)

RECOMMENDED CASSETTES

Wild, Fiedler, Boston Pops Orchestra (RCA, 1961)

Siegel, Slatkin, Saint Louis Symphony (Vox Cum Laude, 1974)

COMMENTS

Wild takes off like a whirlwind, and Fiedler's Bostonians keep up with him all the way for a razzle-dazzle performance. Litton, as both pianist and conductor, is infectiously vibrant and colorful. Siegel and Slatkin perform with lots of spirit but also with elegance.

AN AMERICAN IN PARIS

An American in Paris is a warmly melodic and amiable "orchestral rhapsody" (as Gershwin called it) about Paris in the 1920s, scored for large orchestra plus four automobile horns, and orchestrated by Gershwin himself (unlike the *Rhapsody in Blue*). At the time of its premiere, the 30-year-old Gershwin told an interviewer that his piece "portrays the impressions of an American visitor as he strolls about Paris, listens to its various street noises, and absorbs the French atmosphere." Gershwin also admitted that some of the music reflects a sort of "homesick blues," which is, however, overcome in the exuberant, merry finale. (A considerably rearranged and reorchestrated version of Gershwin's original score was used for the climactic ballet sequence of the Academy Award-winning 1951 film *An American in Paris*.)

RECOMMENDED CDs

Bernstein, New York Philharmonic (CBS, 1959)

Dutoit, Montreal Symphony (London, 1989)

RECOMMENDED LP

Bernstein, New York Philharmonic (CBS, 1959).

RECOMMENDED CASSETTES———
Bernstein, New York Philharmonic
(CBS, 1959)
Dutoit, Montreal Symphony (London,
1989)

COMMENTS————————
Bernstein's performance has lots of dash and color, although its late '50s sound has been surpassed by later but interpretively less-interesting versions. Dutoit is less bluesy than Bernstein but is otherwise debonair. A good Schwarz-Seattle recording of the original version (Delos, 1989) shows Gershwin was wise to trim the finale as he later did.

FOR FOLLOW-UP CONSIDERATION

PORGY AND BESS The book for this 1935 "Negro folk opera" has long divided critics—and civil rights partisans who feel it reflects outdated stereotypes of black Americans. But Gershwin's score has been universally hailed as one of his most inspired—in fact, some consider it the best American opera yet written. The story, laid in Catfish Row, a waterfront tenement section of Charleston, South Carolina, centers on a crippled black beggar's love for the woman of a stevedore whom he subsequently kills.

The original production of *Porgy and Bess* in 1935 lost money, and though a 1942 revival did better, the opera really didn't win worldwide acclaim until a 1952 production starring Leontyne Price and William Warfield, which first toured Vienna, Berlin, London, Paris, and later the U.S.

A 1959 film version, produced by Samuel Goldwyn and directed by Otto Preminger, was widely criticized as heavy-handed and outdated in its stereotypes. The Gershwin estate was reportedly so unhappy with this movie version that it exercised its option to buy back the music rights, an act which has effectively prevented the rerelease of the film either theatrically or on TV or video.

**RECOMMENDED CD AND LP
(COMPLETE OPERA)**————
Haymon, White, Blackwell, Evans, Rattle, London Philharmonic, Glyndebourne Chorus (Angel, 1989).

RECOMMENDED LP AND CASSETTE (HIGHLIGHTS ONLY)——
Price, Warfield, Boatwright, Henderson, RCA Orchestra & DePaur Chorus (RCA, 1963).

PORGY AND BESS: A SYMPHONIC PICTURE In 1942 the well-known Broadway and radio conductor-arranger Robert Russell Bennett was commissioned by Fritz Reiner (then conductor of the Pittsburgh Symphony) to make a symphonic arrangement of the music from Gershwin's opera. It has since become a popular concert standard, and today completely overshadows a less colorful 1936 orchestral suite Gershwin himself adapted from the opera and called *Catfish Row*.

RECOMMENDED CD, LP AND CASSETTE OF THE BENNETT SUITE——
Dorati, Detroit Symphony (London, 1985).

Slatkin, Saint Louis Symphony (Vox Cum
Laude, 1974).

SECOND RHAPSODY   Although some critics have found it more assured
in technique and more rhythmically inventive than the *Rhapsody in Blue*,
this 1932 work for piano and orchestra has not yet won the favor that its
champions feel it deserves. Based on music Gershwin wrote for an extended
dream sequence for the 1931 film *Delicious*, and for a time known as the
New York Rhapsody, it is an imaginative, appealing piece undeserving of its
neglect.

RECOMMENDED CD, LP, AND
CASSETTE_____
Thomas (pianist and conductor), Los
Angeles Philharmonic (CBS, 1986), a
sparkling, completely engaging performance of the "restored original
version" (in contrast to a re-orches-
trated version published after Gershwin's death and generally used until
Thomas sought out the original in the
Library of Congress).

EDVARD GRIEG

Pronounced: *greeg*. Born June 15, 1843, in Bergen, Norway. Died
September 4, 1907, in Bergen, at age 64.

SIGNIFICANCE   Norwegian composer and pianist, whose Romantic music mainly reflects a sturdy Norse spirit.

BACKGROUND   Although Grieg became—and remains—Norway's most-
famous composer, his family was of Scottish origins, and his father was the
British consul in Bergen at the time of Grieg's birth. Grieg began piano
lessons at the age of six; as a teenager he studied in Leipzig and Copenhagen.
He became a close friend of the composer Rikard Nordraak, and under his
influence became committed to writing music that would be recognized as
Norwegian nationalist music.

He wrote music on Norwegian literary themes (for Ibsen's *Peer Gynt*,
Bjørnson's *Sigurd Jorsalfar*), various Norwegian folk song arrangements,
plus many songs and piano works. He settled mainly in Bergen, and spent
most of his life plagued by poor health. When his health permitted, he
toured as a pianist, particularly as accompanist to his wife Nina, who sang
his songs.

PIANO CONCERTO IN A MINOR

This melodic, rhapsodic concerto is modeled in many ways after Schumann's (also in A minor). Written when Grieg was 25, it has long been one of the most popular of all piano concertos, and has been the source of several pop songs in the 1940s and 1960s. The concerto has also provided the finale for the popular musical play *Song of Norway* (a Broadway hit in the 1940s and still a summer musical favorite) as well as the 1970 biographical film also called *Song of Norway*.

RECOMMENDED CDs
Lupu, Previn, London Symphony (London, 1973)
Rubinstein, Wallenstein, RCA Symphony (RCA, 1962)

RECOMMENDED LPs
Rubinstein, Wallenstein, RCA Symphony (RCA, 1962)
Bolet, Chailly, Berlin Radio Symphony (London, 1985)

RECOMMENDED CASSETTES
Lipatti, Galliera, Philharmonia of London (CBS/Odyssey, late 1940s)
Cliburn, Ormandy, Philadelphia (RCA, 1968)

COMMENTS
Lupu blends breadth, elegance, and technical deftness, and his performance is beautifully recorded. Rubinstein's version (his third) is broadly Romantic and engaging. Cliburn underplays the warhorse flamboyance of the work while Ormandy overemphasizes all sorts of brilliant orchestral colors. Bolet's approach is a bit grandiose, but his performance never flags in interest. Despite its dated sonics, the Lipatti version still has the most uncommon sensitivity and Romantic feeling—and deserves to be kept in the active catalog.

PEER GYNT SUITES

Grieg's incidental music for Ibsen's 1876 poetic drama about a legendary Norwegian rogue has become a popular concert work through two orchestral suites that Grieg drew from the original. Suite No. 1 contains the best-known sections: "Dawn," "The Death of Ase," "Anitra's Dance," and "In the Hall of the Mountain King." Suite No. 2 includes "Ingrid's Lament," "Arabian Dance," "The Return of Peer Gynt," and "Solvejg's Song." The music is by turns brooding, vigorous, dramatic, and colorful. "Solvejg's Song" is for soprano and orchestra, but is most often performed by orchestra alone in concert performances. Similarly, "In the Hall of the Mountain King" and the "Arabian Dance" both have brief choral sections which are usually omitted in concert performances and most recordings.

RECOMMENDED CDs
Marriner, Popp, Academy of St. Martin-in-the-Fields, Ambrosian Singers (Angel, 1983)

DeWaart, Ameling, San Francisco Symphony & Chorus (Philips, 1983)

Marriner, Popp, Academy of St. Martin-in-the-Fields, Ambrosian Singers (Angel, 1983)

Blomstedt, Valjakka, Dresden State Orchestra, Leipzig Radio Chorus (Angel, 1979)

RECOMMENDED CASSETTES

Marriner, Popp, Academy of St. Martin-in-the-Fields, Ambrosian Singers (Angel, 1983)

Blomstedt, Valjakka, Dresden State Orchestra, Leipzig Radio Chorus (Angel, 1979)

COMMENTS

All of the above performances are good if not outstanding, and offer more parts of the incidental music than the standard two suites.

For the traditional suites as outlined above, the best performance on CD and LP is that of Slatkin and the Saint Louis Symphony (Teldec). The best on Cassette is by Ormandy and the Philadelphia (RCA Victrola, 1974).

FOR FOLLOW-UP CONSIDERATION

NORWEGIAN DANCES   These four symphonic dances, based on Norwegian folk themes, have long been familiar pops-concert fare. Some of the themes were used as the basis for songs in the musical play and movie *Song of Norway*.

RECOMMENDED CD, LP, AND CASSETTE

Jarvi, Göteborg Symphony (Deutsche Grammophon, 1987), spirited, well-recorded performances, coupled with Grieg's separate set of *Symphonic Dances*.

GEORGE FREDERICK HANDEL

Pronounced: *han-d'l*. Born February 23, 1685, in Halle, Saxony (Germany). Died April 14, 1759, in London, England, at age 74.

SIGNIFICANCE   German-born composer and organist of the Baroque period, who moved to England in his 20s and stayed to become the most famous composer of English oratorios on Biblical themes.

BACKGROUND   Handel taught himself to play the organ and harpsichord when he was seven. But his father, a Saxon barber, was determined that his son become a lawyer. He discouraged his son's musical ambitions, even after a prominent duke persuaded him to allow the boy to study music together with law. When his father died, Handel, then 18, promptly dropped his law courses and concentrated full-time on music. He served several years' musical apprenticeship in Hamburg, playing violin in the opera orchestra and composing. At 21, following a duel with a rival musician, Handel left Germany for Italy, where he became a close friend of Domenico Scarlatti, the composer and harpsichordist, and began composing operas in the Italian style.

In 1711 Handel was invited to produce his opera *Rinaldo* in London. It was successful, and he stayed in England for the rest of his life—becoming a naturalized British subject in 1726 and formally Anglicizing the spelling of his name (originally Georg Friedrich Händel). For more than ten years he directed opera productions at the Royal Academy of Music, hired the singers, and composed about fifteen Italian-style operas for them. But in the 1730s public enthusiasm for opera waned, and the Royal Academy went bankrupt. Then, at 52, Handel suffered a paralytic stroke.

After long months of rest, as his health improved, Handel became determined to regain his lost prestige—and to do so by way of the oratorio, then little known in England. These large-scale, dramatic musical settings of religious or mythological stories (for solo voices, chorus, and orchestra), sung in the vernacular rather than Latin, were presented in concert style, without scenery or costumes. Although Handel's first two oratorios failed to win the public, *Messiah* (1742) was an enormous success—particularly after King George II rose to his feet at the "Hallelujah Chorus." (It has since become a custom for audiences to stand at this part of *Messiah* performances.) Thereafter Handel produced one, sometimes two new oratorios every year until 1751, greatly expanding both the form and expressive depth of his choral writing.

Illness and finally blindness plagued the last years of his life, but at the time of his death he was England's most popular and respected musician, and he was buried among England's great in Westminster Abbey.

MESSIAH

Messiah is a work of musical majesty and spiritual nobility, best-known for its joyous "Hallelujah Chorus." The oratorio is in three parts, consisting of more than 50 individual pieces—dealing with the prophecy, advent, nativity, mission, sacrifice, atonement, ascension, and resurrection of Jesus.

Over the years its instrumentation and ornamentation have been reworked by various conductors, choral directors, and soloists, so that few performances are ever alike. Moreover, in his own lifetime Handel often modified the score to meet the needs of individual performances or soloists, so that musicologists rarely agree on what the composer himself sanctioned.

RECOMMENDED CDs

Solti, Te Kanawa, Gjevang, Lewis, Howell, Chicago Symphony & Chorus (London, 1984), *complete (two discs); also highlights disc*

Gardiner, Marshall, Robbin, Rolfe-Johnson, Hale, English Baroque Soloists, Monteverdi Choir (Philips, 1982), *complete (three discs); also highlights disc*

RECOMMENDED LPs

Solti, Te Kanawa, Gjevang, Lewis, Howell, Chicago Symphony & Chorus (London, 1984), *complete (three discs); also highlights disc*

Gardiner, Marshall, Robbin, Rolfe-Johnson, Hale, English Baroque Soloists, Monteverdi Choir (Philips, 1982), *complete (three discs); also highlights disc*

RECOMMENDED CASSETTES

Solti, Te Kanawa, Gjevang, Lewis, Howell, Chicago Symphony & Chorus (London, 1984), *complete (three cassettes); also highlights cassette*

Gardiner, Marshall, Robbin, Rolfe-Johnson, Hale, English Baroque Soloists, Monteverdi Choir (Philips, 1982), *complete (three cassettes); also highlights Cassette*

COMMENTS

These are two very different approaches to *Messiah*. Solti's is large-scale, using an all-out modern orchestra and chorus, for an exciting, vivid performance that is almost Wagnerian in its scope and color. Gardiner is more authentically Baroque in his use of period instruments and chamber-music styling, but also quite spirited and forceful. Which approach is best for a newcomer is pretty much a matter of individual taste, although most Americans react more favorably to the larger-scale tradition. In any case, a highlights disc or cassette is recommended for a starter. Both performances above are sung in English.

WATER MUSIC

Originally a suite of 20 short movements, the *Water Music* is a set of rhythmically contrasting orchestral pieces written for a royal festival on London's Thames River in 1717. For many years it was best known in an arrangement of six movements made in 1922 by the late English conductor Sir Hamilton Harty, but in recent years conductors have begun to favor the more complete and authentic version by H. F. Redlich. This edition divides 18 of the pieces into three suites.

The first suite (nine pieces) is made up of the music intended to be played as the King's boat journeyed along the Thames from Whitehall to Chelsea. The second, more intimate suite (four pieces) consists of the pieces written to accompany the royal supper. The third suite (five pieces) is the music intended for the return journey, and introduces trumpets into the music for the first time.

RECOMMENDED CDs

Pinnock, English Concert (Deutsche Grammophon/Archiv, 1983)

Gibson, Scottish Chamber (Chandos, 1985)

RECOMMENDED LPs

Pinnock, English Concert (Deutsche Grammophon/Archiv, 1983)

Gibson, Scottish Chamber (Chandos, 1985)

Pinnock, English Concert (Deutsche Grammophon/Archiv, 1983)

Gibson, Scottish Chamber (Chandos, 1985)

COMMENTS

Pinnock's recording is outstanding for its combination of stylistic authenticity and performance verve, and the sound engineering is splendid. Gibson, more modern stylistically, is also lively, supple, and most attractive.

FOR FOLLOW-UP CONSIDERATION

ROYAL FIREWORKS MUSIC   A set of pieces written to accompany a royal fireworks display (some of the pieces have descriptive titles such as "Peace" and "Rejoicing"). Handel wrote two arrangements: the original one for large wind band and percussion, and a second one for normal Baroque orchestra.

RECOMMENDED CD, LP, AND CASSETTE

Hogwood, Academy of Ancient Music (L'Oiseau Lyre, 1977), a rousing, animated mix of the so-called "outdoor" and "indoor" versions, very well-recorded.

FRANZ JOSEF HAYDN

Pronounced: *high*-d'n. Born March 31, 1732, in Rohrau, Austria. Died May 31, 1809, in Vienna, at age 77.

SIGNIFICANCE   Austrian composer, generally known as the "father of the symphony" because of the way he developed and expanded the form even though he did not invent it. Also a major force in the development of the symphony orchestra.

BACKGROUND   Haydn, at age eight, was sent to Vienna to sing in the boys' choir of St. Stephan's Cathedral. There he also learned to play the violin and other instruments. About the time his voice broke, he reportedly pulled a prank that got him thrown out of the choir school (he cut off the pigtail of a chorister in front of him). He wandered penniless through the Vienna streets, finally joining a group of serenading musicians in order to earn money for food. (It was then a custom in Vienna for people to hire musicians to play under the window of a lady on her birthday or other festive occasion.) Several years later he joined the orchestra of Count Morzin, who had a large estate near Pilsen, in Bohemia (now Czechoslovakia), and for it he composed his first symphony in 1759.

Word of his talent spread among the aristocracy, and in 1761 Haydn was invited to join the service of Prince Esterházy, the richest and most powerful of all the Hungarian nobility, and whose estate was the most elaborate east of Versailles. Haydn was never again to know hunger. He became the Esterházys' musical factotum (or servant), teaching the prince's family, organizing concerts, and training various performers in what one biographer has called "a cushioned prison." Haydn remained with the Esterházy family for almost 30 years, conducting and composing more than 60 symphonies, 11 operas, five masses, and hundreds of chamber works. As the fame of his symphonies spread throughout Europe, instrumental music became the chief symbol of 18th-century Germanic culture, just as vocal music was of Italian.

After Prince Nikolaus Esterházy died in 1790, Haydn accepted an invitation to visit England. There he received an honorary degree from Oxford, and heard some of Handel's oratorios for the first time. Under their influence, he wrote his own oratorio, *The Creation*. For a London concert manager, J. P. Salomon, Haydn also wrote his last 12 symphonies (since known as the "London" or the "Salomon" symphonies, which are considered among his finest and most fully developed ones)—bringing the total to 104! As his health failed, he went into retirement. His death in 1809 is said to have been partly caused by the shock of Vienna's bombardment by the French during Napoleon's conquests.

SYMPHONY No. 94 IN
G MAJOR ("SURPRISE")

As a whole, the 94th splendidly represents the uncomplicated melodies and clear-cut rhythms that distinguish Haydn's music. It was nicknamed the "Surprise" Symphony because there is a loud chord in the midst of the quiet and peaceful second movement that Haydn is reported to have puckishly said "will make the ladies jump," referring to the fact that the noble ladies often fell asleep during the long concert programs fashionable in the late 18th century. It is the best-known of the 12 last symphonies Haydn wrote for the London impresario Salomon.

RECOMMENDED CDs————
Bernstein, Vienna Philharmonic (Deutsche Grammophon)
Hogwood, Academy of Ancient Music (L'Oiseau Lyre)

RECOMMENDED LPs————
Bernstein, Vienna Philharmonic (Deutsche Grammophon)

Hogwood, Academy of Ancient Music (L'Oiseau Lyre)

RECOMMENDED CASSETTES——
Bernstein, Vienna Philharmonic (Deutsche Grammophon)
Hogwood, Academy of Ancient Music (L'Oiseau Lyre)

Bernstein has long had a special knack for making the most of the contrasting "courtly" and "peasant" elements in Haydn's music, and he brings out both aspects splendidly with the Vienna orchestra known for its long tradition of Haydn performances.

Hogwood's spirited performance has the added musicological benefit of using a new performing edition prepared by the conductor from his research into Haydn's notes and manuscripts.

SYMPHONY No. 83 IN G MINOR ("LA POULE" OR "THE HEN")

This is one of six so-called "Paris" symphonies that Haydn composed in the mid-1780s, when he was in his early 50s. The commission came from the esteemed *Loge Olympique*, whose concerts were frequently attended by Marie Antoinette and her fashionable ladies-in-waiting. The orchestral players were required to wear brocaded coats, lace ruffles, and swords. This, of course, was the decade in which the excesses of the French aristocracy were stirring up resentments that would soon erupt in the French Revolution. Yet, whatever the social injustices or outright evils that may have supported the French Court at this time, much of its art (and especially its music) reflected an unabashed optimism and *joie de vivre*.

Moreover, the ensemble made available to Haydn in Paris was much larger than the one for which he had composed up to then at Esterháza—and, in fact, it would be larger than Salomon's orchestra in London, for which Haydn would write his last symphonies a few years later.

The Parisian audience nicknamed this symphony "La Poule" ("The Hen") because of the gently clucking sound of the oboe in the first movement.

RECOMMENDED CDs
Colin Davis, Amsterdam Concertgebouw (Philips, 1987)
Karajan, Berlin Philharmonic (Deutsche Grammophon, 1987)

RECOMMENDED LPs
Bernstein, New York Philharmonic (CBS, 1964)
Karajan, Berlin Philharmonic (Deutsche Grammophon, 1987)

RECOMMENDED CASSETTE
None presently available.

COMMENTS
Davis' performance is one of his finest to date, with the fairly large body of Amsterdam strings playing with almost chamber-music clarity.

The spirited Bernstein and more suave Karajan versions are available only in complete sets of all six "Paris" symphonies.

SYMPHONY No. 44 IN E MINOR ("TRAUER" OR "MOURNING")

The symphony that Haydn himself is believed to have nicknamed *Trauersymphonie* (Symphony of Mourning) is one of the best examples of Haydn's middle period, which some annotators call his *Sturm und Drang* (storm and stress) period. Our own era's foremost Haydn scholar, H. C. Robbins Landon, has written that, with this work (composed at Esterháza when Haydn was 39), Haydn created "a new kind of symphony which is neither a chamber work nor a grand one with trumpets and timpani. Here Haydn finally achieved the form he had sought so long, for the emotional world of the church sonata was successfully transferred to 'normal' symphonic structure."

Robbins Landon has also called the slow movement "one of the outstanding slow movements in all the Haydn symphonies." Haydn himself liked it so much that soon after its first performance in 1771 he expressed the wish that it be played at his funeral (and thus the source of the title). Thirty-eight years later, shortly after Haydn's death in 1809, that movement was indeed played at a special Haydn memorial concert in Berlin. But the overall mood of the rest of the symphony is far from funereal or mournful. The opening and closing movements are energetic and occasionally even turbulent, while the minuet is relaxed and quietly lyrical.

RECOMMENDED CDs_____
Orpheus Chamber Orchestra (Deutsche Grammophon, 1985)
Lubbock, St. John's of Smith Square Orchestra, London (MCA Classics, 1985)

RECOMMENDED LPs_____
Orpheus Chamber Orchestra (Deutsche Grammophon, 1985)
Lubbock, St. John's of Smith Square Orchestra, London (MCA Classics, 1985)

RECOMMENDED CASSETTES_____
Orpheus Chamber Orchestra (Deutsche Grammophon, 1985)
Lubbock, St. John's of Smith Square Orchestra, London (MCA Classics, 1985)

COMMENTS_____
Both performances are respectably crisp and clean, although not as penetrating as the recording by Marriner and the Academy of St. Martin-in-the-Fields (Philips, 1975), which is regrettably available only in a six-LP set with twelve of Haydn's "name" symphonies.

The Orpheus version is coupled with Haydn's Symphony No. 49 in F minor ("*La Passione*") from the same period, whereas the Lubbock version is coupled with Haydn's later Symphony No. 77 in B-flat major.

FOR FOLLOW-UP CONSIDERATION

DIE SCHÖPFUNG (THE CREATION)   The most famous work of Haydn's late years, this oratorio was composed between 1796 and 1798, and is based on the Biblical book of Genesis and on Milton's *Paradise Lost*. Most critics regard the work more highly for its solo passages (especially those for Adam and Eve) than for its choral writing, although one very popular chorus, "The Heavens Are Telling," has become part of the standard choral repertory.

CHARLES IVES

Born October 20, 1874, in Danbury, Connecticut. Died May 19, 1954, in New York City, at age 79.

SIGNIFICANCE American composer and insurance executive who wrote some of the most ruggedly individualistic music of the early 20th century —full of challenging harmonies, advanced ideas, and occasionally wild humor.

BACKGROUND Ives lived most of his life in western Connecticut. He studied music at Yale, but when he realized that he could not support his wife except by writing the kind of music he did not believe in, he went into the insurance business in 1898. He eventually became one of New York's most successful insurance executives. In his spare time between 1900 and 1920, he continued to write music, and occasionally paid musicians to come to his Connecticut house to play it. When they had difficulty getting through his complex instrumentation, he despaired of ever having his work publicly performed. After 1920 he lived in precarious health in virtual isolation, and composed little. It was not until 1946 (when he was 71) that he heard any of his orchestral music played in public.

When he won the Pulitzer Prize in 1947 for his Third Symphony (written in 1904) he scorned the award as coming too late to interest him. In the 1950s Leonard Bernstein and others began to play Ives' music regularly. By the 1960s, Ives was widely recognized as one of the greatest American composers to date, and by 1970 all his major works had been recorded. Some of them antedate Schoenberg, Stravinsky, Bartók, and others in musical ideas, including experimentation with multiple rhythms, polytonality, note clusters, and tone rows. He also mixed hymn tunes, patriotic songs, college songs, ragtime, etc., into a jigsaw of sound patterns, sometimes seriously, sometimes for humorous effect. As Leonard Bernstein has said, "We have suddenly discovered our musical Mark Twain, Emerson, and Lincoln all rolled into one."

THREE PLACES IN NEW ENGLAND

One of the most moving inquiries into Americana by any U.S. composer, these three short symphonic pieces were written between 1903 and 1914, yet they were never performed until 1931 (and then not very often until the late 1950s). They are stream-of-consciousness reflections about the history of places in New England known to Ives.

The first movement, " 'St. Gaudens' in Boston Common — Col. Shaw and His Colored Regiment," is a sombre meditation on the Civil War (in which Shaw's regiment served), with songs of that war quoted in various, often distorted guises. The second movement, "Putnam's Camp, Redding, Connecticut" is a wild and raucous vision (during a Fourth of July celebration) of Gen. Israel Putnam's Revolutionary army on the march; it is based in part on the *1776* overture Ives sketched for an opera about John André and Benedict Arnold, and weaves several Revolutionary period songs into its complex texture, plus some of later vintage ("The Battle Cry of Freedom," "Massa's in de Cold, Cold Ground," Sousa's "Semper Fidelis," etc.). The third movement, "The Housatonic at Stockbridge," is an enigmatic scene by the Housatonic River in the Berkshires, beginning with misty orchestral hues and then building to a climax of overpoweringly melancholy intensity which unexpectedly returns to the original mood and then ends abruptly.

RECOMMENDED CDs
Thomas, Boston Symphony (Deutsche Grammophon, 1970)
Davies, St. Paul Chamber Orchestra (Pro Arte, 1983)

RECOMMENDED LP
Ormandy, Philadelphia Orchestra (CBS, 1964)

RECOMMENDED CASSETTE
Davies, St. Paul Chamber Orchestra (Pro Arte, 1983)

COMMENTS
Ormandy's performance is more intense and more lushly played than Davies' leaner, smaller-scaled, but very effective one. Davies also has more current sound engineering. The LP version of Thomas' splendid Boston recording was withdrawn in the mid-'80s, but a remastered CD-only version was re-released in 1988, and remains the best version yet, with a more naturally swinging "Putnam's Camp at Redding" section than either Ormandy or Davies.

SYMPHONY No. 3 ("THE CAMP MEETING")

Gustav Mahler, during his years as conductor of the New York Philharmonic (1909–11), saw the score for this symphony and told Ives he would like to play it. But Mahler died before he could arrange to do so. The Third Symphony would not be publicly performed until 1946 (by the Little Symphony of New York, conducted by Lou Harrison). When that performance led to a Pulitzer Prize for Ives, the symphony was published—from a faded pencil score (Ives had lost the final ink score) pieced together without Ives' active collaboration because of his failing eyesight. Later editions, including one by composer Henry Cowell, sought to correct mistakes or misinterpretations. Finally, with the formation of the Charles Ives Society in 1974 and the cataloging of the full range of manuscript materials assembled in the Ives Collection at Yale, a new "critical edition" (edited by Kenneth Singleton) has recently been prepared, using material not available to Harrison or Cowell.

The symphony is essentially quiet and austere, with the quality of a church service—not surprisingly, since Ives himself noted that the themes are mostly based on hymns and organ pieces he played at New York's Central Presbyterian Church in 1901. The first and last movements, in fact, were originally written as solo organ pieces. In orchestrating them for this symphony, Ives gave them the titles "Old Folks Gatherin'" and "Communion." The livelier second movement is titled "Children's Day."

RECOMMENDED CD————————
Thomas, Amsterdam Concertgebouw (CBS, 1985)
Bernstein, New York Philharmonic (CBS, 1965)

RECOMMENDED LPs————————
Thomas, Amsterdam Concertgebouw (CBS, 1985)
Bernstein, New York Philharmonic (CBS, 1965)

RECOMMENDED CASSETTES——
Thomas, Amsterdam Concertgebouw (CBS, 1985)
Bernstein, New York Philharmonic (CBS, 1965)

COMMENTS————————
Both Thomas and Bernstein are dedicated Ivesians, and both performances are excellent. Thomas has the advantage of more up-to-date sound engineering, and he also is the first conductor to record the new "critical edition."

FOR FOLLOW-UP CONSIDERATION

SYMPHONY No. 2   The Second Symphony has been described by Leonard Bernstein as "a sound image of Ives' world" at the turn of the century. Those images include the music of Brahms, Beethoven, and Wagner, plus the local American music Ives knew—hymns, folk songs, college songs, patriotic songs, and marches. "All this," says Bernstein, "can be found in this symphony, from Beethoven's Fifth to 'Turkey in the Straw' and 'Columbia, the Gem of the Ocean.' But it all comes out Ivesian, transmogrified into his own personal statement."

RECOMMENDED CD, LP, AND CASSETTE————————————
Thomas, Concertgebouw Orchestra

(CBS), a vivid performance using the new "critical edition."

HOLIDAYS SYMPHONY Subtitled "Recollections of a Boy's Holidays in a Connecticut Town," this is really a suite of related pieces rather than a symphony in the formal sense. Its four parts were written between 1904 and 1913, and were placed together by Ives in a folder marked "4 New England Holidays" with a note that "these movements may be played as separate pieces . . . [or] lumped together as a symphony." The pieces are kaleidoscopic views of four American holidays and the four different seasons in which they occur. The first movement, "Washington's Birthday" (1909), evokes the mood of Whittier's "Snowbound" with its feeling of cold and solitude, broken for a brief spell by a barn dance. The second movement, "Decoration Day" (1912), describes the gathering of flowers for the day's memorial ceremony and a town parade. The third, "Fourth of July" (1912–1913), is (to quote Ives) "a boy's Fourth—no historical orations, with a patriotism nearer kin to nature than jingoism"; it explodes in a cacophonous finale of firecrackers. The fourth, "Thanksgiving and/or Forefathers' Day" (1904), is based on two earlier organ pieces by Ives, culminating in a short choral setting of the Forefathers' Day Hymn found in many Protestant hymnals; it represents (according to Ives) "the sternness and strength and austerity of the Puritan character."

RECOMMENDED CD, LP, AND CASSETTE
Thomas, Chicago Symphony Orchestra and Chorus (CBS, 1986/88). Longtime Ives champion Thomas leads a vibrant, intensely expressive performance; his is also the first recording to use the newly published critical edition of the score as prepared by Yale's Ives Society. A fascinating bonus: Thomas also includes both the original (1906) and revised (1930) versions of Ives' short masterpiece *The Unanswered Question*.

AMERICAN SONGS Ives composed many songs about the American scene as he saw it, to poems by Thoreau, Holmes, Whittier, Whitman, and others.

RECOMMENDED CD, LP, AND CASSETTE
Roberta Alexander with Crone, pianist (Etcetera, 1984). Another excellent LP, as sung by Evelyn Lear and Thomas Stewart and titled *American Scenes, American Poets* (CBS, 1969), has been withdrawn from the catalog but still may be found in some collectors' shops.

FRANZ LISZT

Pronounced: *list*. Born October 22, 1811, in Raiding, near Odenburg, Hungary. Died July 31, 1886, in Bayreuth, Germany, at age 75.

SIGNIFICANCE Hungarian pianist, conductor, and composer, who used the term "symphonic poem" to describe extended orchestral pieces that translated into musical terms the content of a specific poem, story, or painting.

BACKGROUND Liszt was the son of a disappointed musician who served as land steward to the noble Esterházy family of Hungary. After he showed prodigious talent as a pianist at the age of nine, a group of Hungarian counts subscribed a six-years' annuity on the boy's family for him to study in Vienna. Liszt started giving successful piano recitals at the age of 12, became a salon idol as a young man, and later won recognition throughout Europe as the first of the great piano virtuosos.

After the age of 40, however, he stopped playing publicly except on rare special occasions, and concentrated on conducting and composing. From 1848 to 1859 he was court music director at Weimar, making it one of Europe's most important music centers and using the post to become a patron of new composers such as Berlioz, Schumann, Grieg, and Wagner. Although he never married, Liszt caused a great public scandal by living for long periods of time with, first, the Countess d'Agoult (from 1833 to 1844), with whom he had four children (one daughter, Cosima, later married Richard Wagner), then with the Princess Sayn-Wittgenstein (from 1848 to 1861).

In 1865 Liszt took minor orders as an abbé of the Roman Catholic Church from Pope Pius IX, and sought unsuccessfully for many years to become Vatican music director. In 1870 he gave up the religious life to teach in Weimar and Budapest, and to become one of Wagner's staunchest supporters in establishing Bayreuth as the capital of Wagnerian opera. He died in Bayreuth in 1886.

As a composer, Liszt is best known for his two piano concertos, some nineteen Hungarian Rhapsodies for piano, of which six exist in orchestral versions as well, and thirteen symphonic poems.

PIANO CONCERTO No. 1 IN E FLAT MAJOR

From its strong, assertive opening chords, this concerto surges with Romantic fervor and rhapsodic melody. The piano dominates throughout, but the orchestral writing is more colorful and more varied than in most concertos up to that time. It is interesting that Liszt, the most acclaimed piano virtuoso of his day, was so preoccupied with orchestral harmonies and tonal effects that he refused to publish a piano concerto until he was 44, when he felt he had finally begun to master orchestral techniques. (He *had* written earlier concertos and performed them in his 20s and 30s, but they were not published and most are apparently lost.) This first published concerto is sometimes nicknamed the "Triangle" Concerto, because of the use Liszt makes of a struck triangle in the final movement, a use that was highly controversial in Liszt's time. There is no break between the concerto's movements, which are linked thematically by what Liszt called the "transformation of themes" (a method of repeating and developing themes in various guises throughout a work), which some critics believe influenced Wagner in developing the *leitmotif* concept in his operas.

RECOMMENDED CDs————————
Arrau, Colin Davis, London Symphony
  (Philips, 1979)
Richter, Kondrashin, London Symphony
  (Philips, 1962)

RECOMMENDED LPs————————
Arrau, Colin Davis, London Symphony
  (Philips, 1979)
Bolet, Zinman, Rochester Philharmonic
  (Vox Cum Laude, 1979)

RECOMMENDED CASSETTES———
Arrau, Colin Davis, London Symphony
  (Philips, 1979)
Bolet, Zinman, Rochester Philharmonic
  (Vox Cum Laude, 1979)

COMMENTS————————————
Richter's 1962 performance is arguably the best the Soviet pianist ever made in the West — offering an impressive blend of lyrical poetry and dazzling virtuosity. But, sonically, the recording is no match for the later one by Arrau, whose performance is almost as compelling and poetic. Bolet, long a specialist in Liszt's music, underplays the flamboyance of the concerto while never losing its surging, dynamic thrust. All three performances are coupled with Liszt's Piano Concerto No. 2 in A major.

LES PRÉLUDES (SYMPHONIC POEM No. 3)

This best known and most popular of Liszt's 14 symphonic poems is a colorful, dramatic work expressing Romantic musical ideas, but with an unexplicit "program" that permits the listener great freedom in interpreting the meaning. Originally written in 1848 as a prelude to a choral work, *The Four Elements*, it was revised several times in succeeding years, until it reached its final form in 1854 as an independent orchestral work.

Although Liszt used some of the thematic material of *The Four Elements*, he related the final version to the poem "Les Préludes" from Lamartine's *Méditations Poétique* (Poetic Meditations): "What is our life but a series of preludes to that unknown song whose first solemn note is sounded only by death?" Liszt depicts man's struggle for existence through various interconnected episodes: first, love ("The Enchanted Daybreak"), then the harshness of the real world ("Storms Whose Killing Breath Dispel Lovely Illusion"), a pastoral interlude ("A Pleasant Rest Amidst Nature's Moods"), a call to battle ("The Trumpets' Loud Clangor . . . The Post of Danger . . ."), and finally, self-recognition.

RECOMMENDED CDs_____
Muti, Philadelphia (Angel, 1983)
Conlon, Rotterdam Philharmonic (Erato, 1985)

RECOMMENDED LPs_____
Barenboim, Chicago Symphony (Deutsche Grammophon, 1987)
Conlon, Rotterdam Philharmonic (Erato, 1985)

RECOMMENDED CASSETTES_____
Barenboim, Chicago Symphony (Deutsche Grammophon, 1987)

Conlon, Rotterdam Philharmonic (Erato, 1986)

COMMENTS_____
Muti's performance is exceptionally spirited and full-blooded. Barenboim's is vivid, warm, and beautifully spacious. Conlon's is lively and dramatically forceful.

FOR FOLLOW-UP CONSIDERATION

TOTENTANZ (DANCE OF DEATH)   A rousingly dramatic and colorful set of variations for piano and orchestra, *Totentanz* is based on the traditional Dies Irae theme from the Mass for the Dead. Liszt's piece was inspired by Vorcagna's 14th-century frescoes "The Triumph of Death," which Liszt saw at Pisa.

RECOMMENDED CD, LP, AND CASSETTE_____
Bolet, Fischer, London Symphony Or-

chestra (London, 1984), a tautly gripping performance that emphasizes the work's many contrasts.

PIANO MUSIC   As his generation's foremost piano virtuoso, Liszt wrote many showpieces for that instrument, as well as many subtler, beautifully lyrical piano pieces.

RECOMMENDED CDs AND LPs____
Watts (Angel, 1986), *Liszt Piano Music Vol. 2*, in which the American pianist of partly Hungarian parentage combines his technical flair and interpretive insight in an outstanding program that includes Liszt's Sonata in B minor, the Transcendental Etude No. 10, "Un Sospiro," "Valse oubliee No. 1," and the Nocturne "En reve." Bolet (London, 1982), just one of many fine Liszt

sets he has recorded, this one particularly worthwhile for showing several different sides of Liszt's writing and including "La Campanella," "Liebestraume," "Mephisto Waltz No. 1," "Funerailles," "Hungarian Rhapsody in C-sharp-minor," and "Concert Paraphrase from Verdi's *Rigoletto*," all splendidly played. (No cassette presently available.)

GUSTAV MAHLER

Pronounced: *mah*-ler. Born July 7, 1860, in Kalischt, Bohemia. Died May 18, 1911, in Vienna, at age 50.

SIGNIFICANCE   Bohemian composer and conductor, last of the great Romantic symphonists; a composer of massive, intensely expressive and profound orchestral music and song cycles.

BACKGROUND   Mahler, the son of a poor Jewish innkeeper, studied music in Prague and Vienna, winning both piano and composition prizes at the Vienna Conservatory. In his thirties he became one of Europe's most famous conductors—first in Prague, then in Budapest and Hamburg. In 1900 he became director of the Vienna State Opera, and set standards of performance over the next six years that were the talk of Europe. But he grew increasingly unpopular with many of his colleagues—partly because of the era's anti-Semitism and partly because of his dictatorial working habits—and he was forced to resign. The following year, the New York Philharmonic named him its music director at what was, to that time, the highest salary ever paid a symphony conductor anywhere: $30,000 a year. But his tenure in New York was to be brief because of illness. Part-way through his second season, he collapsed and returned to Vienna under doctors' orders. He died a few months later.

Throughout most of his life, Mahler led a full conducting schedule during the winter months, but reserved the summer for composing. He gave most of his works a literary or philosophical theme in the Romantic tradition. But he also foreshadowed more modern directions by his use of "progressive tonality" (beginning a movement in one key and leading it toward an ending in another key) and some of the devices of serial music. He sometimes combined instrumental, choral, and solo vocal parts in works of enormous scope. "A symphony is like the world—it must embrace everything," he once said.

During the first half of the 20th century, Mahler's music was rarely performed, except by such disciples as conductor Bruno Walter. "My time will come," Mahler had said—and indeed it did, with enormous impact in the 1950s and 1960s. Impassioned championing by Leonard Bernstein, Dimitri Mitropoulos, and a few others played a big role. So, too, did the coming of the stereo age—for Mahler's massive, often sonically overwhelming symphonies pulled out all the stops not only for an orchestra but also for recording engineers. But most of all, Mahler's emotionally and spiritually complex music seems to speak tellingly today to a generation geared to probing psychological depths and the varied problems of human existence.

SYMPHONY No. 1 IN D ("TITAN")

From his very first symphony, composed when he was in his twenties, Mahler sought to expand the limits of symphonic form. Originally, he subtitled his First Symphony "Titan"—after a novel by Jean-Paul (the pseudonym for Johann Paul Friedrich Richter) "for whose emotional abundance, boundless fantasy, and grotesque humor [Mahler] felt a deep affinity," to quote Bruno Walter.

Mahler also gave descriptive titles to each of its five movements: (1) "Spring without End," (2) "Blumine" ("Flowers"), (3) "Under Full Sail," (4) "The Hunter's Funeral Procession," and (5) "From Inferno to Paradiso." Later he withdrew all the titles except the fourth, and he dropped the "Blumine" movement from the published score (reportedly at his publisher's urging, and reluctantly). However, he continued to defend the use of subtitles as guides to the general atmosphere of a work, saying: "During the first period, when my style may still seem strange and new, the listener gets some word maps and milestones on the journey ... but such an explanation cannot offer more."

Mahler's First is a large-scale symphony of dramatic contrasts. It is full of trumpet calls and marching rhythms. It has quiet, lyrical, pastoral moments and catchy peasant dances (one movement uses the folk song "Frère Jacques" or "Bruder Martin"). It has moments of grotesque black humor ("The Hunter's Funeral Procession" refers to an engraving by Jacques Callot showing a procession of dancing animals escorting the body of a dead hunter to the grave). And in its awesome finale all the major previous themes recur—including the "Blumine,"which some conductors believe justifies restoring the dropped movement—before the movement's own theme finally emerges in blazing glory.

RECOMMENDED CDs
Bernstein, Amsterdam Concertgebouw (Deutsche Grammophon, 1988)
Haitink, Amsterdam Concertgebouw (Philips, 1972)

RECOMMENDED LPs
Haitink, Amsterdam Concertgebouw (Philips, 1972)
Solti, Chicago Symphony (London, 1983)

RECOMMENDED CASSETTES
Haitink, Amsterdam Concertgebouw (Philips, 1972)
Solti, Chicago Symphony (London, 1983)

COMMENTS
Among today's top conductors, Bernstein, Haitink, and Solti head the list as Mahler interpreters—but in very different ways. Bernstein is the most openheartedly passionate in his approach, Haitink the most poetic and penetratingly poignant, Solti the most drivingly dramatic. And those are the qualities clearly in evidence in these recordings. Bernstein's and Haitink's later recordings of this symphony are considerably better than their earlier '60s versions, not only in the sound engineering but also in the depth of the conductors' interpretations.

All of the above performances are of the now-standard four-movement version. Those interested in the five-movement version (with the brief "Blumine") might check out the Rattle-City of Birmingham CD (Angel/EMI, 1993), which places "Blumine" at the disc's start and then presents the standard four movements uninterrupted. This arrangement permits using your CD remote either to bypass "Blumine" or re-program it in its original place as the second movement. But Rattle's overall performance of the symphony is relatively restrained and colorless. An earlier Ormandy-Philadelphia LP and Cassette with "Blumine" (RCA, 1969) has tonal grandeur but not much verve.

SYMPHONY No. 2 IN C MINOR ("RESURRECTION")

If Mahler had written no other work, his Second Symphony (completed in 1894, when he was 34) would certainly place him among the great composers. It is a monumental, mystical, heaven-storming work about nothing less than the meaning of life. To quote annotator William Mann, it "takes the form of a funeral address, dwelling on sorrow and the transitory nature of existence, the hope of better things, the happy memory of past joys, the hectic chaos of competition, and then . . . innocent childish faith which moves mountains and allows the believer to survive, yes to float through, the ultimate ordeal of the Last Judgment."

Nearly an hour and a half long, the symphony requires not only a large orchestra but also a chorus, two vocal soloists, an organ, and an offstage brass band. The first three movements are purely orchestral. The first is an alternately stormy and lyrical dirge (to quote Mahler: "We are standing beside the coffin of one dearly loved . . . [and ask] is it all a hollow dream, or does our life have meaning?"). The second is a gentle Ländler, a triple-time folk dance of Austria. The third is an ironic, despairing scherzo ("A recollection of the world's vulgarities," said Mahler, and its "spirit of negation"). The fourth movement is a hushed and haunting song for mezzo-soprano, "Urlicht" ("Primal Light")—taken from Mahler's earlier song cycle *Des Knaben Wunderhorn* (The Youth's Magic Horn), based on German folk poetry. The fifth movement is an apocalyptic portrait of the Day of Judgment, climaxed by a choral setting of the "Resurrection Ode" by the 18th-century German poet Klopstock (extended by Mahler with words of his own)—ending jubilantly as "an overwhelming Love shines," to quote Mahler, "we know and are."

RECOMMENDED CDs

Bernstein, Ludwig, Hendricks, New York Philharmonic, Westminster Symphonic Choir (Deutsche Grammophon, 1987, two discs)

Slatkin, Forrester, Battle, Saint Louis Symphony & Chorus (Telarc, 1982, two discs)

Slatkin, Forrester, Battle, Saint Louis Symphony & Chorus (Telarc, 1982)
Tennstedt, Soffel, Mathis, London Philharmonic & Chorus (Angel, 1982)

RECOMMENDED CASSETTES
Bernstein, Ludwig, Hendricks, New York Philharmonic, Westminster Symphonic Choir (Deutsche Grammophon, 1987)
Walter, Forrester, Cundari, New York Philharmonic, Westminster Choir (CBS/Odyssey, 1958)

COMMENTS
Bernstein's performance is overwhelming—arguably the finest he has ever recorded of any work. His 1987 recording (his third of this symphony) is taken from a series of live concerts at which he, his outstanding soloists, and the sound engineers were all in top form.

Slatkin's performance may be less profound, but it is thrilling and genuinely moving nonetheless, and the soloists are also splendid.

Tennstedt is tense and driving, yet also uncommonly noble.

Walter's performance was once the touchstone for this symphony, but others have since come to speak just as eloquently for it—and to have the advantage of better sound engineering than Walter had in the 1950s. Yet his performance remains impressive—with a special warmth, nobility, and strength that still shine through.

Due to the length of the symphony (almost an hour and a half), all of the above performances are in two-disc or multiple-cassette sets.

DAS LIED VON DER ERDE (THE SONG OF THE EARTH)

To many, Mahler's song cycles are the essence of Mahler, and *The Song of the Earth* his supreme achievement. Bruno Walter once went so far as to call it the greatest work in all music. Subtitled "A Symphony for Tenor, Contralto (or Baritone), and Orchestra," it is a profoundly moving song cycle based on old Chinese poems about youth, natural beauty, loneliness, life, and death.

Mahler began the work shortly after the death of one of his daughters, and after learning that he himself had an incurable heart ailment. The musicologist and Mahler expert Deryck Cooke has written, "He found himself face-to-face with death as an existential reality—as the imminent cessation of his own life. If his earlier works had been full of *images* of immortality, this one is permeated with the bitter *taste* of mortality."

This is not to imply that the work is filled with despair. On the contrary, it is a loving testament to the mysteries of life—ending with the words: "The dear earth everywhere blossoms in spring and grows green again/ Everywhere and eternally the distance shines bright and blue/Forever . . . forever . . . forever. . . ." In contrast to the massive power of most of Mahler's symphonies, the orchestral texture of *The Song of the Earth* is blended as subtly and sensitively as Chinese watercolors.

RECOMMENDED CDs

Walter, Ferrier, Patzak, Vienna Philharmonic (London, 1952, mono)

Klemperer, Ludwig, Wunderlich, Philharmonia of London (Angel, 1966)

RECOMMENDED LPs

Walter, Ferrier, Patzak, Vienna Philharmonic (London, 1952, mono)

Haitink, Baker, King, Amsterdam Concertgebouw (Philips, 1975)

RECOMMENDED CASSETTES

Walter, Ferrier, Patzak, Vienna Philharmonic (London, 1952, mono)

Haitink, Baker, King, Amsterdam Concertgebouw (Philips, 1975)

COMMENTS

The incomparable Walter-Ferrier recording remains the touchstone for this work. Walter conducted its world premiere six months after Mahler's death in 1911, and he made three recordings of it (1936, 1952, 1960). The nobility and tenderness of Ferrier's singing has yet to be matched by any other version, and Patzak is excellent. London's monaural sound holds up better than some other companies' later stereo, and the CD transfer is remarkably good.

If you must have stereo, Ludwig comes closest to Ferrier, although Baker is also tremendously moving. Wunderlich is the most ardent of the tenors cited, King the least subtle (and shows signs of vocal strain). Haitink brings both poetic depth and surging drama to his version. Klemperer is more emotionally restrained, yet intensely probing.

At present, the only baritone version on CD (Mahler made one of the vocal roles optional for contralto or baritone) is a splendid one by Dietrich Fischer-Dieskau with Bernstein conducting the Vienna Philharmonic (London, 1966).

FOR FOLLOW-UP CONSIDERATION

SYMPHONY No. 4 IN G MAJOR Mahler's shortest symphony, and one of his most melodically appealing. The final movement is a song for soprano and orchestra depicting a child's view of paradise.

RECOMMENDED CD, LP, AND CASSETTE
Welser-Möst, Lott, London Philharmonic (EMI Eminence, 1988), a warm, vibrant performance by the young Austrian conductor.

SYMPHONY No. 5 IN C SHARP MINOR A large-scale mixture of songful melodies, marches, waltzes, and an *adagietto* that must be one of the most beautiful movements any symphony can claim. (It was used as the main background theme for the 1971 Visconti film *Death in Venice*.)

RECOMMENDED CD, LP, AND CASSETTE
Sinopoli, Philharmonia of London (Deutsche Grammophon, 1986), a performance of eloquence and dramatic bite.

SYMPHONY No. 8 IN E FLAT The so-called "Symphony of a Thousand"—because of the huge number of instrumentalists, vocal soloists, and choristers required. Part one is less interesting than part two, a deeply moving setting of the closing scene of Goethe's *Faust* and similar in some ways to the final movement of Mahler's Symphony No. 2.

RECOMMENDED CD, LP, AND CASSETTE

Solti, Harper, Popp, Minton, Watts, Kollo, Shirley-Quirk, Talvela, Chicago Symphony, Vienna State Opera Chorus, Vienna Boys' Choir (London, 1971) —As outstanding a group of singers as has yet been combined for this work with a conductor, orchestra, and choruses that are also outstanding. The performance, recorded in Vienna during a Chicago Symphony European tour, is positively inspired—especially in the expansiveness and glow of the final movement.

SYMPHONY No. 9 IN D A long, brooding, but powerfully expressive, purely orchestral work which some critics call the sphinx among Mahler's symphonies: an enigma poised between Romantic and modern styles.

RECOMMENDED CD

Karajan, Berlin Philharmonic (Deutsche Grammophon, 1982), a live performance of unrelenting intensity and power (and *not* the same as the studio-recorded 1975 Karajan recording on LP and Cassette).

RECOMMENDED LP AND CASSETTE

Haitink, Amsterdam Concertgebouw (Philips, 1969), a deeply probing, eloquent performance.

SONGS OF A WAYFARER (LIEDER EINES FAHRENDEN GESELLEN)

Perhaps the most immediately appealing of Mahler's song cycles—a set of bittersweet, folk-like songs for contralto or baritone and orchestra, written when Mahler was 23.

RECOMMENDED CD AND CASSETTE

Fischer-Dieskau (baritone), Kubelik, Bavarian Radio (Deutsche Grammophon, 1985), a searchingly expressive performance coupled with Mahler's touching *Kindertotenlieder* and four of Mahler's incomparable *Rückert Songs*.

RECOMMENDED LP AND CASSETTE

Baker (contralto), Barbirolli, Halle Orchestra (Angel, 1969), notable for its beauty of musical line and poetic insights, and similarly coupled with *Kindertotenlieder* and five *Rückert Songs*.

BOHUSLAV MARTINŮ

Pronounced: *mar-tee-new*. Born December 8, 1890, in Polička, Bohemia (Czechoslovakia). Died August 28, 1959, in Liestal, Switzerland, at age 68.

SIGNIFICANCE Czechoslovakian composer who lived most of his mature life in France and the United States; a prolific and individualistic composer of rhythmically restless and deeply expressive instrumental and vocal works that often fused Neo-Classicism and Neo-Impressionism with Baroque forms and structures.

BACKGROUND Martinů was born in the belfry of the Church of Saint Jacob in the small eastern Bohemia town of Polička, where his father, a cobbler, had the job of fire-watchman. Sickly for the first six years of his life, Martinů spent most of those years in his parents' rooms in the belfry, which overlooked the busy town marketplace. Some biographers believe this psychologically shaped his lifelong detached view of the world and his sense of isolation from the mainstream. As one annotator has put it, "Composers sometimes have retreated into metaphysical ivory towers. Martinů reversed the process by beginning his life in one."

Martinů's musical studies began at age six. At 12 he was admitted to the Prague Conservatory, but he did not take well to its academic discipline and was expelled twice. In his early twenties he joined the Czech Philharmonic Orchestra as a second violinist, and composed in his spare time for ten years. His predilection for French music of this period led him to move to Paris in 1923 to study with Albert Roussel. He supported himself by teaching and playing in chamber groups. He also fell in love with a young dressmaker and married her. By 1938 his compositions, clearly influenced by the French Neo-Classicists but still strongly Czech in character, had won the attention of Charles Munch, Ernest Ansermet, and other conductors, and appeared with increasing frequency on concert programs.

With the Nazi occupation of Czechoslovakia and the coming of World War II, Martinů, an outspoken anti-Nazi, became a man without a country. He and his wife escaped from Paris with only one suitcase on the very day that city fell to German troops in June of 1940, and they eventually secured passage from Lisbon on a ship to America.

The Martinůs settled in New York, where his works were soon championed by such important conductors as Koussevitzky, Rodzinski, Szell, and Ormandy. Martinů's American years turned out to be the most productive of his life, and it was here that he composed all six of the symphonies that now rank him with Sibelius, Vaughan Williams, and Shostakovich among this century's greatest symphonists. He also taught for brief periods at Princeton, the Curtis Institute, and the Berkshire Music Center at Tanglewood.

Soon after the war, Martinů was invited to return to Prague as a full professor at the same conservatory that had twice expelled him as a student. But he decided against it after the Communist takeover of the Czech government and the murder of Foreign Minister Jan Masaryk (who had befriended Martinů before the war in Paris and spent time with the Martinůs in America during the inauguration of the United Nations in 1945). Martinů chose to remain in the U.S. until 1956. Eventually, however, a combination of ill health (later diagnosed as stomach cancer) and his growing dislike of what he considered the overly hectic quality of American life led Martinů to move to Switzerland. He died a few years later. In 1979 his remains were transferred to his native Czechoslovakia.

SYMPHONY No. 6 (FANTAISIES SYMPHONIQUES)

Martinů's last symphony is one of his finest and most charismatic works. It was written for and is dedicated to conductor Charles Munch, about whom Martinů said at the time of the work's 1956 premiere, "I wished to write something for Munch. I am deeply impressed by his spontaneous approach to music, in which a composition is free to acquire its form, and flows in an unforced manner proportional to its movement—and I like that. A barely perceptible slowing down or acceleration immediately fills the melody with life."

That also describes Martinů's symphony. He says he started out to compose a *Symphonie Fantastique* with three pianos, but that once he got under way he "came down to earth." Well, not entirely. The pianos were dropped, but the score that finally emerged is dreamlike in its basic feeling—an imaginatively colorful, constantly flowing, often shimmering and warmly evocative example of Martinů's mosaic-like Neo-Impressionism at its most fascinating.

RECOMMENDED CDs
Flor, Berlin Symphony (RCA, 1988)
Jarvi, Bamberger Symphony (BIS/ Hungaroton, 1988)

RECOMMENDED LP
Munch, Boston Symphony (RCA, 1957)

RECOMMENDED CASSETTE
Flor, Berlin Symphony (RCA, 1988)

COMMENTS
Claus Peter Flor's vivid, evocative performance marks the Western recording debut of this rising young East German conductor; it's coupled with an equally impressive performance of Martinů's more dancelike Fifth Symphony.

Jarvi's performance, part of his first-rate series of all the Martinů symphonies, is wonderfully surging and sparkling, with excellent sound. Munch's is slightly more expansive and colorful, and the early stereo sound is still quite good. (Munch's version was one of the first Boston Symphony stereo recordings, but it was originally released only in a monaural edition, until 1980 when the stereo master was "rediscovered" in RCA's vaults and a stereo version was finally released.) All of these performances are preferable to a stolid Neumann-Czech Philharmonic one (Supraphon, 1976).

DOUBLE CONCERTO FOR TWO STRING ORCHESTRAS, PIANO, AND TIMPANI

If ever a musical composition was written under clouds of impending doom, it is this Double Concerto. Yet what emerged is one of the strongest and most compelling of Martinů's many works. Martinů completed the score on the very day (September 28, 1938) of the signing of the fateful Munich Pact which doomed his homeland to the Nazis. Throughout the preceding summer, Martinů had worked on the Double Concerto at the Swiss mountain retreat of conductor Paul Sacher, as he and his wife listened daily to radio reports about the deteriorating international situation. Of all Martinů's orchestral works, the Double Concerto is the only one to end on an unresolved chord. Yet, as the composer himself noted, the basic emotion of the piece is not despair "but rather revolt, courage, and unshakeable faith in the future."

The form is that of a Neo-Classical Concerto Grosso. Two string orchestras challenge each other with persistent rhythms, and there is a constant sense of forward motion and tension.

RECOMMENDED CDs _____
Mackerras, Prague Radio Symphony (Surpaphon, 1982)
Belohlavek, Czech Philharmonic (Chandos, 1990)

RECOMMENDED LP _____
Mackerras, Prague Radio (as above)

RECOMMENDED CASSETTE _____
Belohlavek, Czech Philharmonic (Supraphon, 1990)

COMMENTS _____
Mackerras' performance bristles with nervous energy and tension. Belohlavek is less taut but still quite engaging.

FOR FOLLOW-UP CONSIDERATION

SYMPHONY No. 1   Like Brahms, Martinů delayed writing a symphony until many years after he had begun to win international recognition. He was in his fifties when he finally completed his First Symphony in 1942, on a commission from Serge Koussevitzky for the Boston Symphony Orchestra. It is distinctively and unmistakably Martinů from the first measures—with nervous, gliding, motoric rhythms and almost elegaic, folk-like melodies.

RECOMMENDED CD _____
Jarvi, Bamberger Symphony (BIS/ Hungaroton, 1987), a driving, impassioned, eloquent performance, splendidly recorded.

THE FRESCOES OF PIERO DELLA FRANCESCA One of Martinů's most arresting late works, composed in 1954 after he saw some of the 15th-century artist's frescoes on a visit to Italy. "I tried to express in music," said Martinů, "the kind of festively solemn, frozen calm and the opaque, colored atmosphere full of strange, peaceful, and touching poetry." There are three movements. The first derives from a fresco in which the Queen of Sheba kneels before the Sacred Wood with her ladies-in-waiting around her. The second depicts a dream in which King Constantine sees the Sign of the Cross in Heaven. The third is a battle scene, in which Constantine routs the army of Maxentius.

RECOMMENDED CD AND LP⸺
Mackerras, Prague Radio Symphony (Supraphon, 1982), a luminous, richly detailed performance. (No Cassette presently available.)

FELIX MENDELSSOHN

Pronounced: *men*-dell-son. Born February 3, 1809, in Hamburg, Germany. Died November 4, 1847, in Leipzig, at age 38.

SIGNIFICANCE German composer, conductor, pianist, and organist. In his elegant and finely sculptured music, he sought to reconcile Romantic content with Classical form.

BACKGROUND Compared to some early 19th-century composers, Mendelssohn led a uniquely happy, comfortable, and successful life. He was the grandson of Jewish philosopher Moses Mendelssohn, who waged a lifelong battle to reconcile Christians and Jews, and the son of a Hamburg banker who used the name Mendelssohn-Bartholdy to distinguish himself as a Christian. Young Mendelssohn began formal study of music at the age of ten, and became widely known as a child prodigy. On Sundays a small orchestra performed at his father's rambling house in Berlin, and it eventually became a vehicle for young Mendelssohn's composing and conducting. At 20, he conducted the first public performance since Bach's death of the *St. Matthew Passion*, and began a great crusade to take Bach out of obscurity and gain him the reputation he now holds.

By 26 Mendelssohn held the most important musical post in Germany at that time: director of the Leipzig Gewandhaus Orchestra. In 1841 he married the daughter of a French Protestant clergyman, and they subsequently had five children. He traveled frequently to conduct in Berlin and Dresden, and to perform as both pianist and organist. Some of his works were inspired by his travels (the "Scottish" Symphony, the "Italian" Symphony, the "Hebrides" Overture). He also wrote works that reflected his dual religious loyalties (the "Reformation" Symphony dedicated to Martin Luther, and the oratorio *Elijah*).

Returning from a successful English tour in 1847, he was mistaken for a Dr. Mendelssohn wanted for revolutionary political activity, and he was detained and interrogated at the Prussian border. A few hours after his release he learned suddenly that his most beloved sister Fanny had died. He collapsed with a ruptured cerebral blood vessel. He never recovered, and died a few months later.

VIOLIN CONCERTO IN E MINOR

One of the most popular and immediately appealing of all violin concertos with, as one Mendelssohn biographer once said, "the charm of eternal youth." It is Romantic in mood but Classical in form—except that there are no breaks between its three movements. The concerto moves instead in a continuous line, but with changing melodies and rhythms.

RECOMMENDED CDs————————
Zukerman (violinist and conductor), Saint Paul Chamber Orchestra (Philips, 1983)
Perlman, Haitink, Amsterdam Concertgebouw (Angel, 1984)

RECOMMENDED LPs————————
Zukerman, Bernstein, New York Philharmonic (CBS, 1969)
Perlman, Haitink, Amsterdam Concertgebouw (Angel, 1984)

RECOMMENDED CASSETTES————
Zukerman (violinist and conductor), Saint Paul Chamber Orchestra (Philips, 1983)

Perlman, Haitink, Amsterdam Concertgebouw (Angel, 1984)

COMMENTS————————————
Zukerman's latest version, as both soloist and conductor, is dashingly beautiful, with evident respect for the concerto's Classical line. In its absence on LP, Zukerman's earlier version (his debut recording at age 21) is almost as good, except for its less contemporary sonics.

Perlman's version is more broadly lush and beautifully expressive, with a splendid-sounding accompaniment from Haitink.

SYMPHONY No. 4 IN A MAJOR ("ITALIAN")

Mendelssohn himself once called this "the most sportive piece I have composed." He began it on a lengthy holiday in Italy in 1831 (during his twenty-first year), visiting Rome, Naples, Capri, Sorrento, and Amalfi. In general, it is a sunny symphony, filled with appealing melodies and spirited rhythms. Its slow movement has a "walking bass" figure that depicts a religious procession or pilgrims' march.

Although commonly called Mendelssohn's Fourth symphony (because it was the fourth to be published), it was actually his third—*if* you count only the five symphonies Mendelssohn composed as an adult and not the twelve or more he wrote as a teenager, mostly works for strings alone. (For the record, the correct compositional sequence of the Mendelssohn symphonies is as follows, with the numbers referring only to the order in which they were published: No. 1 in C minor, 1824; No. 5 in D minor, the "Reformation," 1832; No. 4 in A major, "Italian," 1833; No. 2, "Lobgesang," with voices, 1840; and No. 3 in A minor, "Scottish," 1842.)

RECOMMENDED CDs————————
Sinopoli, Philharmonia of London (Deutsche Grammophon, 1984)
Abbado, London Symphony (Deutsche Grammophon, 1986)

RECOMMENDED LPs————————
Sinopoli, Philharmonia of London (Deutsche Grammophon, 1984)
Szell, Cleveland Orchestra (CBS, 1962)

RECOMMENDED CASSETTES———
Sinopoli, Philharmonia of London (Deutsche Grammophon, 1984)
Szell, Cleveland Orchestra (CBS, 1962)

COMMENTS————————
It's curious that the two sunniest, most animated performances are by Italian conductors working with English orchestras—for a symphony about Italy by a German composer. And next best, with a splendid balance between melodic flow and rhythmic incisiveness, is a Hungarian conductor with an American orchestra. (Not surprising, I suppose, in this age of internationalized music-making.)

FOR FOLLOW-UP CONSIDERATION

A MIDSUMMER NIGHT'S DREAM (INCIDENTAL MUSIC)   This charming, airily merry set of pieces to accompany Shakespeare's play was begun when Mendelssohn was 17—and was added to in his later years. The "Wedding March" is its most famous part, although the overture is often programmed separately on concert programs and recordings. Although English was Mendelssohn's second language, he wrote this score to a German translation of selected verses from Shakespeare's play, to accompany German productions of the play.

RECOMMENDED CD, LP, AND CASSETTE————————
Ormandy, Blegen, von Stade, Philadelphia Orchestra, Mendelssohn Club of Philadelphia Women's Voices (RCA,

1977), a warm and fluent performance, sung in German and omitting only a few minor parts of the complete score.

SYMPHONY No. 3 IN A MINOR ("SCOTTISH")   An alternately dark and spirited symphony, the "Scottish" mixes romantic, pastoral images with those of combative Scottish clans. Although inspired by a visit that Mendelssohn made to the ruins of Mary Stuart's Holyrood Castle in 1829, the symphony was not completed until 13 years later—partly in Italy, partly in Berlin.

RECOMMENDED CD, LP, AND CASSETTE
Andrew Davis, Bavarian Radio Sym-phony (CBS, 1987), a first-rate, vivid performance.

OLIVIER MESSIAEN

Pronounced: mess-ee-*yahn*. Born December 10, 1908, in Avignon, France. Died April 27, 1992, in Paris.

SIGNIFICANCE French composer, organist, and teacher, who once described his complex, mystical, often exotic musical language as "like a rainbow of rhythms and harmonies"; a pioneer in blending both early and late Western music with Indian and Oriental ideas, and in recreating musically the non-human (bird and animal) noises of the animate world.

BACKGROUND The son of French poetess Cécile Sauvage, Messiaen spent his childhood in Grenoble, near the French Alps, and often said he preferred to compose in mountain regions. He entered the Paris Conservatory at age 11, winning first prizes in five different areas of study before his graduation in 1930. He became organist at Trinity Church in Paris in 1931, holding the post for more than 40 years and writing for it some of the most original and important organ music of this century.

In 1936 Messiaen co-founded a Paris musical group, La Jeune France (Young France), to play "young, free works as much estranged from trite revolutionism as from trite academicism." While fighting with French forces in World War II, he became a prisoner of war and was interned by the Nazis for two years. After the war, he combined composing with teaching, primarily at the Paris Conservatory.

Messiaen's wartime experiences deeply intensified his religious feelings and attitude about the role of the creative artist in life. A Roman Catholic, he has said that music should communicate "lofty sentiments . . . and, in particular, the loftiest of all: religious sentiments." This is reflected in the titles of some of Messiaen's best-known scores—such as *The Ascension*, *Three Petite Liturgies on the Divine Presence*, and his last big-scale work, the opera *Saint Francis of Assisi* (premiered in Paris in 1983). As composer-annotator Phillip Ramey has commented, "True music to him is an act of faith." Yet his music is usually considered more sensuous, exotic, and iridescent than other, more traditional Catholic models. French critic André

Hodier has described Messiaen's music as, paradoxically, "a voluptuous, ingrown world of subtle thrills."

L'ASCENSION (THE ASCENSION)

Subtitled "Four Symphonic Meditations for Orchestra," this was originally composed as an organ work in 1934 and later orchestrated. It remains one of Messiaen's most profoundly moving works—and a good introduction to his music.

Messiaen has said that the work as a whole is meant to depict mystical *feelings* about the ascension of Jesus, rather than being a musical depiction of it. Each of the four meditations bears a Biblical quotation in addition to the following subtitles: (1) "Majesty of Christ Beseeching His Glory of the Father"; (2) "Serene Alleluias of a Soul Yearning for Heaven"; (3) "Alleluias on the Trumpets, Alleluias on the Cymbals"; (4) "Prayer for Christ Ascending to the Father."

RECOMMENDED CD
Stokowski, London Symphony Orchestra live performance (Intaglio, 1970)

RECOMMENDED LP
Stokowski, London Symphony Orchestra studio recording (London Phase-4, 1970)

RECOMMENDED CASSETTE
None presently available.

COMMENTS
Stokowski, long a master interpreter of this score, first recorded a fine LP version in 1947 with the New York Philharmonic (Columbia, deleted). He re-recorded it in 1970 in much superior sound as part of London's then-state-of-the-art Phase-4 Concert Series. That studio version is the one on LP and Cassette, but not on CD. The CD version (on the Italian import label Intaglio) is taken from a live London concert just before the recording session, and while equally as intense a performance is not quite so awesome sonically.

TURANGALÎLA SYMPHONY

This mammoth, ten-movement symphony (pronounced too-rahn-gah-*lee*-lah) was commissioned by Serge Koussevitzky and the Boston Symphony Orchestra, and was introduced by that orchestra in 1949 under Leonard Bernstein's direction. Since then it has been much talked about, but seldom performed. Its title is a Sanskrit word symbolizing (at one and the same time) love, joy, time, rhythm, life, and death.

The symphony itself is, in part, an exotic hymn to transcendental love as part of the game of life and death, and key sections use a theme from Wagner's *Tristan und Isolde*. Besides numerous other themes introduced in each of the ten movements, the symphony contains four cyclic themes that recur in one way or another throughout the work. All in all, *Turangalîla* is a complex work that few can expect to understand fully in all its subtleties and total dimensions in one hearing. But the exotic, orgiastic nature of much of the music, its rhythmic inventiveness, and its often mesmerizing aura of Neo-Impressionism give it a unique fascination and accessibility on even a first hearing.

The composer has also related the feeling of the music to the paintings of the French artist Chagall. The symphony makes extensive use of the Ondes Martenot (an electronic wave generator) and a solo piano.

RECOMMENDED CDs————————
Salonen, Philharmonia of London (CBS, 1987)
Rattle, City of Birmingham Symphony (Angel, 1987)

RECOMMENDED LP————————
None presently available.

RECOMMENDED CASSETTE————
Salonen, Philharmonia of London (CBS, 1987)

COMMENTS————————
It's especially encouraging to find Eu-

rope's two most talked-about young conductors *both* recording complete versions of this not exactly commercially "sure-fire" work. Both versions are excellently performed and recorded, although the Salonen has the edge because of its more effective integration of the Ondes Martenot into the overall sonic design.

A first-rate LP version by Seiji Ozawa and the Toronto Symphony (RCA, 1969) is no longer in the active catalog, but may still be found in some collectors' shops or libraries.

FOR FOLLOW-UP CONSIDERATION

ET EXPECTO RESURRECTIONEM MORTUORUM (AND I AWAIT THE RESURRECTION OF THE DEAD) Partly inspired by the works of St. Thomas Aquinas and written in 1964 to a commission by André Malraux (the noted author and DeGaulle's culture minister), this is a shatteringly moving and mystical sound picture of man's last days on earth. Scored for a large orchestra of woodwinds, brass, and percussion, the work embraces many of the compositional techniques which have made Messiaen's work so distinctive—including the use of religious plainsong, Oriental harmonies, birdsong, and irregular rhythms. It is arguable whether any recording can ever fully capture its gigantic, shattering final climax for gongs and full orchestra.

RECOMMENDED LP————————
Boulez, Domaine Musicale Orchestra of Paris, Strasbourg Percussion Ensemble (CBS, 1967), a brilliantly and subtly etched performance. Another fine performance, by Haitink and the Am-

sterdam Concertgebouw Orchestra, was released in Europe during the 1970s but not in the U.S., although it may be available through record shops that specialize in imports. (No CD or Cassette presently available.)

WOLFGANG AMADEUS MOZART

Pronounced: *moh-tsart*. Born January 27, 1756, in Salzburg, Austria. Died December 5, 1791, in Vienna, Austria, at age 35.

SIGNIFICANCE Austrian composer generally recognized as the greatest 18th-century Classicist. He wrote 41 symphonies, 27 piano concertos, 23 string quartets, 18 Masses, more than ten operas, and numerous other chamber and solo works—most of them unequaled in their Classical style, elegance, subtlety, and melodic imaginativeness.

BACKGROUND Mozart began to show his musical genius at the ripe young age of three in his native Salzburg, where his father was a well-known violinist and composer (Leopold Mozart, composer of the popular "Toy Symphony," a work long wrongly attributed to Haydn). When he was seven, Mozart was taken by his father on a tour to Paris, London, Amsterdam, and other cities, chiefly as a harpsichord prodigy. The young Mozart delighted royalty and impressed musicians with his feats of sight-reading and improvisation. By the age of 12 he had composed an opera (*Bastien and Bastienne*), a Mass, an oratorio, and several sonatas, and had made his debut as a conductor.

In his teens he traveled to Italy to study and concertize, and then returned to Salzburg to settle in the service of the archbishop and his court. After a quarrel, he left this service in 1781 (at age 25), moved to Vienna, married, and had a difficult time over the following years making ends meet for his wife and six children—even though he continued to compose prolifically and to have his works performed. His greatest successes included the operas *The Marriage of Figaro* (Vienna, 1786), *Don Giovanni* (Prague, 1787), and *The Magic Flute* (Vienna, 1791). Despite favor at court, his income was meager and he died penniless at age 35, and was buried in an unmarked pauper's grave. The circumstances of his death have long been controversial, with many annotators suggesting foul play; but the evidence has always been vague at best. (The popular play and film *Amadeus* fictionalized some of that controversy.)

A note about those K. numbers: In the 19th century the Austrian scholar Ludwig von Köchel compiled a complete catalog of Mozart's works in the correct compositional sequence (revised in this century by Alfred Einstein), and it is now standard to refer to Mozart's works as "K. (followed by a number)"—for example, Piano Concerto No. 23, K. 488 (the German usage is sometimes "K.V." for Köchel-Verzeichnis—that is, Köchel Index).

SYMPHONY No. 35 IN D MAJOR, "HAFFNER" (K. 385)

The ease with which Mozart apparently tossed off masterpieces is illustrated by the story of the origin of this symphony: In 1782, Mozart's father Leopold was asked by one of Salzburg's prominent citizens, Sigmund Haffner, to write an orchestral serenade for a special festivity. Leopold Mozart turned the commission over to his son, who had recently married and needed the money. Young Mozart wrote a six-movement serenade in two weeks and sent it to Haffner. Some months later, Mozart needed a new symphony for a concert program he was to conduct in Vienna, and wrote to his father urgently requesting the score of the serenade, to see if any of the material could be adapted to the symphony. When Mozart conducted his new symphony a few weeks later, it consisted basically of four of the six movements of the serenade, rescored for a larger orchestra. It was so well received at its first performance that it had to be repeated—and has remained one of Mozart's most popular works ever since.

The "Haffner" is generally a bright, energetic, lighthearted work, and is perhaps the most immediately appealing of Mozart's great symphonies.

RECOMMENDED CDs
Bernstein, Vienna Philharmonic (Deutsche Grammophon, 1985)
Bohm, Vienna Philharmonic (Deutsche Grammophon, 1966)

RECOMMENDED LPs
Bernstein, Vienna Philharmonic (Deutsche Grammophon, 1985)
Tate, English Chamber (Angel, 1985)

RECOMMENDED CASSETTES
Bernstein, Vienna Philharmonic (Deutsche Grammophon, 1985)
Tate, English Chamber (Angel, 1985)

COMMENTS
The proper size of the orchestra in Mozart performances is always a debatable question; conductors vary widely in the number of players they use. Bernstein opts for large-scale Mozart, and within that context his performance is wonderfully warm and buoyant, and beautifully recorded. Bohm, with the same orchestra (some 19 years earlier) is equally fervent and a bit more animated, and the older sound engineering is still quite good. Tate uses a smaller orchestra for his more intimate, nicely detailed, and elegantly expressive performance. (The coupling for Bernstein is Mozart's Symphony No. 41, the "Jupiter"; for Bohm, the Symphony No. 29; and for Tate, the Symphonies No. 32 and 39.)

SYMPHONY No. 41 IN C MAJOR, "JUPITER" (K. 551)

A London publisher nicknamed Mozart's last symphony the "Jupiter" because of its "loftiness of ideas and nobility of treatment." Its nobility is evident throughout, along with Mozart's special ability to contrast forceful and gentle themes. The fugue in the last movement is considered one of the great achievements in Classical counterpoint.

RECOMMENDED CDs

Bernstein, Vienna Philharmonic (Deutsche Grammophon, 1985)

Mackerras, Prague Chamber (Telarc, 1986)

RECOMMENDED LPs

Bernstein, Vienna Philharmonic (Deutsche Grammophon, 1985)

Mackerras, Prague Chamber (Telarc, 1986)

RECOMMENDED CASSETTES

Bernstein, Vienna Philharmonic (Deutsche Grammophon, 1985)

Tate, English Chamber (Angel, 1985)

COMMENTS

As with other Mozart symphonies, preferences will vary between larger-scaled and smaller-scaled performing forces. Bernstein's is in the first category, and his is a performance of exceptional strength, grandeur, and nobility. Mackerras and Tate opt for smaller ensembles, and each brings considerable vitality and more of a feeling of spontaneity to their performances. (Bernstein's coupling is the Symphony No. 35; both Mackerras' and Tate's is the Symphony No. 40.)

PIANO CONCERTO No. 20
IN D MINOR (K.466)

Critic Alfred Einstein once called Mozart's piano concertos "the peak of all his instrumental achievement." And of all Mozart'.s piano concertos, this one, ever since its first performance by Mozart himself in 1785, has ranked near or at the top of the list in critical esteem and audience popularity. Beethoven was so fond of this concerto that he frequently performed it in concerts, and even composed cadenzas for it (since none of Mozart's own have ever been found). As with Mozart's other late piano concertos, this one mixes elegance and an intimate expressiveness with great subtlety, delicacy, and rhythmic spirit.

RECOMMENDED CDs

Perahia (conductor and pianist), English Chamber Orchestra (CBS, 1977)

Barenboim (conductor and pianist), English Chamber Orchestra (Angel, 1987)

RECOMMENDED LPs

Perahia (conductor and pianist), English Chamber Orchestra (CBS, 1977)

R. Serkin, Abbado, London Symphony (Deutsche Grammophon, 1983)

RECOMMENDED CASSETTES

Perahia (conductor and pianist), English Chamber Orchestra (CBS, 1977)

Brendel, Marriner, Academy-of-Saint-Martin-in-the-Fields (Philips, 1973)

COMMENTS

Perahia is supple, poetic, and beautifully contemplative, in one of the best recordings of this concerto. Barenboim is close behind him, with a fluent, elegant, and animated performance. Both Serkin and Brendel offer a larger-scaled, more

Beethovenian approach, which also works well.

Also highly recommended is a 1970 London recording that has been remastered for CD, with the late English pianist Clifford Curzon, and with composer Benjamin Britten conducting the English Chamber Orchestra. Theirs is a most romantic approach, very *"sturm* and *drang"* as one English critic has put it —but delightfully so.

LE NOZZE DI FIGARO (THE MARRIAGE OF FIGARO) (K. 492)

One of the greatest, if not *the* greatest, of all comic operas, Mozart's *Figaro* is distinguished by its wealth of melody, its wit, and its spirited, stylish sense of fun. In its time, Beaumarchais' original French comedy (on which the libretto was based) did not sit well with much of the aristocracy because of its sardonic view of their manners and amatory escapades. Bans against its public performance merely helped spread its popularity throughout Europe (Marie Antoinette is reported to have delighted in attending a private performance). Mozart's librettist, Lorenzo da Ponte, persuaded the Austrian emperor to rescind the ban in Vienna, where the opera achieved only a mild success in 1876 (partly because of intrigues involving some of Mozart's enemies). Shortly afterward it scored a major hit in Prague, and led to the Prague Opera's commissioning another opera from Mozart, *Don Giovanni. Figaro* later went on to become one of the most popular of all operas in the repertories of virtually every opera company in the world.

As with most operas, a highlights recording is recommended for newcomers, although the complete opera (usually on three or four discs or cassettes) is easily digested the first time around and has that much more to delight a listener.

RECOMMENDED CDs_____
Bohm, Janowitz, Mathis, Troyanos, Fischer-Dieskau, Prey, Berlin Deutsche Oper (Deutsche Grammophon, 1986), *complete (three discs)*
Solti, Te Kanawa, Popp, von Stade, Ramey, Moll, London Philharmonic (London, 1981), *complete (three discs)*

RECOMMENDED LPs_____
Colin Davis, Norman, Freni, Minton, Wixell, Ganzarolli, BBC Symphony (Philips, 1972), *complete (four discs) and highlights*

Bohm, Janowitz, Mathis, Troyanos, Fischer-Dieskau, Prey, Berlin Deutsche Oper (Deutsche Grammophon, 1986), *complete (four discs)*

RECOMMENDED CASSETTES_____
Colin Davis, Norman, Freni, Minton, Wixell, Ganzarolli, BBC Symphony (Philips, 1972), *complete (three cassettes) and highlights*
Bohm, Janowitz, Mathis, Troyanos, Fischer-Dieskau, Prey, Berlin Deutsche Oper (Deutsche Grammophon, 1986), *complete (three cassettes) and highlights*

Bohm brings both Mozartean elegance and warmth to his performance and all his singers are excellent. Davis leads a spirited and elegantly playful performance, in which the women singers are better than the men. Solti's performance has the most up-to-date sound, but his performance and that of his singers is uneven, although the good moments are very good indeed.

FOR FOLLOW-UP CONSIDERATION

EINE KLEINE NACHTMUSIK (A LITTLE NIGHT MUSIC) Formally, Mozart's Serenade No. 13 in G major for strings (K. 525), and considered by some to be the epitome of graceful 18th-century Classicism.

RECOMMENDED CD AND LP ____
Leppard, Scottish Chamber Orchestra (Erato, 1980s) a spirited and stylish performance.

RECOMMENDED CASSETTE ____
Karajan, Berlin Philharmonic (Deutsche Grammophon, 1982), an equally delightful, slightly creamier performance.

ALSO RECOMMENDED ON CD, LP, AND CASSETTE ____
Hogwood, Academy of Ancient Music (L'Oiseau Lyre, 1983), performed by a smaller ensemble using instruments closer to the originals of Mozart's day; Hogwood leads an especially animated performance, and the coupling is one of Mozart's most popular other serenades, the beautiful *Serenata Notturna* (Serenade No. 6).

VIOLIN CONCERTO No. 5 IN A MAJOR (K. 219) Although best-known as a pianist, Mozart was also an accomplished violinist, and his five concertos for that instrument have long been favorites of soloists. (Several other concertos attributed to Mozart are regarded as suspect by most scholars.) No. 5 is sometimes nicknamed "The Turkish," because of a section in the final movement marked "*alla Turca*" (in the Turkish manner).

RECOMMENDED CD, LP, AND CASSETTE ____
Perlman, J. Levine, Vienna Philharmonic (Deutsche Grammophon, 1983), played with delicacy, sensitivity, and warmth.

SINFONIA CONCERTANTE IN E FLAT MAJOR FOR VIOLIN, VIOLA, AND ORCHESTRA (K. 364) Although the origins of this work are uncertain (some believe Mozart composed it for his father and himself to perform in Salzburg in 1779), it remains one of Mozart's most beautiful three-movement instrumental pieces.

RECOMMENDED CD, LP, AND CASSETTE ____
Perlman, Zukerman, Mehta, Israel Philharmonic (Deutsche Grammophon, 1983), a most cordial teaming of these two strongly individualistic soloists for a first-rate performance.

PIANO CONCERTO No. 21 IN C MAJOR (K. 467)   This is the concerto that shot into popularity two decades ago as the "Elvira Madigan Concerto," when its slow movement was used as the principal theme of the hit 1967 Swedish film *Elvira Madigan*. It is stylistically similar to No. 20 (previously discussed) and just as delightful.

RECOMMENDED CD, LP, AND CASSETTE——————————
Perahia (conductor and pianist), English Chamber Orchestra (CBS, 1976), a fresh-sounding, always elegant performance, with a particularly plaintive slow movement.

DON GIOVANNI   Some critics call this opera the Western world's finest single piece of musical art. There is no doubt that it is one of Mozart's most mature achievements. Based on a Spanish version of the Don Juan legend, Mozart's opera (with an Italian libretto by Lorenzo da Ponte) was begun as a comic opera, but was broadened into a drama of profound human irony, dealing with Don Juan after his luck as a lover has run out. In some ways it remains essentially a comic opera with a serious beginning and a tragic ending—and, accordingly, it creates many difficult challenges for singers and conductors in the way of interpretation. Musically, the opera includes some of Mozart's finest melodies, supported by some of his subtlest orchestral writing.

RECOMMENDED CD, LP, AND CASSETTE——————————
Maazel, Moser, Te Kanawa, Berganza, Riegel, Raimondi, Van Dam, Paris Opera (CBS, 1978), with the same cast as the excellent 1978 film version, available on CD only in a three-disc complete version, but in both complete and single-highlights editions on LP and Cassette.

MODEST MUSSORGSKY

Pronounced: muh-*sorg*-skee. Born March 21, 1839, in Karevo, Ukraine. Died March 28, 1881, in St. Petersburg, Russia, at age 42.

SIGNIFICANCE   Russian composer, a leading opponent of traditional formalism and a supporter of nationalism in music.

BACKGROUND   Mussorgsky was the son of impoverished Russian nobility. As a youth he studied the piano, but for economic reasons he prepared first for an army career, then became a civil servant in St. Petersburg. He continued to compose, however, and became a member of the so-called

"Mighty Five" (with Balakirev, Borodin, Cui, and Rimsky-Korsakov). Their aim: to use Russian folk elements and Russian subjects for their works.

Mussorgsky's life was an almost continual struggle against poverty and alcoholism, and his works are marked by a primarily morbid mood. He died in a St. Petersburg military hospital after an epileptic fit.

Following his death, some of his colleagues, seeking to promote his music, encouraged "corrections" to smooth out what they considered its too jagged harmonies. Most controversial has been Rimsky-Korsakov's revision of the opera *Boris Godunov*, which is still the preferred version in many opera houses today (including Moscow's Bolshoi) even though the original version of *Boris*, published in 1928, is considered more strikingly individual by most musicologists, especially in the way the music follows natural speech inflections.

PICTURES AT AN EXHIBITION

Originally a set of ten piano pieces, *Pictures* was written following a memorial exhibition of drawings and watercolors by Mussorgsky's close friend, the painter Victor Hartmann. Two orchestrations of Mussorgsky's piano suite were made in the 1920s, and became popular in the concert hall and later on recordings—one by Leopold Stokowski (for the Philadelphia Orchestra), the other by Maurice Ravel (on commission from Serge Koussevitsky for the Boston Symphony Orchestra). The latter has become one of the most popular orchestral showpieces of the stereo age. In more recent years, there have been still other orchestrations of the piano *Pictures*, including one by the Soviet composer Sergei Gortchakov and another by the Russian pianist-conductor Vladimir Ashkenazy. In all these versions, *Pictures* becomes an exceptionally effective orchestral showpiece, with each section successfully capturing the mood of each of the paintings.

Among the *Pictures* are: "The Old Castle" (a dreamy serenade by a medieval troubadour before an old Italian castle); "Bydlo" (a Polish ox-cart lumbering down a muddy road); "The Market Place at Limoges" (depicting the lively chatter of French housewives at the market stalls); "Ballet of the Unhatched Chickens" (a lighthearted interlude full of chirps and twitters); "Catacombs" (a dark and solemn tone picture of the ancient Roman sepulchres); "Samuel Goldenberg and Schmuyle" (contrasting a rich merchant and a beggar of the Polish ghetto); "The Hut on Fowl's Legs" (an eerie portrait of the legendary Russian witch, Baba Yaga); and "The Great Gate at Kiev" (a majestic finale depicting a procession of medieval nobles entering the ancient capital in splendor).

RECOMMENDED CDs——————
Dutoit, Montreal Symphony (London, 1985)

Slatkin, National Philharmonic (RCA/ BMG, 1991)

RECOMMENDED LPs _____

Dutoit, Montreal Symphony (London, 1985)

Chailly, Amsterdam Concertgebouw (London, 1986)

RECOMMENDED CASSETTES ___

Dutoit, Montreal Symphony (London, 1985)

Chailly, Amsterdam Concertgebouw (London, 1986)

COMMENTS _____

Dutoit, Slatkin, and Chailly perform the Ravel orchestration and their recordings have resplendent sound, especially in the finale. Dutoit brings out more subtle orchestral colors, while Chailly and Slatkin have more of a visceral impact.

An interesting alternative is the recording by Vladimir Ashkenazy (London, 1982), in which he is the soloist in a first-rate piano version and then (on the same disc or tape) conducts his own orchestral version with the Cleveland Orchestra. The latter has many fascinating coloristic differences from the Ravel version and is distinctly more "Russian-sounding" overall—while not surpassing the masterliness of the Ravel.

Similarly, a teaming of Sviatislav Richter's exciting piano version (from a live 1958 performance in Sofia, Bulgaria) with the Ravel orchestral version is available on CD and Cassette (Sony Classical), but the Szell-Cleveland coupling is cool and unengaging.

Gortchakov's darkly vivid, burly 1950 version has been championed by Kurt Masur, whose excellent CD is with the London Philharmonic (Teldec, 1990).

Leif Segerstam and the Finnish Radio Symphony make a good case for the more poetically somber and less colorful but long underrated 1922 version by Finnish conductor Leo Funtek (BIS CD, 1986).

Stokowski omits two pictures (Limoges, Tuileries) in his version with the New Philharmonia (London, 1967). While his CD is more "Stokowskian" in some of its coloristic excesses, he creates many marvelous orchestral effects overall.

BORIS GODUNOV

The only opera that Mussorgsky completed is a stupendous nationalist epic based on the tragic life of a Russian czar who reigned between 1598 and 1605. Mussorgsky based his libretto on a Pushkin play. The original version, submitted to the Imperial Opera in St. Petersburg in 1869, was rejected because (among other reasons) it had almost no music for female singers. Mussorgsky rewrote the opera, changing the order of the scenes and adding a romantic episode between a Polish princess and Boris' rival for the throne—and it was finally produced in 1874.

Several years after Mussorgsky's death, Rimsky-Korsakov completed and orchestrated another Mussorgsky opera, *Khovantchina*, and its success led Rimsky-Korsakov to decide to edit and reorchestrate *Boris* for its first Moscow production in 1888. Four years later Rimsky-Korsakov made further revisions, and in 1896 and 1908 he went even further with his surgery, making major changes in harmonies, modulations, and counterpoint. These reworkings brought the opera new popularity both in and outside Russia. But it also stirred controversy among those preferring Mussorgsky's original version—a controversy that has lasted to today.

In the U.S., the original, the Rimsky-Korsakov version, and a Shostakovich version from the 1950s have all been produced at major opera houses at various times. Whatever the version, the opera is best known for its massive choruses and for providing one of the most dramatic bass roles in all opera.

RECOMMENDED CDs————————
Cluytens, Christoff, Lear, Lanigan, Paris Conservatory, Sofia Opera Chorus (Angel, 1964), *complete on 4 discs*
Fedoseyev, Verdernikov, Arkhipova, Masurok, USSR Radio & TV Orchestra & Chorus (Philips, 1978), *complete on 4 discs*

RECOMMENDED LPs————————
Karajan, Ghiaurov, Vishnevskaya, Maslennikov, Talvela, Vienna Philharmonic, Sofia Radio Chorus, Vienna State Opera Chorus (London, 1971), *complete on 4 discs*
Fedoseyev, Verdernikov, Arkhipova, Masurok, USSR Radio & TV Orchestra & Chorus (Philips, 1978), *complete on 3 discs*

RECOMMENDED CASSETTES————
Cluytens, Christoff, Lear, Lanigan, Paris Conservatory, Sofia Opera Chorus (Angel, 1964), *single-cassette highlights*
Fedoseyev, Verdernikov, Arkhipova, Masurok, USSR Radio & TV Orchestra & Chorus (Philips, 1978), *complete on 3 cassettes*

COMMENTS————————————
For most newcomers, starting with a highlights disc or cassette of *Boris'* great bass arias and choral scenes (including the Coronation Scene) is probably preferable to attempting to digest the whole gloomy opera. But there is only one recommendable highlights album in the catalog at present—and it is on cassette only.

The three complete recordings on CD and LP are decidedly uneven. Among the title-role interpreters, Christoff offers the most impressively mature characterization overall, while Ghiaurov is imposing for his combination of dramatic intensity and vocal strength. Verdernikov is dramatically powerful but vocally not quite the equal of his competitors.

All of the cited versions are sung in Russian and use the Rimsky-Korsakov edition.

FOR FOLLOW-UP CONSIDERATION

A NIGHT ON BALD MOUNTAIN Mussorgsky's only symphonic poem is a short orchestral fantasy based on Gogol's *Saint John's Eve*. The subject is a witches' sabbath (also depicted musically in Liszt's *Totentanz* and the last movement of Berlioz's *Symphonie Fantastique*). The piece begins with the arrival of night and the celebration of a Black Mass by the spirits of darkness. At the height of the orgies, the bells of a nearby village church announce daybreak—and the spirits disappear. Mussorgsky later used the piece as the introduction to Act Three of his unfinished opera *Fair at Sorochintsky*. Still later, Rimsky-Korsakov reorchestrated it, and it has long been a popular concert work (with more than a dozen different performances in the present catalog).

RECOMMENDED CD_____

Ansermet, Suisse Romande (London, 1964), a vividly eerie performance, coupled with Rimsky-Korsakov arrangements of the Prelude and "Dance of the Persian Slaves" from Mussorgsky's unfinished opera *Khovantschina*.

RECOMMENDED LP AND CASSETTE_____

Bernstein, New York Philharmonic (CBS, 1965), a more virtuosic performance.

KRZYSZTOF PENDERECKI

Pronounced: pen-der-ret-skee. Born November 25, 1933, in Krakow, Poland. Now living in Krakow.

SIGNIFICANCE Contemporary Polish composer, whose vivid, adventurous music mixes infinite modern complexity and subtlety with an almost medieval simplicity and directness.

BACKGROUND Penderecki began his study of music in Krakow during years of turmoil and confusion for Poland—first the upheavals of World War II and then the establishment of a Soviet-controlled government after the war. Like a number of other Poles in the arts, Penderecki experimented privately with avant-garde ideas, often without knowledge of similar Western experiments. After 1956, some government restrictions on the arts were eased, allowing cultural exchanges with the West, and Polish avant-garde music came out more into the open.

In 1959, Penderecki anonymously entered three works in the Competition of Young Polish Composers—and won three first prizes. Two years later his *Threnody for the Victims of Hiroshima* was honored by UNESCO's International Tribune of Composers, and became one of the most talked-about pieces of new music of the 1960s.

Since then, Penderecki has written a number of major works with religious themes, including a *Stabat Mater* (1963), the *St. Luke Passion* (1966), and *Dies Irae* (1967), the last one subtitled "Auschwitz Oratorio, in Memory of Those Killed in the Nazi Extermination Camp at Auschwitz." When questioned about his writing religious works in a Communist country, Penderecki told *Musical America's* Bernard Jacobson in 1968, "I am a Catholic . . . and I am concerned with these things in an essentially moral and social way, not in either a political or a sectarian religious way."

During the 1970s, Penderecki also wrote two operas, *The Devils of Loudon* and *Paradise Lost*, which met with mixed receptions. Since 1980 he has turned away from experimenting with the nature of sound (tone clusters, glissandos, and other avant-garde devices), which had dominated much of his previous instrumental music. "I am not interested in sound for its own sake and never have been," he now insists. "Anyone can make sound. A composer, if he be a composer at all, must fashion it into an aesthetically satisfying experience."

For the past decade, Penderecki has divided his time between his homeland and teaching in West Berlin and at Yale University in the United States. In 1988 he was influential in the naming of Gilbert Levine, a former Yale colleague, as the first American conductor to head a major Eastern bloc orchestra, the Krakow Philharmonic.

THRENODY FOR THE VICTIMS OF HIROSHIMA

Few works in the past 30 years have had the impact on listeners that the *Hiroshima Threnody* has had. This ten-minute piece is a searing, violent cataclysm of modern orchestral sound that uses tone clusters, unusually high string registers, and special percussion techniques to depict the horrors of the atomic bombing of Hiroshima during World War II. Scored for an orchestra of 52 strings, it creates a unique web of intense sound colors and an overpowering sense of energy.

RECOMMENDED CD AND CASSETTE
Kawalla, Polish Radio Symphony (Conifer, 1980s)

RECOMMENDED LP
None presently available.

COMMENTS
The Kawalla performance is intense and effective. But the present lack of recordings by any other major orchestra and conductor is a sad commentary on the state of the recording companies' A&R decision-making. Two recordings made in the 1960s and once available in the U.S. on LP were long ago withdrawn, but may still be found in libraries or in stores specializing in cutout LPs. One is by the Rome Symphony conducted by Bruno Maderna (RCA Victrola, 1967); the other (and the better of the two) is by the Warsaw Philharmonic conducted by Witold Rowicki (Philips, 1967). Both include performances of other contemporary works by composers other than Penderecki.

CONCERTO FOR VIOLIN AND ORCHESTRA

"We can still use old forms to write music," Penderecki declared not long after the premiere of this concerto in Switzerland in 1977. Written for and dedicated to the American violinist Isaac Stern, it is a single-movement work that explores three principal themes in a hauntingly dark-hued, essentially brooding but always gripping mood. Passages of intense, sorrowful lyricism are juxtaposed with biting, grotesquely martial rhythms and flashingly virtuoistic figurations that have led some annotators to suspect that the concerto has a secret autobiographical program.

RECOMMENDED CD————————
Kulka, Penderecki, Polish Radio Symphony (Muza, 1979)

RECOMMENDED LP————————
Stern, Skrowaczewski, Minnesota Orchestra (CBS, 1978)

RECOMMENDED CASSETTE————
None presently available.

COMMENTS—————————————
Dedicatee Stern's performance, recorded soon after the American premiere, is arguably definitive—and tremendously moving as well as technically masterful. Skrowaczewski, who has championed Penderecki's music for several decades, makes the most of the alternately knife-edged and melancholy accompaniment.

Kulka's performance, with the composer conducting, is also deeply affecting. At present it is available in the U.S. only in shops that carry imports.

FOR FOLLOW-UP CONSIDERATION

CAPRICCIO FOR VIOLIN AND ORCHESTRA   This eerily striking and expressive 1967 work sounds something like a violin concerto contorted through the sound system of a spaceship in flight.

RECOMMENDED CD AND
CASSETTE————————————
Spivakov (violin and conductor), Moscow Virtuosi (RCA/BMG, 1990), a virtuosic performance, coupled with works by Stravinsky (his 1931 Violin Concerto), Hartmann, Prokofiev, and Schnittke. An outstanding LP performance, by Zukofsky with Foss conducting the Buffalo Philharmonic (Elektra/Nonesuch, 1968), has been withdrawn but may still be found in libraries or in shops specializing in LP cutouts.

FLUORESCENCES   Penderecki in a wry mood, from his sonic experimentation period of the early 1960s. He combines sirens, whistles, an electric bell, a typewriter, a saw, pieces of iron, wood, and glass with orchestral textures for an eerily haunting and occasionally humorous "sound picture." Some may find it merely an exercise in unusual effects, others an imaginative exploration of contemporary sonorities.

RECOMMENDED LP————————
Markowski, Warsaw Philharmonic (Wergo, 1965), which couples the piece with Penderecki's *Stabat Mater* and *From the Psalms of David*. (No CD or Cassette presently available.)

SERGE PROKOFIEV

Pronounced: pro-*kaw*-fee-ef. Born April 23, 1891, in Sonzowka, Russia.
Died March 7, 1953, in Moscow, at age 61.

SIGNIFICANCE   Russian composer and pianist, one of the most lyrical, frequently witty, and rhythmically vibrant of the early 20th-century modernists.

BACKGROUND   Prokofiev began composing when he was five, and tried to write his first opera at nine after having seen one. As a teenager he studied at the St. Petersburg Conservatory with Rimsky-Korsakov and Liadov, stirring controversy there by his experimentations with unconventional, often violent tonalities. Between 1914 and 1921 Prokofiev wrote several scores for Diaghilev's Ballet Russe. One, the barbaric, dissonant *Scythian Suite* (clearly influenced by Stravinsky's *Rite of Spring*), caused a scandal and won considerable sympathy for Prokofiev when a famous critic wrote a review violently attacking the music even though he had not heard it (the work had been withdrawn at the last moment, unknown to the critic).

Prokofiev left Russia after the Communist Revolution. He traveled for a while in the United States and then settled in Paris. In 1934 he decided to return to the Soviet Union permanently. Over the following years he had his ups and downs with the Soviet authorities, who sometimes praised him as the greatest modern Russian composer and at other times denounced him bitterly for writing in "decadent" Western styles.

After World War II Prokofiev suffered a series of strokes which seriously curtailed his activity, though he continued to compose and extensively revise earlier works up to his death—which occurred the same week as that of the Soviet dictator Stalin (and was not announced to the world until after the period of official mourning for Stalin).

ROMEO AND JULIET

Composed in 1935 as a full-length ballet score, Prokofiev's *Romeo and Juliet* was at first rejected by the Leningrad Ballet as "undanceable" (the same charge once made about Tchaikovsky's *Swan Lake*). Since a 1947 Bolshoi production in Moscow, however, it has gone on to become one of the most internationally popular ballets of the 20th century in different Russian, English, Danish, and German productions. Several of them have been turned into films (including one with Ulanova, and another with Fonteyn and Nureyev).

In the late 1930s Prokofiev, despairing of a production of the complete ballet, arranged some of the music into a series of concert suites. He did not just lift sections straight from the ballet, but rather reworked them. These suites have become increasingly popular in the concert hall over the past 40 years. The music is colorful and lyrical, the duel sequences are exciting, the depiction of the Verona aristocracy is grandly sumptuous and bitingly sardonic, and the romantic tragedy of Shakespeare's lovers is eloquently conveyed.

The suites are the basis for most of the recordings of this music, although it has become common for conductors to select different movements from the suites and to perform them in various sequences of their own choosing.

RECOMMENDED CDs ——————
Gergiev, Kirov Orchestra (St. Petersburg) (Philips, 1990)
Dutoit, Montreal Symphony (London, 1989)

RECOMMENDED LPs ——————
Dutoit, Montreal Symphony (London, 1989)
Salonen, Berlin Philharmonic (CBS, 1988)

RECOMMENDED CASSETTES ——
Dutoit, Montreal Symphony (London, 1989)
Salonen, Berlin Philharmonic (CBS, 1988)

COMMENTS ——————
Gergiev, Dutoit, and Salonen all offer lively, impetuously ardent performances, with crisp, colorful playing from their respective orchestras. All three are generous in the number of selections offered from the ballet itself, and all are arranged in a sequence that matches the ballet's action—Gergiev with 25, Dutoit with 24, Salonen with 19.

Of these conductors, Gergiev is the only one who has often conducted performances of the ballet itself and who has recorded its complete score (Philips two-CD set). The group of selections on his single CD are taken from that complete recording with the Kirov Ballet Orchestra, of which he is music director.

CLASSICAL SYMPHONY

Actually Prokofiev's Symphony No. 1, this brief work was written in 1917 "as Mozart or Haydn might have written a symphony if they lived in our day," to quote the composer. It is high-spirited, frequently whimsical, and dissonant, yet a lyrically elegant work of Classical simplicity and clarity.

RECOMMENDED CDs ——————
Bernstein, New York Philharmonic (CBS, 1968)
Jarvi, Scottish National Orchestra (Chandos, 1985)

RECOMMENDED LPs ——————
Bernstein, New York Philharmonic (CBS, 1968)

Jarvi, Scottish National Orchestra (Chandos, 1985)

RECOMMENDED CASSETTES ——
Bernstein, New York Philharmonic (CBS, 1968)
Jarvi, Scottish National Orchestra (Chandos, 1985)

Bernstein is marvelously jaunty and dynamic. He wisely does not rush the first movement and therefore makes the tempo of the finale that much more effective. Jarvi, with more contemporary sound engineering, is not as jaunty but is still stylish and vibrant overall.

SYMPHONY No. 5

Prokofiev called this work, composed in 1944, "a symphony on the greatness of the human spirit." Many inner meanings have been read into it, some of them based on Prokofiev's ups and downs with Soviet officialdom. For example, some say its vigorously marching rhythms and broodingly melancholic melodies relate to the drama of the war years, while others relate them to the battles of men and women with increasingly mechanized and collectivized society. Still others see men and women standing up to the grinding forces that seek to subdue them—and winning. Whatever the interpretation, or whether one prefers to listen to the symphony simply as pure music, this symphony represents Prokofiev at the peak of his musical powers—rhythmically vibrant, deeply lyrical, occasionally sardonic, sweepingly dramatic, and unyieldingly optimistic. It is, indeed, one of the monumental symphonic statements of the 20th century.

RECOMMENDED CDs
Slatkin, Saint Louis Symphony (RCA, 1984)
M. Jansons, Leningrad Philharmonic (Chandos, 1987)

RECOMMENDED LPs
Slatkin, Saint Louis Symphony (RCA, 1984)
M. Jansons, Leningrad Philharmonic (Chandos, 1987)

RECOMMENDED CASSETTES
Slatkin, Saint Louis Symphony (RCA, 1984)
Ashkenazy, Amsterdam Concertgebouw (London, 1985)

COMMENTS
Slatkin builds the first movement to an almost overwhelming climax, and then goes on to deliver even more excitement in the second and fourth movements, and gives proper dramatic urgency to the lyrical third movement.

Jansons, who has succeeded the legendary Mravinsky as a principal conductor of the Leningrad Philharmonic, leads a performance that has exceptional thrust, rhythmic bite, lyrical intensity, and dramatic punch in all the right places.

Ashkenazy is not quite as powerful as Slatkin or Jansons, but his version has a bold forthrightness and eloquence.

PIANO CONCERTO No. 3 IN C MAJOR

This bold, intricate, percussive, yet witty modern concerto was composed in 1921 as a work that the then-30-year-old composer could perform himself on a projected American tour later that year. Prokofiev was living in the small French town of Saint Brevin on the coast of Brittany—uncertain about his future in the West and homesick for his homeland. Whatever his personal insecurities at the time, this concerto is one of his boldest, wittiest, most virtuosic scores. Since its premiere by the Chicago Symphony Orchestra, with Prokofiev as the soloist, it has gone on to become one of the most popular of all modern piano concertos. It was featured in the 1980 Richard Dreyfuss-Amy Irving film of two prize-seeking pianists, *The Competition*.

RECOMMENDED CDs——————
Argerich, Abbado, Berlin Philharmonic
  (Deutsche Grammophon, 1967)
Ashkenazy, Previn, London Symphony
  (London, 1974)

RECOMMENDED LPs——————
Argerich, Abbado, Berlin Philharmonic
  (Deutsche Grammophon, 1967)
Graffman, Szell, Cleveland (CBS, 1966)

RECOMMENDED CASSETTES——
Graffman, Szell, Cleveland (CBS, 1966)
Weissenberg, Ozawa, Orchestre de Paris
  (Angel, 1971)

COMMENTS——————————
Argerich tosses off the most difficult pas-
sages spiritedly and deftly, and also understands that underneath all the dissonances Prokofiev was one of this century's most lyrical composers. She is matched every bar of the way by Abbado's incisive accompaniment.

Graffman, Ashkenazy, and Weissenberg are all crisp, propulsive, and subtle in the right places—with Graffman having the edge in the impressive clarity of his articulation.

Of special historic interest is Prokofiev's own 1932 recording, which is still in the active catalog (InSync). It is, sonically, extremely limited, but shows off the composer's impressive strengths as a pianist, as well as providing a definitive interpretation.

ALEXANDER NEVSKY

This colorful, frequently exciting, massively scored cantata for orchestra, chorus, and mezzo soprano is based on Prokofiev's score for the 1938 Soviet film epic, *Alexander Nevsky*—and it is one of the first film scores from any country to achieve an important life of its own in the concert hall and on records. The film itself, directed by Sergei Eisenstein, is highly propagandistic (and anti-German), but it is also a visually classic account of the Teutonic invasion of Russia in 1240. Its most famous section is the dramatic "Battle on the Ice."

In the mid-1980s, some major symphony orchestras began to incorporate film clips from Eisenstein's movie with their live performances, and efforts were under way in 1988 to re-record the soundtrack of the original film in digital stereo sound.

RECOMMENDED CDs——————
Abbado, Obraztsova, London Symphony
  (Deutsche Grammophon, 1980)
Chailly, Arkhipova, Cleveland (London,
  1983)

RECOMMENDED LP——————
Slatkin, Carlson, Saint Louis Symphony
  (Vox Cum Laude, 1977)

RECOMMENDED CASSETTES_____
Slatkin, Carlson, Saint Louis Symphony (Vox Cum Laude, 1977)
Schippers, Chookasian, New York Philharmonic (CBS/Odyssey, 1961)

COMMENTS_____
Both Abbado and Chailly are rousingly dramatic, and both have the advantage of Russian mezzo sopranos who know how to get to the heart of the plaintive

"Field of the Dead" (in which a woman searches for her soldier-lover). Together with their respective sound engineers, they also make the most of the slashing "Battle on the Ice."

Slatkin's and Schippers' performances are also exciting, although Carlson and Chookasian are not as affecting as their Russian counterparts, and the sound engineering is not up to the later versions.

FOR FOLLOW-UP CONSIDERATION

LIEUTENANT KIJÉ Prokofiev drew this light and bubbly suite from his score for the 1934 Soviet film *The Czar Sleeps*—a satire about government bureaucracy, in which a group of army officers invents adventures for a nonexistent Lieutenant Kijé to cover up a typographical error. ("Kijé" is roughly the Russian equivalent for "whatchamacallit".) Woody Allen later used this music in a film of his own, the 1975 comedy *Love and Death* (set in his own peculiar version of Old Russia).

RECOMMENDED CD_____
Tennstedt, London Philharmonic (Angel, 1983), in which Tennstedt (usually associated with the heavier meditations of Bruckner, Wagner, and Brahms) shows a surprisingly supple light side, with lots of marvelously witty detail.

RECOMMENDED LP AND CASSETTE_____
Slatkin, Voketaitis, Saint Louis Symphony (Vox Cum Laude, 1979), which includes the rarely heard baritone solos, sung in Russian by Voketaitis with just the right mock seriousness.

VIOLIN CONCERTO No. 2 IN G MINOR An alternately vivacious and pensive, beautifully lyrical, modern concerto.

RECOMMENDED CD, LP, AND CASSETTE_____
Heifetz, Munch, Boston Symphony (RCA, 1950s), a stunning, impeccable performance from this century's greatest

violin virtuoso. If you must have more up-to-date sonics, then try Perlman, Rozhdestvensky, BBC Symphony (Angel, 1983), also topnotch.

PETER AND THE WOLF Although this piece was designed as a musical fairy tale for children, its humor, charm, and vitality have long kept it an adult favorite, too. Its narration has been assayed for recordings in English over the years by such diverse personalities as Eleanor Roosevelt, David Bowie, Boris Karloff, Sean Connery, Wilfred Pickles, Beatrice Lillie, Mia Farrow, William F. Buckley Jr., Tom Seaver, Itzhak Perlman, Hermione Gingold, Sting, Lina Prokofiev, and others.

GIACOMO PUCCINI

Pronounced: poo-chee-nee. Born December 22, 1858, in Lucca, Italy.
Died November 29, 1924, in Brussels, at age 65.

SIGNIFICANCE   Italian opera composer, one of the most fluent and heartfelt melodists of all opera, an advocate of dramatic realism (*verismo*) and
intimacy in opera production (in contrast to the heroic, mythological, or
historical "grand" style of earlier opera).

BACKGROUND   The son of a poor family of locally eminent church
musicians, Puccini studied in Milan and wrote his first operas for production
there. In 1884, after the premiere of his one-act *Le Villi*, one of Milan's best-
known critics wrote: "We seem to have before us not a young student, but
. . . the composer for whom Italy has long been waiting." It was nine years,
however, before Puccini produced his first widely recognized success, *Manon
Lescaut*.

There followed over the next dozen years *La Bohème* (1896), *Tosca*
(1900), and *Madama Butterfly* (1904)—not all of them well received at
first, but all eventually winning international fame and popularity for Puccini.
While in the U.S. in 1907 for the Metropolitan Opera's first production of
Madama Butterfly, he accepted the Met's commission to write an opera on
an American subject. The result was *La Fanciulla del West* (*Girl of the Golden
West*)—the first operatic "western." (At the premiere in 1910, Toscanini
conducted and Enrico Caruso and Emmy Destinn headed the cast.)

Puccini's later operas—*La Rondine, Suor Angelica, Il Tabarro*, and *Gianni
Schicchi*—failed to win the popular success of his earlier works, and he
died before completing the last scenes of *Turandot*, his most ambitious
blending of orchestral, choral, and solo vocal writing. He worked almost
exclusively in opera, and once declared: "The only music I can or will make
is that of small things . . . so long as they are true and full of passion and
humanity and touch the heart."

LA BOHÈME

One of the four or five most popular of all operas, *La Bohème* (pronounced boh-*aim* and translated as "The Bohemian Life") is based on a French novel by Henri Murger about student artist life on the Left Bank of Paris in the 1830s — the days of cobblestone streets and cold, candlelit garrets. The story involves a penniless group of young artists, and ranges from their gay camaraderie and "seventh heaven" romances to heartbreak and despair — "a sentimental romantic comedy with a sad ending," as one annotator has called it.

To some critics, the characters are Puccini's most sharply etched and well rounded, and his music is some of the most warmly melodic and appealing in all opera. In *Puccini: A Biography*, George R. Marek goes further: "Puccini accomplished something in the opera. He combined his gift for writing good tunes with a new ability to set weekday conversations to music." To those who criticized the opera for its sentimentality, Puccini replied: "It is said that sentimentality is a sign of weakness. However, I find such weakness beautiful."

RECOMMENDED CDs

Solti, Caballé, Blegen, Domingo, Milnes, Raimondi, London Philharmonic, Alldis Chorus (RCA, 1974), *complete*

Karajan, Freni, Harwood, Pavarotti, Panerai, Ghiaurov, Berlin Philharmonic, Berlin Deutsche Oper Chorus (Deutsche Grammophon, 1973), *complete*

RECOMMENDED LPs

Solti, Caballé, Blegen, Domingo, Milnes, Raimondi, London Philharmonic, Alldis Chorus (RCA, 1974), *complete*

Karajan, Freni, Harwood, Pavarotti, Panerai, Ghiaurov, Berlin Philharmonic, Berlin Deutsche Oper Chorus (Deutsche Grammophon, 1973), *complete and highlights*

RECOMMENDED CASSETTES

Solti, Caballé, Blegen, Domingo, Milnes, Raimondi, London Philharmonic, Alldis Chorus (RCA, 1974), *complete*

Karajan, Freni, Harwood, Pavarotti, Panerai, Ghiaurov, Berlin Philharmonic, Berlin, Deutsche Opera Chorus (Deutsche Grammophon, 1973), *complete and highlights*

COMMENTS

Since *La Bohème* is such a dramatically compact opera without any dull musical moments, and since it fits easily on two discs or cassettes, a complete performance is recommended over a single highlights album.

There are probably more good performances of *La Bohème* in the catalog than of any other opera, but the Solti and Karajan versions have the best combination of beautiful singing and outstanding sound engineering. Freni and Pavarotti convey the most youthfully ardent feeling, while Caballé and Domingo are the most tender and lyrical.

Several older performances still in the catalog deserve commendation, despite their aging sonics. A 1960 Tebaldi-Bergonzi recording conducted by the legendary Serafin (London CD and Cassette) has some voluptuously creamy singing by the leads, and Gianna D'Angelo is a most delightful Musetta. A mid-1950s mono recording conducted by Beecham (Angel LP and Cassette) has long been a favorite of many critics for the lyrical beauty of its singing by De los Angeles and Bjoerling, and its overall lack of gushiness.

A 1946 Toscanini recording (RCA LP and Cassette) is taken from two live broadcasts for the fiftieth anniversary of the opera's premiere (which Toscanini, at age 27, had conducted). It is an exciting performance by some standards, a horror by others—for, in addition to poignant singing by Licia Albanese and Jan Peerce, there is an additional singer whom neither Puccini nor the broadcast engineers had planned on: Toscanini himself, who hums, groans, and sings along audibly throughout the performance. Although originally released in mono, the recording was "electronically rechanneled" for stereo in 1968, somewhat improving the dead acoustics of the original—and it is the stereo version that is now in the catalog.

TOSCA

Puccini saw Sarah Bernhardt act the title role of Sardou's melodramatic play *Tosca* five years before he set it to music. In between, there were a series of intrigues involving Puccini, his librettist, and his publishers before the rights could be cleared—and in the process Puccini earned the undying enmity of another composer, Alberto Franchetti, who had originally owned the rights. (Verdi was also reportedly interested in the rights at this same time.) Puccini and his librettists turned Sardou's play into one of the most taut and exciting operas ever written, with a title role that has become a favorite of almost every prima donna—which is not surprising, since the title character is a temperamental prima donna.

The music is colorful and often beautiful, even though the opera was considered brutal in its time because of its depiction of police torture, an attempted rape, and an onstage execution, among other things. The action takes place in Rome in June of 1800, and is based on historic events during Napoleon's fight to control the Italian states. A Roman prima donna (Floria Tosca) and her lover, a painter with republican sympathies, become involved in the political skulduggery of the despotic chief of Rome's police (Baron Scarpia), and it all ends most melodramatically.

RECOMMENDED CDs
DeSabata, Callas, DiStefano, Gobbi, La Scala Orchestra & Chorus (Angel, 1953), *complete*
Mehta, L. Price, Domingo, Milnes, New Philharmonia of London, Alldis Chorus (RCA, 1973), *complete*

RECOMMENDED LPs
DeSabata, Callas, DiStefano, Gobbi, La Scala Orchestra & Chorus (Angel, 1953), *complete*

Mehta, L. Price, Domingo, Milnes, New Philharmonia of London, Alldiss Chorus (RCA, 1973)

RECOMMENDED CASSETTES
DeSabata, Callas, DiStefano, Gobbi, La Scala Orchestra & Chorus (Angel, 1953), *complete*
Mehta, L. Price, Domingo, Milnes, New Philharmonia of London, Alldis Chorus (RCA, 1973)

COMMENTS

As with *La Bohème*, *Tosca* is such a tightly constructed, dramatically riveting opera that a complete performance is recommended over a highlights album—especially since the complete opera fits on two discs or cassettes.

Despite its 35-year-old monophonic sound, the Callas set remains one of the unequivocal gems of opera recordings. Its recent CD transfer is eminently satisfying, and the musical performance has yet to be equalled in any format. Callas recorded *Tosca* twice (1953, 1965) and the earlier one finds her voice in much better shape and her dramatic use of it peerless. Similarly Gobbi (the villainous Scarpia in both Callas versions) is at his considerable best in the earlier edition, while DeSabata's conducting has excitement and flair.

Among later stereo versions, Leontyne Price's (her second recording of the role, ten years after the first) stands out for her fine vocal colleagues, Mehta's driving direction, and, most of all, the special Price warmth, intensity, and vocal beauty.

Both versions cited are sung in the original Italian.

TURANDOT

Puccini's uncompleted last opera is his most ambitious and exotic blending of orchestral, choral, and solo vocal lines—and, in a good performance, its beauties can be spellbinding. The title role is regarded as one of the most devilishly difficult in opera (one of the reasons that for many years it was not performed too often). The opera also lends itself to spectacular stage productions.

The story, which takes place in China in legendary times, concerns a beautiful but cold-blooded princess who has promised to marry any man of noble blood who can solve three special riddles. Whoever fails, forfeits his head. She meets her match in the son of a dethroned Tartar king.

Puccini finished the opera up to the last two scenes of Act Three; those were completed by Franco Alfano from Puccini's sketches. However, following the premiere in 1926 under Arturo Toscanini's direction, the famous conductor made extensive cuts in Alfano's scenes—and it has been this abridged version that has been sung and recorded in the years since then. However, in the 1980s a number of opera companies, including the New York City Opera, have begun to restore the full Alfano version—but there is not yet a worthy performance on either disc or tape.

RECOMMENDED CDs, LPs AND CASSETTES

Mehta, Sutherland, Caballé, Pavarotti, Ghiaurov, London Philharmonic, Alldis Chorus (London, 1974)

Leinsdorf, Nilsson, Tebaldi, Bjoerling, Tozzi, Rome Opera Orchestra & Chorus (RCA, 1959)

COMMENTS

The star-studded casts assembled for these two versions have rarely been equalled and, best of all, they come through with exciting, superbly sung, well-integrated performances. The London version is superior sonically. Both are sung in the original Italian.

FOR FOLLOW-UP CONSIDERATION

MADAMA BUTTERFLY   A tragic, sentimental, and exotic work which has become one of the most popular of all operas. It is also a great lyric *prima donna's* opera, for the tenor disappears in the first act and returns only briefly in the last. Adapted from an American play by David Belasco (based, in turn, on a reportedly true story by John Luther Long), the opera is set in Japan in 1900, and tells the story of a Japanese girl who marries an American Navy lieutenant with tragic results. Although Puccini used several authentic Japanese themes and coloristic effects in the opera, the work is essentially Italian in mood and musical approach.

RECOMMENDED CDs

Leinsdorf, Leontyne Price, Elias, Tucker, RCA Italiana Orchestra & Chorus (RCA/BMG, 1973)

Karajan, Callas, Danieli, Gedda, La Scala Orchestra & Chorus (Angel, 1955)

RECOMMENDED LP AND CASSETTE

Leinsdorf, Leontyne Price, Elias, Tucker, RCA Italiana Orchestra (RCA, 1973)

Price soars with intense emotion and vocal beauty, for a deeply touching performance. Callas sings a distinctively colored, occasionally shrill, but compellingly dramatic title role. The CD editions are complete on two discs, the LP and Cassette editions on three discs or tapes. There is a single disc and cassette highlights album of the Price performance.

PIANO PARAPHRASES   One of the most striking piano CDs of recent years—and, understandably, a classical bestseller of the mid-'90s—is *The Puccini Album: Arias for Piano*, by the young American pianist John Bayless (Angel, 1993). Somewhat in the manner of Liszt's operatic "paraphrases" a century ago, Bayless weaves stunningly vibrant, colorful piano improvisations around themes from six Puccini operas: *La Bohème, Tosca, Turandot, Madama Butterfly, La Rondine,* and *Gianni Schicchi*. Bayless not only lets loose with cascades of flashy pianistic fireworks but also makes the quieter moments equally memorable as he gets to the heart of Puccini's soaring melodies with appropriate tenderness and dramatic feeling.

SERGEI RACHMANINOFF

Pronounced: rahkh-*mahn*-in-ahff. Born April 1, 1873, in Novgorod, Russia. Died March 28, 1943, in Beverly Hills, California at age 69.

SIGNIFICANCE   Russian composer, pianist, and conductor; one of the last great Romantics, combining a gift for beautiful though often melancholy melody with a unique understanding of tone color.

BACKGROUND   Rachmaninoff showed musical talent at an early age, as well as an intense dislike for practicing. He entered the Moscow Conservatory at the age of 12, and won a number of prizes as both pianist and composer during his teens. By twenty, he had written the Prelude in C sharp minor, which rapidly became one of the most popular of all piano works. Several years later the first performances of his First Symphony and First Piano Concerto fared badly, and he went into a long period of deep depression, convinced he had no real talent. Partly through the efforts of a hypnotist, he regained his confidence, composing a second piano concerto which was an enormous success.

Rachmaninoff reentered the concert field, and became one of the great piano virtuosos of the first half of the 20th century. He also conducted widely, including a year as conductor for Moscow's Bolshoi Theater. Following the Russian Revolution in 1917, Rachmaninoff went into exile, eventually becoming a U.S. citizen. A man of deep emotions, he endured the dual ironies of being a Russia-loving aristocrat forced to live in exile because he could not accept life in Russia under the Communist system, and of being a conservative composer in an age when music was developing in radically new directions with which he was not in sympathy. After 1920 he composed fewer and fewer works (the major ones on commission from the Philadelphia Orchestra) which, in general, looked back nostalgically at a world that *was*. He was one of the first composers to record most of his works as either conductor or piano soloist.

PIANO CONCERTO No. 2 IN C MINOR

Its use in numerous movies and TV shows has made this concerto one of the most widely familiar of all concertos. Several popular songs based on its themes have also become pop standards over the years. Composed in 1900 and 1901, when Rachmaninoff was in his mid-twenties, the concerto is richly melodic, alternating between a strongly heroic mood and a more melancholy tenderness. Its contrasting movements show how uniquely Rachmaninoff understood the modern piano's potential for tonal color. The orchestration is also brilliant, indicating that Rachmaninoff viewed a piano concerto as essentially a symphony led by or dominated by the piano soloist.

RECOMMENDED CDs
Ashkenazy, Haitink, Amsterdam Concertgebouw (London, 1986)
Richter, Wislocki, Warsaw Philharmonic (Deutsche Grammophon, 1961)

RECOMMENDED LPs
Ashkenazy, Haitink, Amsterdam Concertgebouw (London, 1986)
Rubinstein, Ormandy, Philadelphia (RCA, 1972)

Ashkenazy, Haitink, Amsterdam Concertgebouw (London, 1986)
Rubinstein, Ormandy, Philadelphia (RCA, 1972)

COMMENTS

Ashkenazy's 1986 recording (his third, and best) is a compelling, deeply felt performance, exciting and beautifully poetic by turns, with a perfectly matched accompaniment from Haitink and superb sonics. (Ashkenazy's 1971 recording, with Previn and the London Symphony, is also still in the catalog, but it is less impressive overall than either the '86 version or an earlier one from '63, with Kondrashin and the Moscow Philharmonic, no longer available.)

Rubinstein also recorded the concerto at least three times. The last, with Ormandy's Philadelphians, has a more lush orchestral accompaniment than the 1950s RCA recording with Reiner and the Chicago Symphony (also still in the catalog), although Rubinstein's elegantly lyrical, dynamic performance is impressive in both versions.

Rachmaninoff's own recording, dating from 1929, is still in several LP-only albums on the RCA label. It has more than historic worth, for the performance (with the Philadelphia Orchestra conducted by Stokowski) remains one of the most expressive anyone has recorded, despite its dated sonics.

PIANO CONCERTO No. 3 IN D MINOR

This concerto was written for Rachmaninoff's first U.S. tour in 1909, during which one of the New York performances was conducted by Gustav Mahler (whose accompaniment Rachmaninoff warmly described as "perfection"). For many years the Third Concerto languished in the shadow of the more immediately popular Second—even though many critics from the start considered the Third superior. Recently, however, the Third has become one of the most popular of all piano concertos, thanks in part to Van Cliburn, who played it in the Moscow competition of 1958 that turned him into an American cultural hero. Technically one of the most demanding of modern concertos (the sort that separates the champs from the pretenders), it is full of surging melodies, a ceaseless rhythmic drive, and vivid tonal colors.

RECOMMENDED CDs

Horowitz, Ormandy, New York Philharmonic (RCA, 1978)
Collard, Plasson, Toulouse Orchestra (Angel, 1977)

RECOMMENDED LPs

Horowitz, Ormandy, New York Philharmonic (RCA, 1978)
Cliburn, Kondrashin, Symphony of the Air (RCA, 1958)

RECOMMENDED CASSETTES

Horowitz, Ormandy, New York Philharmonic (RCA, 1978)

Cliburn, Kondrashin, Symphony of the Air (RCA, 1958)

COMMENTS

The Rachmaninoff Third was long a Horowitz specialty and his 1978 recording (at age 72) is formidable indeed, often breathtakingly so.

Collard combines exceptional verve with romantic grace and expressiveness for an exciting performance.

Cliburn's recording is taken from the homecoming concert he gave in New York's Carnegie Hall on his return to the U.S. in triumph as winner of the first

International Tchaikovsky Competition in Moscow in 1958. Soviet conductor Kondrashin flew in at Cliburn's request to conduct the concert with what was then left of the former (and once great) NBC Symphony Orchestra. The result: a performance of exceptional musical excitement. Cliburn plays the Third with sweep and grandeur, building toward a brilliant and increasingly electric final movement. He has long insisted that he will never re-record this concerto.

SYMPHONY No. 2 IN E MINOR

This richly melodic, unabashedly Romantic work was composed while Rachmaninoff was living in Dresden, Germany, during 1906 and 1907—an exceptionally productive period that also resulted in his Piano Concerto No. 3 and the tone poem *The Isle of the Dead*. Composer-annotator Phillip Ramsey believes that Rachmaninoff, in composing the symphony, was especially influenced during this period by the German symphonic-narrative tradition. "Like many of Mahler's symphonies," says Ramey, "this lengthy, diffuse symphony gives the impression of having a secret, highly personal and emotional program—of being a musical psycho-drama." Other commentators also see in it elements of the long-breathed, melodic, Tchaikovsky tradition of Rachmaninoff's native Russia. For many years, the length of the symphony (nearly one hour) led most conductors to perform and record it with cuts sanctioned by the composer, although the trend in recent years has been to perform the increasingly popular complete version.

RECOMMENDED CDs
Bychkov, Orchestre de Paris (Philips, 1991)
Previn, Royal Philharmonic (Telarc, 1985)

RECOMMENDED LPs
Previn, Royal Philharmonia (Telarc, 1985)
Ormandy, Philadelphia (RCA, 1974)

RECOMMENDED CASSETTES
Previn, Royal Philharmonic (Telarc, 1985)
Ormandy, Philadelphia (RCA, 1974)

COMMENTS
All of the recommended performances here are of the complete version. Both Previn and Ormandy recorded cut versions earlier, but their later ones are not only complete but also better interpretively and sonically. Previn's is the most broadly expansive, Ormandy's the most luxuriantly lush, and Bychkov's the most strikingly dramatic.

FOR FOLLOW-UP CONSIDERATION

SYMPHONIC DANCES Rachmaninoff's last orchestral work (1941) may well be his finest—a richly melodic, colorful score whose three sections were originally titled "Youth," "Maturity," and "Old Age," then "Morning," "Noon," and "Night," before Rachmaninoff abandoned all subtitles. Some believe that Rachmaninoff knew this would be his valedictory work, for he incorporates into it themes (or fragments of themes) from earlier works that held special significance to him. Perhaps most conspicuously, the final movement makes prominent use of the "Dies Irae" ("Day of Wrath") motif of the Catholic Mass for the Dead, a theme that obsessed Rachmaninoff for much of his life. At its climax, Rachmaninoff lets a theme from the Russian Orthodox chant "Blessed be the Lord" win out over the "Dies Irae."

RECOMMENDED CD, LP, AND CASSETTE——————————— Ashkenazy, Amsterdam Concertgebouw (London, 1983), a tautly surging performance, with outstanding sound.

RHAPSODY ON A THEME BY PAGANINI Rachmaninoff's last major work for piano and orchestra, composed in 1934, takes as its theme the last of *24 Caprices* by the Italian violinist-composer Niccolo Paganini (1782–1840)—the same theme which Schumann, Brahms, and Liszt also used for solo piano works. Rachmaninoff uses it for a set of 24 colorful variations, divided into three general sections (corresponding to the three movements of a conventional piano concerto). In some of the variations, he combines Paganini's lighthearted theme with the ominous "Dies Irae" ("Day of Wrath"). For the 18th variation, Rachmaninoff inverts the original Paganini theme and develops it into the lush melody for which the work is best known (the 18th variation is sometimes played separately at pops concerts).

RECOMMENDED CD, LP, AND CASSETTE——————————— Graffman, Bernstein, New York Philhar- monic (CBS, 1964), a technically brilliant, rhythmically vivid performance.

PRELUDES FOR SOLO PIANO Twenty-four brief but expressive pieces which beautifully show the pianist-composer's sense of musical colors for the solo piano.

RECOMMENDED CD——————— Ashkenazy (London, 1974–75, 2 discs).

RECOMMENDED CASSETTE——— Weissenberg (RCA, 1970). (No complete LP set presently available.)

MAURICE RAVEL

Pronounced: *rah-vell*. Born March 7, 1875, in Ciboure, France. Died December 28, 1937, in Paris, at age 62.

SIGNIFICANCE French composer, pianist, and conductor; a master of Impressionistic orchestration and piano sonorities, whose music is usually marked by elegance, wit, and extraordinary virtuosity.

BACKGROUND Although he was raised in Paris, Ravel made much of his partly Basque ancestry and the influence of Spanish music on his development. At 14 he entered the Paris Conservatory, where he was greatly influenced by Erik Satie. With a series of works (including *Miroirs*, 1905, *Rapsodie Espagnole*, 1907, and *Daphnis and Chloé*, 1912), Ravel became, next to Debussy, the most popular French composer in the years just before World War I.

The war affected him deeply, and in 1920 he wrote *La Valse*, interpreted by many as a musical depiction of the collapse of the "Old Europe" order with the war. He visited the U.S. in the 1920s, and became fascinated by the jazz he heard, incorporating jazz elements into his last two piano concertos and a few other works. When George Gershwin asked if he could come to Paris to study with him, Ravel said that it was *he* who should study with Gershwin.

Ravel, a lifelong bachelor, was renowned in Paris for his generally withdrawn, fastidious, aristocratic behavior. He also developed a sense of perfectionism about his work that limited his output.

In 1928, Ravel's *Bolero*, written for the dancer Ida Rubinstein, quickly became one of the most popular orchestral scores of the era; six different recordings appeared within a year, it was played frequently on radio, and its title was bought for a 1932 Hollywood movie.

In 1932 Ravel was injured in an automobile accident, and it led in subsequent years to his losing his powers of coordination. He died following brain surgery in 1937.

LA VALSE

One of the century's great orchestral showpieces, *La Valse* begins as a nostalgic daydream and ends as a snarling, chaotic nightmare. Some see it as much more than a dramatic exercise in three-quarter time. They view it as a reflection of Ravel's deep feelings about the collapse of the 19th century's social and political structures following World War I. Others see it as a broader symbolic dissection of contemporary life generally—particularly of the folly of "waltzing" through life oblivious to the realities around us.

On its own musical merits, *La Valse* is a masterpiece of orchestral rhythm and tone color—beginning quietly and lightly as the waltz emerges as if through a mist, then building in vibrance and intensity as it whirls along, until a series of strident chords signal a change of mood from joyful abandon to despair and final tragedy. The orchestral version is the best known, but there is also a piano version.

RECOMMENDED CDs————————
Dutoit, Montreal Symphony (London, 1981)
Munch, Boston Symphony (RCA, 1962)

RECOMMENDED LPs————————
Dutoit, Montreal Symphony (London, 1981)
Munch, Boston Symphony (RCA, 1962)

RECOMMENDED CASSETTES———
Dutoit, Montreal Symphony (London, 1981)
Munch, Boston Symphony (RCA, 1962)

COMMENTS————————————
Dutoit's interpretation clearly has been influenced by that of his mentor, the great Swiss conductor Ernest Ansermet, who was for many years the work's most probing interpreter and twice recorded it in much less crystalline sound than Dutoit has.

La Valse was one of the great showpieces of Munch's repertory and his 1962 recording (the third of four he made) is best—a performance of enormous sweep, color, and bite. RCA's recent digital remastering is an incredible improvement on the original, muddy "Dynagroove" sound.

It's a shame that Munch never recorded *La Valse* in tandem with Ravel's earlier *Valses Nobles et Sentimentales*, which he frequently performed together in concert in the same sequence in which they're used in Balanchine's popular ballet *La Valse*. It's a very effective combination, with *La Valse* seeming to grow out of the dying notes of the *Valses Nobles*. The best available CD coupling of the two works in sequence is by Ansermet and the Suisse Romande (London, 1961 and 1963), as part of an all-Ravel program.

DAPHNIS AND CHLOÉ

One of the most popular of all 20th-century orchestral works, *Daphnis and Chloé* met a decidedly mixed reception at the 1912 Paris premiere of the original ballet for which Ravel composed the score. Disagreements plagued that production—disagreements between Ravel and the impresario Diaghilev over Ravel's insistence on using a small chorus in parts of the score; between the choreographer Fokine and the dancer Nijinsky (who danced the part of Daphnis); and among the corps de ballet, which found the fast irregular rhythms of the finale difficult to dance. The critics also were not kind to the scenario, loosely based on an ancient Greek legend about a young woman who is abducted by pirates and rescued by a young Greek shepherd. But some were lavish in their praise of Ravel's score.

Ravel extracted two concert suites from the ballet, and the second of these soon became a popular orchestral showpiece. The Suite No. 2 comprises the final three scenes of the original ballet and bears the following subtitles: "Daybreak," "Pantomime," and "General Dance." It is only in recent years that the complete ballet score has found favor with some conductors for concert programs and recordings—and although there are many beautiful moments throughout the score, the Suite has the best parts and is thus recommended for newcomers. Some conductors now perform the suite with the choral sections restored from the original ballet, and that is also recommended.

RECOMMENDED CDs

Slatkin, Saint Louis Symphony & Chorus (Telarc, 1980), *suite*
Dutoit, Montreal Symphony & Chorus (London, 1980), *complete*

RECOMMENDED LPs

Slatkin, Saint Louis Symphony & Chorus (Telarc, 1980), *suite*
Bernstein, New York Philharmonic (CBS, 1961), *suite*

RECOMMENDED CASSETTES

Munch, Boston Symphony, New England Conservatory Chorus (RCA, 1962), *complete; also suite*
Bernstein, New York Philharmonic, Schola Cantorum (CBS, 1961), *suite*

COMMENTS

Slatkin's atmospheric, rhythmically alive performance is the best of the suite versions with chorus in up-to-date digital sound. Dutoit's tonally more subtle performance and more driving finale make his the best of the complete versions.

Munch once set the standard for this work, and his second Boston recording (1962) is still exceptionally vivid. It is now available only on cassette. His performance on an RCA/BMG CD is his earlier, not quite so lustrous '55 recording.

Bernstein's suite is edited from a complete recording (no longer available), and it is a fine one, with the fastest final dance on records or tapes.

BOLERO

Few pieces of modern orchestral music have won such instantaneous and widespread popularity as Ravel's *Bolero*—nor such subsequent abuse at the hands of both classical, jazz, and popular musicians, choreographers, and movie-makers.

Ravel composed *Bolero* in 1928 on a commission from the dancer Ida Rubinstein for a dance-pantomime with a Spanish setting. He conceived the work as a technical exercise in a gradual, steadily building *crescendo*, repeating one rhythmic melody by passing it continuously from solo instruments to instruments in groups and then, finally, to the full orchestra. He insisted it was a simple work, not a virtuosic one. He also took issue with those conductors (including Toscanini) who played it faster than the fifteen-minute duration specified by him in the score.

RECOMMENDED CDs

Muti, Philadelphia (Angel, 1982)
Slatkin, Saint Louis (Telarc, 1980)

RECOMMENDED LPs

Muti, Philadelphia (Angel, 1982)
Slatkin, Saint Louis (Telarc, 1980)

Muti, Philadelphia (Angel, 1982)
Karajan, Berlin Philharmonic (Deutsche
  Grammophon, 1987)

COMMENTS_____
All of the above performances are at the

tempo Ravel specified. Muti and Karajan
have the most tonally resplendent and
virtuosic orchestras, but Slatkin is a bit
more sinuous and builds to a more vibrant finale.

FOR FOLLOW-UP CONSIDERATION

PIANO CONCERTO IN G MAJOR This exuberant, vivacious concerto
was written, according to the composer, "in the spirit of Mozart and Saint-
Säens"—even though it is clearly of the 20th century, including the use of
some of the jazz rhythms Ravel had heard on a trip to America a few years
earlier. Said Ravel: "I believe a concerto can be gay and brilliant, that there
is no necessity for it to aim at profundity or big dramatic effects." That,
indeed, is the type of concerto Ravel composed here, from the crack of the
whip that begins it, on through the "moonlit" slow movement, to the dashing
finale that makes fantastic technical demands on the soloist.

RECOMMENDED CDs_____
Rogé, Dutoit, Montreal Symphony (Lon-
  don, 1982).
Lortie, Fruhbeck, London Symphony
  (Chandos, 1989)

RECOMMENDED LP AND
CASSETTE_____
Argerich, Abbado, Berlin Philharmonic
  (Deutsche Grammophon, 1967). Both
  Rogé and Lortie give uncommonly
  clean-lined, elegant performances.
  Argerich is equally impressive, but has
  more dated sound.

PIANO CONCERTO FOR THE LEFT HAND ALONE Written for the
Austrian pianist Paul Wittgenstein, who lost his right hand in World War I,
this relatively brief concerto has been interpreted by some as an attempt
by Ravel to depict musically the forces of war and peace battling for control
of man's destiny. A theme resembling the nursery tune "Three Blind Mice"
is pitted against a sinister march, but in the finale an initially introspective
solo cadenza builds defiantly to an ending that seems to assure that life can
and will go on.

RECOMMENDED CD_____
Collard, Maazel, French National Orchestra (Angel, 1980), a deeply probing, eloquent performance.

RECOMMENDED CASSETTE_____
Gavrilov, Rattle, London Symphony

(Angel, 1985), a more rhythmically
biting, dramatic performance. (No
recommended LP presently available.)

GASPARD DE LA NUIT (THE DEVIL OF THE NIGHT) A splendid example of Ravel's distinctively Impressionistic solo piano music. Ravel based his three-part piece on prose poems by the French Romantic poet Aloysius Bertrand (1807–1841), who had said they were written by the devil (thus the title). The three musical portraits are of "Ondine" (a water nymph), "Le Gibet" (an eerie corpse hanging from a gibbet), and "Scarbo" (a devilish dwarf who frightens people and then vanishes).

RECOMMENDED CD, LP, AND CASSETTE
Pogorelich (Deutsche Grammophon, 1983), an interpretively imaginative, tonally virtuosic performance.

NIKOLAI RIMSKY-KORSAKOV

Pronounced: *rim-skee-kor-suh-koff*. Born March 18, 1844, in Novgorod, Russia. Died June 21, 1908, near St. Petersburg, at age 64.

SIGNIFICANCE Russian composer, conductor, and teacher, perhaps best known as the most exotic, colorful orchestrator of his day. He wrote a book on orchestration that remains a classic text — and particularly influenced for several decades the composers of Hollywood movie scores.

BACKGROUND Though he began studying piano at the age of six and wrote his first composition at nine, Rimsky-Korsakov's aristocratic family insisted that he undertake a career as a Russian naval officer. He continued to study music in his spare time, especially after a meeting with composer-conductor Mily Balakirev convinced him he had talent. In 1865 Balakirev introduced Rimsky-Korsakov's First Symphony (written partly at sea) at a St. Petersburg concert. Eight years later, after he had composed several other works, including an opera, Rimsky-Korsakov resigned from the navy to devote himself fully to music.

Despite his lack of formal music education, he became a professor at the Saint Petersburg Conservatory — sometimes teaching lessons to himself first to keep one jump ahead of his pupils. He learned to play many instruments in order to improve his understanding of orchestration and conducting. He turned out more than a dozen operas, mostly based on Russian stories or legends, and various orchestral works that made his name synonymous with rich orchestration.

In 1905 he was dismissed from his professorship after he had spoken out against the czar's use of armed forces to suppress student political gatherings. In reaction, other prominent faculty members, including Glazunov and Liadov, also resigned. Rimsky-Korsakov was later reinstated, when Glazunov became the Conservatory's director. Three years later Rimsky-Korsakov's opera *Le Coq d'Or* (*The Golden Cock*) was banned by the czar's censors as a thinly veiled satire on imperial despotism. Many believe the censorship controversy triggered the sudden heart attack which caused the composer's death in 1908.

SCHEHERAZADE

Although he was known as a man of fastidious habits and an ultramethodical mind, Rimsky-Korsakov wrote some of the most fanciful, extravagant music of any 19th-century composer—and none more fanciful and extravagant than *Scheherazade*. Its melodic charm and rich colors have kept it a concert favorite for nearly a century (in 1988 there were more than 25 different recordings available).

Scheherazade, composed in 1888, was inspired by the tales of the *Arabian Nights*. The composer wrote this foreword to his score: "The Sultan Schariar, convinced of the faithlessness of all women, vowed to put each of his wives to death after the first night of marriage. But the Sultana Scheherazade saved her life by entertaining him with tales which she told for a thousand and one nights. Pricked by curiosity, the Sultan postponed his wife's execution from day to day, and finally gave up his bloodthirsty plan altogether."

Rimsky-Korsakov's work is in four movements, with the following subtitles: (1) "The Sea and Sinbad's Ship"; (2) "The Tale of the Kalandar Prince"; (3) "The Young Prince and Princess"; (4) "Festival at Baghdad and Shipwreck on the Rock Surmounted by the Bronze Warrior." However, Rimsky-Korsakov provided no program beyond the titles, saying: "I meant these hints only to direct the hearer's fancy on the path that my own fancy had traveled ... and to carry away the impression that it is beyond doubt an Oriental narrative of varied fairy-tale wonders." The musical connecting link is a violin theme representing the storyteller Scheherazade, heard in each of the movements and emerging triumphant at the end.

RECOMMENDED CDs————————
Kondrashin, Amsterdam Concertgebouw (Philips, 1979)
Ashkenazy, Philharmonia of London (London, 1985)

RECOMMENDED LPs————————
Kondrashin, Amsterdam Concertgebouw (Philips, 1979)

Ashkenazy, Philharmonia of London (London, 1985)

RECOMMENDED CASSETTES————
Kondrashin, Amsterdam Concertgebouw (Philips, 1979)
Dutoit, Montreal Symphony (London, 1983)

COMMENTS————————
Kondrashin's performance is full-blooded, vivid, and colorful. Ashkenazy is not quite so propulsive but still dra-matic, with a particularly imposing ship-wreck climax. Dutoit is more subtly shaded and vivacious.

FOR FOLLOW-UP CONSIDERATION

RUSSIAN EASTER OVERTURE   This colorful musical evocation of the Easter celebrations of the Russian Orthodox Church was designed, according to the composer, to show the "transition from the gloomy and mysterious evening of Passion Saturday to the joyous pagan-religious merrymaking of the morn of Easter Sunday." Rimsky-Korsakov makes use in the overture of several melodies he took from the *Obikhod*, a collection of the best-known canticles of the church, and in some performances a vocal soloist (or soloists) sings these sections.

RECOMMENDED CD AND LP———
Slatkin, Saint Louis Symphony (Telarc, 1981), a rousingly colorful performance.

RECOMMENDED CASSETTE———
Stokowski, Chicago Symphony (RCA Victrola, 1968), also colorful, if marked by some typically Stokowskian tonal exaggerations and retouchings of the orchestration.

CAPRICCIO ESPAGNOLE (SPANISH CAPRICE)   Rimsky-Korsakov orig-inally planned a work on Spanish themes for violin and orchestra, but he changed his mind and decided to make it a display piece for the entire orchestra. An opening "Alborado" (morning song) sets the Spanish mood right from the start. Then follows a set of variations, a gypsylike melody, and, for the finale, a rhythmically vibrant Andalusian fandango.

RECOMMENDED CD AND CASSETTE————————
Dutoit, Montreal Symphony (London), a brilliant, exhilarating version.

RECOMMENDED LP————————
Bernstein, New York Philharmonic (CBS, 1959), more rousing but recorded less well.

GIOACCHINO ROSSINI

Pronounced: roh-see-nee. Born February 29, 1792, in Pesaro, Italy. Died November 13, 1868, in Passy, France, at age 76.

SIGNIFICANCE The most successful Italian opera composer of the early 19th century, especially noted for his comic operas.

BACKGROUND The only son of a trumpeter father and a singer mother, Rossini was apprenticed at a young age to a blacksmith, but he much preferred to sing in churches, and by age 13 he had joined a theater company as a singer and accompanist. Two years later he entered Bologna's Liceo Musicale, where he distinguished himself as a fast-learning "young Mozart" and wrote his first opera. He was still a teenager when Venice's Teatro San Moisé commissioned him to write a comic opera, and then followed it with two more commissions. By age 21, after the successes of *La Scala di Seta* and *L'Italiana in Algeri*, Rossini was the idol of Italy's opera lovers.

Over the next 25 years, Rossini composed hit after hit—including *Il Turco in Italia* (1814), *Il Barbiere di Siviglia* (1816), *La Cenerentola* (1817), *La Gazza Ladra* (1817), and *Semiramide* (1823). He married the Spanish soprano Isabella Colbran, who starred in many of his operas. In 1822 he left Italy to live in Vienna for two years, and then moved to Paris. There his fortunes seemed to change when his most ambitious opera, *Guillaume Tell* (*William Tell*), was a failure. France's Charles X named him court composer, but the commission was cancelled when the revolution of 1830 forced the king to abdicate. A series of legal disputes over the cancelled commission and problems involving the break-up of his marriage embittered Rossini deeply.

At this point Rossini stunned the music world by announcing, at age 37, his retirement. He continued to live in luxury in Paris (his two decades of opera hits had made him a wealthy man), and mainly indulged his love for good food and wine for the next 38 years. He also married Olympe Pélissier in 1846, some 16 years after the beginning of their relationship caused his separation from his first wife. Only occasionally did he compose again— mostly religious works, such as the *Stabat Mater* (1842) and *Messe Solenelle* (1864).

OVERTURES

Ironically, considering the popular successes of Rossini's operas in the 19th century, it is primarily their overtures that have remained popular, rather than the operas themselves. And many leading conductors love to play and record them. The reason is not hard to understand—for the overtures are brimming with rhythmic vitality, a wealth of melody, and, quite frequently, they are well-laced with delightful humorous touches.

RECOMMENDED CDs
Chailly, National Philharmonic (London, 1981), *William Tell, La Scala di Seta, La Gazza Ladra, Il Turco in Italia, Il Signor Bruschino, Il Turco in Italia, Viaggio a Rheims, L'Italiana in Algeri*
Muti, Philadelphia (Angel, 1980), *William Tell, The Barber of Seville, The Seige of Corinth, Semiramide, Viaggio a Rheims, La Scala di Seta*

RECOMMENDED LPs
Muti, Philadelphia (Angel, 1980), *William Tell, The Barber of Seville, The Seige of Corinth, Semiramide, Viaggio a Rheims, La Scala di Seta*
Chailly, National Philharmonic (London, 1981), *The Barber of Seville, The Seige of Corinth, Torvaldo ed Dorliska, Otello, Tancredi, Semiramide*

RECOMMENDED CASSETTES
Muti, Philadelphia (Angel, 1980), *William Tell, The Barber of Seville, The Seige of Corinth, Semiramide, Viaggio a Rheims, La Scala di Seta*
Chailly, National Philharmonic (London, 1981), *The Barber of Seville, The Seige of Corinth, Torvaldo ed Dorliska, Otello, Tancredi, Semiramide*

COMMENTS
Chailly and Muti both bring considerable verve to their respective sets, with the better of Chailly's two sets presently limited to CD only. The Chailly sets are also a bit more generous in the number of overtures, and have the edge in sound engineering.

FOR FOLLOW-UP CONSIDERATION

THE BARBER OF SEVILLE (IL BARBIERE DI SIVIGLIA)   Generally agreed to be the masterpiece among Rossini's comic operas (or *opera buffa*). Rossini, who idolized Mozart, took as his libretto an earlier Beaumarchais episode involving three of the major characters of *The Marriage of Figaro*—specifically, the Count of Almaviva's wooing of Rosina (later the Countess of Mozart's opera) and Figaro's involvement in his maneuvers. In Rossini's comic operas, the leading characters usually get at least one tongue-twisting or musically high-riding aria, and in *The Barber* the best known are Figaro's "Largo al factotum" ("Room for the Factotum") and Rosina's "Una voce poco fa" ("A Little Voice I Hear"). But there are many other delightful arias and comic turns too. Rossini wrote the role of Rosina originally for a mezzo soprano, but in 1826 the popular soprano Henrietta Sontag, with Rossini's blessing, sang the role in Paris and thereafter it has most often been sung by sopranos.

RECOMMENDED CD, LP, AND CASSETTE
Marriner, Baltsa, Allen, Araiza, Lloyd,

Academy of Saint-Martin-in-the-Fields, Ambrosian Chorus (Philips, 1982), a spirited, well-sung recording, with mezzo Baltsa and baritone Allen the standouts. The CD edition takes three discs, the LP four discs, and the Cassette three cassettes. A single-disc highlights album is available only in the CD format.

STABAT MATER   One of the most beautiful 19th-century settings of medieval devotional poems about the vigil of Mary by the Cross following the crucifixion of Jesus.

RECOMMENDED CD————
Muti, Malfitano, Baltsa, Gambill, Howell, Maggio Musicale (Florence) Orchestra & Chorus (Angel, 1982), an un-abashedly operatic approach to the score but a most effective one. (No recommended LP or Cassette.)

LA BOUTIQUE FANTASQUE (THE FANTASTIC SHOP)   A ballet score adapted from Rossini's music by the Italian composer Ottorino Respighi in 1919. It was commissioned by the great ballet impresario Serge Diaghilev, after he came across a collection of rarely played piano pieces that Rossini had written late in his life and had dubbed *Sins of My Old Age*. Respighi orchestrated some of them and arranged them in a score that is alternately witty and lovely, spirited and lyrical. The ballet is set in a doll shop.

RECOMMENDED CD————
Bonynge, National Philharmonic (London, 1981), a lively, thoroughly charming performance, coupled with the pleasant ballet suite *Matinees Musicales*, which Benjamin Britten arranged from other Rossini pieces.

RECOMMENDED CASSETTE———
Gardelli, London Symphony (Angel/Ser-aphim, 1979), a less crisply played version with older sound, coupled with a spirited performance of the ballet suite *Gaité Parisienne*, based on music by Jacques Offenbach as arranged by Manuel Rosenthal. (No recommended LP presently available.)

CAMILLE SAINT-SAËNS

Pronounced: san-*sawn*. Born October 9, 1835, in Paris. Died December 16, 1921, in Algiers, at age 86.

SIGNIFICANCE   French composer, pianist, and organist, who emphasized elegance, charm, and form in contrast to the German emphasis during the same period on heavier, more emotionally profound styles.

BACKGROUND   Orphaned in his infancy, Saint-Saëns was brought up by an aunt who gave him his first piano lessons when he was three years old. By the age of 11 he was giving public piano recitals in Paris. At 13 he entered the Paris Conservatory, where he won prizes in organ and composition. He went on to enjoy a long and successful career as both a pianist and composer, although his first successes as a composer were not in France but in Leipzig and Weimar. Eventually his Liszt-influenced piano concertos and symphonic poems caught on in France, and helped restore purely orchestral music to eminence at a time when opera dominated French music.

In addition to his world tours as a pianist, Saint-Saëns taught music and archaeology in Paris for many years—and still managed to compose prolifically, writing three symphonies, five piano concertos, three violin concertos, two cello concertos, about a dozen operas (including *Samson and Delilah*), four symphonic poems (including *Danse Macabre* and *Phaeton*), church music, songs, piano pieces, and chamber pieces. His works were once so popular and so overplayed that there has been something of a tendency in the past 50 years to disdain them unfairly.

SYMPHONY No. 3 IN C MINOR

Nicknamed the "Organ Symphony" because of its extensive part for that instrument, Saint-Saëns' Third was dedicated by the composer to the memory of Franz Liszt. It indeed has a Lisztian mood about it, but tempered with a distinctive French elegance and tonal transparency. Saint-Saëns also borrows from Liszt the idea of "thematic transformation," whereby a basic theme or motto is used throughout the work but undergoes numerous changes in color and character. The symphony has become a stereo showpiece work for its mixture of orchestra, organ, piano, and percussion sounds in all sorts of combinations.

RECOMMENDED CDs————————
Dutoit, Hurford (organ), Montreal Symphony (London, 1983)
Munch, Zamkochian (organ), Boston Symphony (RCA, 1960)

RECOMMENDED LPs————————
Barenboim, Litaize (organ), Chicago Symphony (Deutsche Grammophon, 1976)
Munch, Zamkochian (organ), Boston Symphony (RCA, 1960)

RECOMMENDED CASSETTES———
Dutoit, Hurford (organ), Montreal Symphony (London, 1983)

Munch, Zamkochian (organ), Boston Symphony (RCA, 1960)

COMMENTS————————
It was with the Saint-Saëns Third that Munch conquered New York and Boston during his first U.S. appearances following World War II, and it remained a Munch specialty for years thereafter. His last recording of it with the Bostonians remains an exciting, lyrically glowing performance that none of the others quite equals interpretively. But since much of the appeal of this symphony is in its sonic impact, the later versions now have an edge—but only an edge.

The clarity of the Dutoit recording is especially thrilling, though the interpretation is less pungent. Barenboim's vividly propulsive performance also has impressive sound—and is an outstanding example of the synchronization skills of modern recording engineers, since the organ part was separately recorded on the great organ of the Chartres Cathedral in France.

PIANO CONCERTO No. 2 IN G MINOR

Written in 17 days for a Paris concert in 1868 at which Saint-Saëns was to be piano soloist (with his friend Anton Rubinstein conducting), this concerto quickly became one of Saint-Saëns' most popular and successful works. The speed with which it was written may explain its generally one-sided form —for the piano clearly dominates throughout, with the orchestra merely underlining or embellishing the various themes introduced or developed by the pianist. Those themes are mostly bright, melodic, and immediately appealing.

RECOMMENDED CDs————
Collard, Previn, Royal Philharmonic (Angel, 1987)
Roge, Dutoit, Royal Philharmonic (London, 1987)

RECOMMENDED LPs————
Ciccolini, Baudo, Orchestre de Paris (Angel, 1971)
Entremont, Ormandy, Philadelphia (CBS, 1965)

RECOMMENDED CASSETTES——
Ciccolini, Baudo, Orchestre de Paris (Angel, 1971)
Entremont, Ormandy, Philadelphia (CBS, 1965)

COMMENTS————
The newer Collard and Rogé performances are both bright and debonair, with excellent sound. Ciccolini's fine version has less sonic sparkle, and Entremont's is more percussive than lyrical.

FOR FOLLOW-UP CONSIDERATION

PIANO CONCERTO No. 5   This one is sometimes dubbed "The Egyptian Concerto" because one of its main themes is based on a Nubian love song that Saint-Saëns first heard while vacationing at Luxor on the Nile— and also because it is filled with color accents of a decidedly Near-Eastern character. The finale is especially flashy.

RECOMMENDED CD AND LP————
Collard, Previn, Royal Philharmonic (Angel, 1987), a dashing, thoroughly engaging performance. (No Cassette presently available.)

CARNIVAL OF THE ANIMALS   Originally composed as a private joke for some of Saint-Saëns' friends, this delightfully satiric work for two pianos and orchestra was not performed publicly until after Saint-Saëns' death. But over the past half-century it has become widely popular for its cosmopolitan blend of fun and appropriately picturesque music. During the 1940s the American poet Ogden Nash wrote special verses to be recited with the music, and they have since been recorded by Noel Coward, Beatrice Lillie, Itzhak Perlman, and a few others.

RECOMMENDED CD——————
Previn, Villa, Jennings, Pittsburgh Symphony (Philips, 1980).

RECOMMENDED LP——————
Rogé, Ortiz, Dutoit, London Sinfonietta (London, 1980).

RECOMMENDED CASSETTE———
Weissenberg, Ciccolini, Pretre, Paris Conservatory (Angel, mid-1960s).

RECOMMENDED CD, LP, AND CASSETTE (OF THE VERSION WITH NASH'S VERSES)——————
Mehta, Labeque Sisters, Perlman (narrator), Israel Philharmonic (Angel, 1984). All of these performances are delightful and well-recorded. Worth mentioning also is the inimitable, if vintage, Coward recording from the late 1940s, with Kostelanetz and Hambro & Zayde, which is still available on LP only (CBS, mono only).

ARNOLD SCHOENBERG

Pronounced: she(r)n-berg. Born September 13, 1874, in Vienna. Died July 13, 1951, in Los Angeles, California, at age 76.

SIGNIFICANCE   Austrian composer and teacher, whose theories of pan-tonal and 12-tone music made him one of the most influential and controversial composers of this century.

BACKGROUND   Schoenberg grew up in a Vienna waltzing to Johann Strauss while still dwelling on memories of the days of Schubert and Beethoven. Schoenberg started to study the violin and cello at an early age. At 16, after his father's death, he went to work orchestrating operettas to help support his family. But his chief love was chamber music, and on his own time he began to write chamber works that would have the emotionalism of Wagner's operas. After turning to teaching in the early 1900s, first in Vienna and then in Berlin, Schoenberg became convinced that the tonality and key structure on which Western music was based had become exhausted. He set out to devise a new vocabulary and grammar for music that would liberate melody and harmony from what he felt was the tyranny of traditional modes.

He became the father of "pan-tonal" music—more familiarly known, despite Schoenberg's objections, as atonal music—music without a specific key relationship for its notes. The difference lies in the focus of the words: pan-tonal means using *all* tones, while atonal implies that *no* tone is a focal point or key note. In 1912 Schoenberg created a sensation with his pan-tonal song cycle *Pierrot Lunaire*, which also introduced *Sprechstimme* (lit-erally, speaking voice), a vocal line that is half-sung, half-spoken. Schoenberg was also the innovator of 12-tone (dodecaphonic) music, in which the seven white and five black notes of a piano octave (the thirteenth note makes the octave) are subjected to an ordered relationship as equals, unlike the major-minor key system of traditional music.

Schoenberg's theories aroused enormous controversy in Europe and the U.S., revolutionizing the direction of 20th-century music. Driven out of Germany and Austria by the Nazis because he was a Jew, Schoenberg came to the U.S., teaching (primarily at the University of California at Los Angeles) until his death. Despite vigorous championing by many conductors, critics, and music educators, Schoenberg's works have won a place in the repertory of most major orchestras only begrudgingly as far as the majority of the audience is concerned. Yet Schoenberg's influence on post-World War II composers has been undeniably significant.

TRANSFIGURED NIGHT (VERKLÄRTE NACHT)

This tone poem for string orchestra pre-dates Schoenberg's controversial pan-tonal and 12-tone musical theories. In fact, its musical vocabulary is very much that of 19th-century Romanticism, in a direct line from Wagner's *Tristan and Isolde*.

Schoenberg originally composed *Transfigured Night* as a sextet (for violins, violas, and cellos) in 1899 when he was 24 years old. Eighteen years later he arranged it for string orchestra, changing nothing of the work's harmony or melody. Another 26 years later, in 1943, Schoenberg revised it again, thinning out the orchestral texture overall, and modifying some of the score's more expansively Romantic expression marks.

The work was inspired by a poem by Richard Dehmel, which describes two lovers who find in each other the happiness to transform a bleak winter night into a thing of beauty. The poem was considered quite daring in its time, but today both the poem and Schoenberg's piece are viewed more as tender, evocative expressions of an almost-conservative late Romanticism.

RECOMMENDED CDs————————
Chailly, Berlin Radio Symphony (Lon-don, 1987)
Boulez, Ensemble Intercontemporaine (CBS, 1983)

RECOMMENDED LPs————————
Stokowski, Stokowski Orchestra (Angel, 1960)

Boulez, Ensemble Intercontemporaine (CBS, 1983)

RECOMMENDED CASSETTES———
Stokowski, Stokowski Orchestra (Angel, 1960)
Boulez, Ensemble Intercontemporaine (CBS, 1983)

Chailly and Stokowski perform the 1915 orchestral version with fervor and rich orchestral textures. Boulez leads the original chamber version, in a driving performance that belies the frequent charge that Boulez is cold and unromantic. Boulez's earlier (1979) recording of the orchestral version with the New York Philharmonic has been, regrettably, withdrawn, but it still may be available in some collectors' shops or in public-library collections.

FIVE PIECES FOR ORCHESTRA

This is one of Schoenberg's most important early explorations of pan-tonality (it is not yet into his 12-tone theories). A set of brief, self-contained, highly expressive pieces, it is concerned with individual instrumental color rather than massive orchestral sound. Written in 1909, and revised in 1949 (primarily to reduce the orchestral requirements), the pieces are designed to express inner emotional states — not a surprising purpose for an avant-garde work written in Vienna at a time when Sigmund Freud was a leading figure.

A program note for the work's London premiere in 1912 stated: "This music seeks to express all that dwells in us subconsciously like a dream ... [and] is built upon none of the lines that are familiar to us. . . . [But it] has a rhythm, as the blood has its pulsating rhythm, as all life in us has a rhythm; has a tonality, but only as the sea or the storm has its tonality; has harmonies, though we cannot grasp or analyze them nor can we trace its themes." Not unexpectedly, such a work merely baffled most audiences for many years. But since the 1960s it has become increasingly appreciated for its tight concentration of expressive thought, even by average listeners unequipped to recognize its structural properties.

The titles of the five pieces are: (1) "Premonitions"; (2) "Yesteryears"; (3) "Summer Morning by a Lake — Colors" (originally this piece was called "The Changing Chord"); (4) "Peripeteia" (meaning the sudden reversal of a dramatic action); and (5) "The Obligatory Recitative."

RECOMMENDED CDs

J. Levine, Berlin Philharmonic (Deutsche Grammophon, 1988)
Dorati, London Symphony (Mercury/ Philips, 1962)

RECOMMENDED LPs

Boulez, BBC Symphony (CBS, 1976)

RECOMMENDED CASSETTES

None presently available.

COMMENTS

Both Levine's and Dorati's recordings are intense and colorful. The Boulez, however, is even better, and it is coupled with three other Schoenberg works, including the 12-tone *Variations* and the gripping, World War II-inspired *A Survivor of Warsaw*.

FOR FOLLOW-UP CONSIDERATION

GURRELIEDER (SONGS OF GURRE)   Even if he had never "invented" 12-tone music and become one of this century's most influential revolutionaries, Schoenberg's place in music history would have been assured by the early (1900–03), sweepingly Romantic, epic symphonic cantata *Gurrelieder*. The text (by the Danish poet and botanist Jens Peter Jacobsen) deals with a legendary, tragic love affair between Denmark's King Waldemar IV and a beautiful commoner, Tove, at the castle at Gurre. The first two parts of Schoenberg's setting are unabashedly and richly Romantic, but part three, composed some ten years later, foreshadows stylistically some of the directions Schoenberg's later works would take—including a speaker whose lines are notated by pitches that are to be approximated by his speaking voice rather than sung.

RECOMMENDED CD _____
Chailly, Fassbaender, Dunn, Jerusalem, Hotter, Berlin Radio Symphony, Berlin and Dusseldorf choruses (London, 1990), a performance of, alternately, sweeping dramatic urgency and lush expressiveness, with especially impressive singing by Jerusalem and Fassbaender, and with Hotter incomparable as the Speaker. (No recommended LP or Cassette.)

VARIATIONS FOR ORCHESTRA   Schoenberg's first orchestral work (1928) to be composed strictly within the 12-tone scheme. Says critic Alfred Frankenstein: "It is a colossal virtuoso study in instrumentation.... Since the 12-tone philosophy is essentially one of variation, the use of the episodic variation form [in this work] exposes its essential logic with the utmost clarity and precision; the music is wonderfully lithe and energetic too."

RECOMMENDED CD _____
Boulez, Chicago Symphony (Erato, 1991), a forthright, meticulous performance by a master of this type of music. The earlier and almost as good Boulez-BBC Symphony version once on LP is also now on CD (CBS, 1976).

PIERROT LUNAIRE (MOONSTRUCK PIERROT)   This setting of twenty-one Symbolist poems by Albert Giraud for voice and eight instruments, composed in 1912, is one of the most controversial of revolutionary landmarks in 20th-century music. Even after eight decades, its appeal is still quite limited—but it is a work that anyone seeking a broad view of 20th-century music should at least investigate and recognize for its historical significance, whether one ends up liking the work or not. The Giraud poems are basically decadent and macabre (one describes Pierrot smoking his tobacco out of a human skull). One critic has called the piece "German Expressionism at its most paranoid, half-mad best." This was the first work to use half-sung, half-spoken *Sprechstimme*, which has become a basic device of much avant-garde music ever since.

FRANZ SCHUBERT

Pronounced: *shoo*-bert. Born January 31, 1797, in Lichtenthal, near
Vienna. Died November 19, 1828, in Vienna, at age 31.

SIGNIFICANCE Austrian composer, an important bridge between Classical and Romantic music, and the first great master of the Romantic 19th-
century German art song.

BACKGROUND One of 14 children of a village schoolmaster in Lichtenthal, Schubert became a choirboy in the Vienna court choir and a member
of its student orchestra when he was 11. By 15 he had written many songs
and piano pieces, by 16 his first symphony, and by 17 his first Mass. To
avoid military conscription he became a teacher for several years, but he
hated the routine, and was frequently reprimanded for scribbling music in
his notebooks during classes.

He composed quickly, and had written six symphonies by age 21. But
he was badly paid by his publishers, and was involved in a number of
financially disastrous stage productions, and so he lived most of his life on
the verge of starvation. His health finally could not stand the pace of his
daytime writing frenzy combined with too little food and too much nighttime
revelry, and he died at age 31. So little was he appreciated at his death that
the 500 manuscripts found in his room were valued at the equivalent of
just a few dollars by the investigating authorities. It was not until many years
later that the significance of his works was recognized, partly through the
efforts of Mendelssohn and Schumann.

SYMPHONY No. 8 IN B MINOR ("UNFINISHED")

Musicians and scholars have long debated why this symphony was never
completed—if indeed it was ever meant to be. Schubert died six years after
composing its only two movements, and composed many other works (including another, much longer, symphony) during those six years.

Some contend that Schubert, unconcerned about traditional form, *intended* the symphony to be in only two movements rather than the custom-

ary four. Others argue that Schubert's disordered working habits kept him from completing it, as well as other works. A piano sketch of most of a projected third movement was found among Schubert's papers many years after his death (and was orchestrated and recorded in the 1960s by Australian conductor Denis Vaughan). But most scholars feel that the content of the sketch is so inferior to the first two movements that Schubert himself probably abandoned it as unworthy. Critic-annotator Michael Steinberg believes that Schubert "was at a loss how to go on after he had produced two movements that were altogether new in melodic style"—especially since Beethoven's symphonies of that period had made heroic endings *de rigeur* and Schubert couldn't solve the problem of how to write a heroic finale to a symphony in a minor key. (Interestingly, virtually all of Schubert's unfinished works are in a minor key.)

In any case, Schubert sent the first two movements to the Styrian Musical Society in Graz in 1823, presumably as a thank-you for the Diploma of Honor it had awarded him the previous year. It would be another 40 years before the symphony's first performance, after the manuscript's discovery in Graz. Then, ironically, the "Unfinished" became an immediate success.

From its soft, reflective, dark-hued opening, the symphony is full of melting melody. It is one of the most immediately appealing and popular of all early Romantic works, as attested to by more than 30 recordings in the present catalog.

RECOMMENDED CDs————————
Solti, Vienna Philharmonic (London, 1984)
Sinopoli, Philharmonia of London (Deutsche Grammophon, 1984)

RECOMMENDED LPs————————
Solti, Vienna Philharmonic (London, 1984)
Sinopoli, Philharmonia of London (Deutsche Grammophon, 1984)

RECOMMENDED CASSETTES————
Solti, Vienna Philharmonic (London, 1984)
Sinopoli, Philharmonia of London (Deutsche Grammophon, 1984)

COMMENTS————————
Solti's performance is (for him) surprisingly relaxed and mellow—and the Vienna musicians play with the uniquely warm glow for which they are famous. Sinopoli's performance is more intense, and also beautifully played.

Of curiosity value is the Neville Marriner/Academy of Saint Martin-in-the-Fields recording (Philips, mid-1980s), since it includes a "completed performing version" of the third movement by Brian Newbould, based on Schubert's sketches. The movement is only moderately interesting, and Marriner's performance of the familiar parts of the symphony are routine.

SYMPHONY No. 9 IN C ("GREAT")

The nickname "Great" is used primarily to distinguish the Ninth from an earlier, smaller-scaled Schubert symphony in the same key (No. 6, usually called the "Little" C major). However, the Ninth's nickname applies as much to the grand sweep and monumental strength of the music. Next to Beethoven's symphonies, it represents the large-scaled early 19th-century symphony at its most eloquent.

Ironically, the first performance, scheduled the year Schubert died, was cancelled because the musicians considered the symphony too long and too difficult. The premiere did not take place until 11 years later, when Mendelssohn conducted it in Leipzig—in an abridged version. Following the first Paris performance in 1851, Berlioz wrote that "it is, to my thinking, worthy of a place among the loftiest productions of our art."

RECOMMENDED CDs
Solti, Vienna Philharmonic (London, 1981)
Levine, Vienna Philharmonic (Deutsche Grammophon, 1984)

RECOMMENDED LPs
Solti, Vienna Philharmonic (London, 1981)
Szell, Cleveland (CBS, 1957)

RECOMMENDED CASSETTES
Solti, Vienna Philharmonic (London, 1981)
Szell, Cleveland (CBS, 1957)

COMMENTS
Solti's performance has thrust, nobility, and impressive clarity. Levine's, with the same orchestra, is almost as eloquent—and is more genial than an earlier Levine recording with the Chicago Symphony (still on Deutsche Grammophon LP and Cassette).

This symphony was for a long time one of Szell's specialties, and he projected it with exceptional excitement—particularly in his 1957 version.

Of historic interest is a version remastered for CD with Furtwangler and the Berlin Philharmonic (Deutsche Grammophon, 1951). It remains surgingly individual and fascinating in interpretation, despite its aging sound.

FOR FOLLOW-UP CONSIDERATION

SYMPHONY No. 5 IN B-FLAT MAJOR From its opening measures, this is a genial, joyous classical symphony, with one of Schubert's loveliest slow movements. Schubert was 19 when he composed it.

RECOMMENDED CD
Barenboim, Berlin Philharmonic (CBS, 1987), a thoroughly engaging performance, coupled with Schubert's less frequently heard Symphony No. 3.

RECOMMENDED LP AND CASSETTE
Solti, Vienna Philharmonic (London, 1984), a spirited but unfrenetic, beautifully played performance.

DIE SCHÖNE MÜLLERIN (THE FAIR MAID OF THE MILL) This cycle of 20 vividly beautiful *lieder*, composed in 1823, is built on the story of a young miller who loves and loses a beautiful but fickle young woman. It makes a good introduction to Schubert's masterly, warmly expressive songs.

ROBERT SCHUMANN

Pronounced: *shoo*-muhn. Born June 8, 1810, in Zwickau, Saxony. Died July 29, 1856, in Endenich, near Bonn, Germany, at age 46.

SIGNIFICANCE German composer and critic, one of the leading figures in the 19th-century Romantic movement. His compositions, mostly short, poetic works with literary allusions, helped to expand the expressive power of the movement.

BACKGROUND Although Schumann began to study piano at the age of six, the major interest of his early youth seemed to be literature—not too surprising, since his father was a publisher. But during his late teen years, his interest in music grew. On the death of his father, however, his practical-minded mother pushed him to study law. The repression of his musical ambitions strained his nerves almost to the breaking point. Finally he decided to study music despite all opposition. Impatient to improve his piano playing, he invented a device which he believed would strengthen a weak finger on his hand. Instead, it severely crippled the hand and forced him to abandon any hopes for a career as a pianist. He turned to composition.

While boarding at the Leipzig home of one of his composition teachers, Friedrich Wieck, Schumann fell in love with Wieck's teenage daughter, Clara, a piano student. Wieck was determined to block their marriage, partly because he considered his daughter's talent greater than Schumann's. After a long series of legal battles, Schumann and Clara Wieck received court permission to marry shortly after her twenty-first birthday. Meanwhile, she had gone on to become one of Europe's most successful pianists, and frequently played Schumann's works on her programs. Their romance became one of the most famous of the period.

In addition to composing, Schumann also founded a music journal (thus combining his musical and literary interests), and became one of Europe's foremost critics. His writings helped win public recognition for Chopin and Brahms, and to give increased importance to the Romantic movement.

In 1853, signs of emotional instability, which had also appeared in 1833 and 1845, forced Schumann to retire from public life. In 1854, after trying to commit suicide, he was committed to a mental hospital near Bonn, where he died two years later. Clara went back to concertizing, and became a legend over the next 40 years for her continued devotion to her husband's works.

PIANO CONCERTO IN A MINOR

Although Schumann wrote many works for solo piano, he composed only one piano concerto—and that one didn't start out to be a concerto. A few months after his marriage in 1841, Schumann composed especially for his wife a "Fantasie" in A minor for piano and orchestra. Four years later he added an "Intermezzo" and a "Finale," thereby turning it into a three-movement concerto. The work reflects Schumann's comment, "I cannot write a concerto for the virtuoso; I must plan something else." His "something else" is more poetic and intimate than flashy, and interweaves piano and orchestral sound in a manner more often found in chamber music.

RECOMMENDED CDs
Brendel, Abbado, London Symphony (Philips)
Zimerman, Karajan, Berlin Philharmonic (Deutsche Grammophon, 1982)

RECOMMENDED LPs
Bolet, Chailly, Berlin Radio Symphony (London, 1985)
Rubinstein, Giulini, Chicago Symphony (RCA, 1967)

RECOMMENDED CASSETTES
Bolet, Chailly, Berlin Radio Symphony (London, 1985)
Lipatti, Karajan, Philharmonia of London (CBS/Odyssey, 1948)

COMMENTS
Lipatti's recording ranks as one of the great recordings of the century. Made three years before his untimely death, it combines strength and sensitivity in a performance that is profoundly lyrical and beautifully phrased. The sound, of course, is seriously dated (even though the quality of English Columbia's sound was ahead of the field in the late 1940s).

As for the latest recordings, Brendel and Bolet are both in top form, with young Zimerman also breathing a fresh romantic élan into the piece. Rubinstein gives it a more leisurely breadth, but also a suppleness that is most beguiling.

SYMPHONY No. 4 IN D MINOR

This most popular of Schumann's four symphonies was not the fourth to be composed, but rather the second. It dates from 1841, the same year Schumann published his First Symphony ("Spring"). But Schumann held up its publication for ten years, and it was finally published in a rescored version in 1851 as his Fourth Symphony.

Although its sections follow a generally traditional four-movement pattern, there is a unity and flow to the work as a whole that in some ways anticipates the cyclic form used by later 19th-century composers. The music is melodic and dramatic, with a particularly assertive finale.

RECOMMENDED CDs————————
Bernstein, Vienna Philharmonic (Deutsche Grammophon, 1985)
Masur, London Philharmonic (Teldec, 1990)

RECOMMENDED LP————————
Bernstein, Vienna Philharmonic (Deutsche Grammophon, 1985)

RECOMMENDED CASSETTES————
Bernstein, Vienna Philharmonic (Deutsche Grammophon, 1985)

Klemperer, Philharmonia of London (Angel, 1962)

COMMENTS————————————
Bernstein's performance of the 1851 version is vibrant, expansive, and expressive. Masur leads a straightforward but *gemütlich* account of the leaner 1841 version. Klemperer takes his time here with the introduction and the slow movement, but never at the expense of being boring, and he lets loose for an exciting finale.

FOR FOLLOW-UP CONSIDERATION

CARNAVAL   Schumann's most popular work for solo piano, composed when he was 25. It consists of 20 short, contrasting pieces which he said represented different people at a masked ball. Schumann gave each of the movements sometimes hidden, sometimes obvious personal connotations. For example, No. 11, "Chiarina," represents Clara Wieck; No. 13, "Estrella," is Ernestine von Fricken (with whom Schumann had a student romance); Nos. 5 and 6, "Eusebius" and "Florestan," represent Schumann's own alter egos.

RECOMMENDED CD AND LP————
Rubinstein (RCA, 1962), a colorful, sensitive, ingratiating performance. (No recommended Cassette.)

ALEXANDER SCRIABIN

Pronounced: skree-*ah*-bin. Born January 6, 1872, in Moscow. Died April 27, 1915, in Moscow, at age 43.

SIGNIFICANCE   Russian pianist and composer of colorful, sensuous works, often expressing complex mystical concepts about man and the cosmos.

BACKGROUND   Scriabin's mother, a pianist who had studied at the St. Petersburg Conservatory, died when he was still an infant. Since his father was a lawyer in the consular service and frequently traveled, Scriabin was raised by his grandmother and an aunt. Partly because of his devotion to his mother's memory, he became obsessed with the piano as a youth. He worked so intensively at it that the muscles of his right hand became temporarily paralyzed. This kind of excessive zeal for things he believed in was to characterize much of his life — and to make him admired by some as a musical messiah. Boris Pasternak, for example, almost abandoned literature to become a musician under his influence. Others regarded Scriabin as a neurotic charlatan.

Scriabin's early works were influenced by Chopin, Liszt, and Wagner. His later works grew increasingly complex as he sought to make his music express various mystical concepts. And in seeking to expand the impact of his music, he developed a color keyboard for projecting lights on a screen while his music was being performed (a device that was a sort of forerunner of psychedelic light shows and MTV).

In 1912 Scriabin began work on a gargantuan project to create a work that would sum up the history of man from the dawn of time to the final, inevitable cataclysm, and which would use not only sound and sight but also smell. He wanted this work, to be called *Mysterium*, to be performed only in India in a special temple to be built for that purpose. When World War I broke out, he became convinced that this was the cataclysm and that his *Mysterium* was a divine project. His sudden death in 1915 (from gangrene which developed from an untreated carbuncle) left the work unfinished, with very little of its music actually written out.

SYMPHONY No. 4 (POEM OF ECSTASY)

Scored for a very large orchestra, this is lushly colorful, late Romantic music that builds sweepingly to what is one of the loudest final chords in all music (all instruments playing full blast) — which has made the *Poem of Ecstasy* something of a showpiece work in the stereo age.

Some critics interpret the work as being about the joy of artistic creation. Some others regard it as a broader view of love's role in both creation and procreation. And one Scriabin biographer, Faubion Bowers, concludes that "behind this distillation of Scriabin's world-view there was something blunt — sex." Whatever the interpretation, it is worth noting that Scriabin declined to have his text of the poem on which he based the work printed together with the score. "Conductors can always be apprised that there is such a text, but in general I would prefer for them to approach it first as pure music," Scriabin declared.

RECOMMENDED CDs————— Jarvi, Chicago Symphony (Chandos,
Sinopoli, New York Philharmonic   1990)
  (Deutsche Grammophon, 1989)

Abbado, Boston Symphony (Deutsche
  Grammophon, 1971)
Stokowski, Czech Philharmonic (Lon-
  don, 1974)

COMMENTS _____
Both Sinopoli and Jarvi are throbbingly
passionate and make the most of the
virtuoso qualities of their respective orchestras, with Sinopoli bringing out more
subtly detailed touches here and there
but never at the expense of the driving
thrust of his performance. Abbado's older
recording is still perhaps the most tonally
resplendent, if not always as dramatically cogent as the others. Stokowski's
is the most lushly prismatic and more
sensuous than passionate.

FOR FOLLOW-UP CONSIDERATION

SYMPHONY No. 2 IN C MINOR The most interesting of Scriabin's first
three symphonies, this is a five-movement work that dates from 1903. It is
at its best in two hauntingly lovely *andantes*.

RECOMMENDED CD AND LP ___
Jarvi, Scottish National (Chandos, 1986),
  a warmly flowing, beautifully recorded performance. (No recommended Cassette.)

PIANO MUSIC Scriabin wrote some of the most distinctively poetic solo
piano pieces of the past century, and many have been recorded by such
virtuosi as Horowitz, Richter, Ashkenazy, Berman, Glenn Gould, and
others — usually in albums with works by other composers as well. In the
late 1960s and early 1970s, Hilde Somer and Ruth Laredo were, individually,
the first to record multiple sets of Scriabin's piano works in first-rate performances. Only Laredo's (and only some of them) are still in the catalog,
including an excellent 1970 three-disc set on Nonesuch, *LP and Cassette
only*, that includes Scriabin's ten piano sonatas complete, plus a set of etudes.
For a single-disc or single-cassette introduction to Scriabin's piano music,
the first recommendation is for Laredo's marvelously played set of 29 preludes (Desto, 1970s), on *LP and Cassette only*. Also highly recommended is
a single-disc Horowitz program which includes the Sonata No. 10 and seven
etudes (CBS, 1965), on LP only.

DMITRI SHOSTAKOVICH

Pronounced: shoss-tah-*koh*-vitch. Born September 25, 1906, in St. Petersburg, Russia. Died August 9, 1975, in Leningrad, at age 68.

SIGNIFICANCE   Russian composer and pianist, the leading 20th-century symphonist whose best works are marked by a dynamic rhythmic drive, striking harmonies, and a deep, often brooding, lyrical expressiveness.

BACKGROUND   Shostakovich began studying music at the age of nine in St. Petersburg (later Leningrad). His early years were deeply affected by the turbulence of the Communist revolution in Russia. The death of his father intensified his family's poverty, and Shostakovich's own suffering from tuberculosis interrupted his education several times.

He wrote his first symphony as a graduation exercise from the Leningrad Conservatory in 1926, and its tart originality won him fame over the next few years, not only in Russia but also in Europe and the United States. But his next three symphonies and two operas (*The Nose* and *Lady Macbeth of Mzensk*) were attacked by Soviet authorities as "crude, vulgar, decadent," and full of "foreign modernisms." This marked just the beginning of a long series of ups and downs with Soviet officialdom that marked the rest of Shostakovich's life. At times Shostakovich sought to adapt to a role as Soviet musical spokesman, while at other times he boldly (although quietly) continued to assert his own individuality.

He was one of the most prolific symphonists of this century (composing fifteen in all). Three of his most famous (the Seventh, Eighth, and Ninth) were written during World War II, when Shostakovich endured the long, bitter Nazi siege of Leningrad (and sometimes doubled as a fire-fighter); the symphonic trilogy reflects his feelings about the war, from despair to victorious joy. In his later years he collaborated on several occasions with the popular but controversial young Soviet poet Yevtushenko, although one of their works (the Symphony No. 13), protesting Soviet anti-Semitism, was banned in Russia for many years after its first performance.

SYMPHONY No. 1 IN F MINOR

Written when Shostakovich was still a teenaged Leningrad student, this symphony remains one of his most original and immediately attractive scores. It is traditional in form, but is filled with brash and novel harmonies, sharp-edged humor, and, in the third movement, a dark and meditative lyricism.

RECOMMENDED CDs ——————   Haitink, London Philharmonic (London, Jarvi, Scottish National (Chandos, 1986)   1981)

RECOMMENDED LPs_____

Susskind, Cincinnati Symphony (Vox Cum Laude, 1979)

Bernstein, New York Philharmonic (CBS, 1972)

RECOMMENDED CASSETTES_____

Susskind, Cincinnati Symphony (Vox Cum Laude, 1979)

Bernstein, New York Philharmonic (CBS, 1972)

COMMENTS_____

Jarvi and Susskind both capture the sym-phony's mixture of roguish spirit and brooding lyricism exceedingly well, with Jarvi having the better sound-engineering. Haitink's performance is more earthbound in the sprightlier parts, but deeply expressive elsewhere. Bernstein (as he often does with Shostakovich) becomes almost too pensively Mahlerian at times but gives a deeply moving account of the final movements.

SYMPHONY No. 5 IN D MINOR

Since its premiere in 1937, this has been one of the most widely popular of 20th-century symphonies. It marked a significant change in Shostakovich's style, from brashly satiric and clever to suggesting a wider and deeper range of emotions. The Fifth is a big, bold, epic symphony—strikingly dramatic, rhythmically vigorous, occasionally humorous, and, in the slow movement in particular, lyrically intense and even tragic.

RECOMMENDED CDs_____

Rostropovich, National Symphony of Washington, DC (Deutsche Grammophon, 1983)

Haitink, Amsterdam Concertgebouw (London, 1981)

RECOMMENDED LPs_____

Bychkov, Berlin Philharmonic (Philips, 1986)

Bernstein, New York Philharmonic (CBS, 1979)

RECOMMENDED CASSETTES_____

Rostropovich, National Symphony of Washington, DC (Deutsche Grammophon, 1983)

Bernstein, New York Philharmonic (CBS, 1979)

COMMENTS_____

Rostropovich's performance vibrates with drama and feverish power. There is also smoldering intensity and drama in that of the younger Soviet emigré Bychkov. Haitink's performance has exceptional eloquence and force. Bernstein's recording, aging sonically, is passionate and driving, and is known to have greatly pleased the composer himself.

SYMPHONY No. 10 IN E MINOR

Arguably Shostakovich's most deeply probing and compelling symphony, the Tenth, to quote the composer, "expresses the thoughts and aspirations of people who regard man's mission on earth to be creative, not destructive." Some have compared this generally dark-hued work to the sketches of Goya and interpreted it as depicting a lonely man fighting against oppression. Some have also related its moments of boundless motor energy to an affirmation of the human spirit.

In the posthumously published 1979 book, *Testimony: The Memoirs of Dmitri Shostakovich*, editor Solomon Volkov says Shostakovich told him that this symphony describes Stalin. "I wrote it right after Stalin's death," Volkov quotes Shostakovich as saying. "It's about Stalin and the Stalin years. The second part, the scherzo, is a musical portrait of Stalin, roughly speaking. Of course, there are many other things in it, but that's the basis."

RECOMMENDED CDs

Karajan, Berlin Philharmonic (Deutsche Grammophon, 1982)
Slatkin, St. Louis (RCA, 1988)

RECOMMENDED LPs

Karajan, Berlin Philharmonic (Deutsche Grammophon, 1966)
Slatkin, St. Louis (RCA, 1988)

RECOMMENDED CASSETTE

Karajan, Berlin Philharmonic (Deutsche Grammophon, 1966)

COMMENTS

Both of Karajan's recordings are stunning in their darkly dramatic fervor, vivid rhythmic propulsion (especially in the supercharged second movement), and the attention to detail and tonal balances. Slatkin's newer recording is also dramatically vivid. Also recommended: a 1990 Halle Orchestra recording with Stanislaw Skrowaczewski (an outstanding Shostakovich interpreter, though not well represented on records), available on an imported English IMP/Pickwick CD.

FOR FOLLOW-UP CONSIDERATION

CONCERTO IN C MINOR FOR PIANO, TRUMPET, AND STRING ORCHESTRA This generally bright and lighthearted concerto was written in the early 1930s and is scored for string orchestra with a prominent trumpet part in the spirited finale. It represents early Shostakovich at his most ebullient and sportive.

RECOMMENDED CD AND LP.

Maxim Shostakovich, Dmitri Shostakovich, Jr., Musici de Montreal (Chandos), a delightfully spirited performance with the composer's son Maxim conducting and grandson Dmitri at the piano, coupled with Shostakovich's breezy Piano Concerto No. 2, written for Maxim when he was a teenager.

RECOMMENDED CASSETTE

Previn, Bernstein, New York Philharmonic (CBS, 1962), in some respects a more vivacious and pungent performance, but with more dated sound, it is also coupled with a similarly fine performance of the Concerto No. 2.

SYMPHONY No. 8 The second of a trilogy of symphonies Shostakovich wrote during World War II, and arguably the most emotionally profound of all his symphonies. Russian musicologist Marina Sabinina has called it "an epic song about war as the cruelest evil that could ever exist." In a long (80 minutes), relentlessly gripping work that varies from darkly elegiac and somber to ironic and even sardonic, Shostakovich dramatically alternates enormously scored passages with almost chamber-like ones. The five movements range from depicting war as a dance of death with its narcotic-like militaristic fervor, to depicting the tragedy left in the wake of war's horrors and the human courage needed to face them.

RECOMMENDED CDs ———————

COMMENTS ———————

Mravinsky, Leningrad Philharmonic (Philips, 1982)
Kondrashin, Moscow State Symphony (Praga, 1969)

Both are profoundly intense, moving performances. (An imported Eurodisc LP has an equally vivid '67 Kondrashin-Moscow performance. No recommended cassette.)

SYMPHONY No. 15   There is likely to be continued controversy for many years over hidden meanings in this last of Shostakovich's symphonies, composed in 1968 when he was ill with a heart ailment and crippling arthritis and was distressed about world conditions. The principal theme of the first movement is borrowed from one in Shostakovich's First Cello Concerto (written for and dedicated to Rostropovich, who had just recently left the Soviet Union to settle in the West). Shostakovich also uses a theme from Rossini's opera *William Tell*, a theme which many Americans know only from *The Lone Ranger* movies and broadcasts but which, more significantly to those who know the opera, reflects the legendary Swiss hero's fight for freedom from the political tyranny of his day. There are also three quotations from Wagner, including the so-called "Fate" motif from *The Ring*, and, as the Fifteenth quietly fades away, quotations from Shostakovich's Fourth and Seventh Symphonies. However cryptic the composer may have remained about these references, the Fifteenth holds its own strictly as a listening experience—alternately vivacious, elegiac, powerful, sometimes ironic, always deeply expressive.

RECOMMENDED CD AND LP ——

Ashkenazy, Royal Philharmonic (London, 1990), coupled with an equally fine performance of Symphony No. 9.

JEAN SIBELIUS

Pronounced: sih-*bay*-lee-us. Born December 8, 1865, in Tavastehus, Finland. Died September 20, 1957, in Jorvenpäa, Finland, at age 91.

SIGNIFICANCE   Finnish composer, who wrote in a restrained, frequently austere form of late Romanticism, often on nationalistic Finnish subjects.

BACKGROUND   Sibelius started out to be a lawyer, but switched to music in his early twenties, going to Berlin and Vienna to study. He returned to Finland at a time of ruthless suppression of that country by czarist Russia, and he took as his mission to write music in the cause of Finnish liberation.

He became a Finnish national hero with such works as *Kullervo, En Saga, The Swan of Tuonela, Lemminkäinen, Tapiola*, and particularly *Finlandia* — which became the country's national anthem after Finland won independence. His seven symphonies, written between 1898 and 1924, reflect the development of Sibelius' style from one that was ardently melodic to more ruggedly austere.

During the last 32 years of his life he wrote no works for publication, a situation some critics interpreted as evidence that Western tonal music had reached a dead end which even a master like Sibelius could not resolve.

FINLANDIA

This fairly brief tone poem in tribute to Sibelius' homeland does not, as is commonly believed, use any Finnish folk themes. Composed in 1899, when Sibelius was in his mid-thirties, the piece was first performed that year as part of a fund-raising concert for Finnish press representatives who had been forced out of work by Czarist suppression of Finnish newspapers. A year later the piece was performed in France under the title *La Patrie* and in Germany as *Vaterland*, and it was acclaimed for stirringly representing the Finnish character and soul. The Russians promptly banned performances in Finland, until circumstances forced the Czar in 1905 to make far-reaching concessions to the Finns generally. By the time Finland won its independence following the Russian Revolution, *Finlandia* had firmly established itself as a musical expression of the Finns' fight for freedom. The main theme of the piece is hymnlike and builds to a mighty, triumphant climax.

RECOMMENDED CDs
Ashkenazy, Philharmonia of London (London, 1980)
Jarvi, Goteborg Symphony (BIS, 1986)

RECOMMENDED LPs
Ormandy, Philadelphia, Mormon Tabernacle Choir (CBS, 1959)
Jarvi, Goteborg Symphony (BIS, 1986)

RECOMMENDED CASSETTES
Bernstein, New York Philharmonic (CBS, 1965)
Karajan, Berlin Philharmonic (Deutsche Grammophon, 1984)

COMMENTS
Ormandy, a longtime champion of Sibelius' music, is the only one to add a chorus (singing in English) to the final sections — and this creates a tremendously thrilling conclusion to a full-blooded performance, even though the sound is not quite up to present-day standards.

The orchestral-only performances of Ashkenazy and Jarvi have more up-to-date sound, and both are stirringly played. (Interestingly, both conductors were raised in the post-Czarist Soviet Union. Jarvi is from Estonia, which, like

19th-century Finland, has been controlled for years by Russia. Soviet defector Ashkenazy is married to an Icelander.)

Bernstein's and Karajan's older recordings are still very good — with high-voltage playing by both orchestras.

SYMPHONY No. 2 IN D MAJOR

Though Sibelius' music has often been compared to huge icebergs or granite blocks, the Second Symphony, written in Italy in 1901, is a sunny, boldly tempestuous work.

Sibelius declared that none of his symphonies were programmatic, yet some commentators have persisted in attempting descriptions of Sibelius' earliest symphonies, the most Romantic of his works. George Schneevoight, Sibelius' close friend and among the first to conduct his music, said that the first movement of the Second depicted the quiet, pastoral life of the Finns; the second, the timid dawn of patriotic feeling, tempered by thoughts of brutal Czarist repression; the third, the awakening of national hope; and the fourth, an apotheosis of hope and the dream of triumph of Finnish nationalism.

Critic Paul Rosenfeld has related the music more to nature than to politics: "It is blood brother to the wind and silence, to the lowering cliffs and the spray, to the harsh crying of sea-birds and the breath of fog. . . . The musical ideas . . . recall the ruggedness and hardiness and starkness of things that persist in the Finnish winter. . . ."

RECOMMENDED CDs
Ashkenazy, Philharmonia of London (London, 1979)
Bernstein, Vienna Philharmonic (Deutsche Grammophon, 1987)

RECOMMENDED LPs
Colin Davis, Boston Symphony (Philips, 1977)
Bernstein, New York Philharmonic (CBS, 1968)

RECOMMENDED CASSETTES
Colin Davis, Boston Symphony (Philips, 1977)
Bernstein, New York Philharmonic (CBS, 1968)

COMMENTS
Ashkenazy's version has passion and grandeur in a blazingly Romantic interpretation. Bernstein's latest version (from Vienna) is also passionately intense, if a bit more solemn. Both are beautifully recorded.

Colin Davis is cooler yet dramatically alive and penetrating. Bernstein's New York recording is ardent and majestic, and totally absorbing despite aging sound.

Among vintage recordings still in the catalog, Koussevitzky's with the Boston Symphony (RCA, 1950) remains the standout on LP and Cassette — a sweepingly taut, heroic, unforgettable account, despite its limited sonics.

VIOLIN CONCERTO IN D MINOR

Like Beethoven, Brahms, Mendelssohn, and Tchaikovsky before him, Sibelius wrote only one violin concerto—but that one is unlike any other in the repertory. Moreover, Sibelius, unlike the others mentioned, was himself a violinist as a young man. But he gave up the instrument at the age of 25 to concentrate on composing. Thirteen years later (1903) he wrote his violin concerto, and he revised it in 1905.

It is one of the most difficult violin concertos. Yet it does not show off a violinist's technique as much as it challenges his or her ability to spin out a deeply lyrical, richly colored line—more mysterious and introspective in mood than the outgoing warmth and glitter of most 19th-century concertos.

RECOMMENDED CDs _____
Heifetz, Hendl, Chicago Symphony (RCA, 1960)
Kremer, Muti, Philharmonia of London (Angel, 1983)

RECOMMENDED LPs _____
Heifetz, Hendl, Chicago Symphony (RCA, 1960)
Perlman, Previn, Pittsburgh Symphony (Angel, 1979)

RECOMMENDED CASSETTES ___
Heifetz, Hendl, Chicago Symphony (RCA, 1960)

Perlman, Previn, Pittsburgh Symphony (Angel, 1979)

COMMENTS _____
Heifetz's recording ranks as one of the century's gems—and remains peerless for its jewel-like brilliance and clarity, despite somewhat too-closely-miked violin sound.

Kremer and Perlman are both outstanding in different ways. Kremer is more individualistically sensitive and dynamic, Perlman more soaringly songful and expansive.

FOR FOLLOW-UP CONSIDERATION

SYMPHONY No. 1 IN E MINOR A sweepingly dramatic, eloquently melodic symphony—the most unabashedly Romantic of all of Sibelius' symphonies.

RECOMMENDED CD _____
Segerstam, Danish National Radio Symphony (Chandos, 1992), a broadly

paced interpretation that stresses both the work's rugged majesty and its dark, melodic nobility.

SYMPHONY No. 5 IN E FLAT MAJOR Stylistically more lean and introspective than Sibelius' earliest symphonies, the Fifth is nonetheless grippingly dramatic, with one of Sibelius' most broadly eloquent finales.

RECOMMENDED CD _____
Rattle, City of Birmingham Symphony

(Angel, 1986), an intensely moving, incisive performance.

RECOMMENDED LP AND CASSETTE

Kondrashin, Amsterdam Concertge-bouw (Philips, 1976), a vividly urgent, dramatic performance, recorded during a live concert.

FOUR LEGENDS FROM THE KALEVALA   The second of the *Legends*, the darkly atmospheric *Swan of Tuonela*, is often performed (and recorded) as a separate piece. But it is most fascinating in the context of the other orchestral *Legends*, all of them based on ancient Finnish tales about Lemminkäinen, warrior hero of the Kalevala (Land of Heroes). The other three *Legends* are titled *Lemminkäinen and the Maidens of Saari*, *Lemminkäinen in Tuonela*, and *Lemminkäinen's Homeward Journey*.

RECOMMENDED CD, LP, AND CASSETTE

Ormandy, Philadelphia (Angel, 1979), a tonally luscious, sweepingly Romantic performance.

BEDRICH SMETANA

Pronounced: *smeh*-ta-nuh. Born March 2, 1824, in Leitomischl, Bohemia. Died May 12, 1884, in Prague, at age 60.

SIGNIFICANCE   Bohemian (Czech) composer, conductor, pianist, regarded as the founder and greatest exponent of the Czech nationalist style, which was strongly influenced by folk music.

BACKGROUND   Smetana, the son of a brewery manager, first sought a career as a pianist, but that ended in financial disaster. With help from Franz Liszt, he opened a successful music school in Prague. But Smetana, an intense Bohemian nationalist, found it difficult to live in the repressive political environment that followed the unsuccessful 1848 revolt against Austrian rule. So he went to Sweden, where he continued to compose actively. In 1859 the Austrians, following their defeat by Italian armies, granted Bohemia political autonomy. Smetana returned to Prague to become one of the leading figures in the movement to build a national opera house. He composed eight operas for it, including *The Bartered Bride*, an international success. But disputes over his policies as a director of the house, aggravated by growing deafness, eventually forced his resignation.

He continued to compose, and after going completely deaf completed his most famous work: the six symphonic poems that make up the cycle *Ma Vlast* (*My Country*). The last six years of life were marked by mental illness, and he was sent to an asylum a few weeks after his sixtieth birthday. He died there two months later.

Today Smetana is revered in Czechoslovakia as that country's greatest composer. If his international reputation is less than Dvořák's it is because he was primarily an opera composer whose librettos, in Czech, are not widely known outside his homeland. Dvořák, in contrast, composed mainly for orchestra. Each spring the famous Prague Festival traditionally begins with a complete performance of *Ma Vlast*, which today has the stature of a national epic in Czechoslovakia.

THE MOLDAU (VLTAVA)

Next to Johann Strauss' *Blue Danube Waltz*, the most famous piece ever written about a river is surely Smetana's ten-minute symphonic poem *Vltava*—better known by its German name, *The Moldau*. It forms the second movement of Smetana's epic cycle *Ma Vlast* (*My Country*), but is often performed as a separate work.

Smetana follows the flow of the river from its twin sources in the Sunava forest, past villages along the way to Prague, ending as it passes the great Vyšehrad rock outside Prague (from which the river continues on to join the Elbe). The music begins as a trickle, gradually swelling into a mighty and majestic force. Along the way, Smetana incorporates the sounds of a village wedding with its lively polka, a moonlit scene in which Rusalkas (legendary water nymphs) play on the waters, and the turbulence of the rapids of St. John. As the river reaches Prague, the majestic Vyšehrad theme of *Ma Vlast's* first movement recurs, as it does in the last movement of the complete cycle.

RECOMMENDED CDs
Kubelik, Czech Philharmonic (Supraphon, 1990)
Stokowski, RCA Orchestra (RCA, 1960)

RECOMMENDED LPs
Kubelik, Boston Symphony (Deutsche Grammophon, 1971)
Szell, Cleveland (CBS, 1963)

RECOMMENDED CASSETTES
Stokowski, RCA Orchestra (RCA, 1960)
Kubelik, Boston Symphony (Deutsche Grammophon, 1971)

COMMENTS
The Czech-born Kubelik leads a lyrical, soaringly colorful performance, recorded live upon his emotion-packed return to Prague following the fall of communism (and after a 42-year exile from his former orchestra). It is part of his complete 1990 performance of the Czech national epic *Ma Vlast* on a single CD. The earlier Kubelik-Boston performance is also reflectively heartfelt, and is available either as part of a complete *Ma Vlast* or coupled with several short works by Dvořák and Liszt. (Both versions are superior interpretively and sonically to an even earlier Kubelik-Vienna Philharmonic recording on London Records.)

Stokowski's is played with marvelous lilt, color, and tonal beauty, with the opening passage literally oozing out of the orchestra. Szell's version is almost as good, and its CD transfer is also respectable.

RECOMMENDED CD, LP, AND CAS-
SETTE (COMPLETE) _____
Kubelik, Bavarian Radio Symphony (Orfeo, early 1980s), as compelling a case
for the entire cycle as anyone could
make.

FOR FOLLOW-UP CONSIDERATION

THE BARTERED BRIDE: OVERTURE AND DANCES Light, appealing,
and lively instrumental excerpts from the comic opera of 1863–70, still one
of the most popular of all operas in central Europe.

RECOMMENDED CD _____
James Levine, Vienna Philharmonic
  (Deutsche Grammophon, 1988), a
  warm and vivid performance, beautifully recorded.

RECOMMENDED LP _____
Bernstein, New York Philharmonic (CBS,

1963), a spirited performance with
serviceable sound.

RECOMMENDED CASSETTE _____
Kertesz, Israel Philharmonic (London,
  1963), a crisp and colorful account
  with good sound.

RICHARD STRAUSS

Pronounced: *shtrows*. Born June 11, 1864, in Munich, Germany. Died
September 8, 1949, in Garmisch, (West) Germany, at age 85.

SIGNIFICANCE German conductor and composer of late Romantic symphonic poems and operas. (No relation to Johann Strauss, the Viennese
"waltz king".)

BACKGROUND As a student, Strauss became a fierce disciple of Wagner,
even though his father, a celebrated horn player, had organized bitter intrigues against Wagner and his music. Three years after leaving the University
of Munich in 1882, Strauss became assistant to the well-known conductor
Hans von Bülow, and eventually he became chief conductor at Weimar,
Berlin, and Munich.

Between 1887 and 1898, Strauss wrote a series of symphonic poems
(sometimes called tone poems) that were strikingly original in their use of
large orchestral forces—*Macbeth, Don Juan, Death and Transfiguration,
Till Eulenspiegel's Merry Pranks, Thus Spake Zarathustra, Don Quixote*, and
A Hero's Life. He turned primarily to opera after 1900, first with a series of
heavily scored works on texts that were considered daring or even shocking

in their time (*Salomé, Elektra*), then with more subtle works that combined the tonal colors of Romanticism with more Classical elegance and simplicity (*Der Rosenkavalier, Ariadne auf Naxos, Arabella*). He also wrote some of the finest *lieder* since Schubert.

In his later years, controversy followed Strauss' acceptance of an official music post under the Nazi regime of Adolf Hitler in 1933, even though he resigned it in 1935 because the Nazis opposed his continuing to work on an opera with a libretto by Stefan Zweig, who was Jewish. He lived in virtual retirement in Bavaria during World War II, turning down repeated invitations to conduct ceremonial performances that the Nazis considered important.

In 1940, however, he did accept a government commission to write a short orchestral work for a festival honoring the Japanese emperor (then allied with the Germans in World War II), though Strauss later insisted he had accepted the commission only in return for a safe-passage visa to Switzerland for his daughter-in-law, who was part Jewish.

After the war, an Allied military court formally cleared Strauss of charges of having collaborated with the Nazis. He wrote a number of new instrumental works, including one for the American oboist John De Lancie, and traveled to England. Soon after celebrations of his eighty-fifth birthday, he suffered a series of heart attacks, and died a few weeks later.

TILL EULENSPIEGEL'S MERRY PRANKS

The character of Till Eulenspiegel is as familiar to German children as Robin Hood is to English-speaking children. But Till's origins seem to be much more in doubt. Some say there really was a Till Eulenspiegel, and that he was Flemish (others say German) and that he lived in the 14th or 15th century. Stories about him began to appear in 15th-century German folk literature, and were frequently related to the growing peasant rebellion against the authority of church and state. Till even appears in 16th-century English literature as Tyl Owlglass (*Eulenspiegel*, in German, means owl's mirror). Whatever his origins, Till is now the legendary prototype of the gaily rebellious imp, prankster, or rapscallion—boldly and continually upsetting the respectable life of the conformist establishment.

Strauss' musical characterization of Till is lusty and colorful, witty and lively. The 15-minute work, composed in 1895, calls for unusually large orchestral forces. Before its premiere, Strauss withdrew the literary program he had prepared. However, he did confide to one conductor that various episodes depict Till upsetting a marketplace, assuming the disguise of a monk and giving a mock sermon, trying to make love to a girl who isn't interested, twitting a group of pompous professors, being arrested and brought to trial for flouting authority, then thumbing his nose at his executioners in the belief that they are merely playing a joke on him—followed by a sudden strangled squeak and a deadly drum roll as Till plunges through the gallows' trap door. But the work does not end grimly, for suddenly Till's spirit reappears, defiantly demonstrating his immortality.

RECOMMENDED CDs————————
Haitink, Amsterdam Concertgebouw (Philips, 1981)
Abbado, London Symphony (Deutsche Grammophon, 1983)

RECOMMENDED LPs————————
Abbado, London Symphony (Deutsche Grammophon, 1983)

RECOMMENDED CASSETTES——
Abbado, London Symphony (Deutsche Grammophon, 1983)

Maazel, Cleveland (CBS, 1979)

COMMENTS————————————
Haitink brings sparkle and ardor to his *Till*, Abbado a bit more robustness. Both of their couplings are two other Strauss symphonic poems, *Don Juan* and *Death and Transfiguration*, in equally good performances.

ALSO SPRACH ZARATHUSTRA (THUS SPAKE ZARATHUSTRA)

This 40-minute tone poem has become enormously popular in recent years—partly because of its use for the soundtrack of the now-classic 1968 film *2001: A Space Odyssey*, and partly because of its reputation as a stereo soundbuster. Its opening is one of the most dramatic in all music, and just the sort to show off the qualities of a good audio system—with the lowest C of the organ laying down a solid bass while trumpets and timpani herald ever-building sonorities that soon explode in an awesome climax. As to the quality of the music that follows, banalities jostle with great moments of beauty and cleverness—all held together by Strauss' enormous skill as an orchestrator of enticing sonorities.

The title is taken from the book of the same name by the 19th-century German philosopher Nietzsche. Strauss' tone poem, written in 1896 when the composer was 32, is not a literal setting of that book, but a symbolic tribute to some of Nietzsche's ideas. The work ends enigmatically on an unresolved chord, indicating that for all of Zarathustra's philosophy, life will always remain a mystery.

RECOMMENDED CDs————————
Solti, Chicago Symphony (London, 1975)
Ozawa, Boston Symphony (Philips, 1981)

RECOMMENDED LPs————————
Reiner, Chicago Symphony (RCA, 1962)
Karajan, Berlin Philharmonic (Deutsche Grammophon, 1984)

RECOMMENDED CASSETTES——
Reiner, Chicago Symphony (RCA, 1962)
Steinberg, Boston Symphony (Deutsche Grammophon, 1971)

The Solti CD is a knockout sonically, especially in the clarity and impact of the opening "Sunrise" section. All of the other performances are interpretively outstanding and well-recorded, with Solti and Steinberg the most propulsive and exuberant, Karajan and Ozawa the most tonally opulent. Reiner recorded the work twice with the Chicago Symphony (1954, 1962) and both recordings are still in the active catalog; the second Reiner version is sonically superior in its details and was for many years *the* stereo showcase of its era and still impresses in both its LP and Cassette editions, as well as in a remastered RCA Papillon Collection CD.

FOUR LAST SONGS

After Mahler, Strauss was unquestionably the past century's greatest writer of art songs (*lieder*), in addition to being a masterly composer of operas and symphonic poems. The *Four Last Songs* that Strauss composed in his final years are among his most profound and most beautiful. All four treat the approach of life's end with various metaphors.

"Frühling" (Spring), to a text by the Nobel Prize-winning writer Hermann Hesse, looks back on the joys and beauties of spring from dusk-dim vaults. "September," also to a Hesse text, describes "golden leaves dropping down as a fading summer lingers among the roses, yearning for rest." "Beim Schlafengehen" (Before Sleeping), again to a Hesse text, reflects on "senses longing to settle into slumber." "Im Abendrot" (At Dusk), with a text by the Romantic poet Josef von Eichendorf, describes an old couple who finds that "around us the valleys are waning, the sky is darkening — it's nearly time for us to sleep." This last song includes musical quotations from Strauss' earlier *Death and Transfiguration* and *Der Rosenkavalier*.

The *Four Last Songs* (so titled by Strauss' publisher after his death) actually turned out to be not quite his last. Shortly before his death, Strauss wrote a short song, "Malven" (Mallows), and sent it to the soprano Maria Jeritza in New York. Jeritza had for years been closely identified with some of Strauss' operas and, after the war, had financially helped Strauss when he was hard-pressed to pay for medical treatment. The song turned up among her papers after her death in 1982, and has since been performed and recorded.

RECOMMENDED CDs
Norman, Masur, Leipzig Gewandhaus (Philips, 1982)
Schwarzkopf, Szell, Berlin Radio Symphony (Angel, 1967)

RECOMMENDED LPs
Norman, Masur, Leipzig Gewandhaus (Philips, 1982)

Schwarzkopf, Ackermann, Philharmonia of London (Angel, 1950s), *mono*

RECOMMENDED CASSETTES
Norman, Masur, Leipzig Gewandhaus (Philips, 1982)
Flagstad, Furtwangler, Philharmonia of London (Turnabout, 1950), *mono*

COMMENTS————————
Norman's and Schwarzkopf's recordings are classics in their own individual ways. Norman brings an almost awesome depth and dignity as well as vocal beauty to the songs, and Masur's accompaniments are perfectly matched. Schwarzkopf floats the notes of these songs ravishingly while also conveying the unique depth of feeling that made her her generation's greatest Strauss *lieder* singer. She has a bit more vocal bloom in the earlier recording with Ackermann, but she had learned to phrase certain lines even more beautifully and expressively by the time of the later recording with Szell, whose accompaniment is especially lustrous.

Flagstad premiered the songs in 1950 with Furtwangler, and that performance has been preserved, though only on cassette at present. Her performance is not as subtle as either Norman's or Schwarzkopf's, but it is still touchingly beautiful and clear-voiced, and the Flagstad sound is still matchless.

FOR FOLLOW-UP CONSIDERATION

A HERO'S LIFE (EIN HELDENLEBEN)   Strauss said that this alternately boistrous and beautifully lyrical tone poem was about "an average man whose heroism lies in his triumph over the inward battles of life." But because of the work's musical quotations from some of Strauss' best-known earlier works, it is usually interpreted as symbolically autobiographical — with one critic of Strauss' day calling it "a blatant blowing of his own horns, all eight of them." Whatever its autobiographical or even egotistical intent, it is one of Strauss' finest and most sumptuously orchestrated works.

RECOMMENDED CD————————
Karajan, Berlin Philharmonic (Deutsche Grammophon, 1988).

RECOMMENDED LP AND CASSETTE————————
Ormandy, Philadelphia (RCA, 1978).

Karajan and the Berliners have long made this one of their showpiece specialties, and their performance is ardent, luminous, and exciting. Ormandy's Philadelphians also give a tonally glowing, dramatic performance.

DER ROSENKAVALIER (THE CAVALIER OF THE ROSE)   Strauss' great opera contains two of the most beautiful duets and one of the most beautiful trios ever written for female voices, and its waltz sequences have long been a concert favorite. But there are also many lengthy scenes which may seem less interesting to a newcomer at first, yet whose dramatic and musical subtleties grow with familiarity. Strauss called *Der Rosenkavalier* "a comedy for music" — but it is a comedy of rare maturity and psychological depth. In some ways, *Der Rosenkavalier* blends the farce style of Viennese operetta with refined orchestral grand opera. The plot involves the complications of love among the nobility of mid-18th-century Vienna, but much more significant is the way the characters emerge (through both text and music) as human beings. A single-disc or single-cassette highlights album is recommended for a newcomer, but the versions cited here are also available in complete performances by the same artists.

IGOR STRAVINSKY

Pronounced: strah-*vin*-skee. Born June 17, 1882, in Oranienbaum, Russia. Died April 6, 1971, in New York City, at age 88.

SIGNIFICANCE Russian-born composer and conductor, a dynamic innovator in a number of different styles, and one of the most influential composers of the 20th century.

BACKGROUND After studying with Rimsky-Korsakov in St. Petersburg, Stravinsky went to Paris in 1908 to work with Diaghilev's Ballet Russe. There he created a sensation with the *Firebird* in 1910 and *Petrushka* in 1911. *Firebird* blended elements of Impressionism with more colorful, folklike Russian elements; *Petrushka* was more strikingly original in its rhythms and harmonies. His third work for Diaghilev, the massively savage, howling *The Rite of Spring* (*Le Sacre du Printemps*) was so electrifyingly unorthodox that it caused a riot at its Paris premiere in 1913—but promptly established itself as a landmark of orchestration, rhythm, and polytonality.

The ever-unpredictable Stravinsky then switched directions in the 1920s and 1930s, moving toward a more austere Neoclassicism (*Oedipus Rex, Apollo, Symphony of Psalms*), espousing this as the most reasonable option in opposition to the more radical directions in which Schoenberg and the serialists were leading 20th-century music. But then, in the 1950s, Stravinsky stunned the music world by embracing serialism, the system to which his music had been the major "alternative" for nearly 40 years. His last works (*Agon, Canticum Sacrum, Requiem Canticles*) were highly original explorations of new approaches to serial composition.

The composer Nicholas Nabokov has written, "Despite his many twists and turns, Stravinsky became the unquestioned leader of Western music [in our time]. . . . Stravinsky and Schoenberg remain the lonely founding fathers of the strangely eccentric and highly anarchic state of modern music."

From the 1930s until his death, Stravinsky was active in the recording studios—becoming one of the first composers to have virtually all of his works recorded under his own direction, as a conductor, pianist, or just on-the-scene supervisor.

THE FIREBIRD

Few pieces of 20th-century music have become so widely popular as Stravinsky's *Firebird*, composed when Stravinsky was 27. This ballet, based on Russian folktales about the Firebird and the evil magician Katschei, had first been commissioned from the Russian composer Liadov in 1909 by the great ballet impresario Diaghilev. But Diaghilev became dissatisfied with Liadov's progress and turned to the young Stravinsky, whose short orchestral works had impressed him. Although Stravinsky later admitted that "the *Firebird* did not attract me as a subject," he accepted the offer and produced the score in less than six months. It was an immediate success, and launched Stravinsky's international career.

Critics hailed its brilliant colors and ingenious instrumental combinations. Stravinsky himself remained its severest critic. "I was more proud of some of the orchestration than of the music itself," he later wrote. "The *Firebird* belongs to the style of its time. It is more vigorous than most of the 'composed' folk music of the period, but it is also not very original. These are all good conditions for a success," he said.

Stravinsky twice revised parts of the score—first in 1919, then again in 1945 (partly for copyright reasons). He sometimes referred to it as "that great audience lollipop," but he rarely failed to include it on programs he conducted in both Europe and the United States, and he himself recorded music from the *Firebird* on four different occasions.

Newcomers may prefer to start with the 25-minute suite, which includes the ballet's best music. But since the complete score is less than 50 minutes and fits on a single disc or cassette, recommendations are also included for the complete version.

RECOMMENDED CDs───────────
Shaw, Atlanta Symphony (Telarc, 1978), *suite, 1919 version*
Muti, Philadelphia (Angel, 1979), *suite, 1919 version*
Dutoit, Montreal Symphony (London, 1987), *complete, 1910 version*
Boulez, New York Philharmonic (CBS, 1975), *complete, 1910 version*

RECOMMENDED LPs───────────
Stravinsky, Columbia Symphony (CBS, 1967), *suite, 1945 version*
Muti, Philadelphia (Angel, 1979), *suite, 1919 version*
Dutoit, Montreal Symphony (London, 1987), *complete, 1910 version*
Colin Davis, Amsterdam Concertgebouw (Philips, 1978), *complete, 1910 version*

Stravinsky, Columbia Symphony (CBS, 1967), *suite, 1945 version*
Muti, Philadelphia (Angel, 1979), *suite, 1919 version*
Dutoit, Montreal Symphony (London, 1987), *complete, 1910 version*
Colin Davis, Amsterdam Concertgebouw (Philips, 1978), *complete, 1910 version*

COMMENTS_____
Stravinsky's own recording of the suite is taken at a faster clip than most others and has dramatic punch if less sense of mystery and tonal sheen. Muti's is the most tonally luxurious, but it is not as cleanly recorded as Shaw's, which also has a slight interpretive edge.

As for the complete versions, Dutoit's is not only sonically gorgeous but also superbly detailed and subtly colored, without losing the score's dramatic thrust. Boulez is also outstanding for rhythmic detail and overall mood, and is the most sensuous in some of the quieter sections. Davis brings splendid color and vitality to his version.

PETRUSHKA

Close to *The Firebird* in popularity, but much more original, is *Petrushka* (1911) — sometimes spelled *Petrouchka* (the French transliteration of Stravinsky's title as used at the Paris premiere). The ballet is set in St. Petersburg in 1830, during the Shrovetide Fair preceding Lent. A puppeteer has set up a booth for performances by three of his life-size puppets which he has, through magic, imbued with human feelings. Inevitably, there is a romantic conflict between the three (the frail but spirited Petrushka, the large and bullyish Blackamoor, and the fickle Ballerina) — with Petrushka ending up the loser. Or is he?

To tell the ballet's tragicomic story, Stravinsky used a number of catchy Russian folk themes, a colorful orchestration, and an intriguingly mechanical kind of rhythm. But most significant, and controversial, were Stravinsky's harmonic innovations. He boldly combined chords of the most distant keys to create a new *bitonality* (sometimes, but not always accurately, called *polytonality*). He also varied time signatures and even used different ones simultaneously. For all such technical inventiveness, the music is immediately appealing to the listener.

The music from *Petrushka* exists in several forms: the original 1911 score, a revised 1947 edition (in which Stravinsky thinned down some of the orchestration and made other alterations), a suite of dances (mainly the carnival scenes) from the complete score, and a 1921 piano transcription of three scenes. The complete score is about 45 minutes long, and is recommended over the suite (which, by focusing on the carnival music, fails to convey either the full drama or musical flavors of the complete score).

RECOMMENDED CDs_____
Thomas, Philharmonia of London (CBS, 1980), *1911 version*

Abbado, London Symphony (Deutsche Grammophon, 1981), *1911 version*

RECOMMENDED LPs_____
Abbado, London Symphony (Deutsche Grammophon, 1981), *1911 version*
Bernstein, New York Philharmonic (CBS, 1969), *1947 version*

RECOMMENDED CASSETTES_____
Thomas, Philharmonia of London (CBS, 1980)
Abbado, London Symphony (Deutsche Grammophon, 1981), *1911 version*

COMMENTS_____
Regrettably, the two best recorded versions to date are no longer in the active catalog: Ansermet's mid-1960s recording (his second) on the London label, and Stravinsky's 1960 recording for CBS. If either should be reinstated, they would

deserve consideration over any of the versions listed above. Ansermet's, in particular, brings out all sorts of rhythmic and coloristic subtleties that other conductors rarely even hint at, and his rhythmic pulse is unerring, whatever the score's complexities. Stravinsky's own performance is jauntier, with many wonderful touches, both humorous and dramatic.

Meanwhile, the versions listed above are still most recommended. Thomas and Bernstein have a real flair for this music, and bring out both the wit and pathos better than most. (Bernstein's New York version, incidentally, is preferable to his later Israel Philharmonic version on Deutsche Grammophon.) Abbado's is rhythmically vibrant and colorful.

THE RITE OF SPRING (LE SACRE DU PRINTEMPS)

Few musical works of this (or any) century have created quite the sensation Stravinsky's *Rite* did at its premiere in 1913 — or have changed the direction of subsequent orchestral music so significantly. Pierre Boulez has called the *Rite* "the cornerstone of modern music" and "a manifesto work."

Coming at a time when Romantic and Impressionistic music had made rhythm subordinate to form, expression, or mood, the *Rite* boldly asserted the preeminence of rhythm and rhythmic impulse. It did so with a work designed to depict the celebration of primitive, pagan rites in old Russia. Its barbaric, almost convulsive power, rhythmic invention, tension, and decibel intensity were unlike anything Western music had ever known before. Inevitably, some critics at first attacked it as "a blasphemous attempt to destroy music as an art" or as "the precise exploitation of violence." But over the years, understanding of the *Rite's* freshness and inventiveness has grown — while the electric excitement of the work rarely fails to affect audiences. The Paris premiere of 1913 ended in a near-riot with half the audience scrambling for the exits. In contrast, a half-century later, in 1965, the largest audience ever known to attend a single symphony concert to that time — estimated at 75,000 people — turned out in New York's Central Park to hear Leonard Bernstein lead Stravinsky's *Rite* and Beethoven's *Eroica* with the New York Philharmonic. The ballet for which Stravinsky wrote his score is divided into two parts: (1) "The Adoration of the Earth," which depicts the gradual emergence of spring and the celebration of the new season through pagan ceremonies and dances; (2) "The Sacrifice," which depicts the selection of the chosen virgin whose sacrifice will fertilize the earth, and her frenetic dance of death.

RECOMMENDED CDs———————
Mehta, New York Philharmonic (CBS, 1977)
Dutoit, Montreal Symphony (London, 1984)

RECOMMENDED LPs———————
Stravinsky, Columbia Symphony (CBS, 1960)
Boulez, Cleveland (CBS, 1966)

RECOMMENDED CASSETTES———
Stravinsky, Columbia Symphony (CBS, 1960)
Boulez, Cleveland (CBS, 1966)

COMMENTS———————————
Stravinsky's own recording remains unforgettably vivid. It is tauter and leaner-sounding than most others (except Boulez's), but propulsively exciting. Boulez

brings astonishing clarity and definition to his version. His is a more clinically intellectual view of the score, but without ever sacrificing the work's rhythmic pulse, energy, or tension. (Boulez's Cleveland version is infinitely superior in both orchestral execution and sound engineering to an earlier one he made in France that's still in the catalog.)

Among the CDs, Dutoit's has by far the most outstanding sound, though interpretively Dutoit is more restrained and less biting than Mehta, who is more willing to let loose with the score's gut power.

For history buffs, there is a performance still in the catalog by Pierre Monteux, who led the 1913 premiere. His 1950s recording with the Boston Symphony (RCA, mono, CD, cassette) still has considerable power and impact.

FOR FOLLOW-UP CONSIDERATION

SYMPHONY IN THREE MOVEMENTS   Composed in 1945 at the end of World War II, this symphony has no program, but the composer admitted that its mood and rhythms were affected by the war. The last movement, in particular, he said, was inspired by newsreels Stravinsky had seen of goose-stepping Nazi soldiers and then of "their overturned arrogance when their war machine failed." The more serene second movement is based on part of a score Stravinsky began but never completed for the 1944 film *Song of Bernadette*.

RECOMMENDED CD, LP, AND CASSETTE———————————
Conlon, Rotterdam Philharmonic (Er-

ato, 1985), rhythmically alive and crisply forceful.

SYMPHONY OF PSALMS   A deeply eloquent work in Latin for chorus and orchestra, based on Biblical psalms, and composed a year after Stravinsky's return to the Russian Orthodox Church in 1928.

RECOMMENDED CD AND CASSETTE———————————
Chailly, Berlin Radio Symphony & Cho-

rus (London, 1984), a spacious, moving performance.

Festival Chorus (CBS, 1960s), a more propulsive performance.

CONCERTO IN D MAJOR FOR STRING ORCHESTRA Best-known as the music for Jerome Robbins' ballet *The Cage* (in the repertory of the New York City Ballet since the 1950s), this is a rhythmically vibrant yet touchingly lyrical score, composed in 1946. It remains one of the most appealing of Stravinsky's "dry" Neo-Classical works.

RECOMMENDED LP AND
CASSETTE
Colin Davis, English Chamber Orchestra (London, 1962), a taut, gripping

performance — one of Davis' first recordings and still one of his best. (No recommended CD.)

PETER ILYICH TCHAIKOVSKY

Pronounced: chi-*koff*-skee. Born May 7, 1840, in Votkinsk, Russia. Died November 6, 1893, in St. Petersburg, at age 53.

SIGNIFICANCE Russian composer and conductor; the leading 19th-century Russian Romantic composer of symphonies and ballets.

BACKGROUND Tchaikovsky did not take up music seriously until he was 22, after studying law and entering the government civil service. But in 1863 he gave up his boring job as a clerk in the czar's Ministry of Justice to enter the newly founded St. Petersburg Conservatory. There he was at first considered rather foppish, and his inability to win approval for some of his early works led to a nervous breakdown. He moved to Moscow, where he became a music critic and teacher and continued to compose. A brief, unsuccessful marriage when he was 34 led to another nervous collapse.

At about this time his serious financial plight was resolved by a wealthy widow, Madame Nadejda von Meck, who became Tchaikovsky's patroness and gave him a handsome annual allowance — even though they had never met and probably never did meet. They corresponded extensively over the next 13 years. Then, for reasons that have never been clear (contrary to the fictionalized Ken Russell movie *The Music Lovers*, of 1971) she abruptly withdrew her support. By this time Tchaikovsky was a world-famous composer.

In 1891 he visited the U.S. to conduct at the opening concert of New York's Carnegie Hall, and then conducted in Baltimore and Philadelphia.

Two years later he died suddenly, after drinking unboiled water in cholera-infested St. Petersburg. Controversy has long raged over whether or not he did it deliberately, but most scholars now believe it was accidental.

PIANO CONCERTO No.1 IN B FLAT MINOR

The majestic opening of this concerto has long been one of the best-known themes in all music — at least among Americans. It has been used as the basis for several popular songs, and in innumerable movies and TV shows. The whole concerto is brimful of melody after melody, and also reflects Tchaikovsky's love of color and contrast.

Written during one of the happiest periods of his life (when he was in his mid-thirties), the concerto is permeated with a joy of living. The piano solo is bold and sometimes florid, and the orchestral accompaniment is full-blooded and dramatic. Tchaikovsky used two Ukrainian folk songs for major themes, and the finale is full of a Russian folklike, dancing verve. Every four years since 1958 — when Van Cliburn won the First International Tchaikovsky Piano Competition in Moscow — all of the young first-place winners, and some of the second-placers as well, have dutifully recorded this concerto (Ashkenazy, Ogdon, Sokolov, Dichter), swelling the already plentiful number of available versions (at one count there were 40 listed in the Schwann catalog, including nearly every top-ranking soloist).

RECOMMENDED CDs————————
Argerich, Dutoit, Royal Philharmonic
    (Deutsche Grammophon, 1971)
Rubinstein, Leinsdorf, Boston Symphony (RCA, 1963)

RECOMMENDED LPs————————
Rubinstein, Leinsdorf, Boston Symphony (RCA, 1963)
Pogorelich, Abbado, London Symphony
    (Deutsche Grammophon, 1986)

RECOMMENDED CASSETTES————
Argerich, Dutoit, Royal Philharmonic
    (Deutsche Grammophon, 1971)
Rubinstein, Leinsdorf, Boston Symphony (RCA, 1963)

COMMENTS————————————
Argerich combines majestic sweep and poetic intimacy in a unique way — bringing a remarkably fresh approach to this most overplayed of concertos, and Dutoit's rapport with her is splendid. Rubinstein's performance is sweepingly grand and singing, in the manner that was his trademark, and Leinsdorf's accompaniment is beautifully matched. Young Pogorelich dares to be individualistic about certain passages and, for the most part, they work — for an arresting, impressive performance.

Also in the catalog is Van Cliburn's historic 1958 recording, the first Classical LP ever to sell more than a million copies. It is available on LP and Cassette and has been re-mastered for CD (RCA), and it remains a performance of exceptional grandeur and spaciousness, if less compelling dramatically than the versions cited above.

ROMEO AND JULIET (OVERTURE-FANTASIA)

Of the many musical works based on Shakespeare's story, Tchaikovsky's is the most popular and the most frequently performed. Tchaikovsky does not follow the order of the play, but instead seeks to recreate in music the basic atmosphere of Shakespeare's romantic tragedy. After a solemn introduction (Friar Laurence meditating on the plight of the lovers), the work divides itself between two main themes — a "Battle Theme" representing the struggle for power between the Capulet and Montague families, and a "Love Theme" representing the two young lovers — and the interplay of those themes.

Although originally planned in the traditional 19th-century overture form (introduction, development, coda), Tchaikovsky reworked the score so extensively between the time of its first performance in 1870 and its publication in 1881 that he finally called it an "overture-fantasia" (the term "fantasia" indicates a work of freer form).

RECOMMENDED CDs——————
Chailly, Cleveland (London, 1984)
Bernstein, New York Philharmonic (CBS, 1959)

RECOMMENDED LPs——————
Chailly, Cleveland (London, 1984)
Munch, Boston Symphony (RCA, 1961)

RECOMMENDED CASSETTES——
Chailly, Cleveland (London, 1984)
Munch, Boston Symphony (RCA, 1961)

COMMENTS——————
Chailly's is clearly the best-sounding by today's standards. His performance has warmth and breadth, if not as much orchestral color and passion as either Bernstein's or Munch's. If up-to-date sound is not your first consideration, then the super-charged Munch or the fervent Bernstein performances may please you more. Chailly is coupled with another Tchaikovsky orchestral work about doomed Italian lovers, *Francesca da Rimini*; Munch with Tchaikovsky's lovely *Serenade for Strings*; and Bernstein with the *1812 Overture* and *Marche Slav*.

VIOLIN CONCERTO IN D MAJOR

Like so many works that have won enduring popularity, Tchaikovsky's sole violin concerto was not well received when it first appeared. First, Leopold Auer, the celebrated violinist to whom Tchaikovsky had intended to dedicate the score, pronounced it "unplayable." Then at its premiere in Vienna, the leading critic, Eduard Hanslick, denounced it as "vulgar" and "music that stinks in the ear."

This was undoubtedly because of the freedom with which Tchaikovsky had moved away from the more Classical forms of Beethoven, Brahms, and others. But over the years violinists, critics, and especially audiences have come to view the concerto differently, so that in 1988 there were more than 24 different recordings of the concerto in the Schwann catalog—marking it as one of the most popular of all concertos. Its soaring melodies and the variety of its Romantic moods surely account for that popularity.

RECOMMENDED CDs————————

Perlman, Ormandy, Philadelphia (Angel, 1979)

Chung, Dutoit, Montreal Symphony (London, 1981)

RECOMMENDED LPs————————

Perlman, Ormandy, Philadelphia (Angel, 1979)

Stern, Ormandy, Philadelphia (CBS, late '50s)

RECOMMENDED CASSETTES————

Perlman, Ormandy, Philadelphia (Angel, 1979)

Oistrakh, Ormandy, Philadelphia (CBS, 1959)

COMMENTS————————————

It would seem that Ormandy and his Philadelphians recorded this concerto with nearly every soloist over the past 30 years—and with good reason, for they have been arguably the world's best in conveying the warm, richly flowing Romanticism of this kind of work. But, of course, it's the solo violinist who counts most in the final analysis.

For more than a generation Oistrakh and Stern were the concerto's finest performers—with their fervently singing tone and glowing Romantic feeling. But now Perlman has become their equal interpretively, and he has more up-to-date sound engineering.

Chung's recording (her second) is less sentimental and faster in the finale, with the best engineering of all.

SYMPHONY No. 4 IN F MINOR

One of the most forceful and dramatic of Romantic symphonies, Tchaikovsky's Fourth was composed during a period of enormous personal turmoil for him. Following his unsuccessful marriage and a suicide attempt, Tchaikovsky was taken by his brother to Switzerland to rest and recover from what appeared to be almost a complete nervous collapse. As a result, some analysts have speculated on the Fourth Symphony as providing both a cathartic escape and a rehabilitative anchor for Tchaikovsky during a year of severe emotional trauma.

Tchaikovsky himself saw his Fourth as a musical expression of "the triumph of sensibility over attacks of fate." "Although there is no actual musical resemblance, the work is modeled after Beethoven's Fifth," he said. A dramatic brass fanfare (sometimes called the "Destiny Fanfare," which Tchaikovsky related to fear of the unknown) opens the symphony, dominates the first movement, and recurs again in the finale, thus binding the whole symphony together. The first and second movements are filled with contrasts, from profound melancholy to marchlike assertiveness. The third movement is one of the most famous of any symphony—a satirical scherzo for strings played *pizzicato* (plucked with the fingers rather than bowed).

The fourth movement is defiantly heroic — one of the most swashbuckling, kinetic finales in all music.

RECOMMENDED CDs——————

Karajan, Vienna Philharmonic (Deutsche Grammophon, 1985)
Solti, Chicago Symphony (London, 1984)

RECOMMENDED LPs——————

Karajan, Vienna Philharmonic (Deutsche Grammophon, 1985)
Solti, Chicago Symphony (London, 1984)

RECOMMENDED CASSETTES——

Karajan, Vienna Philharmonic (Deutsche Grammophon, 1985)
Solti, Chicago Symphony (London, 1984)

COMMENTS——————

Karajan's latest recording (his fourth) attests anew that he is the best Tchaikovsky conductor in the West. And also the fastest for the Fourth's all-stops-out finale (though not quite as fast as the legendary Mravinsky-Leningrad Philharmonic recording of the 1950s). Karajan also makes the brooding Romantic themes of the first movement really brood, and the martial sections really march along. Solti's version is also exciting, with fewer contrasts in mood but a bit more brilliant sound.

SYMPHONY No. 6 IN B MINOR ("PATHÉTIQUE")

"As far as I am concerned, I am more proud of it than of any other work of mine," wrote Tchaikovsky of his Sixth Symphony. "While composing it I frequently shed tears." Many listeners still do the same — especially those to whom the *Pathétique* has come to be *the* Romantic symphony.

Tchaikovsky at first designated it "The Program Symphony (No. 6)," but added that none but he would know the program. The morning after the Moscow premiere, however, he decided the title was unfair because "I do not intend to expound any meaning." He sought instead a title that would convey the symphony's general mood. His brother Modest suggested *Pathétique*, meaning "affecting the emotions," particularly tender or sorrowful emotions. Whatever the original program of the Sixth Symphony was, Tchaikovsky took it to his grave — for a week after the premiere he was dead, a victim of a cholera epidemic.

The symphony is, broadly speaking, a mixture of melody and dramatic conflict, of lamentation and defiance. Structurally, it diverges from the traditional symphonic pattern in several ways that were unusual for its time: the first movement is more like a symphonic poem with separate sections; the second movement was one of the first to use a 5/4 rhythm (a rhythm which 20th-century composers have used extensively), and was first mocked as a waltz to be danced by a three-legged man; the third movement has qualities of both a scherzo and a march (different conductors perform it with different emphases); and instead of a lively, grand finale, the fourth movement is a melancholy *adagio lamentoso* that ebbs away in desolation.

RECOMMENDED CDs_____
Karajan, Vienna Philharmonic (Deutsche Grammophon, 1985)
Ashkenazy, Philharmonia of London (London, 1987)

RECOMMENDED LPs_____
Karajan, Vienna Philharmonic (Deutsche Grammophon, 1985)
Ormandy, Philadelphia (CBS, 1960)

RECOMMENDED CASSETTES_____
Karajan, Vienna Philharmonic (Deutsche Grammophon, 1985)
Ormandy, Philadelphia (CBS, 1960)

COMMENTS_____
Karajan's latest recording (his fifth) still sets the standard (like his earlier ones) for this work. It is a deeply expressive, passionately poignant performance, with an especially stirring third movement. Ashkenazy's is almost as good, with well-conceived dramatic contrasts and lyrical intensity. Ormandy's 1960 version (his third of four recordings) is on the more lushly Romantic side, tremendously moving and superbly played by the Philadelphians.

FOR FOLLOW-UP CONSIDERATION

1812 OVERTURE This unabashed rouser has become both a popular stereo showpiece (and apartment lease-breaker) and a sure-fire concluding piece for outdoor concerts (often combined with fireworks during the overture's final section). Although called an overture, it is really a symphonic poem, commemorating the Russian defeat of Napoleon in 1812 (strains of the French anthem "La Marseillaise" are heard, as well as the Russian hymn "Save, O God, Thy People"). The score, originally written for the Moscow Exhibition in 1882, calls for a large orchestra plus a military band, all sorts of bells and chimes, and cannon shots. Some performances even add a chorus to some sections.

RECOMMENDED CD_____
Solti, Chicago Symphony (London, 1986), as high-voltage and exciting a performance, sonically and interpretively, as you're likely to get.

RECOMMENDED CD, LP AND CASSETTE_____
Ormandy, Philadelphia, Mormon Tabernacle Choir (CBS, 1959), another spectacular performance, if not as well recorded, but with the added choral parts making it most memorable.

THE NUTCRACKER This perennial holiday favorite contains some of Tchaikovsky's most delightfully unpretentious music. It exists in several versions: (1) the complete ballet score; (2) the more familiar *Nutcracker Suite*, which includes most of the short dances from the ballet's Act Two; and (3) the less-familiar *Nutcracker Suite No. 2*, which includes several other dances, the "Snow Journey" sequence from Act One, and the ballet's Grand Finale. Normally I would recommend the first suite for a start-up collection, but if you have seen the ballet (either as a youngster or an adult) then you will probably want favorite sections not included in the suite, and since the complete ballet fits onto two discs or cassettes, that may be more appropriate.

RECOMMENDED CD, LP, AND CASSETTE OF THE COMPLETE SCORE
Slatkin, Saint Louis Symphony (RCA, 1985), played with marvelous sparkle, color, and elan.

RECOMMENDED CD AND CASSETTE OF THE SUITE
Slatkin, Minnesota (Pro Arte, 1982), a different performance from the complete one cited above, but with the same essential qualities, and coupled with a fine set of excerpts from Tchaikovsky's ballet *Swan Lake*.

RECOMMENDED LP OF THE SUITE
Dutoit, Montreal Symphony (London, 1986), a thoroughly delightful, beautifully recorded performance, coupled with Tchaikovsky's *Capriccio Italien* and *Marche Slav*.

SYMPHONY No. 5 IN E MINOR Along with Tchaikovsky's Fourth and Sixth, the Fifth has long been among the most popular symphonies in the concert repertory, and it is similar to them in its mixture of haunting melody and swashbuckling rhythms — although it is more optimistic (even heroic) in mood.

RECOMMENDED CD, LP, AND CASSETTE
Karajan, Vienna Philharmonic (Deutsche Grammmophon, 1985), a warmly dramatic, thrilling performance.

RALPH VAUGHAN WILLIAMS

Pronounced: vawn *will-yims.* Born October 12, 1872, in Down Ampney, England. Died August 26, 1958, in London, at age 85.

SIGNIFICANCE English composer, whose music has been described by some as late-Romantic with a "typically English" restraint, and whose works are sometimes strongly influenced by his own extensive research into early English folk music.

BACKGROUND The son of a country vicar, Vaughan Williams became interested in music at an early age and studied at both London's Royal College of Music and at Cambridge. He also later studied orchestration privately in Paris with Ravel. Soon after college, Vaughan Williams joined the English Folk Song Society, and he traveled extensively around England on behalf of the society doing research and collecting material, often with composer Gustav Holst (*The Planets*), who became a close lifelong friend. Vaughan Williams' growing reputation in this field led to his being chosen music editor, in 1904, of the new English Hymnal of the Anglican Church, a project which occupied him for the next two years.

Following military service in the Middle East during World War I, Vaughan Williams settled into the academic life as a professor at the Royal College of Music, work which provided him and his wife with the security he needed to continue composing. Over the next 40 years he turned out symphonies, concertos, operas, film scores, and song collections that rank among this century's most noble, dignified, and profound.

FANTASIA ON "GREENSLEEVES"

The song "Greensleeves" is one of the oldest of English tunes — certainly pre-dating Shakespeare's allusions to it in *The Merry Wives of Windsor* (by Mrs. Ford in Act II, and again by Falstaff in Act IV). In 1929 Vaughan Williams used the melody in his opera *Sir John in Love* — Sir John, of course, being Falstaff, and the libretto coming straight out of *The Merry Wives*. A short time later, Vaughan Williams adapted the "Greensleeves" episode of his opera into a five-minute instrumental fantasia for concert performance, and it quickly became one of his best-known works.

RECOMMENDED CDs————————
Slatkin, Saint Louis Symphony (Telarc, 1982)
Marriner, Academy of Saint-Martin-in-the-Fields (Argo, 1972)

RECOMMENDED LPs————————
Slatkin, Saint Louis Symphony (Telarc, 1982)
Marriner, Academy of Saint-Martin-in-the-Fields (Argo, 1972)

RECOMMENDED CASSETTES——————
Marriner, Academy of Saint-Martin-in-the-Fields (Argo, 1972)
Boult, London Symphony (Angel, 1977)

COMMENTS————————
All three of these performances are played with a serene, dignified atmosphere, with Slatkin's slightly warmer in orchestral tone.

FANTASIA ON A THEME BY THOMAS TALLIS

In his researches as the editor of the new English Hymnal in the early 1900s, Vaughan Williams discovered a long-forgotten psalm book dating back to the year 1567. The psalm book had been suppressed by Queen Elizabeth I after the official re-establishment of Protestantism. In it, Vaughan Williams found nine melodies by Thomas Tallis, a predecessor of both William Byrd and Henry Purcell. In 1909, Vaughan Williams decided to use one of these Tallis melodies as the basis for an orchestral fantasy for double string orchestra. Since its first performance that year by the London Symphony in

Gloucester Cathedral, it has remained one of Vaughan Williams' most admired works.

The Fantasia may look back for its theme, but the piece also looks ahead in the way it is scored—to the Stereo Age of the last half of the 20th century. Vaughan Williams divides his orchestra into three groups: a first orchestra of massed strings, a second orchestra of just nine players, and a quartet of solo strings. The score directs that the two orchestras be placed as far apart as practical. Vaughan Williams obviously had in mind the Renaissance practice of separating two or more choirs within the expanses of a church or cathedral. But, at the same time, he also anticipated certain aspects of modern recording.

RECOMMENDED CDs

Slatkin, Saint Louis Symphony (Telarc, 1982)

Marriner, Academy of Saint-Martin-in-the-Fields (Argo, 1972)

RECOMMENDED LPs

Slatkin, Saint Louis Symphony (Telarc, 1982)

Marriner, Academy of Saint-Martin-in-the-Fields (Argo, 1972)

RECOMMENDED CASSETTES

Slatkin, Saint Louis Symphony (Telarc, 1982)

Marriner, Academy of Saint-Martin-in-the-Fields (Argo, 1972)

COMMENTS

Both Slatkin's and Marriner's recordings are breathtakingly beautiful, with Slatkin's having a slight edge in overall tonal color.

SYMPHONY No. 2
("A LONDON SYMPHONY")

This stoutly melodic musical evocation of London remained Vaughan Williams' own favorite among his nine symphonies. But before a 1920 performance of the then eight-year-old symphony, he told an interviewer that perhaps he had misnamed it, that a more accurate subtitle would have been "Symphony by a Londoner." On other occasions, however, he did give rather specific clues to the relationship of parts of the symphony to places or aspects of London. For example, he declared that the first movement, after a slow prelude that ends with the notes of Big Ben's chimes, "leads to a vigorous allegro which may perhaps suggest the noise and hurry of London." On another occasion, he referred to the slow second movement as an evocation of Bloomsbury Square on a November afternoon. For the third movement, marked Scherzo-Nocturne, he suggested that the listener imagine himself or herself "standing on Westminster Embankment at night, surrounded by the distant sounds of the Strand." As for the final movement, just a few months before his death he said (in a letter to Michael Kennedy) that its coda or epilogue was associated in his mind with the Thames: "The river passes. London passes. England passes."

RECOMMENDED CDs_____

Haitink, London Philharmonic (Angel, 1987)

Previn, Royal Philharmonic (Telarc, 1986)

RECOMMENDED LPs_____

Boult, London Philharmonic (Angel, 1977)

RECOMMENDED CASSETTES_____

Boult, London Philharmonic (Angel, 1977)

COMMENTS_____

Haitink's performance is one of the best he has ever recorded—heartfelt, noble, dramatically moving. Previn's is more restrained in comparison, but still quite genial and sensitive. Boult was long this symphony's foremost champion.

FOR FOLLOW-UP CONSIDERATION

SYMPHONY No. 6   Since Vaughan Williams composed this work between 1944 and 1947, many have felt it reflects the explosiveness and tensions of the war years—from its growling, marchlike opening movement, on through a frenzied scherzo that is interrupted by a brief, parodistic jazz tune, to the solemn, meditative last movement in which the composer seems to challenge the listener to ponder the meaning of life itself. But Vaughan Williams rebuked those critics who tried to dub the Sixth his "War Symphony," and specifically denied that the last movement had any relation to the world after a nuclear holocaust (as some reviewers had suggested). Instead, he said the symphony's last movement could best be understood by reading Prospero's speech from Shakespeare's *The Tempest*—the speech that concludes, "We are such stuff as dreams are made of." Whatever the composer's specific thoughts or inspiration, there is little doubt that the Sixth reflects a deep spiritual struggle and is one of his greatest works.

RECOMMENDED CD, LP AND CASSETTE_____

Previn, London Symphony (RCA, 1968),

a darkly dramatic, profoundly touching performance.

GIUSEPPE VERDI

Pronounced: *vair-dee*. Born October 10, 1813, in Le Roncole, near Busseto, Italy. Died January 27, 1901, in Milan, at age 87.

SIGNIFICANCE   Italian composer of the grandest of grand operas, noted for their melodic vigor, idealized arias, and resourceful orchestration.

BACKGROUND Verdi was the son of a poor innkeeper. At first, he was rejected as a student by the Milan Conservatory. But unwilling to give up, he studied with private teachers, meanwhile attending as many operas at Milan's La Scala Opera as he could. He began composing at age 23, but most of his earliest works met with failure. Following the death of his wife and two of his children, all within three months when he was 27, Verdi's grief was so great that he renounced composing. But two years later, the director of La Scala persuaded him to come to the rescue of a work another composer (Nicolai) had turned down. Verdi agreed, and the result was *Nabucco*—his first success. Over the following years Verdi wrote opera after opera, becoming Italy's most popular composer with *Rigoletto, La Traviata, Il Trovatore, Aïda, Don Carlo, Otello*, and *Falstaff*. The last two were written when he was more than 70 and reflect a changing stylistic tendency to avoid the set arias of his earlier works.

Because he was known throughout his life as a fierce nationalist, patriot, and democrat, Verdi's early operas frequently ran into censorship problems because of their suspected political implications. Later, from 1860 to 1865 Verdi sat as a deputy in that part of Italy already unified. When he died, he left the bulk of his fortune to found a home for aged musicians in Milan.

AÏDA

Aïda (pronounced ah-*ee*-dah) is the most impressive combination of theatrical spectacle and personal drama in all opera. The music is noble, powerful, melodic, and passionate—as Verdian and Italian as *Tristan und Isolde* is Wagnerian and German. *Aïda* was commissioned by the Khedive of Egypt to open his new Grand Opera House in Cairo at the time of the dedication of the Suez Canal in 1871.

Set in ancient Egypt at the time of the pharaohs, the opera tells the story of an Egyptian war hero who spurns the love of the king's daughter for that of a captive Ethiopian princess (Aïda). But he is tricked by her father into a treasonous revelation of secret battle plans, and is condemned to be buried alive. At the end he finds Aïda has secreted herself in the burial tomb to die with him.

Verdi's plan for the opera permits all the pomp and ceremony of its historical period to blend with his human drama—including a spectacular Triumphal March in Act Two and several exotic dance sequences. This, of course, has led to lavish stage productions recreating ancient Egyptian palaces and temples. But in the final analysis it is the beauty and eloquence of the music that makes *Aïda* great.

Complete performances of *Aïda* usually require three LPs or Cassettes, but a recent CD release fits it on two discs. For most newcomers to the opera, a single-disc or single-cassette highlights version may be preferable.

RECOMMENDED CDs

Leinsdorf, Leontyne Price, Domingo, Bumbry, Milnes, London Symphony & Chorus (RCA/BMG, 1971), *complete (two discs) and highlights*

Serafin, Callas, Tucker, Barbieri, Gobbi, La Scala Orchestra & Chorus (Angel, 1955), *complete (three discs)*

RECOMMENDED LPs

Leinsdorf, Leontyne Price, Domingo, Bumbry, Milnes, London Symphony & Chorus (RCA, 1971), *complete (three discs) and highlights*

Muti, Caballé, Domingo, Cossotto, Ghiaurov, New Philharmonia & Chorus (Angel, 1974), *complete (three discs)*

RECOMMENDED CASSETTES

Leinsdorf, Leontyne Price, Domingo, Bumbry, Milnes, London Symphony & Chorus (RCA, 1971), *complete and highlights*

Perlea, Milanov, Bjoerling, Barbieri, Warren, Rome Opera Orchestra & Chorus (RCA Victrola, 1951), *complete (three cassettes), mono*

COMMENTS

Price is *the* great Aïda of the past two or three decades—and her second recording (1971) finds her proud and ringing where required, and heartbreakingly melting in the more tender moments. Her colleagues are all exceptionally good, too, even if Leinsdorf never lets go as movingly as other conductors do.

Next to Price, Caballé's is the most beautifully sung title role—ravishingly so. Her colleagues are also quite good, although Muti paces some scenes routinely and the sound engineering is not as good as RCA's Price recording.

The Callas version is the most dated sonically, and her performance makes up in dramatic intensity and vividness what it lacks in sheer vocal beauty. Tucker, Barbieri, and Gobbi all help make this a memorable set.

Milanov's vintage recording remains one of the most beautiful performances any singer has ever given in *any* recorded opera. Bjoerling, Barbieri, and Warren are also in top form. Perlea pushes the tempos a bit, but not to any serious detriment. The mono sound is serviceable. (Both a highlights disc and a complete edition on three discs have been transferred to CD by RCA/BMG.)

LA TRAVIATA

La Traviata (pronounced lah *trah*-vee-*ah*-tah) is one of Verdi's most lyrically expressive works, and for many years it has remained one of his most popular. The title is translatable roughly as "The Woman Gone Astray." The story, based on Alexandre Dumas' romantic tragedy *La Dame aux Camélias* (*The Lady of the Camellias*, better known in America as *Camille*), concerns a Parisian courtesan whose love for a young nobleman is thwarted by the social taboos of her time (the early 1700s, although the opera is often presented in 19th-century settings).

Complete performances of *La Traviata* vary from two to three CDs, LPs, or Cassettes. For most newcomers to this opera, a single-disc or single-cassette highlights version may be preferable.

RECOMMENDED CDs

Bonynge, Sutherland, Pavarotti, Managuerra, National Philharmonic & London Opera Chorus (London, 1979), *complete (three discs) and highlights*

Carlos Kleiber, Cotrubas, Domingo, Milnes, Bavarian Radio Symphony (Deutsche Grammophon, 1977), *complete (two discs)*

RECOMMENDED LPs

Bonynge, Sutherland, Pavarotti, Managuerra, National Philharmonic & London Opera Chorus (London, 1979), *complete (three discs) and highlights*

Previtali, Moffo, Tucker, Merrill, Rome Opera & Chorus (RCA, 1960), *complete (two discs)*

RECOMMENDED CASSETTES

Bonynge, Sutherland, Pavarotti, Managuerra, National Philharmonic & London Opera Chorus (London, 1979), *complete (three cassettes) and highlights*

Ceccato, Sills, Gedda, Panerai, Royal Philharmonic, Alldis Chorus (Angel, 1972), *complete (three cassettes) and highlights*

COMMENTS

Judgments on performances of *Traviata* hinge mainly on attitudes about the soprano singing the title role, and all of the sopranos above are controversial in one way or another.

Sutherland is one of the greats of our time in vocal agility, but usually at the expense of diction and dramatic comprehensibility. All that is evident in her *Traviata*, but it is still the most stunning overall version to date, thanks to Pavarotti's ardent partnering, Bonynge's alert pacing, and first-rate sound engineering.

Moffo's career was lamentably cut short by vocal problems, but few are evident in this recording aside from a couple of thinnish top notes. She, Tucker, and Merrill bring the most vocal colors and ardor to their recording, and the sound engineering is quite good.

Cotrubas and Sills are lighter voiced than Sutherland or Moffo, and come off better in some parts than others — but those good parts are impressive indeed. Cotrubas has the stronger partners, especially in the fervent Domingo, but Kleiber's conducting is not as animated as one might have expected from him. The Cotrubas-Kleiber complete version fits onto two discs and cassettes by making cuts in the opera itself.

REQUIEM

Composed in memory of the Italian poet and patriot Alessandro Manzoni (1785–1873), this is probably the most theatrically operatic of settings of the Roman Catholic Mass. But there is no denying its powerful religious spirit and the sincerity of Verdi's expressive outpouring. Since Verdi was no orthodox churchgoer, it is not surprising that his Requiem should be highly individualistic, and that he should employ the operatic idiom he knew best (just as many composers in our own century have employed folk, jazz, and rock musical idioms for the Mass and other religious works). The floating beauty of the "Libera me" and the apocalyptic fury of the "Dies Irae" sections are easily the equal of anything Verdi ever composed — and the latter has become famous as a stereo showpiece with few equals in purely sonic respects.

RECOMMENDED CDs

Solti, Leontyne Price, Baker, Luchetti, Van Dam, Chicago Symphony & Chorus (London, 1977), *two discs*

Muti, Studer, Zajic, Pavarotti, Ramey, La Scala Opera & Chorus (Angel, 1987), *two discs*

RECOMMENDED LPs

Solti, Leontyne Price, Baker, Luchetti, Van Dam, Chicago Symphony & Chorus (London, 1977), *two discs*

Karajan, Freni, Ludwig, Cossutta, Ghiaurov, Berlin Philharmonic & Chorus (Deutsche Grammophon, 1972), *two discs*

RECOMMENDED CASSETTES

Solti, Leontyne Price, Baker, Luchetti, Van Dam, Chicago Symphony & Chorus (London, 1977), *two cassettes*

Karajan, Freni, Ludwig, Cossutta, Ghiaurov, Berlin Philharmonic & Chorus (Deutsche Grammophon, 1972), *two cassettes*

COMMENTS

All of the above performances are beautifully sung, well-conducted, and splendidly recorded. From a purely sonic point of view, Solti's "Dies Irae" makes the most impact.

FOR FOLLOW-UP CONSIDERATION

IL TROVATORE (THE TROUBADOUR)   Since its first production in Rome in 1853, *Il Trovatore* (pronounced eel troh-vah-*tor*-eh) has remained one of the most popular of all operas. It is an exciting and richly melodious opera in four acts, in which the verve and beauty of Verdi's music manage to overcome an unbelievable, over-melodramatic plot (which Gilbert and Sullivan burlesqued, in part, in *Ruddigore* and the Marx Brothers used as the opera they mangle at the climax of the classic film comedy *A Night at the Opera*). Briefly, the story concerns twin brothers—one the powerful Count di Luna, the other Manrico, a wandering troubadour who had been kidnapped as a baby and raised by the gypsy Azucena. The two men end up as opposing leaders in a civil war in 15th-century Aragon, and in love with the same lady-in-waiting at the Court of Aragon (Leonora). Both are eventually destroyed by events linked (what else?) to a witch's curse! What counts most is the wealth of thrilling music—providing more great arias and ensembles for its principal singers than two or three average operas, as well as one of the most famous choruses in all opera: the "Anvil Chorus," sung by the gypsies working at their forges.

RECOMMENDED CD, LP, AND CASSETTE

Giulini, Plowright, Domingo, Zancaro, Fassbaender, Santa Cecilia (Rome) Orchestra & Chorus (Deutsche Grammophon, 1987), complete (three discs or three cassettes, or single highlights disc or cassette; one of Giulini's few opera recordings in many years and showing anew that, with a good cast, he has few equals.

Cellini, Milanov, Bjoerling, Warren, Barbieri, RCA Orchestra, Robert Shaw Chorale (RCA, early 1950s), two discs, complete (with cuts), mono; still the most beautifully and thrillingly sung of recorded versions, although the sound is quite dated.

OTELLO   Composed when Verdi was in his seventies, *Otello* is considered by many critics and music lovers to be Verdi's most mature and perfectly realized opera. In contrast to Verdi's earlier works, there are few set arias or ensembles and more emphasis on achieving characterization through music, a change which some credit to the influence of Richard Wagner's music dramas. The libretto is based on Shakespeare's tragedy about a 15th-century Moor in the service of Venice who is destroyed by jealousy and deception.

**RECOMMENDED   CD, LP, AND
CASSETTE**
J. Levine, Scotto, Domingo, Milnes, National Philharmonic of London, Ambrosian Chorus (RCA, 1978), complete on two CDs, three LPs or cassettes; a stirring, dramatic performance, with today's greatest Otello (Domingo). The only recommended highlights version is at present on cassette only: Barbirolli, Jones, McCracken, Fischer-Dieskau, New Philharmonia of London, Ambrosian Chorus (Angel, 1969), excitingly sung by McCracken, with Fischer-Dieskau a most subtly sinister Iago.

ANTONIO VIVALDI

Pronounced: vee-*vahl*-dee. Born March 4, 1678, in Venice. Died July 28, 1741, in Vienna, at age 63.

SIGNIFICANCE   Italian priest, composer, and violinist, one of the masters of Italian Baroque music, and the principal hero of the Baroque revival of recent decades.

BACKGROUND   The term Baroque (from the Portuguese *barocco*, a pearl of irregular shape) is sometimes simplified to mean a type of music that is "elegantly and irregularly fashioned" (like the gilt scroll ornamentation that decorates Baroque architecture). One of the most prolific of the composers of such music was Vivaldi. He wrote many oratorios, operas, and several hundred instrumental pieces, most of them concertos for almost every instrument known at that time (as well as combinations of them).

According to harpsichordist Igor Kipnis, "A wag once observed that

Vivaldi didn't write 400 concerti, but merely wrote one concerto 400 times; though exaggerated, the comment has a slight touch of truth."

Baroque composers did indeed frequently rework their own material, as well as that of other composers, not because of lack of imagination but as a common compositional procedure of the period to use and re-use easily recognizable musical idioms. Bach so admired Vivaldi that he transcribed or extended more than a dozen of Vivaldi's works for different instruments; for example, Bach's Concerto for Four Harpsichords and Strings is a transcription of Vivaldi's Concerto for Four Violins and Strings.

Little is known about Vivaldi's life. His father was a violinist at San Marco in Venice, and presumably Vivaldi's first music teacher. Sometime before 1703 he entered the Roman Catholic priesthood, but he continued his musical studies at the same time. In 1703 he became a teacher at a Venice school for foundling girls, the Seminario Musicale dell' Ospitale della Pietà, where he had the nickname of the "Red Priest" (for the color of his hair). In 1709 he became director of the school's concerts, and remained at least nominally in that post until about 1740. He is known to have traveled extensively throughout Italy and other parts of Europe between 1725 and 1736, performing his own works. In 1740 he settled in Vienna, hoping to win favor at the court of Charles VI as a composer. He died there a year later, unsuccessful in his goal and apparently in poverty.

After his death, most of his music slipped into obscurity, lying forgotten in libraries and various archives until the Baroque revival of recent years led scholars and others to seek it out. Since then there has been a virtual explosion of Vivaldi performances and recordings, filling more pages of the record catalog today than any other Baroque composer except for Bach.

THE FOUR SEASONS (LE QUATTRO STAGIONI)

Perhaps the most popular of all Baroque instrumental works, *The Four Seasons* is a series of four short violin concertos in the Baroque style, each concerto representing one of the seasons (Spring, Summer, Fall, Winter). The strict fast-slow-fast scheme of the Baroque concerto is maintained for each of the successive movements, and Vivaldi's score is sprinkled with terms designed to set the mood of specific sections. For example, the phrase "languidezza per il caldo" (languidness because of the heat) appears over the opening bars of the second concerto, "Summer."

In 1950 there were two recordings of *The Four Seasons* listed in the Schwann catalog; by 1988 there were 58—dramatic testimony to the recent Baroque revival.

RECOMMENDED CDs

Loveday, Marriner, Academy of St.-Martin-in-the-Fields (Argo, 1970)

Perlman, Mehta, Israel Philharmonic (Deutsche Grammophon, 1983)

RECOMMENDED LPs

Fasano, Virtuosi di Roma (Angel, 1961)

Perlman, Mehta, Israel Philharmonic (Deutsche Grammophon, 1983)

RECOMMENDED CASSETTES

Fasano, Virtuosi di Roma (Angel, 1961)

Perlman, Mehta, Israel Philharmonic (Deutsche Grammophon, 1983)

COMMENTS

The Virtuosi di Roma long specialized in Vivaldi's music, and their recording is exceptionally good—vibrant, expressive, and with beautiful ensemble playing. The Loveday-Marriner edition is a bit more opulent in string tone, with noteworthy continuo playing by Simon Preston. Violinist Perlman is the most showmanlike, but delightfully so; the version in which he leaves the conducting to Mehta is preferable to two others in which he acts as both soloist and conductor (one with the London Philharmonic, the other with the Israel Philharmonic).

For those seeking a version using original period instruments and following more scholarly Baroque performing practices, the recommended version on CD, LP, and Cassette is that of Hogwood with four different violin soloists and the Academy of Ancient Music (L'Oiseau-Lyre, 1983).

FOR FOLLOW-UP CONSIDERATION

CONCERTO IN D FOR GUITAR AND ORCHESTRA Originally written for the lute, but usually played today by concert guitarists.

RECOMMENDED CD

Romeros, Brown, Academy of Saint-Martin-in-the-Fields (Philips, 1984).

RECOMMENDED LP AND CASSETTE

Williams (guitar and conductor), English Chamber Orchestra (CBS, 1968).

Both are attractive, animated performances. A recording of the original lute version is also available on LP and Cassette: Julian Bream, Bream Consort (RCA, 1975), a brilliantly played performance by the contemporary lute master.

CONCERTOS FOR FLUTE AND ORCHESTRA Six short, lively, but similar concertos, which may be a bit too much of the same for listening to on one disc or cassette—unless, of course, only one or two of the concertos are played at a time.

RECOMMENDED CD, LP, AND CASSETTE

Rampal, Scimone, Soloisti Veneti (CBS, 1980s), in which the masterly Rampal shows why he has few rivals on the flute today.

CONCERTO IN A MINOR FOR TWO VIOLINS AND ORCHESTRA Vivaldi wrote no fewer than 23 double violin concertos, obviously intrigued with the possibilities of adding to the virtuoso aspects of different harmonies and counterpoint not possible with a single soloist.

RECOMMENDED CD AND LP_____
Stern, Zukerman, Saint Paul Chamber (CBS, 1981), a lively performance by two well-matched virtuosos.

RECOMMENDED CASSETTE_____
Midori, Zukerman, Saint Paul Chamber (Philips, 1986), a less characterful performance by the teenaged Japanese virtuoso, but still most impressive.

GLORIA IN D   One of the best examples of Vivaldi's musical settings of a religious text.

RECOMMENDED CD_____
Corboz, Lausanne Chamber Orchestra & Vocal Ensemble (Erato).

RECOMMENDED LP AND CASSETTE_____
Preston, Academy of Ancient Music,

Christ Church Cathedral Chorus (L'Oiseau-Lyre). The Preston is more stylistically correct, but the Corboz is a bit livelier. Both performances are sung in the original Latin.

RICHARD WAGNER

Pronounced: *vahg*-ner. Born May 22, 1813, in Leipzig, Germany. Died February 13, 1883, in Venice, Italy, at age 69.

SIGNIFICANCE   German composer and conductor, who wrote "music-dramas" in which he combined complex orchestral and vocal elements built out of combinations of hundreds of individual themes (called *leitmotivs*, or leading motives). These themes represent characters, objects, moods, situations, or ideas, which Wagner changed in rhythm, form, etc., according to the dramatic requirements.

BACKGROUND   Wagner's father, a Leipzig police actuary, died when Wagner was quite small, and his mother took in boarders to support her family. One of the boarders was an actor whom she eventually married. Through his stepfather, Wagner became fascinated with the theater, and as a teenager he determined to become a poet for the stage. Then he saw a production of Beethoven's opera *Fidelio*. "From that moment," he wrote, "my life acquired its true significance" — he would, he decided, write poetic dramas for the *musical* stage.

He borrowed books on music and began to teach himself composition, finally beginning formal music training at age 17 at the Leipzig university. By 21 he had written two operas (*Die Feen, Das Liebesverbot*) and managed to get them produced. They were both failures. Wagner married an actress, became a theater conductor, and continued to write operas. Finally, in the early 1840s, the first performances of his *Rienzi* and *The Flying Dutchman* (*Der Fliegende Holländer*) were successful and Wagner was made conductor of the opera house in Dresden.

He remained there, producing *Tannhäuser* and *Lohengrin*, until he got into political difficulties when he threw in his lot with the socialist revolutionaries of 1848. A warrant was issued for his arrest, but he escaped to Weimar. There Franz Liszt sheltered him in his house and gave him money to go to Switzerland. Wagner spent 12 years in exile in Switzerland, writing a book on *Art and Revolution*, composing *Tristan und Isolde*, and beginning a mammoth four-opera cycle, *The Ring of the Nibelungs* (*Der Ring des Nibelungen*).

The *Ring*, based on his own adaptations of Teutonic legends, occupied Wagner off and on for more than 25 years (1848–74). During these years, Wagner experienced many ups and downs. His exile was finally ended and he was allowed back to Germany as a conductor. But he accumulated large debts that almost landed him in debtor's prison, and his personal habits won him as many enemies as friends. Some considered him the most amoral, self-absorbed egotist of all time and a vituperative anti-Semite. Particularly scandalous at this time was his love affair with Liszt's daughter, Cosima. She bore him three children before they could be married, which came only after Wagner's first wife died and Cosima divorced her husband, the famous conductor Hans von Bülow.

Finally, when his personal fortunes seemed at their lowest ebb, the 19-year-old King Ludwig II of Bavaria came to Wagner's rescue, becoming his patron and encouraging his plans to build his own theater big enough for his grandiose scheme of opera production. Despite widespread controversy over Wagner's works, philosophy, and personal life, there were enough pro-Wagner societies to raise the funds to complete the theater in the town of Bayreuth, in the foothills of the Bavarian Alps. He devoted his last years to Bayreuth, producing for it not only the *Ring* but his last opera, *Parsifal*.

ORCHESTRAL MUSIC

Since Wagner's operas tend to be long and complex, a good introduction to them is through their orchestral music — some of the most resplendent, dramatic, and exciting music in all opera. Conductors renowned for their performances of Wagnerian opera have frequently played orchestral excerpts on their concert programs (Toscanini, Furtwangler, Szell, Bohm, Solti, Barenboim, etc.). Several have prepared extensive "orchestral syntheses" of individual operas for concert performances (Stokowski, Leinsdorf)—although, unfortunately, few of the latter have been recorded.

Since the selections on individual recordings of Wagner's orchestral music vary considerably from recording to recording, more than two recommended choices are listed below.

RECOMMENDED CDs

Karajan, Berlin Philharmonic (Deutsche Grammophon, 1984) *Tannhauser Overture & Venusberg Music, Tristan and Isolde Prelude & Liebestod, Meistersinger Prelude Act III*

Solti, Chicago Symphony (London, 1972) *Tannhauser Overture & Venusberg Music, Tristan and Isolde Prelude & Liebestod, Flying Dutchman Overture*

Tennstedt, Berlin Philharmonic (Angel, 1983) *Tannhauser Overture & Venusberg Music, Meistersinger & Lohengrin Preludes, Rienzi Overture*

Walter, Columbia Symphony (CBS, 1959–61) *Tannhauser Overture & Venusberg Music, Lohengrin and Meistersinger Preludes, Flying Dutchman Overture*

RECOMMENDED LPs

Karajan, Berlin Philharmonic (Deutsche Grammophon, 1984) *Tannhauser Overture & Venusberg Music, Tristan and Isolde Prelude & Liebestod, Meistersinger Prelude Act III*

Bohm, Vienna Philharmonic (Deutsche Grammophon, 1975) *Tannhauser Overture, Meistersinger, Parsifal, & Lohengrin Preludes, Flying Dutchman Overture*

Sinopoli, New York Philharmonic (Deutsche Grammophon, 1986) *Flying Dutchman Overture, Lohengrin and Meistersinger Preludes, Siegfried Idyll*

Klemperer, Philharmonia of London (Angel, 1962), *Rienzi, Flying Dutchman, Tannhauser, & Meistersinger Overtures*

RECOMMENDED CASSETTES

Karajan, Berlin Philharmonic (Deutsche Grammophon, 1984) *Tannhauser*

Overture & Venusberg Music, Tristan and Isolde Prelude & Liebestod, Meistersinger Prelude Act III

Solti, Chicago Symphony (London, 1972) *Tannhauser Overture & Venusberg Music, Tristan and Isolde Prelude & Liebestod, Flying Dutchman Overture*

Tennstedt, Berlin Philharmonic (Angel, 1983) *Tannhauser Overture & Venusberg Music, Meistersinger & Lohengrin Preludes, Rienzi Overture*

Bohm, Vienna Philharmonic (Deutsche Grammophon, 1975) *Tannhauser Overture, Meistersinger, Parsifal & Lohengrin Preludes, Flying Dutchman Overture*

COMMENTS

The *Tannhauser Overture & Venusberg Music* begins with the devotional "Pilgrim's Chorus," then moves into the voluptuous "Venusberg Music," and (in most concert versions) ends with a recall of the "Pilgrim's Chorus." The *Tristan and Isolde Prelude & Liebestod* is Wagner at his most broodingly and surgingly romantic. The *Flying Dutchman* and *Rienzi* overtures are alternately dramatic and stirring curtain-raisers, as is the Act III Prelude to *Lohengrin*. The *Parsifal* and *Lohengrin* Act I Preludes are more serene, and the *Meistersinger* Prelude is Wagner at his most noble.

Karajan's performances are the most tonally sumptuous and dramatically intense. Solti's and Bohm's are sharper and more animated, Tennstedt's the most tense and pulsating. Walter is expensive yet forceful, Klemperer strikingly stately. You can't go wrong with any of these well-recorded albums.

TRISTAN AND ISOLDE

This is *the* Romantic masterpiece in German opera—an intense, soaringly beautiful, elaborately scored music-drama based on a tragic Celtic legend dating from the thirteenth century. Its libretto is Wagner's most complicated and subtle—filled with secret love potions, royal intrigue, etc.—causing critic Ernest Newman to write, "While there are few operas more popular, there probably is not one that is the subject of so much misconception on the part of its admirers."

The opera's popularity rests clearly on its music, particularly the fervid, impassioned Love Duet of Act Two and the poignant *"Liebestod"* ("Love-Death") of Act Three.

Since the complete opera usually requires five CDs, LPs, or cassettes, a single-disc or single-cassette of highlights is recommended for most newcomers.

RECOMMENDED CDs

Bohm, Nilsson, Windgassen, Ludwig, Wachter, Bayreuth Festival Orchestra & Chorus (Deutsche Grammophon, 1966), *complete (three discs)*

Furtwangler, Flagstad, Suthaus, Thebom, Fischer-Dieskau, Philharmonia of London, Royal Opera Chorus (Angel/Seraphim, 1952, mono), *complete (four discs)*

RECOMMENDED LPs

Bohm, Nilsson, Windgassen, Ludwig, Wachter, Bayreuth Festival Orchestra & Chorus (Deutsche Grammophon, 1966), *complete (five discs) and highlights*

Bernstein, Behrens, Hofmann, Minton, Weikl, Bavarian Radio Symphony & Chorus (Philips, 1981), *complete (five discs) and highlights*

RECOMMENDED CASSETTES

Bohm, Nilsson, Windgassen, Ludwig, Wachter, Bayreuth Festival Orchestra & Chorus (Deutsche Grammophon, 1966), *complete (five cassettes) and highlights*

Bernstein, Behrens, Hofmann, Minton, Weikl, Bavarian Radio Symphony & Chorus (Philips, 1981), *complete (five cassettes) and highlights*

COMMENTS

Although its sound is not quite up to present-day standards, the 1966 Bohm-Bayreuth recording remains possibly the best ever made of any Wagnerian opera. Taken from a series of performances and rehearsals for that year's Bayreuth Festival, it has a first-rate cast headed by Nilsson, the Wagnerian superstar of the '60s (and still unsurpassed by any of today's singers). But it is Bohm's pacing, dramatic emphases, and ardent expressiveness that is at the core of the album's triumph. He draws from Nilsson, in particular, one of the most impressive performances she has ever given anywhere. The single highlights album includes the Love Duet and "Liebestod" (Love Death).

Bernstein's recording has more up-to-date sound, but the performance is much, much slower and more earthbound. Behrens and Hofmann are properly intense, and once you get used to Bernstein's tempos the dramatic emphases are riveting.

The vintage Flagstad-Furtwangler version is still a classic in its own right, capturing two of the greatest of the pre-1950s Wagnerian interpreters in decent monaural sound (though certainly not as good as stereo would bring just a few years later). Flagstad brings a cool, clear vocal beauty to the role of Isolde. And, yes, the secret has long been out and this is the famous album for which a young Elisabeth Schwarzkopf (whose husband produced the sessions) dubbed in a high note that was eluding Flagstad at that stage of her career.

ALSO RECOMMENDED_____
An orchestral "symphonic synthesis" of the so-called Love Music from this opera, made in the 1930s by Leopold Stokowski and recorded several times by him. His 1960 version, with the Philadelphia Orchestra (CBS/Odyssey, LP and cassette only), is still a glorious introduction to the music of this opera despite a few typically Stokowskian excesses in tonal color and altered orchestration.

THE RING OF THE NIBELUNGS
(ORCHESTRAL EXCERPTS)

The *Ring* is a cycle of four long (*very* long) music-dramas that Wagner began in his mid-thirties and completed soon after he turned sixty. Its complex libretto (by Wagner himself) is based in part on a number of legends of Germanic, Scandinavian, and Icelandic origin — and it is peopled with mythical gods, giants, dwarfs, warrior maidens, and superheroes who are all affected by a curse that falls upon gods and mortals alike after the magic gold of the Rhine is stolen by a mortal who hopes to gain the power to rule the world through a ring forged from that gold.

The plot has long been subjected to widely varying interpretations, including a politically controversial one in the updated Patrice Chereau staging of the 1980 *Ring* at Bayreuth, which was taped in its entirety and has been shown on U.S. television (conducted by Boulez, with Hofmann, Altmayer, Jones, and Jung in major roles). If you have seen and enjoyed that telecast, then you may want to investigate individual recordings of the four operas directly, especially that 1960 Boulez version (Philips, LP only) or the superb 1960s' version conducted by Solti (London, CD and Cassette only), with a remarkable cast that includes Nilsson, Flagstad, Crespin, Windgassen, Svanholm, Fischer-Dieskau, and Hotter.

However, more accessible to most record collectors will be an album of orchestral excerpts from the *Ring*. Beginning with Wagner himself, such orchestral excerpts have become a standard part of most symphony orchestra's repertories and there are now many recordings of them.

RECOMMENDED CDs_____
Szell, Cleveland (CBS, 1969)
Solti, Vienna Philharmonic (London, 1982)

RECOMMENDED LPs_____
Szell, Cleveland (CBS, 1969)

Solti, Vienna Philharmonic (London, 1982)

RECOMMENDED CASSETTES_____
Szell, Cleveland (CBS, 1969)
Solti, Vienna Philharmonic (London, 1982)

COMMENTS

Both performances are blazingly crisp and expressive, although Szell offers a bit more music. He includes the final sections of "Brünnhilde's Immolation" (which actually ends the *Ring*) in addition to the "Entrance of the Gods into Valhalla" (from *Das Rheingold*), the "Ride of the Valkyries" and "Magic Fire Music" (from *Die Walküre*), "Forest Murmurs" (from *Siegfried*), and "Siegfried's Rhine Journey" and "Siegfried's Funeral Music" (from *Gotterdammerung*), also included in Solti's performance.

FOR FOLLOW-UP CONSIDERATION

DIE WALKÜRE (THE VALKYRIE) The second music-drama in the *Ring* cycle is in many ways the most accessible to those who want to graduate from the orchestral excerpts of the *Ring* to the vocal parts. The Sieglinde-Siegmund Love Duet in Act One is especially attractive (and even exciting), as are the "Ride of the Valkyries" (with the vocal parts) and "Wotan's Farewell" in Act Three.

RECOMMENDED CD (OF THE COMPLETE OPERA)

Janowski, Norman, Altmeyer, Jerusalem, Minton, Adam, Dresden Staatskapelle (Eurodisc), *five discs.*

RECOMMENDED LP AND CASSETTE (OF THE COMPLETE OPERA)

Solti, Nilsson, Crespin, King, Ludwig, Hotter, Vienna Philharmonic (London, 1965), four discs, digitally remastered.

RECOMMENDED LP AND CASSETTE (OF HIGHLIGHTS ONLY)

Leinsdorf, Brouwenstejn, Vickers, London Symphony (London), actually only one highlight: the Act One Siegmund-Sieglinde Love Duet.

ALSO RECOMMENDED ON CD, LP, AND CASSETTE

The vintage excerpt-only recording by Toscanini, Traubel, Melchior, and the NBC Symphony (RCA, 1941, mono), whose dated sound cannot completely veil the superb singing of Traubel and Melchior in the Act One Love Duet, nor the electricity of Toscanini's conducting of that scene plus the Act Three "Ride of the Valkyries" (orchestral only).

ANTON VON WEBERN

Pronounced: vay-burn. Born December 3, 1883, in Vienna, Austria. Died September 15, 1945, in Mittersill, near Salzburg, at age 61.

SIGNIFICANCE Austrian composer and conductor, who distilled the essence of 12-tone music in works of remarkable sensitivity, transparency, economy, and precision.

BACKGROUND After studying composition and musicology at the University of Vienna, Webern earned his living by conducting in small opera houses and theaters in Austria. He met Arnold Schoenberg in 1904, and studied privately with him for the next six years. Later he founded, with Schoenberg, the Society for Private Musical Performances in Vienna, which first presented many of the works of the revolutionary Schoenberg school.

After 1924, Webern composed only in the 12-tone idiom. But, in contrast to Schoenberg and Berg, he composed in a more tightly knit, more economical style. He became active as a conductor of modern works in Germany and Austria, and in 1929 served as a guest conductor with the British Broadcasting Company (BBC) in London. During World War II, he lived quietly in Austria in what some commentators have called an "inner exile." Just a few months after the war's end, he was accidentally killed by a soldier on patrol duty at night in the American occupation zone when he lit a cigarette while walking near his son-in-law's home.

SIX PIECES FOR ORCHESTRA

These short, spare pieces, composed in 1910, have been compared by many critics to miniature jewels. The entire score takes only ten minutes to perform, and only one of the Six Pieces requires more than a minute. But in each piece Webern distills the essence of some of the new musical ideas being advanced in the early 1900s by his mentor, Schoenberg.

This is music that renounces a traditional tonal center and thematic structure, but it is neither a 12-tone composition nor a serial work. Those aspects were to come later in Webern's output.

The Six Pieces have strong emotional undertones, but with uncommon sensitivity and prismatic orchestral colorings—of the sort that were to influence a whole generation of later composers, especially Boulez. The individual pieces are marked: (1) *Langsam* (Slowly); (2) *Bewegt* (Propulsive); (3) *Mässig* (Moderate); (4) *Sehr mässig* (Very Moderate); (5) *Sehr langsam* (Very Slowly); and (6) *Langsam* (Slowly).

RECOMMENDED CD————

Levine, Berlin Philharmonic (Deutsche Grammophon, 1988)

Boulez, London Symphony (CBS/Sony Classical, 1969)

RECOMMENDED LPs————

Boulez, London Symphony (CBS, 1969)

Karajan, Berlin Philharmonic (Deutsche Grammophon, 1974)

RECOMMENDED CASSETTE————

None presently available.

COMMENTS

All three performances are completely absorbing in their sensitivity, perceptiveness, and dramatic contrasts. Regrettably, both the Boulez and Karajan LP versions are available at present only in multiple sets. Boulez's is in a three-LP collection of Webern works, many of which will have little interest to a newcomer. Karajan's is part of a four-LP album of music by Schoenberg, Berg, and Webern. The Karajan set actually includes the cream of those three composers' orchestral music, so it may be a worthwhile extravagance for someone who has been exposed to some of this music and likes it. It is too bad, however, that the discs are not available singly for more economy-minded newcomers.

FOR FOLLOW-UP CONSIDERATION

IM SOMMERWIND (IN THE SUMMER WIND) This short tone poem, composed in 1904, was not discovered until some 15 years after Webern's death, when it turned up in a collection willed by Webern's eldest daughter to the Moldenhauer Archive of Spokane, Washington. Begun in 1903, just before Weburn met Schoenberg, the piece was inspired by a poem by Bruno Willie, published in 1901, which describes in highly metaphorical language a summer landscape in northern Germany. In Webern's tone poem there is, at first, just the whisper of a light summer breeze. It grows in strength to what the original poem describes as "the jubilant, organlike roar of the wind," and then subsides into total silence. The title is sometimes translated into English as *Summer Breezes*.

RECOMMENDED CD

Chailly, Amsterdam Concertgebouw (London, 1989), tonally lush and interpretively vivid.

RECOMMENDED LP AND CASSETTE

Ormandy, Philadelphia (CBS, 1963), beautifully atmospheric.

FIVE PIECES FOR ORCHESTRA Composed between 1911 and 1913, these short, delicate, and kaleidescopically colored pieces extend the type of music Webern wrote in his *Six Pieces* of 1910, with a particular emphasis on expressing the nuances of soft dynamic levels. The longest of the Five Pieces is about a minute and a half, the shortest being about 30 seconds. As one critic has appropriately noted, "Webern conveys much by means of the least."

RECOMMENDED CD AND LP

Boulez, London Symphony (CBS, 1967), a most transparent and sensitive performance—but (as noted in the comments on the Six Pieces) regrettably available only in a three-CD or LP set of Webern's works. A good if less subtle 1962 recording by Dorati and the London Symphony (Mercury/Philips) was once available as part of a single LP, titled *Vienna 1908–1914*, and was reissued on CD in 1994. (No Cassette presently recommended.)

AN EXTRA NOTEWORTHY DOZEN

There are, of course, many other composers of interest beyond the 50 discussed in the preceding pages. Some have written works that have become popular sonic showpieces of the stereo age. Some have been overshadowed by others writing in similar styles. Some have only recently begun to win or re-win renown for the individual qualities of their works.

Here are brief notes and recording recommendations on an additional dozen such composers, primarily from our own century.

LEONARD BERNSTEIN

Pronounced: *burn*-stine. Born August 25, 1918, in Lawrence, Massachusetts. Died October 14, 1990, in New York City.

In addition to being one of the most popular conductors of his generation, Bernstein composed three symphonies, several ballets, five Broadway musicals (the most famous, *West Side Story*, was also an award-winning film), a controversial Mass, and other works notable for their melodic vigor, jazz influences, and unabashed theatricality.

CHICHESTER PSALMS   Written in 1965 for England's Chichester Festival, this is Bernstein's finest concert piece to date — an eloquently simple, disarmingly melodic, compellingly rhythmic, and deeply moving work for chorus and orchestra. The text, sung in Hebrew, is taken from six Old Testament Psalms (2, 23, 100, 108, 131, 133) concerning war and peace.

RECOMMENDED CDs, LPs AND CASSETTES
Bernstein, New York Philharmonic, Camerata Singers (CBS/Sony Classical, 1966)
Bernstein, Israel Philharmonic, Vienna Boys' Choir (Deutsche Grammophon, 1978)

COMMENTS
Conductor Bernstein is not the only one who has recorded his *Chichester Psalms*, but his remain the most eloquent, heartfelt, and (in the appropriate places) thrilling. The newer Israel version has marginally better sound, but is not quite as glowing a performance. The New York

recording is available with different CD couplings; a 1991 edition, titled *Leonard Bernstein: A Tribute*, also includes the Symphonic Dances from Bernstein's *West Side Story*, Gershwin's *Rhapsody in Blue*, Ives' *Unanswered Question*, and Mahler's Adagietto from Symphony No. 5; the other has Poulenc's *Gloria* and Stravinsky's *Symphony of Psalms*. The Israel CD's coupling is Bernstein's more recent but less interesting *Songfest*, with vocal soloists Dale, Elias, Williams, Gramm, Reardon, and Rosensheim.

BENJAMIN BRITTEN

Pronounced: *brit*-ten. Born November 23, 1913, in Lowestoft, England. Died December 4, 1976, in Aldeburgh, England, at age 63.

One of England's most prolific composers of orchestral works, concertos, song cycles, and, particularly, operas — many of the latter based on well-known literary themes, such as Herman Melville's *Billy Budd*, Henry James' *The Turn of the Screw*, and Thomas Mann's *Death in Venice*. Late in his career he also became active as a conductor for recordings of some of his own works.

VARIATIONS ON A THEME BY PURCELL   Also known as the *Young Person's Guide to the Orchestra*, but increasingly performed without its "educational" narration and under the first title, so as not to be mistaken as strictly a "kiddie" piece, which it is certainly not musically. Composed for a 1945 documentary film explaining the various instruments of a symphony orchestra, this is a marvelously inventive score, sometimes lightly droll and frolicsome, at other points expressively lyrical and dramatic. It is the score for one of Jerome Robbins' most popular ballets, *Fanfare*, in the repertory of the New York City Ballet since 1953.

RECOMMENDED CDs————————
Britten, London Symphony (London, 1964)
Ormandy, Philadelphia (RCA, 1974)

RECOMMENDED LPs————————
Ormandy, Philadelphia (RCA, 1974)
Giulini, Philharmonia of London (Angel, 1964)

RECOMMENDED CASSETTES————
Ormandy, Philadelphia (RCA, 1974)
Ozawa, Chicago Symphony (RCA, 1967)

COMMENTS————————
All the above versions are without the narration that is sometimes added (most often for youngster-aimed recordings that couple this piece with Prokofiev's *Peter and the Wolf*). The composer leads an especially lively performance. Ormandy's Philadelphians, Giulini's Londoners, and Ozawa's Chicagoans all make the most of the score's virtuosic turns, with Ormandy having marginally better sound.

JOHN CORIGLIANO

Pronounced: *kor*-ill-*yah*-no. Born February 16, 1938, in
New York. Now living there.

Composers are not generally noted for generous compliments about other
composers. Yet the often-crusty Aaron Copland declared a few years before
his death that "John Corigliano is the real thing. His music is individual,
imaginative, expertly crafted, and aurally quite stunning." Corigliano grew
up in a predominantly musical atmosphere (his father was concertmaster
of the New York Philharmonic for 23 years), and he supported his early
composing career by working as a continuity writer for New York radio
stations WQXR and WBAI, and by writing orchestrations for pop recordings.
Since the 1960s he has won increasing recognition for primarily tonal, neo-
Romantic works in a wide range of forms—from a Sonata for Violin and
Piano (which won first prize in the 1969 Spoleto Chamber Music Competition judged by Samuel Barber, Walter Piston, and Gian-Carlo Menotti) to
concertos for piano, clarinet, and oboe respectively, to numerous orchestral,
choral, and solo instrumental pieces, as well as several film scores (including
1981's *Altered States*). He is best known, however, for two of the most
critically lauded works of recent years: the opera *The Ghosts of Versailles*
(premiered by the Metropolitan Opera in 1992) and his Symphony No. 1
(known as the "AIDS Symphony," commissioned by the Chicago Symphony
and played to international acclaim on its 1992 European tour).

SYMPHONY NO. 1 Corigliano says his symphony, dedicated to the
memory of friends and colleagues who have died of AIDS, was inspired in
part by the AIDS Memorial Quilt and "was generated by feelings of loss,
anger, and frustration." The symphony is a powerfully emotional, rawly
expressive, even gut-wrenching work, whose three movements range from
terror, rage, and anguish to a final chaconne of dignity, consolation, and
serenity amid the prevailing atmosphere of grief. Colorful, nostalgic evoc-
ations of a number of well-known musicians who died of AIDS are linked
quilt-like throughout with themes Corigliano identifies with them.

**RECOMMENDED CD
& CASSETTE**
Barenboim, Chicago Symphony (Erato,
1990)

COMMENTS
A searing, intensely dramatic performance of stunning impact, recorded
live. Winner of the 1992 Grammy
Award for Best Orchestral Performance
and the 1992 Grammy for Best Contemporary Classical Composition.

MANUEL DE FALLA

Pronounced: *fye-yah*. Born November 23, 1876, in Cadiz, Spain. Died November 14, 1946, in Córdoba, Argentina, at age 69.

Spain's most internationally renowned composer in this century, noted at first for his Impressionistic, folk-influenced ballets and vocal scores, and later for more Neo-Classical works.

THE THREE-CORNERED HAT   One critic has described this 1919 ballet score as treating the orchestra "like a gigantic Spanish guitar." A rhythmically vibrant, elegant, and colorful work, it uses elements of Spanish folk music in an Impressionistic manner. Although a set of three dances from the ballet has long been popular concert fare, the complete score has only recently come into its own as a concert work—partly through LP recordings, which became popular stereo showpieces in the 1960s, especially for the opening section with its choral "olés" and strongly accented castinet and percussion beats.

RECOMMENDED CDs
Dutoit, Boky, Montreal Symphony (London, 1983)
Ansermet, Berganza, Suisse Romande (London, 1961)

RECOMMENDED LPs
Dutoit, Boky, Montreal Symphony (London, 1983)
Batiz, Salinas, Mexico State Symphony (Varese/Sarabande)

RECOMMENDED CASSETTE
Dutoit, Boky, Montreal Symphony (London, 1983)

COMMENTS
Dutoit has the best sound and leads the most rhythmically vibrant performance, with many subtle touches. Ansermet, who conducted the ballet's premiere in 1919 and remained a master of the score throughout his life, is also marvelous with coloristic details, if less exciting overall. Batiz is rhythmically animated but the orchestral playing is not as polished as the others.

MORTON GOULD

Pronounced: *goold*. Born December 10, 1913, in Richmond Hill, New York. Now living in Great Neck, New York.

American composer, conductor, pianist, and music administrator. His career as a prolific, imaginative composer of symphonies, concertos, ballet scores, and other forms of concert music has sometimes been obscured by his parallel career as a composer for Broadway, Hollywood, and television. In his twenties and thirties, Gould was also one of the busiest conductors on network radio and an arranger-conductor of best-selling recordings of popular standards. Most of his serious works (*Fall River Legend, Spirituals for Orchestra, Dance Variations for Two Pianos and Orchestra, Jekyll and Hyde Variations, Burchfield Gallery*, etc.) have a "Made in America" quality that is fresh, warmly melodic, rhythmically arresting, and almost always purposely accessible. In 1987 he was elected president of ASCAP (the American Society of Composers, Authors and Publishers) and served in that position until 1994, the first classical composer since Deems Taylor in the 1940s to head that prestigious performing-rights organization.

SPIRITUALS FOR ORCHESTRA   A brilliantly orchestrated, deeply moving and stirring work in which Gould does not use any actual spirituals, but mirrors their moods in vividly contemporary patterns. At the time of the work's premiere in 1941, Gould noted that "a good part of American folk material is made up of spirituals, both black and white. Their emotions and moods run a wide gamut, ranging from songs which are escapist in feeling or light and gay, to those having tremendous depth and tragic implications. They are the singing soul of a people." The five movements are subtitled: (1) Proclamation, (2) Sermon, (3) A Little Bit of Sin, (4) Protest, and (5) Jubilee.

RECOMMENDED CDs
Hanson, Eastman-Rochester Orchestra (Mercury/Philips, 1966)

RECOMMENDED LP
Gould, Chicago Symphony (RCA, 1965)

RECOMMENDED CASSETTE
Gould, Chicago Symphony (RCA, 1965)

COMMENTS
Hanson's performance is gripping and moving. Gould's own version stands out both in the dramatic intensity and festiveness of the performance, and in the exceptionally crisp, clean sound. After twenty-plus years, the "Protest" section can still knock you right off your seat (depending, of course, on your stereo equipment).

PAUL HINDEMITH

Pronounced: *hin*-deh-mitt. Born November 16, 1895, in Hanau, Germany.
Died December 28, 1963, in Frankfurt, Germany, at age 68.

Distinguished as a violinist, violist, conductor, teacher, and theoretician as well as a composer in Germany in the years following World War I. In 1934 the Nazis banned his music, partly because his wife's family was "non-Aryan," partly because of the anti-authoritarian theme of his opera *Mathis der Maler*. He spent the rest of his life teaching, successively, in Turkey, the U.S., and Switzerland. Much of his music has been called "Gebrauchsmusik"—"workaday" or "utility" music—because it was composed for a specific function in schools, cabarets, movies, etc. But his best scores continue to be respected for their straightforward, tonal expressiveness.

SYMPHONIC METAMORPHOSES (ON THEMES OF CARL MARIA VON WEBER)
Composed in the U.S. in 1943 and the most popular of Hindemith's "American" works. Its four movements are based mainly on themes from some virtually forgotten piano music by Weber (1786–1826), which Hindemith transformed into a witty, sophisticated, ingeniously orchestrated set of variations, ending with a somewhat macabre mock-march which builds to a brilliant climax that completes the metamorphosis of all the previous themes.

RECOMMENDED CD————————
Davies, Stuttgart Staatsorchester (Musicmasters, 1987)

RECOMMENDED LPs————————
Abbado, London Symphony (London, 1969)
Bernstein, New York Philharmonic (CBS, 1970)

RECOMMENDED CASSETTES———
Abbado, London Symphony (London, 1969)
Bernstein, New York Philharmonic (CBS, 1970)

COMMENTS————————
Davies and Abbado are the liveliest and best-recorded. Bernstein is rhythmically propulsive and ebullient. The Abbado and Bernstein performances are coupled with different but good other works by Hindemith; Davies' coupling is the rarely played but attractive Variations and Fugue on a Theme by J.A. Hiller, by Max Reger (1873–1916). (Hiller was a German composer and critic who died in 1804.)

GUSTAV HOLST

Pronounced: *hohlst*. Born September 21, 1874, in Cheltenham, England.
Died May 25, 1934, in London, at age 59.

English composer of Swedish descent, best-known for his orchestral suite *The Planets*, and one of the most influential English music teachers of his generation.

THE PLANETS A colorful, impressionistic orchestral suite about space—written between 1914 and 1917, long before movie composers made clichés of some of Holst's ideas. The seven sections bear descriptive astrological titles, such as "Mars, the Bringer of War," "Venus, the Bringer of Peace," "Mercury, the Winged Messenger," "Neptune, the Mystic."

RECOMMENDED CDs————
Dutoit, Montreal Symphony (London, 1986)
Karajan, Berlin Philharmonic (Deutsche Grammophon, 1981)

RECOMMENDED LPs————
Dutoit, Montreal Symphony (London, 1986)
Karajan, Berlin Philharmonic (Deutsche Grammophon, 1981)

RECOMMENDED CASSETTES————
Dutoit, Montreal Symphony (London, 1986)

Karajan, Berlin Philharmonic (Deutsche Grammophon, 1981)

COMMENTS————
Of the many first-rate recordings of this popular sonic showpiece, these two—by today's two finest orchestral tone colorists—head the list, with each bringing out the varying moods of each section brilliantly. But none of the recordings now in the catalog can quite match the sinister undercurrent that Haitink brings to the opening "Mars" section in his regrettably deleted 1971 LP for Philips.

CARL ORFF

Pronounced: *orf*. Born July 10, 1895, in Munich, Germany. Died March 29, 1982, in Munich, at age 86.

Orff was the advocate of an essentially neo-primitive musical style—going back to old legends and medieval literature for the texts of his operas and cantatas, and writing music that dispenses with counterpoint and tradition in favor of a kind of straightforward rhythmic declamation, often accompanied by large percussive forces.

CARMINA BURANA This secular cantata was composed in the 1930s and is based on drinking songs and love poems of defrocked medieval monks. Parts of its hedonistic text, sung in Latin, may be in questionable taste (if not downright offensive to some), but there is no denying the impact and appeal of this directly physical music, or the fact that it has become one of the most popular works of recent years. It is full of blazing brass and biting percussive effects, full-blooded choral sections, and alternately lusty and tender sections for soprano, tenor, baritone, and orchestra.

RECOMMENDED CDs

Thomas, Blegen, Riegel, Binder, Cleveland Orchestra & Chorus (CBS, 1974)
Mata, Hendricks, Aler, Hagegard, London Symphony & Chorus (RCA, 1980)

RECOMMENDED LPs

Thomas, Blegen, Riegel, Binder, Cleveland Orchestra & Chorus (CBS, 1974)
Ozawa, Mandac, Kolk, Milnes, Boston Symphony, New England Conservatory Chorus (RCA, 1969)

RECOMMENDED CASSETTES

Muti, Auger, Van Kesteren, Summers, Philharmonia Orchestra & Chorus (Angel, 1980)
Mata, Hendricks, Aler, Hagegard, London Symphony & Chorus (RCA, 1980)

COMMENTS

All of the above recordings have good sound and rousingly lusty performances, with Muti and Thomas having a slight edge in bite and excitement. All are sung in the original Latin.

OTTORINO RESPIGHI

Pronounced: res-*pee*-ghee. Born July 9, 1879, in Bologna, Italy. Died April 18, 1936, in Rome, at age 56.

Best-known in the U.S. for a series of tonally resplendent orchestral tone poems about Rome, but equally well-known in Italy for works based on old Classical structures (including a piano concerto in the Mixolydian mode and a violin concerto based on Gregorian chant).

THE PINES OF ROME   One of a trilogy of lushly colorful tone poems about Rome that Respighi wrote between 1917 and 1928. Its four sections depict: (1) noisy children playing in the pine groves of the historic Villa Borghese; (2) the deserted, pine-shadowed entrance to an ancient Roman catacomb; (3) a moonlit night among the pines of the Janiculum Hill's gardens; and (4) ancient Roman soldiers marching up the pine-lined Appian Way to enter the Capitoline Hill triumphantly. The last section, building steadily from soft percussion and winds to trumpet flourishes and then to blaringly full orchestral sounds, is a popular stereo showpiece.

RECOMMENDED CDs

Sinopoli, New York Philharmonic (Deutsche Grammophon, 1993)
Muti, Philadelphia (Angel, 1985)

RECOMMENDED CASSETTES

Dutoit, Montreal Symphony (London, 1982)
Muti, Philadelphia (Angel, 1985)

Dutoit, Montreal Symphony (London, 1982)
Muti, Philadelphia (Angel, 1985)

COMMENTS —————

All three performances pull out all the tonal stops brilliantly, with Sinopoli having the best sound engineering. Sinopoli is also one of the few conductors to pace the final Appian Way march to match the gait of foot-soldiers (some other recordings, such as Ozawa's with the Boston Symphony, sound more like Ferraris rolling down the road). All three performances are coupled with Respighi's more gaudily colorful *Roman Festivals* and his more tranquilly glittering *Fountains of Rome*.

WILLIAM SCHUMAN

Pronounced: *shoo*-min. Born August 4, 1910, in New York City. Died in Larchmont, New York, February 15, 1992.

American composer and arts administrator, whose symphonic works "tend to have the sort of long-lined melody, sweep, rhythm, and no-nonsense masculinity that seem quite American in character" (to quote composer-annotator Phillip Ramey). As a young man, Schuman led his own jazz band (Billy Schuman and His Alamo Orchestra) and collaborated with Frank Loesser and others on popular songs—before a scholarship to study at Salzburg in 1935 convinced him to concentrate on classical music. After the early 1940s he combined composing with major academic and administrative posts, including long periods as the president of the Juilliard School and then of the Lincoln Center for the Performing Arts. He wrote ten symphonies, numerous concertos for different instruments, ballet scores, vocal and chorus works, and solo works—and was long one of the most frequently performed of contemporary American composers.

SYMPHONY NO 3.

This symphony's first performance in 1941 (by Serge Koussevitzky and the Boston Symphony) established Schuman a a major figure on the American musical scene, and won the New York Music Critics' Circle Award as the best new orchestral work that year. It remains one of his best. The symphony is in two parts, each with two connected movements marked Passacaglia and Fugue, and Chorale and Toccata. There is no programmatic context, but Leonard Bernstein and others have noted that the symphony reflects the historically wrenching war-year of 1941 and America's growing determination to stand up and fight.

RECOMMENDED CD —————

Bernstein, New York Philharmonic (Deutsche Grammophon, 1985)

(Deutsche Grammophon, 1985)
Bernstein, New York Philharmonic (CBS, 1960)

RECOMMENDED LP —————

Bernstein, New York Philharmonic

RECOMMENDED CASSETTE ——

None presently available.

Bernstein has been a loyal champion of this symphony over the years, and it's interesting how his approach to it has changed between the two recordings. The latest one is much better sonically, but also more deliberate and a bit less buoyant than the earlier one. The 1960 recording is coupled with Schuman's more astringent Symphony for Strings (his Symphony No. 5), while the 1985 recording is coupled with the more folk-like Symphony No. 3 by another American composer Bernstein has long championed, Roy Harris (1898–1979).

SIR WILLIAM WALTON

Pronounced: *wall*-ton. Born March 9, 1902, in Oldham, England. Died March 9, 1983, in Ishia, Italy.

English composer of lyrically patrician, rhythmically animated, sometimes dryly witty, always thoroughly tonal symphonies, concertos, ballets, opera, choral music, and film scores. Both of Walton's parents were Lancashire singing teachers, and he was a mere ten when he won a scholarship to the Christ Church Cathedral Choir School, Oxford. He applied himself so completely to music that he neglected his other courses and was expelled at 16. At Oxford he had become friends with the two sons of Sir Osbert Sitwell, who convinced Walton to move to London to live with the Sitwell family and pursue a musical career. Beginning with some chamber works in the early 1920s, Walton established himself as the musical heir of Elgar and Vaughan Williams in English music — although his meticulousness and slow working habits kept his output relatively small over the next 60 years.

FACADE   Originally written for a private concert at the Sitwells in 1922, *Facade* was devised as a novel kind of highbrow burlesque in which Edith Sitwell recited 18 abstract original poems (that she described as "patterns in sound") to Walton's lightly parodistic, sometimes jazzy score. *Facade* became so well-known in London artistic circles that Walton arranged some of its numbers into an orchestral concert suite that was premiered in 1926, and then followed up its success with a second suite. Between the two suites there are 11 numbers, with titles such as "Tango-Pasodoble," "Tarantella Sevillana," "Scotch Rhapsody," "Swiss Yodeling Song," "Spanish Night," "Popular Song," etc. Walton later revised and expanded the score for a ballet by Sir Frederick Ashton.

RECOMMENDED CD————
Chicago Pro Musica (Reference, 1986),

original chamber version, without narration

RECOMMENDED LPs_____

Chicago Pro Musica (Reference, 1986), *original chamber version, without narration*

Epstein, Janet Bookspan, ensemble (Vox, 1976), *original chamber version, with narration*

RECOMMENDED CASSETTE_____

Epstein, Janet Bookspan, ensemble (Vox, 1976), *original chamber version, with narration*

COMMENTS_____

Fifteen years ago, the only available recordings were of the concert suites—including a monaural Angel LP from the 1950s with Walton himself conducting the Philharmonia of London. Today it's only the original chamber version that's available, both with and without the Sitwell verses.

The version *with* the verses will appeal mostly to people who appreciate the far-out, the witty, and the surrealistic—for that is what Sitwell's poems are. Bookspan's delivery is superb, as she changes voice-tones, tempo, inflections, and even characters as she seeks to convey the sense beyond the nonsense (after all, the piece *is* called "facade").

Others will prefer the music without narration, as infectiously played by the Chicago sextet.

KURT WEILL

Pronounced: *vhile*. Born March 2, 1900, in Dessau, Germany. Died April 3, 1950, in New York City, at age 50.

Together with poet-dramatist Bertolt Brecht, Weill was a major force in revolutionizing German opera and musical theater after World War I, especially in its incorporation of elements of jazz and popular music (*The Three-Penny Opera, Mahagonny*, etc.). After coming to the U.S. in 1935 he composed almost exclusively for Broadway and for films, although several of these works (particularly *Street Scene*) are now regarded as serious, innovative, modern operas.

THE SEVEN DEADLY SINS (*DIE SIEBEN TODSÜNDEN*)   The last Weill-Brecht collaboration (1933), a stinging satire on the corruption the average man or woman must endure (and even contribute to) in order to survive in the modern urban world. Weill's music for this ballet-opera is alternately jazzy and traditional, as it traces the travels of two sisters (or is it the alter egos of one?) to seven American cities to try to get enough money to build their family a "little home down by the Mississippi"—only to find in each city that they can fight sins only with bigger sins. The score is one of Weill's best—harmonically lean, rhythmically vibrant, melodically bittersweet, alternately caustic and tender, and, overall, always cutting into the text's bitter, cynical surface with a feeling of deep humanity. George Balanchine staged the first production in Paris in 1933 and also one for the New York City

Ballet in 1958, with one of the sisters sung, the other danced. Concert performances and recordings use the same singer for both roles.

RECOMMENDED CD _____
Kegel, May, Leipzig Radio Symphony (Polydor, 1967)

RECOMMENDED LP _____
Weil, Milva, Deutsche Oper Berlin (Metronome, 1981)
Bruckner-Ruggeberg, Lenya, unidentified German ensemble (CBS Special Projects, 1955)

RECOMMENDED CASSETTES _____
None presently available.

COMMENTS _____
Lotte Lenya, Weill's widow, remains interpretively definitive in a role she originated and replayed in the '50s and '60s, but the incomparable Gisela May (of Brecht's Berliner Ensemble) is also outstanding, vividly matching Lenya's dramatic pungency and actually singing better; this version has been withdrawn as a Deutsche Grammophon LP but is now on a Polydor CD, coupled with a 1975 London Sinfonietta recording of the 1928 Brecht-Weill radio cantata, *The Berlin Requiem*, commemorating the tenth anniversary of the end of World War I. Milva's *Seven Deadly Sins* is also very good and has the most up-to-date sound engineering; like May, Milva sings the work (in German) in a style that is closer to cabaret than the concert hall, but appropriately so.

"NEW AGE" AND OTHER CONTEMPORARY COMPOSERS

At present, classical music is also branching out in significant new directions beyond those represented by the composers on the preceding pages. It is too early to know which of the new composers, and which of their works, will eventually rank alongside those of the great masters of the past. But some are currently finding an enthusiastic audience—and are even drawing people into investigating other areas of concert music. Interest in new music is surprisingly on the upswing, particularly among young people, after several decades of widespread, unalloyed disdain.

For a while, it looked as if classical composers in the 20th century would continue to be divided essentially into serialist and anti-serialist camps (see page 7), as they had been since the 1920s. After World War II, the atonal, cerebral serialists seemed to be in the dominant position —at least among academics, though definitely not among audiences at large. For a time, it also seemed as if every composer was just trying to outdo every other composer in more complex, convoluted ideas. And heaven forbid that any composer should use a recognizable tune or rhythmic pattern, or repeat an identifiable idea from a previous work (which would be greeted by many critics as "lack of growth"). The result was more and more music that lost touch with what the vast majority of listeners could assimilate or appreciate. For them, contemporary music became a challenge to be endured rather than enjoyed. Even many performing musicians came to dislike much of the new music they played.

Through all this, a Neo-Romantic movement of sorts managed to carry on the basically conservative, melodic style represented mid-century by Samuel Barber and a few others—but with elements of Stravinskian or Bartókian modernism also worked in, to make it clear that they were composing in the second half of the 20th century. This Neo-Romantic influence expanded most noticeably in the 1970s, and has been reflected in the work of such American composers as John Corigliano (b. 1938), David Del Tredici (b. 1937), Jacob Druckman (b. 1928), Joseph Schwantner (b. 1943), Joan Tower (b. 1938), and Ellen Taaffe Zwilich (b. 1938). Although they write in quite individualistic and often eclectic styles, there is a common demoninator among them: they compose music to which audiences can relate, and which they want to hear again—not music that scares them away at first hearing. Jacob Druckman prefers to call it "the New Romanticism."

By the 1980s, an even more decisive musical reaction against serialism had made itself felt. Just as Impressionism and Neo-Classicism had appeared nearly a century earlier as a reaction against the excesses of Romanticism, so a Neo-Primitive movement took hold as a reaction against music that had become too complicated and cerebral.

Significantly, this movement coincided with changes that were also taking place in popular music—especially in reaction to the increasingly extreme and abrasive styles of rock music that appeared in the '70s and early '80s. Although the movements were largely separate, there have been some shared aspects along the way—particularly in the infusion of non-Western musical ideas, including Indian, African, and Oriental, and in the use of electronic instruments and sounds, including synthesizers.

The use of electronics in contemporary classical music dates back, of course, to well before the 1970s. The German composer Karlheinz Stockhausen (b. 1928), working at the Electronic Music Studio of the West German Radio at Cologne in the 1950s, was one of the first "serious" composers to record works using synthetic electronic sounds (often involving sonically altered layers of tape). In the 1960s Stockhausen taught at the University of Pennsylvania in the United States, at the Basel Conservatory in Switzerland, and at the influential International Summer School for New Music at Darmstadt, West Germany. His experiments with ear-bending electronic sounds and with the spatial relationships of music, often in combination with serial techniques, put him in the forefront of the avant-garde for many years, and won him worldwide fame (or notoriety, depending on the viewpoint), especially among young people.

For at least a dozen years, Deutsche Grammonphon regularly released LPs of just about every new Stockhausen piece or "realization." These releases have slowed down over the past decade and, as of 1991, few have turned up on CD in the United States. But among those still available on LP, the 1960 work *Kontakte* (*Contacts*) remains one of the best introductions to both Stockhausen and electronic music in general. The piece involves "contacts" between electronic and instrumental sound groups (in this case, piano and percussion).

In a 1971 *New York Times* interview, Stockhausen spoke of the composer as a spiritual guide for the new generation. "Young people ... feel that we have reached the beginning of a new age. They don't believe anymore in the old systems, and they are right. These systems can't go on the way they are." Stockhausen went on to say that he was trying to produce "music that brings us to essentials." So too were the composers he influenced.

Although Stockhausen has always had a much larger following in Europe and Japan than in the United States, he exerted a major influence on a number of American composers, particularly in the area of tape manipulation of sounds. Among them: Terry Riley (b. 1935) and Steve Reich (b. 1936), who used some of Stockhausen's ideas and techniques in the development of the repetitive, pattern-oriented musical style that has come to be called Minimalism (previously mentioned briefly in Part One, on page 7).

Minimalism became a major musical force in the 1970s with the compositions of Reich and Philip Glass (b. 1937)—although there are some, such as author-broadcaster and "new sounds" specialist John Schaefer, who in his landmark book *New Sounds* (1987) traces its origins to certain works in the 1950s of John Cage (b. 1912) and La Monte Young (b. 1935). At first, most Minimalist pieces were built around simple musical fragments which repeated over and over in a way that mutated very slowly and subtly with each repetition. For some listeners, enormous patience was needed as much as an open mind and open ears. As the 1970s progressed, both Reich and Glass moved away from what some critics called their original "stripped down" primitive style, and towards music not only richer in textures but also more melodic.

Although Reich's works were among the first to turn up on the programs of major symphony orchestras (including those of the New York Philharmonic in 1971 and the Boston Symphony in 1972), it was Glass who generally attracted wider audiences with the 1976 theater-piece *Einstein on the Beach* and the operas *Satyagraha* (1980) and *Akhnaten* (1984)—and, most of all, with two distinctive film scores, *Koyaanisqatsi* (1983) and *Mishima* (1985). All of these works have been released on records or tapes. For a newcomer, however, I would recommend the album *Philip Glass Dance Pieces* (CBS CD and LP, 1987), which contains rhythmically propulsive and lyrically compelling music for two recent ballets, Twyla Tharp's *In the Upper Room* and Jerome Robbins' *Glass Pieces*.

The Minimalist who has had the greatest impact in the concert hall to date, however, and whose works seem potentially to have the most chance of becoming concert staples, is John Adams (b. 1947). In contrast to Reich and Glass, Adams' music, in addition to a Minimalist rhythmic pulse, exhibits a flair for lyricism and some of the climactic ebb-and-flow of traditional, even Romantic-era melody. To quote Adams directly, "What sets me apart from Reich and Glass is that I am not a modernist. I embrace the whole musical past, and I don't have the kind of systematic language they have. I rely a lot more on my intuitive sense of balance." Adams has also said that many of his pieces "seem to involve the influence of popular music of the 1950s and 1960s, specifically rock, and to subtly internalize elements of that music's phrasing, melody, harmonic progressions, and continuous rhythmic drive."

The premiere of John Adams' opera *Nixon in China* was a major musical event in 1987—and it became one of the few contemporary operas to be not only taped for television but also promptly recorded (on Nonesuch CD, LP, and Cassette). Fascinating though the opera may be, I would recommend that a newcomer to Adams' music start with a 28-minute orchestral work from 1988, *Fearful Symmetries,* which has had enormous success as the score for Peter Martins' ballet of that title in the repertoire of the New York City Ballet. It is a rhythmically propulsive and harmonically colorful example of Adams' way of "layering" motifs so that they merge, submerge, and reemerge throughout a work in constantly riveting ways. Adams himself conducts an excellent recording with the Orchestra of St. Luke's (Elektra/Nonesuch CD and Cassette).

Also recommended as a follow-up is *Harmonielehre* (1984–85), a longer, three-movement work that shows an even wider range of Adams' musical palette, from insistent motoric energy to slower episodes that the composer has described as "full of longing" and with harmonies "that revolve like a slow kaleidoscope." *Harmonielehre* has been recorded by De Waart and the San Francisco Symphony (ECM CD, LP, and Cassette, 1986).

Minimalism has sometimes been linked in the media with so-called New Age music—a linkage that may have helped draw some young listeners into our concert halls or into investigating contemporary classical composers on records, but a linkage which is marginal at best. New Age is essentially a pop phenomenon, a most successful one in many ways. Part of its success may be related to the fact that the term New Age is vague enough to mean different things to different people—from the music of Japanese synthesizer player Kitaro, to the Swiss electro-acoustic harpist Andreas Vollenweider, to the British ambient-sounds pioneer Brian Eno, to the solo pianists and guitarists of America's Windham Hill label or the ensemble of the eclectic Paul Winter Consort. These and other New Age musicians are now heard on some classical music radio stations that still avoid playing Schoenberg, Ives, Messiaen, Penderecki, and other contemporary composers.

Some New Age music resembles that of the classical Minimalists in its use of repetitive rhythmic patterns and slow-moving melodies. But New Age music is much more than that. Generally speaking, it can be defined as electronic and/or acoustic instrumental music that is essentially serene, relaxing, and mellow, and which combines certain aspects of rock, jazz, folk, non-Western, and Western classical music. It may involve solo instruments, ensembles, synthesizers, or a mixture of some or all of these. Most significantly, it is an easy-to-listen-to music that *New York Times* critic Jon Pareles had called "a refuge from the assaultive 20th century." Some of its exponents also attribute to it meditative or spiritual values (shades of Stockhausen's view of the composer as "a spiritual guide"). Record industry hype has also turned New Age into what Pareles calls "a trendy commodity." Quite a few other critics dismiss it as 1980s–1990s "wallpaper music" or "Muzak with synthesizers."

But New Age music has at least helped to re-establish a relationship (marginal though it may be) between present-day classical and popular music. Haydn and Mozart did not hesitate to use elements of the folk or popular music of their day, nor Mahler the *ländler* of his day, and so on through the use of jazz by Ravel, Stravinsky, Copland, Bernstein, Gould, and others in the '20s, '30s, and '40s. With the '60s, however, classical music and popular music seemed to grow more separate than ever, with little crossfertilization. The 1980s and '90s have changed that—in *both* directions. Just how much and to what lasting effect remains to be seen. But through recordings and audio equipment today, we have the means to hear, probe, absorb, reject, accept, or, most of all, enjoy it all like no previous generation in music history.

A "NEW AGE" FOR RECORDING LABELS TOO?

The corporate mergers of the late 1980s and early 1990s are reflected in the sometimes confusing name changes of a number of major record labels. For decades, the two best-known American classical labels were RCA Victor and CBS Masterworks (the latter originally Columbia). But no more. RCA Victor is now part of the German communications giant BMG (Bertelsmann Music Group), which plans to market releases internationally as *BMG Classics*. Similarly, CBS Masterworks is now part of the Japanese electronics giant Sony, with its new record label name of *Sony Classical*.

These changes took effect too late to amend all the individual RCA and CBS listings in this book. Moreover, both companies say they expect to continue to sell recordings under their original labels for some time to come, and that many releases will include both the old and the new company designations to minimize consumer confusion.

PART THREE

MAJOR RECORDING ARTISTS ON CDs, LPs, AND CASSETTES

Have you ever heard a piece of music and then gone to buy a recording of it—only to open up the record catalog and be overwhelmed by a long list of names with which you aren't familiar? How do you choose?

There's no foolproof system, of course. But knowing who the major conductors and soloists are, something about their background, and what types of music they're usually best at, can at least provide a start.

That is the purpose of this section. It is not a complete "Who's Who" of the concert world by any means. It includes most of the established recording artists plus some of today's most promising newcomers.

(Pronunciations are for the closest approximation of the Anglicized version of each name.)

CLAUDIO ABBADO

(pronounced: ah-*bah*-doh)

Conductor. Born June 26, 1933, in Milan, Italy. Studied at the Verdi Conservatory in Milan and the Vienna Academy. Won first prize in a conducting competition at Tanglewood (Massachusetts) in 1958, and was an assistant to Bernstein with the New York Philharmonic in 1963. In the 1970s he was music director of the Vienna Philharmonic, and then music director of the Vienna State Opera. Named music director, Berlin Philharmonic, 1989. A particularly forceful and incisive interpreter of both 19th- and 20th-century works.

RECOMMENDED RECORDINGS Stravinsky *Petrushka* (Deutsche Grammophon); Debussy *Nocturnes* (Deutsche Grammophon).

GEZA ANDA

(pronounced: *ahn*-dah)

Pianist and occasional conductor. Born November 19, 1921, in Budapest, Hungary. Studied at the Budapest Academy of Music, winning its coveted Franz Liszt Prize at age 18. Has lived in Switzerland since 1942, and became a Swiss citizen in 1955. Best known for his performances of Classical and early Romantic works. In the 1960s, became the first pianist to record all of Mozart's piano concertos as both pianist and conductor.

RECOMMENDED RECORDINGS Mozart Piano Concerto No. 21 (Deutsche Grammophon). Shumann Piano Concerto (Deutsche Grammophon).

MARIAN ANDERSON

Contralto. Born February 17, 1902, in Philadelphia, Pennsylvania. One of the first American blacks to overcome long-standing obstacles to a major concert career. First gained prominence in the 1920s as winner of a contest to appear with the New York Philharmonic. Left the U.S. from 1930 to 1935, scoring numerous triumphs in Europe. In 1939 the D.A.R. refused to let her give a concert at Constitution Hall in Washington, D.C., whereupon the President's wife, Eleanor Roosevelt, and others arranged a concert for her on the steps of the Lincoln Memorial—and it became one of the most famous concerts in Washington's history. In 1955 she became the first black to sing a major role (Ulrica in Verdi's *Un Ballo in Maschera*) at the Metropolitan Opera. Retired from active concertizing in 1965. Noted for her deeply expressive singing of Brahms, Schubert, and Schumann, and for her eloquent interpretations of spirituals. Died April 10, 1993.

RECOMMENDED RECORDINGS Treasury of Immortal Performances —Marian Anderson (RCA, *mono only*). *He's Got the Whole World in His Hands*, an album of spirituals (RCA).

ERNEST ANSERMET

(pronounced: *ahn*-sayr-may)

Conductor. Born November 11, 1883, in Vevey, Switzerland. Died February 20, 1969, in Geneva. A mathematics professor who turned to conducting in 1914. For many years principal conductor of Diaghilev's Ballet Russe de Monte Carlo, premiering numerous works by Stravinsky, Ravel, Prokofiev, and others. In 1918, founded l'Orchestre de la Suisse Romande at Geneva, Switzerland, and remained its conductor for 49 years—raising it to major international status through recordings following World War II. One of the century's masters of tonal subtlety, particularly in Impressionistic and Neo-Classical works.

RECOMMENDED RECORDINGS Stravinsky *Petrushka* (London); Ravel *La Valse, Valses nobles et sentimentales* (London).

MARTHA ARGERICH

(pronounced: *ahr*-geh-ritch)

Pianist. Born June 5, 1941, in Buenos Aires, Argentina. Studied in Europe with Friedrich Gulda, Mme. Dinu Lipatti, and others. Won first prize at 1965 International Chopin Competition in Warsaw. Subsequent career has been marked by major critical acclaim as a dynamic pianist with a special affinity for works with a strong rhythmic pulse.

RECOMMENDED RECORDINGS Prokofiev Piano Concerto No. 3 (Deutsche Grammophon); Tchaikovsky Piano Concerto No. 1 (Deutsche Grammophon).

CLAUDIO ARRAU

(pronounced: *ahr-rowh*)

Pianist. Born February 6, 1903, in Chillan, Chile. Studied in Berlin and taught at Berlin's Stern Conservatory, 1925–27. Won Grand Prix Internationale des Pianistes in Geneva, 1927. Since 1941 a permanent U.S. resident, and a U.S. citizen since 1979. One of the century's great pianists, particularly renowned for his Beethoven. Died June 9, 1991, in Mürzzuschlag, Austria.

RECOMMENDED RECORDINGS Beethoven Piano Concerto No. 5 ("Emperor") (Philips); Liszt Piano Concerto No. 1 (Philips).

VLADIMIR ASHKENAZY

(pronounced: ash-keh-*nah*-zee)

Pianist and conductor. Born July 6, 1937, in Gorky, Russia. Studied at Moscow Conservatory. In 1950 won Queen Elisabeth of Belgium Competition. In 1964 co-winner of the Tchaikovsky International Competition in Moscow. Since his marriage in 1961 to an Icelander, he has maintained residences in Reykjavik and London, declining to return to the Soviet Union. Became active as a conductor in 1970s, but also still active as pianist. Principal conductor of London's Royal Philharmonic since 1987 and of (West) Berlin Radio Symphony since 1989. A particularly penetrating and poetic interpreter of Mozart, Beethoven, Rachmaninoff, Prokofiev, and Sibelius.

RECOMMENDED RECORDINGS As *pianist*—Rachmaninoff Piano Concerto No. 2 & 4 (London); As *conductor*—Sibelius Symphony No. 2 (London).

EMANUEL AX

Pianist. Born June 8, 1949, in Lwow, Poland. Moved to Canada at an early age with parents. Studied in U.S. at Juilliard School and Columbia University. In 1974 won first prize in Artur Rubinstein International Piano Competition in Israel, then in 1979 the Avery Fisher Prize. Renowned as an uncommonly perceptive and technically assured interpreter of the Classical and Romantic repertory, and an adventurous champion of some contemporary works. Married to pianist Yoko Nozaki.

RECOMMENDED RECORDINGS Chopin Piano Concerto No. 1 (RCA); Mozart Piano Concerto No. 17 (Deutsche Grammophon).

SIR JOHN BARBIROLLI

(pronounced: bahr-bih-*roh*-lee)

Conductor. Born December 2, 1899, in London, England. Died in Manchester, England, July 28, 1970. Originally a cellist, then a conductor—first of his own Barbirolli Chamber Orchestra in 1925, then of the Scottish National Orchestra. In 1936, succeeded Toscanini as conductor of the New York Philharmonic, but his tenure was not generally successful with critics or subscribers. After World War II he built Manchester's Hallé Orchestra into one of England's finest, and re-established his international reputation as a warm, tasteful interpreter of 19th- and early 20th-century works. For several years (1961–1967) also music director of the Houston Symphony Orchestra. Knighted in 1949 by King George VI.

RECOMMENDED RECORDINGS Vaughan Williams Symphony No. 2 ("A London Symphony") (Angel). Grieg *Peer Gynt* Suites (Angel/Seraphim).

DANIEL BARENBOIM

(pronounced: *baa*-ren-boym)

Pianist and conductor. Born November 15, 1942, in Buenos Aires, Argentina. At age 10, moved with his parents to Israel and is now an Israeli citizen. Became internationally known as a pianist while still in his teens, after winning the Alfredo Cassella competition in Naples in 1956. Meanwhile, studied conducting. In 1968, made a much-acclaimed, short-notice substitution for Istvan Kertesz as conductor of the touring London Symphony Orchestra in a series of New York concerts. Since then, he has divided his time between the piano and the podium. At his best in the Classical and Romantic repertory, where his intense interpretations are often marked by uncommonly broad pacing. Conductor, Orchestre de Paris, 1975–1990. Music director, Chicago Symphony, since 1991; and of Berlin State Opera (Staatsoper) in Germany, since 1992.

RECOMMENDED RECORDINGS *As pianist*—Brahms Piano Concerto No. 2 (Angel). *As conductor*—Strauss *Alpine Symphony* and *Die Frau ohne Schatten* Symphonic-Fantasy (Erato).

KATHLEEN BATTLE

Soprano. Born Portsmouth, Ohio, August 13, 1948. Studied at College-Conservatory of Music, University of Cincinnati. Debut at Spoleto Festival, 1972; at Metropolitan Opera, 1973. Noted for exceptional cleanness, clarity, and sweetness of her soprano voice, especially in Mozart and Strauss. Also has acquired reputation in music circles as difficult, demanding, and temperamental, and was dismissed by Metropolitan Opera in 1994 over charges involving her behavior.

RECOMMENDED RECORDINGS *Kathleen Battle Sings Mozart* (Angel). Poulenc *Gloria* and French Songs (Philips).

CECILIA BARTOLI

(pronounced: *bar-toll-ee*)

Mezzo-soprano. Born in 1966 in Rome, Italy. Her father and mother were singers in Rome Opera chorus. Studied at Accademia di Santa Cecilia, and made Rome and La Scala debuts at age 19 in Rossini operas. Quickly rose to international prominence for her exceptionally warm, flexible voice and mastery of coloratura and bel canto technique. Most acclaimed to date for Rossini and Mozart.

RECOMMENDED RECORDINGS: *Cecilia Bartoli Sings Rossini Arias* (London). *Rossini Heroines* (London). *Si tu m'ami: 18th-Century Italian Songs* (London).

SIR THOMAS BEECHAM

(pronounced: *bee*-chum)

Conductor. Born April 29, 1879, in St. Helens, Lancashire, England. Died March 8, 1961, in London. For many years Britain's best-known and most popular conductor. The son of a wealthy patent-medicine manufacturer, the Oxford-educated Beecham first organized his own orchestra, the New Symphony, with family funds in 1906. In 1911, became music director of opera at London's Covent Garden, introducing many new and long-neglected works. In 1932, founded London Philharmonic Orchestra. Left England during World War II, conducting primarily in the U.S. Returned to England and in 1947 founded the Royal Philharmonic Orchestra. A highly individualistic, colorful conductor, particularly noted as a champion of Delius, Handel, and Sibelius.

RECOMMENDED RECORDINGS   *Music of Delius* (Angel). Bizet Symphony in C (Angel).

LEONARD BERNSTEIN

(pronounced: *burn*-styne)

Conductor, pianist, composer. Born August 25, 1918, in Lawrence, Massachusetts. In early 1940s, studied with Boston Symphony director Serge Koussevitzky, and was assistant to Artur Rodzinski, conductor of the New York Philharmonic. In 1943, made a dramatic, last-minute substitution conducting the Philharmonic when Bruno Walter became ill. Soon after, he was hailed as a composer for his ballet *Fancy Free*, his "Jeremiah" Symphony, and the hit Broadway musical *On the Town*. In 1957 he composed *West Side Story*, the landmark musical (later an award-winning film) conceived as part opera and part ballet, with strong jazz influences. In 1959, began a ten-year directorship of the New York Philharmonic, and in 1970 was named its Laureate Conductor for life. One of the best-known and most popular American musicians in history, and one of the first to make extensive use of television and video to foster appreciation of classical music. As a conductor, most noted for his highly dramatic, openly emotional approach to Mahler, Brahms, and early 20th-century works. Died October 14, 1990, in New York City.

RECOMMENDED RECORDINGS   Mahler Symphony No. 2 (Deutsche Grammophon). Brahms Symphony No. 1 (Deutsche Grammophon).

HERBERT BLOMSTEDT

(pronounced: *bloom*-stedt)

Conductor. Born July 11, 1927, in Springfield, Massachusetts. Studied at Royal Academy of Music, Stockholm, and University of Uppsala; also with Igor Markevitch and Leonard Bernstein. Was conductor of Oslo Philharmonic, 1962–68; Swedish Radio Symphony, 1967–1977. Became music director of Dresden State Orchestra, 1975–1983, and the San Francisco Symphony, 1986–1994. A perceptive but often staid interpreter of a wide range of music.

RECOMMENDED RECORDINGS Mozart Symphonies Nos. 38 & 39 (Denon). Hindemith Mathis der Maler (London).

KARL BÖHM

(pronounced: boehm)

Conductor. Born August 28, 1894, in Graz, Austria. Died August 14, 1981 in Salzburg. Early career was in opera in Austria and Germany, as principal conductor of the Graz Opera (1924), Darmstadt (1927), and Hamburg (1931). In 1933, began a long association with the Dresden Opera. After World War II, served for a period as music director of the Vienna State Opera. In later years, active at the Metropolitan Opera and Salzburg Festival. One of the foremost masters of German Classical and Romantic works, especially those of Mozart, Schubert, and Richard Strauss.

RECOMMENDED RECORDINGS Mozart Symphonies Nos. 40 & 41 (Deutsche Grammophon). Strauss *Die Frau ohne Schatten* (The Woman Without a Shadow) (Deutsche Grammophon).

JORGE BOLET

(pronounced: boe-*let*)

Pianist. Born November 15, 1914, in Havana, Cuba. Studied at Curtis Institute, Philadelphia. First recipient of Josef Hofmann Award, 1937. During World War II, served in U.S. Army and became a U.S. citizen. Active recitalist ever since. For many years, headed piano department at Curtis Institute. Renowned for his prodigious technique and dramatic performances of Romantic piano music. Died October 16, 1990, in Mountain View, California.

RECOMMENDED RECORDINGS Liszt Piano Music including Sonata in B minor (London). Liszt *Totentanz* (Dance of Death) (London).

PIERRE BOULEZ

(pronounced: boo-*lezz*)

Conductor and composer. Born March 26, 1925, in Montbrison in southern France. In 1948, became music director of Jean-Louis Barrault-Madeleine Renaud theater company in Paris. In 1954 Barrault agreed to let him use the theater on off-days to present concerts of avant-garde music, and subsequent Domaine Musicale concerts became both well-known and controversial. A series of disputes with the French government led him to move to Germany, where in 1966 he became conductor of the Southwest German Radio Orchestra at Baden-Baden. In 1968, became an associate of George Szell with the Cleveland Orchestra, and in 1971 music director of both the New York Philharmonic and the BBC Symphony Orchestra in London. As a conductor, he is one of the most exacting orchestral technicians of our time, but his unusually analytical, intellectual, and unemotional interpretations have divided critics and audiences. Usually at his best in complex 20th-century works. (For more about Boulez the composer, see p. 58).

RECOMMENDED RECORDINGS   Boulez Conducts Debussy, Vol. 1— *La Mer, Jeux, Prelude to the Afternoon of a Faun* (CBS). Stravinsky *Le Sacre du Printemps* (CBS).

ALFRED BRENDEL

(pronounced: bren-*dell*)

Pianist. Born January 5, 1931, in Wiesenberg, Austria. Studied in Graz and Vienna, with Edwin Fischer, Eduard Steuermann, and others. An active recitalist since the 1950s, particularly renowned for his recitals of the complete Beethoven sonatas and cycles of works by Mozart, Brahms, and Schumann. Winner of many European recording awards for his elegant, probing performances.

RECOMMENDED RECORDINGS   Beethoven Concerto No. 5 (Philips) Beethoven "Moonlight" and "Apassionata" Sonatas (Philips).

JOHN BROWNING

Pianist. Born May 23, 1933, in Denver, Colorado. Studied at Occidental College, California, and at Juilliard in New York, where he was a student of Josef and Rosina Lhevinne. In 1954, won Steinway Centennial Award; in

1955, the Leventritt Award; in 1956, the Queen Elisabeth of Belgium Competition. In 1962, introduced the Pulitzer Prize-winning Piano Concerto by Samuel Barber, and has performed it extensively throughout the U.S. In recent years, in addition to performing concertos and solo works, has also performed with chamber ensembles.

RECOMMENDED RECORDINGS Barber Piano Concerto (BMG). Mussorgsky *Pictures at an Exhibition* (Delos).

SEMYON BYCHKOV

(pronounced: *beech-khuv*)

Conductor. Born November 30, 1952, in Leningrad, U.S.S.R. Studied at Leningrad Conservatory; then, after emigration to the U.S., at Mannes College of Music, New York, in mid-1970s. Became music director of Grand Rapids Symphony in 1980, of Buffalo Philharmonic in 1986. Named music director of Orchestre de Paris, effective 1989. A fast-rising, much-praised conductor, especially noted for dramatic 20th-century works.

RECOMMENDED RECORDING Shostakovich Symphony No. 5 (Chandos). Rachmaninoff Symphony No. 2 (Philips).

MONTSERRAT CABALLÉ

(pronounced: kah-bahl-*yay*)

Soprano. Born April 12, 1933, in Barcelona, Spain. Studied at Liceo Consebfadobi in Barcelona, winning its prestigious Gold Award in 1954. Made her operatic debut in 1957 in Basel, Switzerland (as Mimi in Puccini's *La Bohème*), remaining three years with the Basel company and then two years with the Bremen Opera in West Germany. In 1965 her New York debut with the American Opera Society (in Donizetti's *Lucrezia Borgia*) created a sensation, and led to her Metropolitan Opera debut ten months later. She has since become one of the most popular and most admired singers in both Europe and the U.S. Particularly noted for her remarkably delicate, floating tones and *pianissimos*. Her husband is Spanish tenor Bernabé Martí.

RECOMMENDED RECORDINGS *Bel Canto Arias* (RCA). *Opera Duets*, with Placido Domingo (Angel).

MARIA CALLAS

Soprano. Born December 3, 1923, in New York City. Died September 16, 1977, in Paris. Of Greek parentage, she was taken to Greece as a teenager and studied at the Athens Conservatory. Made her operatic debut at age 13 at Athens Royal Opera House (in Mascagni's *Cavalleria Rusticana*). After World War II, studied with Italian opera conductor Tullio Serafin. In 1947, joined Milan's La Scala Opera, creating sensation after sensation in *Tosca, Norma, Lucia di Lammermoor*, and *I Puritani*. Her international reputation as a great singing actress of extraordinary vocal range and versatility quickly spread, and she was heard with the Paris Opera, London's Covent Garden, Chicago's Lyric Theatre, and New York's Metropolitan over the next ten years. Although some critics found her voice limited in natural beauty, most admired the excitement, skill, and intelligence she brought her roles. Various controversies over her private and professional life kept her one of the most publicized prima donnas of the era.

RECOMMENDED RECORDINGS "La Divina" (Angel, 2-disc set, including a Callas interview). Bizet *Carmen* (Angel).

GUIDO CANTELLI

(pronounced: kahn-*tehl*-lee)

Conductor. Born April 27, 1920, in Novara, Italy. Died in a plane crash near Paris, November 24, 1956. Shortly after making debut as a conductor in Novara in 1941, he was sent to labor camps in Italy and Germany for refusing to work with the Fascists. Escaped in 1944, but was caught while fighting with Italian Partisans and was sentenced to be shot. The American liberation of Italy saved his life. In 1945, became a conductor at Milan's La Scala. Toscanini heard him and invited him to U.S. as principal guest conductor of the NBC Symphony. At the time of his death, he was considered the most promising young conductor of his generation.

RECOMMENDED RECORDINGS Schubert "Unfinished" Symphony and Mendelssohn "Italian" Symphony (Angel/Seraphim).

JOSÉ CARRERAS

(pronounced: cah-*rare*-uss)

Tenor. Born December 5, 1946, in Barcelona, Spain. Studied at the Barcelona Conservatory. Operatic debut, Parma, Italy, 1971; New York City Opera, 1972;

Metropolitan Opera, 1974; La Scala, 1975. Rose quickly to prominence as one of his generation's most lyrical tenors. Career interrupted in late-1980s by leukemia, but resumed limited worldwide performances in 1989.

RECOMMENDED RECORDINGS *Opera Arias* (Philips). Puccini *La Bohème*, with Ricciarelli (Philips).

ROBERT CASADESUS

(pronounced: kah-sah-day-soo)

Pianist. Born April 7, 1899, in Paris, France. Died September 19, 1972, in Paris. Studied at the Paris Conservatory, graduating with first-prize honors in 1913. A professor at conservatories of Genoa (1929–30) and Lausanne (1931–35), then became head of piano department of the American Conservatory at Fontainebleau in 1936. Following World War II, toured both Europe and the U.S. extensively, sometimes giving joint piano recitals with his wife, Gaby. Best known as an elegant, always tasteful interpreter of 18th- and 19th-century composers. He was also a composer of numerous sonatas and several concertos.

RECOMMENDED RECORDINGS D'Indy *Symphony on a French Mountain Tune* and Franck Symphonic Variations (CBS/Odyssey). Mozart Piano Concertos Nos. 21 & 24 (CBS/Odyssey)

PABLO CASALS

Cellist and conductor. Born December 29, 1876, in Vendrell (near Barcelona, in Catalonia), Spain. Died October 23, 1973, in San Juan, Puerto Rico. Started studying the cello at age 11 in Barcelona. In his early twenties, continued studies in Paris, living on money he earned playing in dance halls. Made his concert debut in Paris in 1899 playing Bach's Unaccompanied Cello Suites. Soon won almost legendary acclaim throughout Europe and the U.S. for his broad-lined, intensely singing technique. In 1939, went into voluntary exile from Spain following the Spanish Civil War. Settled in Puerto Rico in 1957, organizing and directing an annual Festival Casals there—appearing primarily as a conductor and only occasionally as a cellist. In his later years, also composed a number of works, including a *Hymn to the United Nations*.

RECOMMENDED RECORDINGS Beethoven Sonata for Cello and Piano, with Kempf (Philips, mono). Casals *Song of the Birds*, with other works by Schumann and Couperin (CBS CSP series, mono).

RICCARDO CHAILLY

(pronounced: shy-yee)

Conductor. Born February 20, 1953, in Milan, Italy. Studied with his father, composer Luciano Chailly, then at Milan's Giuseppe Verdi Conservatory and Perugia Conservatory. Became an assistant conductor at La Scala, 1972. U.S. debut at Chicago Lyric Opera, 1974. Music director, Berlin Radio Symphony, 1982–88. Became principal conductor, Amsterdam Concertgebouw Orchestra, 1988. A forceful, dynamic conductor, at his best in dramatic, colorful works.

RECOMMENDED RECORDINGS Rossini Overtures (London). Bruckner Symphony No. 7 (London). Prokofiev *Alexander Nevsky* (London).

BORIS CHRISTOFF

Bass. Born May 18, 1918, in Sofia, Bulgaria. Studied first in Sofia, then in Rome. Made opera debut in 1946 in Rome. In 1949, made a much-acclaimed debut at London's Covent Garden in Mussorgsky's *Boris Godunov*. He became closely identified with Boris in the 1950s, scoring successes with it in Buenos Aires and San Francisco. A much respected bass, noted for penetrating, subtle characterizations.

RECOMMENDED RECORDING Mussorgsky *Boris Godunov* (Angel).

VAN CLIBURN

(pronounced: kly-burn)

Pianist. Born July 12, 1934, in Shreveport, Louisiana. Studied with his mother from 1937 to 1950, then at Juilliard in New York with Rosina Lhevinne, graduating in 1954 with highest honors. Made recital debut at Shreveport in 1940, and concert debut in 1947 with Houston Symphony. In 1948, won National Music Festival Award, then the Leventritt Award in 1954, and the first Tchaikovsky International Competition in Moscow in 1958. The latter, coming at a significant time in changing U.S.-Soviet relations, made him a national hero. Withdrew from active performing in the late-1970s. One of the most popular American pianists of this century. Best-known for his elegant, clean-lined performances of 19th-century Romantics.

RECOMMENDED RECORDINGS Rachmaninoff Piano Concerto No. 3
(RCA). Tchaikovsky Piano Concerto No. 1 (RCA).

JEAN-PHILIPPE COLLARD

Pianist. Born January 27, 1948, in Mareuil-sur-Ay, France. Graduated from
Paris Conservatory at age 16. Won Gabriel Fauré Award, the Cziffra International Competition, and Laureate Prize in Marguerite Long-Jacques Thibaud Competition while in his teens. U.S. debut in 1973 with San Francisco
Symphony. A pianist with a distinct lyrical style and sensuality, as well as
uncommon tonal subtlety.

RECOMMENDED RECORDINGS Saint-Saëns Piano Concerto No. 2
(Angel). Rachmaninoff Piano Concertos Nos. 1 & 3 (Angel).

SERGIU COMISSIONA

(pronounced: *koh*-mis-ee-*yoh*-nah)

Conductor. Born June 16, 1928, in Bucharest, Rumania. In the late 1940s,
was a violinist in Bucharest Radio Quartet and Rumanian State Ensemble,
becoming conductor of the latter in 1950. In 1955, became principal conductor of Rumanian State Opera, but was dismissed in 1959 after he and
his wife (a ballerina) applied for permission to emigrate to Israel. Became
music director of the Haifa Symphony in Israel in 1961, then of Israel
Chamber Orchestra, which he led on a U.S. tour in 1963. Music director of
the Göteborg (Sweden) Symphony Orchestra in late '60s; Baltimore Symphony 1969–1986; Houston Symphony 1984–88; New York City Opera 1988–
89; Helsinki Philharmonic since 1990.

RECOMMENDED RECORDINGS Britten *Diversions* and Laderman
Concerto for Orchestra (Desto). Ravel *La Valse* and *Daphnis and Chloe* (Vanguard).

JAMES CONLON

Conductor. Born March 18, 1950, in New York City. Studied at the Juilliard
School. Served three years on Juilliard faculty before pursuing conducting
career in 1975. A frequent conductor at Metropolitan Opera since 1976.
Music director, Rotterdam Philharmonic, 1983–91. Became chief conductor

of Cologne Opera in 1989, and of historic Gurzenich Orchestra (Cologne) in 1990. An adventurous, engaging conductor of 19th and 20th-century works.

RECOMMENDED RECORDINGS Liszt "Dante" Symphony (Erato). Stravinsky Symphony in Three Movements (Erato).

DENNIS RUSSELL DAVIES

Conductor, pianist. Born April 16, 1944, in Toledo, Ohio. Studied at the Juilliard School, New York. Co-founder with composer Luciano Berio of the Juilliard Ensemble, and its conductor 1968–74. Music director, Norwalk (Conn.) Symphony, 1968–72; Saint Paul Chamber Orchestra, 1972–1981; Stuttgart Opera, 1980–88. Principal conductor, American Composers Orchestra since 1986, General Music Director of Bonn (Germany) since 1988, principal conductor Brooklyn Philharmonic since 1990, and music director Austrian Radio effective 1996. An insightful specialist in 20th-century music.

RECOMMENDED RECORDINGS Copland *Appalachian Spring* and Ives *Three Places in New England* (Pro Arte). Glass *Akhnaten* (CBS).

ANDREW DAVIS

Conductor, pianist, organist. Born February 2, 1944, in Ashbridge, Britain. Studied at Kings College, Cambridge, and Royal Academy of Music, London; also with Franco Ferrara in Rome. Associate conductor, BBC Scottish Symphony, 1970–73; New Philharmonia Orchestra, London, 1973–76. Music director, Toronto Symphony, 1975–1988; BBC Symphony, London, since 1988. A forthright, animated conductor of a wide repertory.

RECOMMENDED RECORDINGS Duruflé Requiem, with Kiri Te Kanawa (CBS). Mendelssohn Symphony No. 3 ("Scottish") (CBS).

SIR COLIN DAVIS

Conductor. Born September 25, 1927, in Weybridge (Sussex), England. From 1957 to 1959, conductor of the BBC Scottish Orchestra, and then from 1961 to 1965 music director of the Sadler's Wells Opera, London. His international reputation grew during the early 1960s when he shared with Georg Solti the conductorship of the London Symphony Orchestra on several overseas tours. In 1971, succeeded Solti as music director of London's Royal Opera

House at Covent Garden. Principal guest conductor of the Boston Symphony 1972–84. Music director, Bavarian Radio Symphony, Munich, 1986–92; London Symphony, since 1994. A sometimes dramatic, more often stolid, but always tasteful conductor, best-known for Berlioz and Mozart.

RECOMMENDED RECORDINGS Berlioz *Symphonie Fantastique* (Philips). Mozart Requiem (Philips).

ALICIA DE LARROCHA

(pronounced: de lah-*rohk*-oh)

Pianist. Born May 23, 1923, in Barcelona, Spain. Made her recital debut in 1928 at the age of five. In 1943, won the Academia Granados Gold Medal for her stylistic excellence in traditional Spanish music. Since 1947, has performed regularly throughout Europe, and since 1954 throughout the U.S. Ranks as one of the most respected of presentday pianists for her warm, expressive interpretations of a broad range of Classical and Romantic music, but is best-known for her performances of Spanish music (Granados, Turina, Falla, Espla, etc.).

RECOMMENDED RECORDINGS *Piano Music of Granados*, including Concierto di Allegro (London). *Spanish Piano Music of the 20th Century* (London). Mozart Sonatas Nos. 10, 11, 12 (London).

VICTORIA DE LOS ANGELES

(pronounced: de los *anh*-kheh-les)

Soprano. Born November 1, 1923, in Barcelona, Spain. Following study in Barcelona, she made her opera debut in that city in 1945 (as the Countess in Mozart's *The Marriage of Figaro*). Two years later, won first prize in International Singing Competition at Geneva. In the 1950s and early 1960s, sang at London's Convent Garden, the Paris Opera, Milan's La Scala, and New York's Metropolitan Opera—and was much admired for her exceptionally clean-lined, lyrical singing and unsentimental interpretations of major operatic roles. In recent years, has confined herself mostly to recital tours, and has become best-known as an exponent of classical Spanish songs.

RECOMMENDED RECORDINGS *Opera Arias* (Angel). *Spanish Songs of the Renaissance* (Angel/Seraphim). Puccini *La Bohème*, with Bjoerling and Beecham (Seraphim).

EDO DE WAART

(pronounced: de *wahrt*)

Conductor. Born June 1, 1941, in Amsterdam, Holland. At age 23, won one of top prizes in the Mitropoulos International Conducting Competition; served a year in New York as assistant to Leonard Bernstein as part of the prize. Also spent a year studying with George Szell in Cleveland in 1967. Became conductor of the Netherlands Wind Ensemble in 1968 and then of the Rotterdam Philharmonic Orchestra. In 1974, became principal guest conductor of the San Francisco Symphony. Music director, San Francisco Symphony, 1977–1985; Minnesota Orchestra, since 1987. A thoughtful, expressive conductor of a wide repertory, from Mozart to John Adams.

RECOMMENDED RECORDINGS Ravel *Sheherezade*, with Ameling (Philips) and Debussy *La Damoiselle Elue*, with Ameling (Philips). Adams *Harmonielehre* (Nonesuch).

MISHA DICHTER

(pronounced: *dick*-ter)

Pianist. Born September 27, 1945, in Shanghai, China, of Polish parents who had left their homeland at outbreak of World War II. Grew up in Los Angeles, and started studying piano at age 12. In 1966, won second prize in the Tchaikovsky International Competition at Moscow, but delayed full-time concertizing for several years in order to complete his schooling at Juilliard in New York, where he studied with Rosina Lhevinne. Active concertizing since early '70s has won him recognition as one of his generation's most sensitive and probing pianists.

RECOMMENDED RECORDINGS Brahms Piano Concerto No. 1 (Philips). Liszt *Mefisto* Waltz and other piano pieces (Philips).

CHRISTOPH VON DOHNANYI

(pronounced: duff-*nyahn*-yee)

Conductor. Born September 8, 1929, in Berlin, Germany. Studied at Munich's Hochschule für Musik; won Richard Strauss Prize for conducting and composition. Also studied with grandfather, Hungarian-born composer Erno von Dohnanyi, at Florida State University in late 1940s. Conductor, Frankfurt

Opera, 1952–57. Music director, Lübeck Opera, 1957–63; Cologne Radio Symphony, 1964–70; Frankfurt Opera, 1968–77. Principal conductor, Hamburg State Opera, 1977–84. Music director, Cleveland Orchestra, since 1984. An outstanding interpreter of the standard Classical and Romantic repertory. Married to the soprano Anya Silja.

RECOMMENDED RECORDINGS Dvořák Symphony No. 8 (London). Brahms Symphony No. 1 (Teldec).

PLACIDO DOMINGO

(pronounced: doh-*ming*-go)

Tenor and conductor. Born January 21, 1941, in Madrid, Spain. Raised and educated in Mexico City, where his parents were *zarzuela* (operetta) singers. Made his operatic debut in Mexico City in 1961, then spent several years with Tel Aviv Opera in Israel. Became an overnight star at 25 when he sang the title role in the premiere of Ginastera's *Don Rodrigo* at the New York City Opera in 1966. Joined the Metropolitan Opera in 1968, and has since become one of the most popular tenors in both Europe and the U.S., noted for his ringingly strong, expressive singing in a wide range of roles. Since the mid-1970s has also conducted opera performances and recordings.

RECOMMENDED RECORDINGS *Bravissimo Domingo!* Vols. 1 & 2 (RCA). Verdi *Otello* (RCA, 2-disc set).

JACQUELINE DU PRÉ

(pronounced: du *pray*)

Cellist. Born January 26, 1945, in Oxford, England. Died October 19, 1987, in London. Began musical studies at an early age, and made recital debut at age 7. As a teenager, studied in Paris with Paul Tortelier, then in Moscow with Rostropovich. At 15, won Queen's Prize for British Instrumentalists. U.S. debut in 1965, with touring BBC Symphony Orchestra. Won wide acclaim as one of the outstanding cellists of our time, particularly noted for her intensity, soaring tone, and big melodic line. In 1973, she was forced to withdraw from performing because of multiple sclerosis. Was married to pianist-conductor Daniel Barenboim from 1967 to her death.

RECOMMENDED RECORDINGS Haydn Concerto for Cello and Orchestra in D (Angel). Elgar Concerto for Cello and Orchestra (Angel).

CHARLES DUTOIT

(pronounced: doo-*twah*)

Conductor. Born October 7, 1936, in Lausanne, Switzerland. Studied at Lausanne Conservatory; Academy of Music, Geneva; Accademia Musicale, Siena; Beneditti Marcello Conservatory, Venice. Always cites Swiss conductor Ernest Ansermet as his mentor, but never a teacher. Conducting debut with Bern Symphony, 1963. Principal conductor and artistic director, Zurich Radio Orchestra, 1967–75. Principal conductor, Göteborg (Sweden) Symphony, 1975–77. Music director, Montreal Symphony, since 1977; and Orchestre National de la Radio-Television Française (Paris) since 1991. Principal conductor, Philadelphia Orchestra at Saratoga Festival. Principal conductor, Tokyo NHK Radio Symphony Orchestra, effective 1996. A master orchestral colorist and a lively, incisive interpreter of a wide repertory.

RECOMMENDED RECORDINGS Saint-Saens Symphony No. 3 (London). Mussorgsky-Ravel *Pictures at an Exhibition* (London).

PHILIPPE ENTREMONT

(pronounced: *ahn*-tray-mont)

Pianist and conductor. Born June 7, 1934, in Rheims, France. Studied at Paris Conservatory. In 1953, won Marguerite Long-Jacques Thibaud Competition. That same year, made U.S. debut. His tall, handsome appearance, combined with a crisply impressive piano technique, made him something of a "matinee idol" among concert-goers ever since. In 1970, made his debut as a conductor in London. Principal conductor, New Orleans Philharmonic, 1981–84.

RECOMMENDED RECORDINGS Satie Piano Music (CBS). Khachaturian Piano Concerto and Liszt Hungarian Fantasy (CBS).

CHRISTOPH ESCHENBACH

(pronounced: *eh*-shehn-bohkh)

Pianist and conductor. Born February 20, 1940, in Breslau, Silesia, then part of Germany. Earliest years were marked by a series of family tragedies and serious illness in the upheavals of World War II. After the war, studied both piano and conducting in Hamburg and Cologne, winning prizes in several German and European piano competitions before age 17. In the 1960s, became one of the most acclaimed of the younger generation of European pianists, performing frequently in Europe with Karajan and in U.S. with Szell. As a pianist, has been primarily identified with the music of Mozart and Beethoven, and is noted for unusually sensitive, deeply poetic interpretations. Turned increasingly to conducting in 1970s, including performances at New York's Mostly Mozart Festival. Music director of the Zurich Tonhalle Orchestra, 1982–86, and of Houston Symphony, effective 1989.

RECOMMENDED RECORDINGS   As a pianist, Schumann *Kinderscenen* and *Waldscenen* (Deutsche Grammophon). As pianist and conductor, Mozart Concerto in E flat for Two Pianos and Orchestra, with Justus Frantz (Deutsche Grammophon).

RUDOLF FIRKUSNY

(pronounced: feer-*kuhsh*-nee)

Pianist. Born February 11, 1912, in Napajedla, Czechoslovakia. Studied at Brno and Prague conservatories. Debut with Czech Philharmonic in 1922 at age 20. Active recitalist in Europe in 1920s and '30s, then settled in U.S. Resumed worldwide tours after World War II, with U.S. as home base. A much-respected, discerning pianist, best-known for his Mozart, Beethoven, and Czech composers Janáček and Martinů.

RECOMMENDED RECORDINGS   Dvořák Piano Concerto (Vox/Turnabout). Beethoven Sonata No. 8 (London).

DIETRICH FISCHER-DIESKAU

(pronounced: *fihsh*-er *dees*-kow)

Baritone. Born May 28, 1925, in Berlin. Drafted into the German Army at age 16. Later captured by the Americans on the Italian front, and spent the next two years in a prisoner-of-war camp in Italy. When a copy of Schubert's song cycle *Die Schöne Müllerin* was found in the camp, he studied it and gave his first public recital for fellow prisoners. In 1948, became a principal baritone with the Berlin State Opera, and that same year made his debut as a *lieder* singer in Leipzig. U.S. debut, 1955, with Cincinnati Symphony. Although he divides his time between opera and concert appearances, and in 1973 made his debut as a conductor, he is now regarded primarily as a *lieder* singer — the greatest of our time. He is also probably the most widely recorded singer in history. He is especially noted for his mastery of tone color and phrasing.

RECOMMENDED RECORDINGS Schubert *Winterreise*, with Brendel (Philips). Mahler *Songs of a Wayfarer* and *Songs from Ruckert* (Deutsche Grammophon).

KIRSTEN FLAGSTAD

(pronounced: *flahg-stahd*)

Soprano. Born July 12, 1895, in Oslo, Norway. Died December 7, 1962, in Oslo. Studied singing with her mother, an operatic coach. Made her debut at the Oslo Opera in a minor role in 1913. For several years, appeared in operettas and musical comedies in Norway. After joining Göteborg Opera, decided to concentrate on opera. In 1929 she retired following her marriage to a wealthy industrialist, but in 1933 accepted an invitation to sing a minor role at Bayreuth. Her Bayreuth performances led to an audition with the Metropolitan Opera in New York, and she made a sensationally acclaimed debut there in 1935 (as Sieglinde in *Die Walküre*). Over the next few years, repeated her American triumph in London, Paris, Vienna, and Prague, and was widely hailed as the greatest Wagnerian singer of her time. In 1941 she left the U.S. to return to Norway, then occupied by the Nazis, and retired from performing until after World War II. Controversy over her wartime behavior continued for many years, and she made only occasional U.S. appearances after 1949 before her formal retirement in 1955.

RECOMMENDED RECORDINGS Wagner *Tristan und Isolde*, highlights (Seraphim). *The Great Voice of Flagstad* (London).

LEON FLEISHER

(pronounced: *fly-sher*)

Pianist and conductor. Born July 23, 1928, in San Francisco. Made recital debut as a pianist at age 7 in San Francisco, and at 10 was accepted as a pupil by Artur Schnabel. In 1952, won the Queen Elisabeth of Belgium Competition. His busy and successful career was interrupted in the mid-1960s by an ailment affecting his right hand, although he has performed occasionally as soloist in concertos for the left hand alone in recent years. He also began appearing as a conductor in the early 1970s. Since the mid-'80s, a director of the Tanglewood Music Center in Massachusetts.

RECOMMENDED RECORDINGS Beethoven Five Piano Concertos, complete (CBS, 3-D or 4-LP set). Britten *Diversions for Piano Left Hand* (Desto). Ravel Concerto for Left Hand Alone (Sony).

LUKAS FOSS

Conductor, pianist, composer. Born August 15, 1922, in Berlin, Germany. Studied at the Curtis Institute, Philadelphia; also at Tanglewood with Koussevitzky, and Yale with Hindemith. Won a Pulitzer scholarship at age 19. Official pianist of the Boston Symphony, 1944–50. Music director, Buffalo Philharmonic, 1963–80; Milwaukee Symphony, 1981–87; Brooklyn Philharmonic, 1971–1990. Most renowned for his performances of contemporary music.

RECOMMENDED RECORDINGS Irving Fine *Notturno for String Orchestra* (CRI). Schuman *Newsreel*, Copland *Shaker Variations*, Bernstein *Candide* Overture (Pro Arte). Foss *Baroque Variations* (Vox/Turnabout).

MALCOLM FRAGER

(pronounced: *fray*-gher)

Pianist. Born January 15, 1935, in St. Louis, Missouri. Made his recital debut in St. Louis at age 6, and appeared as a soloist with the St. Louis Symphony at 10. Attended Columbia University, 1953–57, majoring in languages and graduating Phi Beta Kappa. Won the Geneva International Competition in 1955, the Leventritt Award in 1959, and the Queen Elisabeth of Belgium Competition in 1960. In subsequent years performed extensively throughout the United States and Europe. Particularly noted for his clean-lined, always tasteful performances of Classical and Neo-Classical works. Died June 20, 1991, in Pittsfield, Massachusetts.

RECOMMENDED RECORDINGS Piano Music of McDowell, Paine, Gilbert, Nevin, others (New World). Prokofiev Piano Concerto No. 2 (RCA Victrola). Weber Piano Concertos Nos. 1 and 2 (RCA, 1977, withdrawn).

RAFAEL FRÜHBECK DE BURGOS

(pronounced: *froo*-beck deh *boor*-gohss)

Conductor. Born September 15, 1933, in Burgos, Spain, Of mixed German and Spanish parentage. Added "de Burgos" to his professional name in the

1960s in order to stress his Spanish upbringing. Started as a child prodigy on the violin and changed to conducting while studying at the Madrid Conservatory. Became conductor of Bilbao Municipal Orchestra in 1959, and the Orquesta Nacional de España (Spanish National Orchestra) in Madrid in 1962—the youngest conductor in its history. Noted internationally for his conducting of Spanish music and 20th-century works with a strong rhythmic pulse.

RECOMMENDED RECORDINGS   Falla *The Three-Cornered Hat* (Angel). Orff *Carmina Burana* (Angel).

WILHELM FURTWANGLER

(pronounced: *foort*-veng-gler)

Conductor. Born January 25, 1886, in Berlin, Germany. Died November 30, 1954, in Eberstein. After success as a conductor in Berlin, Vienna, and Leipzig, made a highly acclaimed U.S. debut with the New York Philharmonic in 1925. In 1936, he was nominated by the Philharmonic to succeed Toscanini as music director; but a public uproar ensued because of his position with the Berlin Philharmonic in Nazi Germany, and the nomination was withdrawn. He continued as head of the Berlin Philharmonic throughout World War II, despite several confrontations with Nazi officials which forced him into "leaves of absence" on two occasions. In 1947 he was officially cleared by Allied investigators of charges of Nazi collaboration, and again became conductor of the Berlin Philharmonic. He and the orchestra were preparing for their first U.S. tour in 1954 when he died. One of the conducting giants of the century, he was a highly individualistic, often profound interpreter of the Classical and Romantic repertory, particularly noted for the unique elasticity of his interpretations.

RECOMMENDED RECORDINGS   Furtwangler Conducts Wagner (Seraphim). Beethoven Symphony No. 9 (Seraphim).

JAMES GALWAY

Flutist and conductor. Born December 8, 1939, in Belfast, Northern Ireland. Studied at Royal College of Music and Guildhall School of Music and Drama, London; also at Paris Conservatory with Jean-Pierre Rampal. Flutist in London Symphony and Royal Philharmonic, London, in late '60s. Principal flutist, Berlin Philharmonic, 1969–75. Began full-time solo career in 1976, and quickly became one of the most popular concert performers in the world.

Renowned for his fluent instrumental technique and lively approach to the classical flute repertory.

RECOMMENDED RECORDINGS Mozart Flute Concertos Nos. 1 & 2 (RCA). *The Man With the Golden Flute* (RCA).

VALERY GERGIEV

(pronounced: *ghehr*-ghee-yev)

Conductor. Born May 2, 1953, in Moscow. Studied at Leningrad Conservatory. Won top prize in Karajan Competition in Berlin in 1976, and made his debut at Kirov Opera a year later. In 1988 became artistic director of the Kirov. Since 1991 he has guest-conducted the Boston Symphony, Chicago Symphony, New York Philharmonic, and Metropolitan Opera to considerable acclaim as an unusually dynamic, exciting conductor.

RECOMMENDED RECORDINGS Prokofiev *Romeo and Juliet* and *War and Peace* (Philips). Borodin *Polovetsian Dances* plus miscellaneous short works collected under the title *White Nights* (Philips).

CARLO MARIA GIULINI

(pronounced: joo-*lee*-nee)

Conductor. Born May 9, 1914, in Barletta, Italy. Studied at Rome's Santa Cecilia Academy, and made his debut as a conductor in Rome in 1944. Became a conductor of the Orchestra of Radio Milan in 1951, and principal conductor at Milan's La Scala Opera in 1953. Following his debut at the Edinburgh Festival (Scotland) in 1955, his international reputation grew rapidly as a sensitive, lyrical conductor of Mozart and the early Romantics. Principal guest conductor of the Chicago Symphony, 1969–1978. Principal conductor, Vienna Symphony Orchestra, 1973–78. Music director, Los Angeles Philharmonic, 1979–84.

RECOMMENDED RECORDINGS Berlioz *Romeo et Juliet,* orchestral excerpts (Angel). Bruckner Symphony No. 8 (Deutsche Grammophon).

GLENN GOULD

Pianist. Born September 25, 1932, in Toronto, Canada. Died October 4, 1982, in Toronto. Studied at Toronto's Royal Academy of Music (1943–52). U.S.

recital debut 1955. A year later, won wide acclaim for a recording of Bach's *Goldberg Variations* and was launched on international career. In late 1960s, announced he would no longer tour, preferring to restrict his playing primarily to recordings. Regarded as a highly individualistic, sometimes eccentric, but most frequently a sensitive and rhythmically animated performer.

RECOMMENDED RECORDINGS Bach *Goldberg Variations* (CBS, either 1955 mono or 1981 stereo version). Brahms Ballades (CBS).

GARY GRAFFMAN

Pianist. Born October 14, 1928, in New York City. Studied at Curtis Institute in Philadelphia (1936–46) and Columbia University. Won the Rachmaninoff Fund Special Award in 1948 and the Leventritt Award in 1948. In the 1960s, played a major role in organizing prominent concert artists to agree to perform only to nonsegregated audiences in the South. In 1970s, an ailment affecting his right hand interrupted his active performing career, but he has continued to appear occasionally in repertory for left hand alone.

RECOMMENDED RECORDINGS Tchaikovsky Piano Concertos Nos. 1, 2, & 3 (CBS). Prokofiev Piano Concertos Nos. 1 & 3 (CBS).

BERNARD HAITINK

(pronounced: *hy*-tink)

Conductor. Born March 4, 1929, in Amsterdam, the Netherlands. Originally a violinist, then a conductor of Netherlands Radio Philharmonic in 1950s. In 1956, took over on short notice when Carlo Maria Giulini was unable to conduct an Amsterdam concert — and subsequent acclaim led to many other appearances, culminating in appointment as Amsterdam Concertgebouw's music director in 1961. Held post to 1987. Also principal conductor of the London Philharmonic, 1967–79. Music director, Glyndebourne Festival, 1978–88. Music director, Royal Opera at Covent Garden, London, 1987–1990. Particularly noted for performances of Mahler and Bruckner. One of the finest all-around conductors of Europe's present "middle generation."

RECOMMENDED RECORDINGS Mahler Symphony No. 4 (Philips). Bruckner Symphony No. 4 (Philips). Shostakovich Symphony No. 15 (London). Vaughan Williams Symphony No. 2 (Angel).

LYNN HARRELL

(pronounced: *har*-rell)

Cellist. Born January 30, 1944, in New York City. Son of late Metropolitan Opera baritone Mack Harrell. Studied at Juilliard School in New York, Curtis Institute in Philadelphia. Principal cellist of Cleveland Orchestra, 1965–71. Co-recipient (with pianist Murray Perahia) of first Avery Fisher Prize, 1975. Artistic Director, Los Angeles Philharmonic Institute, since 1988. Renowned for his warm, broad sound and uncommon sensitivity in both orchestral and chamber works.

RECOMMENDED RECORDINGS Dvořák Cello Concerto (London). Strauss *Don Quixote* (London).

JASCHA HEIFETZ

(pronounced: *hy*-fehts)

Violinist. Born February 2, 1901, in Vilna, Russia. Died December 10, 1987, in Los Angeles. Started playing the violin at age three, entered Royal Music School at Vilna at five, graduating at nine. Later studied at St. Petersburg with Leopold Auer. U.S. debut in 1917. Quickly became one of the most widely acclaimed violinists on the concert stage. After the Russian Revolution, settled permanently in the U.S., becoming an American citizen in 1925. Acted and played in a 1938 Hollywood movie, *They Shall Have Music*, and a frequent radio performer during 1940s. Retired from active concertizing in the early 1960s. One of the century's great violin virtuosos, and considered by most critics to be the personification of impeccable technique combined with impeccable musical taste.

RECOMMENDED RECORDINGS Brahms Violin Concerto (RCA). Sibelius Violin Concerto (RCA).

MARILYN HORNE

Mezzo soprano. Born January 16, 1934, in Bradford, Pennsylvania. Studied at University of Southern California on a voice scholarship. Took part in many Los Angeles radio broadcasts and recorded with Igor Stravinsky, Robert Craft, and the Roger Wagner Chorale, as well as dubbing her voice for Dorothy Dandridge in the title role of the film *Carmen Jones*. In 1957, went to Europe for further study, returning in 1960 to score a triumph with San Francisco Opera (as Marie in Berg's *Wozzeck*). Debut at Milan's La Scala, 1969; at New York's Metropolitan, 1970. Formerly married to conductor Henry Lewis. Admired not only for sumptuousness of her voice, but also for varied range of her performances, including Baroque, *bel canto*, Wagnerian opera, and contemporary music.

RECOMMENDED RECORDINGS *Rossini Arias* (London). *The Great Voice of Marilyn Horne* (London).

VLADIMIR HOROWITZ

(pronounced: *hoh-roh-witz*)

Pianist. Born October 1, 1904, in Kiev, Russia. Died November 5, 1989, in New York City. Made his debut in Russia in 1921, Europe in 1925, the U.S. in 1928. Quickly established himself as a pianist of fantastic virtuosity, with a Romantic flair that made him one of the most acclaimed concert stars of the 1930s and 1940s. Settled in the U.S. and married daughter of Arturo Toscanini. From 1953 to 1965, and again from 1968 to 1971, gave up public performing, partly for health reasons, but continued to make recordings, including one just four days before his death. One of the musical giants of the century.

RECOMMENDED RECORDINGS Horowitz in Concert (CBS, 2-disc set). *Horowitz at the Met, 1981—Scarlatti, Liszt, Chopin, Rachmaninoff* (RCA).

PAUL JACOBS

Pianist. Born June 22, 1930, in New York City. Died September 25, 1983, in New York City. Studied privately with Ernest Hutcheson. From 1951–60, performed primarily in Europe, including unprecedented Paris recital cycle of complete piano works of Schoenberg. Official pianist of New York Philharmonic, 1962–1983. Career cut short by AIDS.

RECOMMENDED RECORDINGS Debussy Etudes (Nonesuch). Works by Bartók, Stravinsky, Messiaen, Busoni (Nonesuch).

BYRON JANIS

Pianist. Born March 24, 1928, in McKeesport, Pennsylvania. Studied in the 1940s with Vladimir Horowitz, who had never previously accepted a pupil.

Made debut with Pittsburgh Symphony in 1944, and New York recital debut in 1948. In 1960, made a much-acclaimed tour of Soviet Union, and in 1962 was first American pianist to record Russian works with a Russian orchestra and an American engineering team. Active career cut short by health problems in 1970s. An intense, virtuoso pianist, most noted for late Romantic and early 20th-century works.

RECOMMENDED RECORDINGS   Rachmaninoff Piano Concerto No. 1 and Strauss *Burleske* (RCA). Rachmaninoff Piano Concerto No. 3 (Philips).

NEEME JARVI

(pronounced: *yehr*-vee)

Born June 7, 1937, in Tallinn, Estonia. Studied at the Tallinn Music School and the Leningrad State Conservatory. In 1963 became chief conductor of the Estonian Radio and Television Orchestra, and later of Opera Theater Estonia. In 1977 he was one of the conductors of the Leningrad Philharmonic on its American tour. He left the Soviet Union in 1980, became a US resident, and was soon guest-conducting major U.S. and European orchestras. In 1982 became principal conductor of Göteborg (Sweden) Symphony and in 1984 Scottish National Orchestra. Since 1990, music director of the Detroit Symphony. A dynamic, robust, often colorful conductor of Romantic and Neo-Classical works, and one of the most-recorded conductors of recent years.

RECOMMENDED RECORDINGS   Scriabin *Poem of Ecstasy* (Chandos). Martinů Symphonies Nos. 1 to 6 (BIS). Shostakovich Symphony No. 7 (Chandos).

HERBERT VON KARAJAN

(pronounced: *kah*-rah-yahn)

Conductor. Born April 5, 1908, in Salzburg, Austria. Died July 15, 1989, in Anif, Austria. First conducted in Salzburg at age 20, then held minor posts in Germany in early 1930s. Joined the Nazi party in 1933, and by 1937 was director of the Berlin State Opera's symphony concerts. In 1942, fell into disfavor with key Nazi authorities, partly because he married (second wife) a woman whose family was part-Jewish. Lived in Italy and Austria 1944–45. After end of World War II, Allied denazification officials barred him from conducting until 1948. In 1954, became conductor of London's Philharmonia Orchestra, and in 1956 music director "for life" of Berlin Philharmonic.

Quickly established himself as one of Europe's most popular and critically acclaimed conductors, noted especially for vibrant, tonally sleek, rhythmically supple performances of German classics. Director of Salzburg Festival, 1956–1989; music director, Vienna State Opera, 1956–64; chief conductor of Orchestre de Paris, 1969–70.

RECOMMENDED RECORDINGS   Beethoven Symphony No. 3 ("Eroica") (Deutsche Grammophon). Tchaikovsky Symphony No. 4 (Deutsche Grammophon). Bruckner Symphony No. 8 (Deutsche Grammophon).

DOROTHY KIRSTEN

(pronounced: *keer*-stehn)

Soprano. Born July 6, 1910, in Montclair, New Jersey. To pay way through Juilliard School in New York, worked as a telephone operator, then as a radio singer. Film star and Metropolitan Opera soprano Grace Moore heard one of her broadcasts, and sponsored further studies for her in Italy. Returned to U.S. to sing with the Chicago Opera, the New York City Opera, and after 1945 the Metropolitan Opera. For the next three decades, remained one of the Met's most popular stars, best known for warmly expressive Puccini heroines (*Madame Butterfly, Tosca, Manon Lescaut, The Girl of the Golden West*). Died November 18, 1992, in Los Angeles.

RECOMMENDED RECORDINGS   *Dorothy Kirsten—By Popular Demand* (CBS Odyssey, *mono only*). *Dorothy Kirsten in Opera and Song* (RCA Victrola, *mono only*).

CARLOS KLEIBER

(pronounced: *kly*-ber)

Conductor. Born July 3, 1930, in Berlin, Germany. Son of conductor Erich Kleiber. Studied in Buenos Aires during 1940s. Conductor at Deutsche Oper am Rhein, Düsseldorf, West Germany, 1956–64; then at Zurich Opera, Switzerland, 1964–66; and at Bavarian State Opera, Munich, since 1968. U.S. debut at San Francisco Opera, 1977. Regarded as one of his generation's outstanding conductors, but has limited his U.S. appearances because of disagreements about time needed for rehearsals.

RECOMMENDED RECORDINGS   Beethoven Symphony No. 5 (Deutsche Grammophon). Brahms Symphony No. 4 (Deutsche Grammophon).

ERICH KLEIBER

(pronounced: *kly*-ber)

Conductor. Born August 5, 1890, in Vienna, Austria. Died January 27, 1956, in Zurich. From 1923 to 1935, one of Berlin's leading symphony and opera conductors. Spent one year (1930–31) as principal guest conductor of the New York Philharmonic, including conducting its first coast-to-coast radio broadcast. In 1935, left Germany, settling first in Salzburg, then Milan, then Buenos Aires. Frequently appeared as a guest conductor in U.S. during World War II. After the war, often conducted Amsterdam Concertgebouw. In 1955, named music director of the (East) Berlin State Opera, but resigned later that same year charging government interference. Died suddenly of a heart attack a few months later. Best known for exciting and highly dramatic performances of Beethoven, Mozart, and Richard Strauss.

RECOMMENDED RECORDINGS Beethoven Symphony No.3 (London, *mono*). Beethoven Symphony No. 5 (London, *mono*).

OTTO KLEMPERER

(pronounced: *klehm*-per-er)

Conductor. Born May 15, 1885, in Breslau, Germany. Died July 7, 1973, in Zurich, Switzerland. Became a conductor of Prague Opera in 1907 at Mahler's recommendation. Later held posts at Cologne Opera (1917–24), Wiesbaden (1924–27), and Berlin State Opera (1927–33). For several years in the mid-1930s, conductor of Los Angeles Philharmonic, and from 1947 to 1950 of the Budapest Opera. A series of debilitating accidents and illnesses plagued his life, and he was partially paralyzed after the 1950s. From 1964 until his death, principal conductor of New Philharmonia Orchestra of London. Highly regarded as an eloquent, penetrating interpreter of Classical and Romantic repertory, although he leaned toward slow, sometimes ponderous tempos that divided many critics.

RECOMMENDED RECORDINGS Brahms *A German Requiem*, with Schwarzkopf, Fischer-Dieskau (Angel, 2-disc set). Bruckner Symphony No. 7 (Angel).

ZOLTAN KOCSIS

(pronounced: *coach*-sees)

Pianist. Born May 30, 1952, in Budapest, Hungary. Studied at Budapest Conservatory. Won a pair of prestigious competitions in Hungary in early 1970s, and began international career several years later. Together with conductor Ivan Fischer, founded Budapest Festival Orchestra in early 1980s. Particularly renowned for his complete survey of Bartók's works, but also as an outstanding interpreter of a broad repertory from Baroque to contemporary.

RECOMMENDED RECORDINGS Bartók Piano Concertos Nos. 1 & 2 (Hungaroton). Wagner Transcriptions from *Tristan and Isolde, Lohengrin, Parsifal*, etc. (Philips).

KIRIL KONDRASHIN

(pronounced: Kon-*drahsh*-een)

Conductor. Born May 5, 1914, in Moscow, Russia. Died March 7, 1981, in Amsterdam, The Netherlands. During late 1930s, an opera conductor in Leningrad, then between 1943 and 1956 principal conductor of the Bolshoi Ballet in Moscow. Chief conductor of Moscow Philharmonic, 1960–74. When Van Cliburn won first International Tchaikovsky Piano Competition in Moscow in 1958, Kondrashin conducted the orchestra and then, at Cliburn's request, conducted the pianist's homecoming concert in New York's Carnegie Hall. Left Soviet Union permanently in 1978, became principal guest-conductor of Amsterdam Concertgebouw. Most admired for his colorful, dramatic performances of Tchaikovsky, Rachmaninoff, and Shostakovich.

RECOMMENDED RECORDINGS Shostakovich Symphonies Nos. 5, 6 & 9 (Philips). Rimsky-Korsakov *Scheherezade* (Philips).

SERGE KOUSSEVITZKY

(pronounced: koo-seh-*vits*-kee)

Conductor. Born July 26, 1874, in Iver, Russia. Died June 4, 1951, in Boston, Massachusetts. Began career as double bass player, and for a long time was considered the world's finest. In 1905, settled in Berlin to study conducting with Nikisch. By 1907, had his own orchestra in Russia—a wedding present from his bride's father, one of Russia's wealthiest merchants. After Russian

Revolution in 1917, his orchestra was disbanded. Became director of Russian State Symphony. In 1920, discouraged by conditions in Soviet Union, left and went to Paris, where he directed Concerts Koussevitzky for several years. From 1924 to 1949, conductor of Boston Symphony Orchestra, rebuilding it into one of the world's great orchestras and founding its summer festival and school at Tanglewood. Through the Koussevitzky Foundation, also established funds for commissioning hundreds of new works. One of the century's great musicians; noted for taut, dramatic, often electric performances of Russian and French music of late 19th and early 20th centuries.

RECOMMENDED RECORDINGS   Sibelius Symphony No. 2 (RCA, *mono*). Harris Symphony No. 3 (CBS, CSP series)

GIDON KREMER

(pronounced: *kray-mir*)

Violinist. Born February 27, 1947, in Riga, Latvia. Studied at Riga School of Music, then at Moscow Conservatory with David Oistrakh. Won first prize in Queen Elisabeth of Belgium Competition, Brussels, 1967, and first prize in Fourth International Tchaikovsky Competition, Moscow, 1970. Since 1980, has lived primarily in the West, maintaining studios in Lucerne, Switzerland, and New York. Founded Lockenhaus Chamber Music Festival in Austria in 1982 to promote new and neglected chamber works. One of his generation's most adventurous and technically outstanding violinists.

RECOMMENDED RECORDINGS   Sibelius Violin Concerto (Angel). Berg Violin Concerto (Philips).

RAFAEL KUBELIK

(pronounced: *koo-beh-lick*)

Conductor, composer. Born June 29, 1914, in Bychory, Czechoslovakia. Son of violinist Jan Kubelik. Accompanist on his father's U.S. tours, 1934 to 1936. Became acting conductor of Czech Philharmonic in Prague in 1936, then first conductor of Brno Philharmonic, 1939. During World War II, principal conductor of Czech Philharmonic, but was in and out of difficulty for his refusal to cooperate with officials of the Nazi occupation. Left Czechoslovakia when Communists took over in 1948. Was music director of Chicago Symphony Orchestra (1950–53), of Covent Garden Opera in London (1955–58), and of Bavarian Radio Orchestra in Munich, Germany, 1961–1986. In

1973, became music director of Metropolitan Opera in New York, but resigned in 1974 after a series of controversies. Best known for refined, somewhat restrained performances of the late Romantics, especially Dvořák, Smetana, and Mahler.

RECOMMENDED RECORDINGS Smetana *Ma Vlast* (My Country), including *The Moldau* (Deutsche Grammophon, 2-disc set). Dvořák Slavonic Dances (Deutsche Grammophon).

RUTH LAREDO
(pronounced: lah-*ray*-doh)

Pianist. Born November 20, 1939, in Detroit, Michigan. Studied with Rudolf Serkin and Mieczyslaw Horszowski at Curtis Institute. Closely associated with Marlboro Festival in Vermont for many years, and toured Europe and the Middle East with the "Music from Marlboro" concerts. A vibrant, clean-lined, subtly detailed pianist, most noted for her interpretations of Ravel, Scriabin, and Rachmaninoff.

RECOMMENDED RECORDINGS Scriabin Preludes (Desto). Barber Sonata, *Souvenirs, Nocturne* (Nonesuch).

ERICH LEINSDORF
(pronounced: *lynss*-dorf)

Conductor. Born February 4, 1912, in Vienna, Austria. Assistant to Arturo Toscanini and Bruno Walter at Salzburg Festival (1934–37). Came to U.S. in 1937, settling permanently and becoming a U.S. citizen in 1942. Chief conductor of Wagnerian opera at Metropolitan Opera (1937–42), then conductor of Cleveland Orchestra (1943–44) until drafted into U.S. Army during World War II. Music director of Rochester Philharmonic (1947–56) and Boston Symphony (1962–69), as well as conducting at both New York City Opera and Metropolitan Opera. An intelligent, perceptive, always tasteful but sometimes emotionally restrained conductor, at his best with Wagner, most German classics. Died September 11, 1993, in Zurich, Switzerland.

RECOMMENDED RECORDINGS Strauss *Death and Transfiguration* and Wagner *Tristan and Isolde* Prelude & Liebestod (Angel/Seraphim). Prokofiev Symphony No. 5 (RCA).

RAYMOND LEPPARD

(pronounced: *leh*-pard)

Conductor, harpsichordist. Born August 11, 1927, in London, England. Studied at Trinity College, Cambridge. Began career as a harpsichord soloist. In 1952, formed Leppard Ensemble, which became famous throughout England for performances of Baroque music. During 1960s, his researches into music by Monteverdi, J.C. Bach, Cavalli, and others resulted in more authentic "performing editions" at Glyndebourne Festivals and elsewhere. Music director, English Chamber Orchestra, 1959–1970. Principal conductor, BBC Northern Symphony, Manchester, 1972–1980. Official resident of U.S. since 1976, now a U.S. citizen. Principal guest-conductor, Saint Louis Symphony Orchestra, 1984–88. Music director, Indianapolis Symphony, since 1987.

RECOMMENDED RECORDINGS   Handel *Royal Fireworks Music* (Philips). Haydn and Mozart Trumpet Concertos, with Wynton Marsalis (CBS).

YOEL LEVI

(pronounced *leh*-vee)

Conductor. Born August 16, 1950, Satu Mare, Rumania. One month later moved with his family to Israel. Studied at Tel Aviv and Jerusalem academies, then played violin in Israel Philharmonic for a year before further music studies in Siena, Rome, and London. Assistant conductor, then Resident Conductor, Cleveland Orchestra, 1981–87. Music director, Atlanta Symphony, since 1988. An exceptionally clean-lined, insightful interpreter of a wide repertory.

RECOMMENDED RECORDINGS   Prokofiev Symphonies No. 1 & 5; Hindemith *Mathis der Maler* Symphony.

JAMES LEVINE

Conductor and pianist. Born June 2, 1943, in Cincinnati, Ohio. Made debut at age 10 as pianist with Cincinnati Symphony. At Juilliard, studied piano with Rosina Lhevinne and conducting with Jean Morel, completing his undergraduate requirements in an unprecedented one year. Following year (1964), was chosen for Ford Foundation's American Conductors Project. Among the judges was George Szell, who invited him to become an assistant conductor of Cleveland Orchestra. Remained in that post for six years. In 1970, made a much-praised debut as a conductor with the Metropolitan Opera, and also appeared as a guest conductor of major U.S. and European orchestras. In 1972, chosen principal conductor of the Met; music director since 1974. Also music director, Cincinnati May Festival, 1973–77; Ravinia Festival summer concerts of Chicago Symphony since 1973. A uniquely brilliant, often exciting conductor, at his best in 19th-century repertory.

RECOMMENDED RECORDINGS Verdi *Otello*, with Domingo, Scotto, Milnes (RCA). Mahler Symphony No. 4, with Blegen (RCA).

ANDREW LITTON

(pronounced: *lit*-ton)

Conductor and pianist. Born May 16, 1959, in New York City. Studied at Juilliard, then at Mozarteum in Salzburg. Served as an assistant conductor for a season at Milan's Teatro alla Scala. Top prize-winner in 1979 Kapell Memorial Piano Competition, and in 1981 was youngest (and first American) winner of BBC/Rupert Foundation International Conductors Competition. In 1982 became assistant conductor to Rostropovich at National Symphony in Washington, then associate conductor. In 1986 he was named principal guest-conductor of England's Bournemouth Symphony, then principal conductor. Became music director of Dallas Symphony in 1994. One of his generation's most dynamic young conductors, widely praised for insightful, rhythmically crisp performances of late-Romantic and 20th-century works.

RECOMMENDED RECORDINGS Gershwin Concerto in F (Virgin Classics) and *Who Cares?* ballet (RPO/MCA). Bernstein *Age of Anxiety* and *Fancy Free* (Virgin Classics). Rachmaninoff Symphonies Nos. 1, 2, 3 (Virgin).

DINU LIPATTI

(pronounced: lee-*pah*-tee)

Pianist. Born March 19, 1917, in Bucharest, Rumania. Died December 2, 1950, in Geneva, Switzerland. Began giving concerts at age 5, and won prize in an international competition in Vienna at 17. Performed only in Switzerland during World War II. In 1946 he was preparing for a U.S. tour when it was discovered he had leukemia. Igor Stravinsky, Charles Munch, and Yehudi Menuhin contributed large amounts of money for expensive cortisone treatments, but he died in 1950 at age 33. The recordings he made in the late 1940s have confirmed his reputation as one of the century's great pianists—a subtle tone colorist, rhythmically vibrant, and with an unequaled evenness of sound.

RECOMMENDED RECORDINGS Chopin Waltzes (CBS/Odyssey, *mono only*). Schumann and Grieg Piano Concertos (CBS/Odyssey, *mono*).

LOUIS LORTIE

(pronounced: *lor-tee*)

Pianist. Born in 1959 in Montreal, Canada. At 16, took first prize in both the Canadian National and CBC Radio competitions. In 1984 he won first prize in the prestigious Busoni International Competition in Italy; followed by concert tours throughout Europe. An uncommonly cleanlined, reflectively poetic interpreter of Ravel, Chopin, Liszt, and Mozart.

RECOMMENDED RECORDINGS   Ravel Piano Music Vols. 1 & 2 (Chandos). Chopin Complete Etudes (Chandos). Mozart Piano Concertos Nos. 12 & 14 (Chandos).

YO-YO MA

Cellist. Born October 7, 1955, in Paris, France, of Chinese parents. Began cello studies at age 4 with father; gave first public recital at age 5. Studied at Juilliard School in New York and at Harvard. Won Avery Fisher Prize, 1978. Has risen rapidly to front rank of cellists, with outstanding technique and a singing tone. Also active in chamber recitals with pianist Emanuel Ax and violinists Young-Uck Kim and Gidon Kremer.

RECOMMENDED RECORDINGS   Haydn Cello Concertos Nos. 1 & 2 (CBS). Shostakovich and Kabalevsky Cello Concertos (CBS).

LORIN MAAZEL

(pronounced: *mah-zehl*)

Conductor and violinist. Born March 6, 1930, in Neuilly, France, of American parents. Raised in the U.S. Became a child prodigy on violin and as a conductor. Conducted at New York World's Fair in 1939 and then Toscanini's NBC Symphony in 1941. As he approached his teens, he was (in his own words) "dropped flat as soon as I lost my market value as a monstrosity." At 15, joined Pittsburgh Symphony as a violinist while studying philosophy and languages at University of Pittsburgh. In the 1950s, became a radio conductor in Italy and Germany, and in 1960 became the first American ever to conduct at Bayreuth Festival. From 1964 to 1972, music director of both the (West) Berlin Radio Symphony and the Berlin Opera. Music director, Cleveland Orchestra, 1971–82. Music director, Vienna State Opera, 1982–84. Since 1988, artistic director, Pittsburgh Symphony. Noted for clarity and balance of orchestral textures in his performances.

RECOMMENDED RECORDINGS Strauss *Don Juan, Till Eulenspiegel,* and *Death and Transfiguration* (CBS). Mozart *Don Giovanni* (CBS).

SIR CHARLES MACKERRAS

(pronounced: mac-*kare*-uss)

Conductor. Born November 17, 1925, in Schenectady, New York. Studied at New South Wales Conservatorium in Australia and at Prague Academy of Music. Conductor, Sadlers Wells Opera, London, 1948–66; Hamburg State Opera, 1966–70. Music director, English National Opera, 1970–77. Principal conductor, BBC Symphony, London, 1978–79; Sydney Symphony, Australia, 1982–85. Since 1987, music director, Welsh National Opera. Knighted by Queen Elizabeth II, 1979. A much-respected all-round conductor, best-known for Slavic and British composers.

RECOMMENDED RECORDINGS Martinů Double Concerto and *Frescoes of Piero della Francesca* (Supraphon). Elgar *Falstaff* and *Enigma Variations* (Angel).

SIR NEVILLE MARRINER

(pronounced: *mar*-in-ir)

Conductor and violinist. Born April 15, 1924, in Lincoln, England. Studied at Royal College of Music, London, and Paris Conservatory. Assistant concertmaster, London Symphony, 1956–58. Founder of the Academy of St. Martin-in-the-Fields, London, in 1959 and its director until 1979. Music director, Los Angeles Chamber Orchestra, 1969–78; Minnesota Orchestra, 1979–86. Renowned as an intelligent, clean-lined, if sometimes bland conductor, at his best in Baroque and Classical repertory.

RECOMMENDED RECORDINGS Handel Six Concerti Grossi (Philips). Mozart Symphonies Nos. 38 & 39 (Angel).

KURT MASUR

(pronounced: mah-*zhur*)

Conductor. Born July 18, 1927, Silesia (then part of Germany). Studied at Hochschule für Musik, Berlin, 1946–48. Conductor, Dresden Philharmonic,

1955–58. Music director, Mecklenburg State Theater, Schwerin, 1959–60; Komische Oper, East Berlin, 1960–64; Leipzig Gewandhaus Orchestra since 1970. Principal guest-conductor, London Philharmonic, 1988–91. Music director, New York Philharmonic, since 1991. A solidly musical, if sometimes unsubtle conductor of German classics, Tchaikovsky, and Shostakovich.

RECOMMENDED RECORDINGS Brahms Symphonies, complete (Philips, 3-disc set). Dvorak Symphony No. 9 (Teldec). Reger *Variations on a Theme by Mozart* (Teldec).

EDUARDO MATA

(pronounced: *mah*-tah)

Conductor. Born September 5, 1942, in Mexico City, Mexico. Studied at National Conservatory of Mexico and at Tanglewood. Conductor, Symphony Orchestra of Guadalajara, 1964–66; Phoenix (Arizona) Symphony, 1970–79. Music director, Dallas Symphony Orchestra, 1979–93. An uncommonly clean-lined, rhythmically incisive interpreter of late-Romantic and 20th-century works.

RECOMMENDED RECORDINGS Bizet Symphony in C and Mozart Divertimento No. 11 in D (RCA). Prokofiev *Love for Three Oranges* Suite and Stravinsky Suites Nos. 1 & 2 (RCA).

ZUBIN MEHTA

(pronounced: *may*-tah)

Conductor. Born April 29, 1936, in Bombay, India. Studied in Vienna and Siena, Italy. In late 1950s, began attracting attention as first major Indian conductor in Europe. Music director, Montreal Symphony Orchestra, 1961–67; Los Angeles Philharmonic, 1968–1978; Israel Philharmonic, since 1968; New York Philharmonic, 1978–1991. Has also conducted opera at Milan's La Scala, Vienna State Opera, London's Covent Garden, and New York's Metropolitan. A virtuoso, facile conductor, at his best in Bruckner and late Romantics and in complex contemporary scores. Married to former Hollywood actress Nancy Kovack.

RECOMMENDED RECORDINGS Strauss *Alpine* Symphony (London). Stravinsky *The Rite of Spring* (CBS).

YEHUDI MENUHIN

(pronounced: *mehn-yoo-in*)

Violinist and conductor. Born April 22, 1916, in New York City. Started playing violin at age 4; was a soloist with San Francisco Symphony at 7, then a child prodigy performing throughout the world. "Retired" for several years in the 1930s, studying with Georges Enescu in Paris, then with Adolf Busch in Switzerland, before resuming career. Has sometimes appeared (and recorded) as a violist. In the 1950s, also turned to conducting, becoming director of the Bath Festival in England (1958–68), and founding the Menuhin Festival Orchestra in Windsor, England, in 1969. As both violinist and conductor, noted for his elegant, sensitive, tasteful performances of Classical and Romantic works.

RECOMMENDED RECORDINGS   Beethoven Violin Concerto (Angel). Mozart Violin Concertos Nos. 3 & 5 (violinist & conductor) (Angel).

ZINKA MILANOV

(pronounced: *mee-lah-nawf*)

Soprano. Born May 17, 1906, in Zagreb, Yugoslavia. Died May 30, 1989, in New York City. Debut with Zagreb, 1927, under maiden name, Zinka Kunc; adopted her husband's name in 1930s. Metropolitan Opera debut, 1937; within a few years, she was one of Met's most popular sopranos. Retired in late 1960s. Her voice at its prime was a soaringly beautiful, warmly expressive, dramatically exciting one, capable of spinning out some of the most lovely soprano sounds of any soprano of this age.

RECOMMENDED RECORDINGS   Verdi *Aida*, complete (RCA Victrola, 3-disc set, mono). Verdi *Il Trovatore*, complete (RCA Victrola, 2-disc set, mono).

NATHAN MILSTEIN

(pronounced: *mihl-styn*)

Violinist. Born December 31, 1904, in Odessa, Russia. Studied with Leopold Auer and Eugene Ysaye. Began touring Russia at age 19, sometimes with Horowitz as pianist. U.S. debut, 1929. Since then, a leading violin soloist throughout U.S. and Europe, much admired for warm, lyrical, silken tone, and generally at his best in the Romantic repertory.

RECOMMENDED RECORDINGS Chausson *Poème*, Beethoven *Romances*, Berlioz *Reverie & Caprice* (Angel/Seraphim). Beethoven and Mendelssohn Violin Concertos (Angel).

SHLOMO MINTZ

(pronounced: mihnts)

Violinist. Born October 30, 1957, in Moscow. Began music studies at an early age in Israel after his family's emigration. Debut with Israel Philharmonic at age 11. Through scholarship grants, studied at Juilliard School in New York. New York debut, 1973. One of his generation's finest violinists, noted for warmth and expressiveness of his playing.

RECOMMENDED RECORDINGS Mendelssohn and Bruch Violin Concertos (Deutsche Grammophon). Prokofiev Violin Concertos Nos. 1 & 2 (Deutsche Grammophon).

DIMITRI MITROPOULOS

(pronounced: mih-*traw*-poo-lohs)

Conductor, pianist, and organist. Born March 1, 1896, in Athens, Greece. Died November 2, 1960, in Milan, Italy. A rehearsal conductor with Berlin Opera in 1920s, then a conductor in Athens. From 1937 to 1948, music director of Minneapolis Symphony, and from 1949 to 1958 of New York Philharmonic. Also active at La Scala (Milan), Vienna State Opera, and New York's Metropolitan Opera. Noted as a dramatic, intense interpreter of Mahler, Strauss, other late Romantic composers, and a dedicated champion of Schoenberg, Berg, Webern, and other early 20th-century composers.

RECOMMENDED RECORDINGS Mahler Symphony No. 5 (New York Philharmonic Radiothon). Gould *Fall River Legend* (New World).

ANNA MOFFO

(pronounced: *mah*-fo)

Soprano. Born June 27, 1934, in Wayne, Pennsylvania. Studied at Curtis Institute in Philadelphia on scholarship. Won Philadelphia Orchestra Young Artists Auditions, 1954. Awarded a Fulbright Fellowship to study in Italy. Made operatic debut in Italian television production of Puccini's *Madama*

Butterfly, then sang at Milan's La Scala, Vienna State Opera, and Paris Opera. U.S. opera debut, 1957, with Chicago Lyric Opera; joined New York's Metropolitan Opera, 1959. One of the most beautiful opera stars of our time, widely praised for her acting ability as well as for sensuous, warmly expressive singing, especially in lyrical music of Puccini and Verdi. Vocal problems in recent years have curtailed operatic appearances, but she appears occasionally on European and U.S. television.

RECOMMENDED RECORDINGS   Cantaloube *Songs of the Auvergne* and Villa-Lobos *Bachianas Brasilieras* No. 5, with Stokowski (RCA). Puccini *La Rondine*, complete (RCA Italiana, 2-disc set, import).

PIERRE MONTEUX

(pronounced: mawn-*tuh*)

Conductor. Born April 4, 1875, in Paris, France. Died July 1, 1964, in Hancock, Maine. A violinist in orchestra of Paris Opéra Comique (1896–1911), then conductor for the Diaghilev Ballet Russe in the years before World War I. Music director, Boston Symphony Orchestra (1919–24), Orchestre Symphonique of Paris (1930–35), San Francisco Symphony (1935–52), and London Symphony (1961–64). In the decade before his death, was one of the most beloved of all conductors, frequently appearing as a guest conductor in Boston, Amsterdam, Tel Aviv, and other cities, and directing a summer music school at Hancock, Maine. Best known as a warm, vibrant, always elegant and tasteful conductor of Brahms, Beethoven, most French composers, and most Romantics.

RECOMMENDED RECORDINGS   Franck Symphony in D minor (RCA). Stravinsky *The Rite of Spring* and *Petrushka* (RCA).

IVAN MORAVEC

(pronounced: more-eh-vetz)

Pianist. Born November 9, 1930, in Prague, Czechoslovakia. Studied in Prague. Attracted international attention in late 1950s with Czech-made recordings that showed his individualistically poetic, penetrating approach to traditional and early 20th-century piano repertory. U.S. debut, 1964. The piano soloist in Milos Foreman's award-winning 1984 film, *Amadeus*.

RECOMMENDED RECORDINGS   Beethoven Piano Concerto No. 3 (Pro Arte). Chopin 5 Mazurkas, 3 Waltzes, 2 Polonaises (Vox).

CHARLES MUNCH

(pronounced: moonch)

Conductor. Born September 26, 1891, in Strasbourg, Alsace (then part of Germany). Died November 6, 1968, in Richmond, Virginia. Began his career as a violinist, first in Strasbourg's orchestra, then as concertmaster of the Leipzig Gewandhaus Orchestra under Furtwängler. Drafted into German Army in World War I; wounded at Verdun. After the war, turned to conducting. In 1933, married an heiress of the Nestlé (Swiss chocolate) family, who helped him found Paris Philharmonic in 1935. Conductor of Paris Conservatory Orchestra, 1938–1947. During World War II secretly active in anti-Nazi Resistance movement, allowing his house to be used as "underground railway" station. Music director, Boston Symphony Orchestra, 1948 to 1962, retiring after a series of heart attacks. In 1967, helped launch new Orchestre de Paris, and was leading it on a U.S. tour when he died. Best known as an exciting, colorful master of Berlioz, Debussy, and Ravel, and as a conductor who sometimes sacrificed details for overall effect but whose rhythmic and coloristic flair has rarely been equaled in this century.

RECOMMENDED RECORDINGS   Ravel *Daphnis et Chloé*, complete (RCA). Berlioz Overtures (RCA) and Symphonie Fantastique (RCA).

RICCARDO MUTI

(pronounced: *mooh*-tee)

Conductor. Born July 28, 1941, in Naples, Italy. Won first prize in Guido Cantelli International Competition, 1967. Principal conductor, Maggio Musicale, Florence, Italy, 1969–1978. U.S. debut, 1972, with Philadelphia Orchestra. Became principal conductor of New Philharmonia Orchestra of London, following the death of Klemperer, 1973. Music director, Philadelphia Orchestra, 1980–1991. A colorful, often exciting conductor, at his best in late Romantic and early 20th-century works.

RECOMMENDED RECORDINGS   Respighi *Pines, Fountains,* and *Festivals* of Rome (Angel). Berlioz *Romeo and Juliet,* complete (Angel).

ANNE-SOPHIE MUTTER

(pronounced: *moo-tehr*)

Violinist. Born June 29, 1963, in Rheinfeldin, West Germany. At age 6, won first prize in a West German music competition. Began active concertizing at age 13, at Lucerne and Salzburg Festivals, under guidance of Herbert von Karajan. U.S. debut, 1980. Also active with Mutter-Rostropovich-Giuranna Trio in chamber performances, and has toured Europe and Japan with pianist Alexis Weissenberg. Noted for uncommonly rich, romantic tone and impressive technique.

RECOMMENDED RECORDINGS Beethoven Violin Concerto (Deutsche Grammophon). Brahms Violin Concerto (Deutsche Grammophon).

BIRGIT NILSSON

(pronounced: *neel-suhn*)

Soprano. Born May 17, 1918, in Karup, Sweden. Studied at Royal Academy of Music, Stockholm. Debut with Stockholm Royal Opera, 1947. Joined Vienna State Opera, 1953. Scored a triumph at Bayreuth (as Elsa in *Lohengrin*), 1954. U.S. debut with San Francisco Opera, 1956 (as Brünnhilde in *Die Walküre*), and joined Metropolitan Opera three years later. Retired in early 1980s. Her powerful, clear soprano made her the most successful Wagnerian soprano of her generation, but unlike her great Wagnerian predecessors, Flagstad and Traubel, she also sang non-Wagnerian roles regularly.

RECOMMENDED RECORDINGS Final Scenes from *Salome* and *Götterdämmerung* (London). Wagner *Tristan und Isolde*, excerpts or complete (Deutsche Grammophon).

JESSYE NORMAN

Soprano. Born September 15, 1945, in Augusta, Georgia. Studied at Howard University, Washington, D.C.; Peabody Conservatory, Baltimore; and University of Michigan. Operatic debut in West Berlin, 1969 (as Elisabeth in *Tannhäuser*), but then concentrated primarily on concerts and recitals for next decade. Metropolitan Opera debut, 1983 (as both Dido and Cassandra in *Les Troyens*). One of most admired and most popular singers in recent years, known for full, rich sound of her voice and the penetrating depth of her interpretations.

RECOMMENDED RECORDINGS Mahler *The Song of the Earth* (Philips). Strauss *Four Last Songs*, other songs (Philips).

GARRICK OHLSSON

(pronounced: *ohl*-son)

Pianist. Born April 3, 1948, in White Plains, New York. Began piano studies at age 8, later studying at Juilliard in New York with Rosina Lhevinne. Won three major international piano competitions between 1967 and 1971: Italy's Busoni Prize, Montreal's International Piano Competition, Warsaw's International Chopin Competition (the first American ever to win the latter). Engagements with leading American orchestras soon followed, and he quickly established himself as a deeply lyrical, probingly expressive pianist.

RECOMMENDED RECORDINGS Chopin Piano Concerto No. 1 and *Krakowiac* (Angel/Seraphim). Liszt Piano Concertos Nos. 1 & 2 (Angel).

DAVID OISTRAKH

(pronounced: oy-strahk)

Violinist, conductor. Born in 1908, in Odessa, Russia. Died October 24, 1974, in Amsterdam. Debut at age 12. In 1937, won first prize in Ysaye Competition in Brussels, and established his international reputation. During 1950s, became an active conductor as well as violinist. His son Igor (born in 1931) is also a gifted violinist, and they occasionally performed together. Admired as a warm, vibrant, intensely lyrical violinist with a full, rich sound; at his best in 19th- and early 20th-century Russian music.

RECOMMENDED RECORDINGS Tchaikovsky Violin Concerto (CBS/Odyssey). Shostakovich Violin Concerto No. 1 (Monitor).

EUGENE ORMANDY

(pronounced: ohr-man-dee)

Conductor. Born November 18, 1899, in Budapest, Hungary. Died March 12, 1985, in Philadelphia. At five and a half, was the youngest pupil of Budapest's Royal Academy of Music; graduated at 14. Came to U.S. in 1921; became a citizen in 1927. Was a violinist, then concertmaster, then conductor of Broadway's Capitol Theatre Orchestra (1922–28). From 1931 to 1936, conductor of Minneapolis Symphony, and then from 1936 to 1980 music director of the Philadelphia Orchestra. A colorful, polished, highly virtuoso conductor, at his best with the music of Rachmaninoff, Sibelius, Strauss, Brahms, and most Romantics.

RECOMMENDED RECORDINGS Mahler-Cooke Symphony No. 10 (CBS). Bartók Concerto for Orchestra (RCA). Tchaikovsky Symphony No. 6 (*Pathétique*) (Delos).

SEIJI OZAWA

(pronounced: oh-*zah*-wah)

Conductor. Born September 1, 1935, in Hoten, Manchuria, of Japanese parents. Studied at Toho School of Music, Tokyo. Won 1959 International Competition of Orchestra Conductors at Besançon, France. Subsequently became an assistant to Herbert von Karajan in Europe and Leonard Bernstein in New York. Rose rapidly to become the first successful Japanese conductor in America. In 1964, became music director of Chicago Symphony's Ravinia Park summer concerts, and then of the Toronto Symphony (1964–69). Music director of San Francisco Symphony, 1970–76. Music director, Boston Symphony Orchestra, since 1973. One of his generation's most kinetic if not often very profound conductors, at his best in late 19th- and early 20th-century works.

RECOMMENDED RECORDINGS Orff *Carmina Burana* (RCA). Stravinsky *The Firebird*, complete (Angel).

LUCIANO PAVAROTTI

(pronounced: poh-voh-*roht*-tee)

Tenor. Born October 12, 1935, in Modena, Italy. Began taking singing lessons at age four. Debut at Milan's La Scala in 1964 (as Rodolfo in Puccini's *La Boheme*). Two years later, created a sensation at London's Covent Garden when, in a production of Donizetti's *Daughter of the Regiment* with Joan Sutherland, he became the first tenor in more than a century to sing "Tonio's" famous first-act aria and *cabaletta* in its original key, hitting every one of its string of high C's. Metropolitan Opera debut in 1968. One of world's most popular tenors, much admired for the brilliance and range of his lyric voice and the warmth and intelligence of his acting.

RECOMMENDED RECORDINGS Puccini *La Bohème*, complete or highlights (London). *Pavarotti — The World's Favorite Tenor Arias* (London).

MURRAY PERAHIA

(pronounced: peh-rye-ah)

Pianist and conductor. Born April 19, 1947, in New York City. Studied at Mannes College of Music, New York. Carnegie Hall debut, 1968. First American to win Leeds International Piano Competition, 1972. Co-winner (with Lynn Harrell) of First Avery Fisher Prize, 1975. Since 1982, co-artistic director, Aldeburgh Festival (founded by the late Benjamin Britten), Aldeburgh, England. In addition to recitals and concerts with orchestras, an active chamber-music performer, dating back to his early affiliation with Marlboro Festival as a teenager. One of his generation's most technically fluent and interpretively sensitive and probing pianists.

RECOMMENDED RECORDINGS Mozart Piano Concertos Nos. 20 & 27 (pianist & conductor) (CBS). Beethoven *Appassionata* Sonata (CBS).

ITZHAK PERLMAN

Violinist. Born August 31, 1945, in Tel Aviv, Israel (then Palestine), son of Polish refugees who had settled there in mid-1930s. Stricken with polio at age four, and still walks with the aid of metal crutches and plays sitting down. Came to U.S. in 1958 to study at Juilliard in New York. Won Leventritt Award in 1964, and has since gone on to become one of the most popular of all violinists, especially noted for warm, strong, singing tone. By mid-1980s, was reputed to be the concert soloist commanding the highest performance fee.

RECOMMENDED RECORDINGS Tchaikovsky Violin Concerto and *Serenade mélancholique* (Angel). Mendelssohn Violin Concerto and Bruch Violin Concerto No. 1 (*Angel*).

MICHEL PLASSON

Conductor. Born October 2, 1933, in Paris, France. Studied at the Paris Conservatory. Won first prize, Besançon International Conducting Competition, 1962. Since 1968, music director of Orchestre du Capitole de Toulouse in southwestern France; has built it into an ensemble of international standing. One of the most respected of present-day French conductors, specializing in French music of the late 19th- and early 20th-centuries.

RECOMMENDED RECORDINGS   Ravel *La Valse, Bolero, Mother Goose Suite, Pavane*, and *Valses nobles et sentimentales* (EMI, import). Franck Symphonic Variations (with Collard) and Symphony in D minor (Angel).

IVO POGORELICH

(pronounced: poh-go-*reh*-lick)

Pianist. Born October 20, 1958, in Belgrade, Yugoslavia. Studied at Moscow Conservatory. Won Cassagrande Competition, Terni, Italy, 1978; first prize, Montreal International Music Competition, 1980. U.S. debut, 1981, at Carnegie Hall, New York. Has risen rapidly to front rank of younger pianists; admired for his probing individuality and the electricity of his performances. Married to Russian pianist Alice Kezeradze, who was one of his Moscow teachers.

RECOMMENDED RECORDINGS   Ravel *Gaspard de la Nuit* and Prokofiev Sonata No. 6 (Deutsche Grammophon). Chopin Piano Concerto No. 2 (Deutsche Grammophon).

ANDRÉ PREVIN

(pronounced: *preh*-vihn)

Conductor and pianist. Born April 6, 1929, in Berlin, Germany. Studied in Paris, then in U.S. after 1938, later becoming a U.S. citizen. From 1950 to 1959, an arranger and conductor, for Metro-Goldwyn-Mayer film studios in Hollywood, later free-lancing for other studios. Won several Academy Awards for his film work (*Gigi, My Fair Lady, Irma la Douce*). During this period, also active as a jazz pianist, mainly on the West Coast. In 1966, decided to concentrate on a symphonic career. Music director, Houston Symphony, 1967–69; London Symphony, 1968–79; Pittsburgh Symphony, 1976–84. Principal conductor, Royal Philharmonic, London, since 1985. Music director, Los Angeles Philharmonic, 1987–89. Generally insightful, intelligent, but often soft-edged and reserved conductor of a broad repertory.

RECOMMENDED RECORDINGS   Rachmaninoff Symphony No. 2 (Telarc). Vaughan Williams Symphony No. 6 (RCA).

LEONTYNE PRICE

Soprano. Born February 10, 1927, in Laurel, Mississippi. A wealthy Laurel family (the Alexander Chisholms) helped put her through Juilliard in New York. Virgil Thomson heard her in a student production, and cast her in a Broadway revival of his opera *Four Saints in Three Acts* in 1951. The following year she scored a triumph as Bess in a production of Gershwin's *Porgy and Bess* that toured Europe under U.S. State Department auspices, and later toured the U.S. In 1955, sang the title role in an NBC-TV production of Puccini's *Tosca*, the first black to perform a major operatic role in a nationwide telecast. Two years later, made her debut with the San Francisco Opera, and appeared with the Vienna State Opera. Joined the Metropolitan Opera in 1961, and quickly established herself as one of the most popular and critically praised sopranos of her time, admired for her creamily beautiful, vibrant, rich-sounding voice, and generally at her best in Verdi, Puccini, and Richard Strauss. Has drastically curtailed performances since mid-1980s.

RECOMMENDED RECORDINGS Verdi *Aïda*, complete or highlights (RCA). Puccini *Madama Butterfly*, complete or highlights (RCA).

JEAN-PIERRE RAMPAL

(pronounced: *rahm-pahl*)

Flutist and conductor. Born January 7, 1922, in Marseilles, France. Studied at Paris Conservatory. First flutist, Paris Opera Orchestra, in the 1950s. Phenomenally successful solo career since the 1960s, performing and recording Baroque works especially. Also active as a chamber-music performer with Stern, Rostropovich, Zukerman, others. His technical mastery of the flute is now legendary.

RECOMMENDED RECORDINGS Vivaldi Concertos (Six) for Flute and Orchestra (CBS). Mozart Flute Concertos Nos. 1 & 2 and *Andante in C* (CBS).

SIMON RATTLE

Conductor. Born January 19, 1955, in Liverpool, England. While in his early teens, played percussion with the Royal Liverpool Philharmonic and won scholarship to London's Royal Academy of Music. Became music director of England's City of Birmingham Symphony in 1980 and has led it to international renown through TV and recordings. Has risen quickly to front rank of conductors of his generation in both popularity and critical acclaim.

RECOMMENDED RECORDINGS Sibelius Symphony No. 5 (Angel). Messiaen *Turangalila* Symphony (Angel). Rachmaninoff Symphony No. 2 (Angel). Gershwin *Porgy and Bess* (Angel).

FRITZ REINER

(pronounced: *rye*-ner)

Conductor. Born December 19, 1888, in Budapest, Hungary. Died November 15, 1963, in Weston, Connecticut. Studied at Budapest's Royal Academy of Music (Bartók was one of his teachers). Conducted at Budapest Opera, 1911–14, and Dresden Opera, 1914–1921. Came to U.S. in 1921; became a U.S. citizen in 1928. Conductor of Cincinnati Symphony, 1922–31; Pittsburgh Symphony, 1938–48; and Chicago Symphony, 1953–63, raising each to significantly high levels of performance and prestige. For many years during the 1930s and 1940s, also headed orchestra and opera departments at Curtis Institute of Music in Philadelphia. Renowned as a demanding orchestral taskmaster, noted for incisive, dramatic performances of a broad repertory from Mozart to Bartók.

RECOMMENDED RECORDINGS Beethoven Symphony No. 6, "Pastoral" (RCA). Strauss *Also Sprach Zarathustra* and Waltzes from *Der Rosenkavalier* (RCA).

SVIATOSLAV RICHTER

(pronounced: *rihkh*-ter)

Pianist. Born in 1915, in Zhitomir, the Ukraine. Started as an assistant conductor with Odessa Ballet in 1930; did not begin formal piano training until 1937. Eight years later, won first prize in U.S.S.R. Competition of Executant Musicians as a pianist. Made first appearances in Western countries in 1960, although his reputation as Russia's finest pianist had preceded him through recordings. Ranks as one of the century's great pianists—a dynamic, subtle, and lyrically expressive performer, called by one critic "the perfect amalgamation of sound, rhythm, and technique." Married to singer Nina Doloyak.

RECOMMENDED RECORDINGS Mussorgsky *Pictures at an Exhibition* (CBS/Odyssey). Rachmaninoff Piano Concerto No. 2 and Prokofiev Piano Concerto No. 5 (Deutsche Grammophon).

MSTISLAV ROSTROPOVICH

(pronounced: rah-strah-poe-vitch)

Cellist and conductor. Born August 12, 1927, in Baku, U.S.S.R. Made recital debut at age of eight. Later studied at Moscow Conservatory. In late 1940s, was first cellist in Moscow Philharmonic, before embarking on a solo career. In the 1960s he was a frequent visitor to the U.S., but in 1971 he was temporarily denied permission to travel or perform because of his defense of Soviet author Solzhenitsyn and other critics of Soviet artistic controls. He and his wife, soprano Galina Vishnevskaya, left the Soviet Union permanently in 1974, settling in the U.S. Music director of the National Symphony of Washington, D.C., since 1977. Co-director of Aldeburgh Festival in England since mid-1980s. Recognized as one of the world's great cellists and a vigorous, dramatic conductor, at his best in the music of Tchaikovsky, Shostakovich, and Prokofiev.

RECOMMENDED RECORDINGS *As cellist* — Dvořák Cello Concerto and Tchaikovsky *Rococo Variations* (Deutsche Grammophon). *As conductor* — Shostakovich Symphony No. 5 (Deutsche Grammophon).

GENNADY ROZHDESTVENSKY

(pronounced: rohj-*dest*-vyen-skee)

Conductor. Born in 1931 in Moscow. Began studying piano at age 8. Entered Moscow Conservatory in 1949. Won a competition to be assistant conductor of Bolshoi Theater, 1951. The following year, became full conductor, leading performances of both ballet and opera. Beginning in 1952, also guest-conducted Leningrad Philharmonic and other orchestras in the Soviet Union and Eastern Europe. During the 1960s, principal conductor of both the Bolshoi Ballet and the Moscow Radio Symphony Orchestra. Gave up the ballet post in 1970 to concentrate on symphonic conducting. Music director, Grand Symphony Orchestra of the Soviet Ministry of Culture, Moscow, since 1982. For several years in mid-1970s, principal conductor of Stockholm Philharmonic — the first Soviet conductor to be allowed to accept a post in a Western country. Held similar post with BBC Symphony in London in early 1980s. Ranks today as foremost Soviet conductor of his generation, much admired internationally for rhythmic suppleness and lyrical qualities of his performances. Married to the pianist Viktoria Postnikova.

RECOMMENDED RECORDINGS Tchaikovsky *The Nutcracker*, selections (Monitor); complete (CBS/Melodiya, 2-disc set). Prokofiev Violin Concertos Nos. 1 & 2, with Perlman (Angel).

ARTUR RUBINSTEIN

(pronounced: *roo-bihn-styn*)

Pianist. Born January 28, 1889, in Warsaw, Poland. Died December 20, 1982, in Geneva, Switzerland. Studied in Warsaw and Berlin, including study of the violin under Joachim in Berlin. Made his debut as a pianist in Warsaw at age six; performed as soloist with Berlin Philharmonic at 13. First U.S. concert in 1906, with Philadelphia Orchestra. Lived in the U.S. after the 1930s; became a U.S. citizen in the 1940s. One of the most popular and respected pianists of the century, particularly admired for his youthful vigor and remarkably sustained abilities in his later years. A performer in the grand tradition—a colorful, frequently exciting, powerfully elegant interpreter of the Romantic standards, particularly Chopin.

RECOMMENDED RECORDINGS Chopin Waltzes (RCA). Grieg Piano Concerto and Tchaikovsky Piano Concerto (RCA).

ESA-PEKKA SALONEN

(pronounced: *sah-loh-nen*)

Conductor. Born June 30, 1958, in Helsinki, Finland. Studied at Sibelius Academy, Helsinki, and in Siena and Milan, Italy. Became conductor of Finnish Radio Symphony in 1982; led it on tour to Australia, 1984. American debut, 1984, with Los Angeles Philharmonic. Has risen quickly to prominence as one of most talented and engaging conductors of his generation, best-known to date for insightful performances of Sibelius and early 20th-century works. Named music director of Los Angeles Philharmonic, 1989.

RECOMMENDED RECORDINGS Sibelius Symphony No. 5 and Pohjola's Daughter (CBS). Prokofiev *Romeo and Juliet*, excerpts (CBS). Messiaen *Turangalila* Symphony (CBS).

THOMAS SCHIPPERS

(pronounced: *ship*-pers)

Conductor. Born March 9, 1930, in Kalamazoo, Michigan. Died December 16, 1977, in Cincinnati, Ohio. Won a national contest to conduct the Philadelphia Orchestra in a youth concert in 1947. Conductor of the Lemonade Opera in New York, 1948. Took over as conductor of Menotti's *The Consul* on Broadway in 1949 when regular conductor became ill. In 1950s, conducted other Menotti operas (*Amahl and the Night Visitors* on NBC-TV, *The Saint of Bleecker Street* on Broadway), and became a conductor at the New York City Opera and at La Scala. One of the founders, with Menotti, of the Spoleto Festival in Italy. Conductor of the Cincinnati Symphony Orchestra, 1970–77.

RECOMMENDED RECORDINGS   Prokofiev *Alexander Nevsky* Cantata (CBS/Odyssey). Barber *Medea's Dance of Vengeance* and other works (CBS/ Odyssey).

ELISABETH SCHWARZKOPF

(pronounced: *shvahrts*-kawpf)

Soprano. Born December 9, 1915, in Poznan, Poland, of German parents. As a teenager, lived in England for a year as a League of Nations exchange student. Studied at Berlin High School for Music. Made opera debut in 1932 with Berlin State Opera in a minor role (in *Parsifal*). Continued to sing minor roles until 1942, when she joined Vienna State Opera as a leading singer. Also gave her first *lieder* recital in Vienna in 1942. Following marriage in 1947 to British recording executive Walter Legge, resumed her career, scoring major triumphs at Milan's La Scala Opera and Vienna State Opera. Overcame antagonisms about her alleged associations with Nazis and became increasingly admired for the sheer beauty of her voice and the depth and patrician sensitivity of her interpretations — especially in German opera and *lieder*. In 1953, made her U.S. debut in a New York *lieder* recital, and in 1955 her U.S. operatic debut with San Francisco Opera as the Marschallin in *Der Rosenkavalier*. That role was to become her most famous over the next decade, and she filmed it in 1960.

RECOMMENDED RECORDINGS   Strauss *Four Last Songs* and other songs (Angel). Strauss *Der Rosenkavalier*, complete or highlights (Angel).

PETER SERKIN

Pianist. Born July 24, 1947, in New York City. Son of pianist Rudolf Serkin. Studied at Curtis Institute in Philadelphia, 1958–64. As a teenager, attracted favorable attention for performances in chamber and solo works at Marlboro Festival in Vermont. Made his New York recital debut in 1959, and has since concertized extensively in the U.S., Europe, and Japan. During late 1960s, acquired a reputation as a young maverick because of his "hip" attire and attitudes, but his reputation as an uncommonly thoughtful, versatile musician has grown steadily in years since then.

RECOMMENDED RECORDINGS Mozart Piano Concertos Nos. 14 and 15 (RCA). Works of Stravinsky, Lieberson, and Wolpe (New World).

RUDOLF SERKIN

Pianist. Born March 28, 1903, in Eger, Bohemia. Made debut at age 12 with Vienna State Symphony. Later studied composition in Vienna with Arnold Schoenberg. Performed throughout Europe in 1920s and 1930s. U.S. debut, 1933. Soon acquired reputation as an intense, nervous, powerful interpreter of Classical and Romantic repertory. In 1936, married daughter of violinist Adolph Busch (with whom he frequently appeared in chamber recitals); their six children include pianist Peter Serkin. For many years, headed piano department at the Curtis Institute, and was the director of the Marlboro Festival in Vermont since the 1960s. Died May 8, 1991, in Guilford, VT.

RECOMMENDED RECORDINGS Beethoven Piano Concerto No. 5, "Emperor" (CBS). Brahms Piano Concerto No. 1 (CBS).

GIUSEPPE SINOPOLI

(pronounced: sih-*nopp*-oh-lee)

Composer, conductor. Born November 2, 1948, in Venice, Italy. Studied medicine and psychiatry at University of Padua, earning degrees in 1971. Also studied music at Benedetto Marcello Conservatory, Venice, and privately with Bruno Maderna. Decided to concentrate on music in mid-1970s. His opera, *Lou Salomé*, premiered at Bavarian State Opera, Munich, 1981. Principal conductor, Rome's Santa Cecilia Orchestra, 1984–87; Philharmonia Orchestra, London, 1983–94. Music director, Dresden Staatskapelle Orchestra since 1992. U.S. conducting debut in 1983 with New York Philharmonic. A dynamic, uncommonly probing and dramatic conductor of 19th-century Romantics and contemporary works.

RECOMMENDED RECORDINGS   Mahler Symphony No. 5 (Deutsche Grammophon). Schubert *Unfinished* Symphony (No. 8) and Mendelssohn *Italian* Symphony (No. 4) (Deutsche Grammophon).

STANISLAW SKROWACZEWSKI

(pronounced: skroh-vah-*chehv*-skee)

Conductor and composer. Born October 3, 1923, in Lwow, Poland. Began composing at age seven. His First Symphony performed by Lwow Philharmonic in 1931. Later became conductor of Wroclaw Philharmonic (1946–47), Katowice National Philharmonic (1949–54), Krakow Philharmonic (1955–56), and Warsaw Philharmonic (1957–59). Invited to U.S. to conduct Cleveland Orchestra by George Szell in 1959. Music director, Minneapolis Symphony (renamed Minnesota Orchestra) 1960–78. Principal conductor, Halle Orchestra, Manchester, England, since 1984. Best known for incisive, elegant, rhythmically vibrant performances of Classical and Neo-Classical composers.

RECOMMENDED RECORDINGS   Stravinsky *Petrushka* and *The Rite of Spring* (Vox). Skrowaczewski Concerto for English Horn and Orchestra, with Thomas Stacy (Desto).

LEONARD SLATKIN

(pronounced: *slat*-khin)

Conductor, pianist. Born September 1, 1944, in Los Angeles, California. Son of conductor Felix Slatkin and cellist Eleanor Aller. Studied with parents, then at Juilliard School, New York. Conducting debut, Aspen Music Festival, 1963. Became assistant conductor (to Walter Susskind) with Saint Louis Symphony in 1968, then associate conductor in 1971, principal conductor in 1974, music director 1979–1995. Music director, Minnesota Orchestra's Sommerfest, 1979–89, Cleveland Orchestra's Blossom Festival since 1991. Music director, National Symphony (Washington, D.C.), 1995—. An exceptionally versatile conductor, at his best in late-19th- and 20th-century works.

RECOMMENDED RECORDINGS   Shostakovich Symphony No. 10 (RCA). Vaughan Williams *Fantasia on a Theme by Thomas Tallis*, Barber *Adagio for Strings*, Satie *Gymnopedies*, Fauré *Pavane* (Telarc).

SIR GEORG SOLTI

(pronounced: *shohl*-tee)

Conductor. Born October 21, 1912, in Budapest, Hungary. In late 1930s, a conductor at Budapest Opera. After the Nazi takeover of Hungary, escaped to Switzerland. In 1942, won Geneva International Piano Competition, and considered pursuing a career as a pianist. In 1944, invited by Ernest Ansermet to be a guest conductor of Orchestre de la Suisse Romande, and has since devoted himself exclusively to conducting. Held several posts as an opera conductor: at Munich (1946–51), Frankfurt (1952–60), and London's Covent Garden (1961–70). Music director of the Chicago Symphony Orchestra from 1969 to 1991, leading it to new heights of national and international prestige. From 1972–75, also director of Orchestre de Paris; also principal conductor, London Philharmonic, 1979–83. Ranks today as one of the world's foremost conductors, best known for dramatic, full-blooded performances of Romantic classics, and especially Wagner.

RECOMMENDED RECORDINGS   Wagner *Orchestral Highlights from The Ring* (London). Mahler Symphony No. 8 ("Symphony of a Thousand") (London).

HILDE SOMER

Pianist. Born February 11, 1930, in Vienna, Austria. Died December 24, 1979, in Freeport, the Bahamas. Made debut at age nine with Vienna Symphony. U.S. debut, 1944, with the New York Philharmonic. Two years later, won a scholarship to study at Curtis Institute with Rudolf Serkin. A warmly expressive, often robust interpreter of a wide range of 19th- and 20th-century music, she was an active champion of Latin American composers (notably Ginastera) and was in the forefront of the 1960s Scriabin revival—often performing his music with light shows.

RECOMMENDED RECORDINGS   Ginastera Piano Concerto and Piano Sonata (Desto). Villa-Lobos *Choros No. 5*, Chavez *Poligonos*, Revueltas *Allegro*, Ginastera *Creole Dance Suite*, Castro *Sonata espagnola* (Desto).

JANOS STARKER

(pronounced: *shtahr*-ker)

Cellist. Born July 5, 1924, in Budapest, Hungary. Studied at Franz Liszt Academy in Budapest. Came to U.S. in 1948, has been an American citizen since 1953. A cellist in Dallas Symphony (1948), Metropolitan Opera Orchestra (1949–53), and first cellist of Chicago Symphony (1953–58), before embarking on solo career. Highly regarded as a darkly lyrical, penetrating interpreter of a broad repertory from Bach to Bartók.

RECOMMENDED RECORDINGS Boccherini Cello Concerto in B flat and Haydn Cello Concerto in D (Angel). Bloch *Schelomo* and *Voice in the Wilderness* (London). Bach Cello Suites, complete (Sefel, two-disc set).

WILLIAM STEINBERG

(pronounced: *styne*-berg)

Conductor. Born August 1, 1899, in Cologne, Germany. Died May 16, 1978 in New York City. In early 1920s, a conductor at Cologne Opera, Prague Opera, and Berlin Opera. Left Germany after Nazi takeover, helping to found the Palestine Symphony (later the Israel Philharmonic). Came to U.S. in 1938 at invitation of Arturo Toscanini to be a guest conductor of NBC Symphony. Music director, Buffalo Philharmonic (1945–52), Pittsburgh Symphony (1952–1976), Boston Symphony (1968–72). For several years in late 1950s, also principal conductor of London Philharmonic. A solid, forceful conductor of most major 19th-century works.

RECOMMENDED RECORDINGS Strauss *Also Sprach Zarathustra* (Deutsche Grammophon). Schubert Symphony No. 9 (RCA).

ISAAC STERN

Violinist. Born July 21, 1920, in Kreminiecz, Russia. Came to the U.S. with parents in 1921. Raised in San Francisco. Began piano studies at age six, turned to violin at eight. Debut at 11, with San Francisco Symphony under Monteux. New York recital debut, 1937. Has since concertized extensively throughout the world. Also active as performer of chamber music. In early 1960s, was leader of the group which fought successfully to block the tearing down of New York's Carnegie Hall (at the time of the building of Lincoln Center), and has since served Carnegie Hall as its president. Ranks as the century's outstanding American-trained violinist. Best known for evenness of tone and warm, vibrant interpretations of Romantic works.

RECOMMENDED RECORDINGS Beethoven Violin Concerto (CBS). Barber Violin Concerto (CBS).

LEOPOLD STOKOWSKI

(pronounced: stoh-*kawf*-skee)

Conductor. Born April 18, 1882, in London, England. Died September 13, 1977, in Nether Wallop, Hampshire, England. Came to U.S. in early 1900s; became a U.S. citizen in 1915. Conductor of Cincinnati Symphony (1909–12). Music director, Philadelphia Orchestra (1912–36), the All-American Youth Orchestra (1940–42), New York City Symphony (1944–45), Hollywood Bowl Symphony (1945–47), and American Symphony Orchestra (1962–72). Most famous for having built the Philadelphia Orchestra into one of the world's greatest orchestras, and for his introduction of much major new music to the U.S. Conducted the music for Walt Disney's *Fantasia* (1941) and several other films. Was long active in efforts to improve sound qualities of recordings. Sometimes criticized for being too much of a showman, but recognized as one of the century's great masters of orchestral color and dramatic effect. Usually at his best in 19th-century and early 20th-century music, and at his most controversial in his own Romantic transcriptions of Bach and other early composers.

RECOMMENDED RECORDINGS Stokowski's Greatest Hits (RCA Victrola). Falla *El Amor Brujo*, with Verrett, and Wagner *Tristan and Isolde* Symphonic Synthesis (CBS/Odyssey).

JOAN SUTHERLAND

Soprano. Born November 7, 1929, in Sydney, Australia. Studied at Sydney Conservatory; made her operatic debut in 1950 in a Conservatory production of Goossens' *Judith*. In 1952, joined London's Covent Garden, singing minor roles for several years. Married Australian-born conductor Richard Bonynge, who coached her in *bel canto* singing, which he believed more appropriate to her voice than the dramatic soprano roles she had been singing. In 1958, scored a triumph at Covent Garden in Donizetti's *Lucia di Lammermoor* and Handel's *Samson*. Since then, has specialized in the Italian lyric and coloratura repertory. U.S. debut in 1961. Ranks as one of the era's most exciting, remarkably agile sopranos, with a more weighty sound than the usual coloratura; particularly noted for her performances of what she has called "the demented dames" of Bellini, Donizetti, and Rossini.

RECOMMENDED RECORDINGS *The Art of the Prima Donna*, arias by Verdi, Mozart, Gounod, Bellini, Delibes, others (London). Donizetti *Lucia di Lammermor*, complete or highlights (London).

GEORGE SZELL

(pronounced: *zehl*)

Conductor. Born June 7, 1897, in Budapest, Hungary. Died July 30, 1970, in Cleveland, Ohio. Originally a pianist; made debut playing a Mozart concerto with Vienna Symphony at age ten. At 18, an assistant conductor at Berlin Opera, then a conductor of Berlin Broadcasting Symphony (1924–29). Principal conductor of Prague German Opera, 1929–38. Just before World War II, came to U.S., spending first years as a teacher and writing orchestral transcriptions for a publisher. In 1941, joined conducting staff of Metropolitan Opera. From 1946 until his death, music director of Cleveland Orchestra, building it into one of the world's finest orchestras. Renowned as exceptionally precise, rhythmically incisive if often unemotional conductor, at his best in late 18th- and 19th-century repertory.

RECOMMENDED RECORDINGS Schubert Symphony No. 9 (CBS/Odyssey). Dvořák Slavonic Dances (CBS/Odyssey).

RENATA TEBALDI

(pronounced: teh-*bahl*-dee)

Soprano. Born February 1, 1922, in Pesaro, Italy. First studied piano at Pesaro Conservatory, then switched to voice at Boito Conservatory in Parma. Made opera debut in 1944 in a minor role in Boito's *Mefistofele* at Roviogo. When Toscanini returned to Milan at the end of World War II, he auditioned Tebaldi and chose her for his re-opening concerts at La Scala. Remained a principal singer at La Scala until 1954. U.S. debut in San Francisco in 1950 (as *Aïda*). In 1955, joined Metropolitan Opera and quickly became one of its most popular stars. Most admired for silken beauty of her voice and for lyrically elegant interpretations of Verdi and Puccini heroines.

RECOMMENDED RECORDINGS Puccini *La Bohème* (London, 2-disc set). *The Great Voice of Renata Tebaldi* (London).

KIRI TE KANAWA

(pronounced: *tay khan-ah-wah*)

Soprano. Born March 6, 1944, in Gisborne, New Zealand, of an Irish mother and Maori father. After singing on New Zealand television as a teenager, won scholarship to study at London Opera Centre. Debut at Royal Opera, Covent Garden, 1970. U.S. debut, Santa Fe, 1971. Metropolitan Opera debut, 1974. Also sings regularly at Paris Opera, Vienna State Opera, Chicago Lyric Opera, San Francisco Opera, Salzburg Festival, others. Made a Dame Commander of the British Empire by Queen Elizabeth II in 1982. One of today's most popular singers, noted for velvety quality of her beautiful voice, but also faulted by some critics as a superficial interpreter.

RECOMMENDED RECORDINGS   *Mozart Arias* (Philips). Ravel *Sheherezade* and Duparc Songs (Angel).

YURI TEMIRKHANOV

(pronounced: tem-eer-*khan*-uhv)

Conductor. Born December 10, 1938, in Nalchik, U.S.S.R. Studied at Leningrad Conservatory. Conducting debut, Leningrad Opera, 1965. Won first prize in All-Union Soviet Conductors Competition, 1966. Principal conductor, Leningrad Symphony, 1968–76. Chief conductor, Kirov Opera and Kirov Ballet, Leningrad, 1978–86. Principal conductor, Leningrad Philharmonic since 1986; music director since 1988. A dynamic, colorful conductor, at his best in 19th-century Russian Romantic music.

RECOMMENDED RECORDINGS   Rachmaninoff Symphony No. 2 (Angel/Seraphim). Khachaturian *Spartacus* and *Gayne* excerpts (Angel).

KLAUS TENNSTEDT

(pronounced: *ten*-shtedt)

Conductor. Born June 6, 1926, in Merseburg, Germany. Studied at Leipzig Conservatory. Concertmaster, Municipal Theater, Halle, East Germany, 1948–58. Conductor, Dresden Opera, 1958–62; Schwerin State Theater, 1962–71. He and his wife, an opera singer, left East Germany permanently in 1971, settling in Kiel, West Germany. U.S. debut, 1974, as guest conductor,

Boston Symphony Orchestra. Principal conductor, North German Radio Orchestra, Hamburg, 1979–82. Music director, London Philharmonic, 1983–87. One of the top postwar specialists in German Classical and Romantic repertory, noted for uncommonly profound, often electric performances.

RECOMMENDED RECORDINGS Brahms Symphony No. 1 (Angel). Bruckner Symphony No. 4 (Angel).

MICHAEL TILSON THOMAS

Conductor, pianist. Born December 21, 1944, in Hollywood, California. Studied at University of Southern California and at Tanglewood. Assistant to Pierre Boulez during 1966 Bayreuth Festival and 1967 Ojai (California) Festival, and for several years led a youth orchestra in Los Angeles. In 1969, a few weeks after he became assistant conductor of the Boston Symphony, he made a dramatic, mid-concert substitution for William Steinberg, who was ill, and conducted more than thirty subsequent concerts in the months before Steinberg's recovery. Music director, Buffalo Philharmonic, 1971–79. Succeeded Leonard Bernstein as director of the New York Philharmonic's televised Young People's Concerts, 1972–77. Principal guest-conductor, Los Angeles Philharmonic, 1981–85. Principal conductor, London Symphony, 1988–92. Music director, San Francisco Symphony, from 1994. Noted for usually vivid performances of late-Romantic and 20th-century composers.

RECOMMENDED RECORDINGS Gershwin *Second Rhapsody* and other works (CBS). Orff *Carmina Burana* (CBS).

ALEXANDER TORADZE

(pronounced: toh-*rahd*-zee)

Pianist. Born May 30, 1952, in Tbilisi, U.S.S.R. Studied at Tbilisi and Moscow conservatories. Debut at age nine with Tbilisi Symphony. Winner of a Soviet piano competition, 1969; Terni Competition, Italy, 1975; Van Cliburn International Competition, 1977. Emigrated to U.S. in 1983, now lives in New York. An individualistic, sensitive yet strongly dramatic pianist, at his best with late 19th-century and early 20th-century Russian music.

RECOMMENDED RECORDING Prokofiev Sonata No. 7, Ravel *Miroirs*, and Stravinsky *Three Scenes from Petrushka* (Angel).

ARTURO TOSCANINI

(pronounced: taw-skah-nee-nee)

Conductor. Born March 25, 1867, in Parma, Italy. Died January 16, 1957, in New York. Made a last-minute substitution for an ill conductor of a touring Italian opera company in Rio de Janeiro in 1886 — and remained a conductor ever after. Before World War I, active at Milan's La Scala and New York's Metropolitan Opera. From 1928 to 1936, music director of the New York Philharmonic. In 1937 the NBC Symphony was organized for him; he remained its conductor until retirement in 1954. For most of the first half of this century, the most famous and most widely respected conductor in the world. Noted for incisive, penetrating, exciting performances of Classical and Romantic works, especially Beethoven, Brahms, Wagner, Rossini, Verdi, Puccini, and Respighi.

RECOMMENDED RECORDINGS   Beethoven Symphony No. 9 (RCA Victrola). *Toscanini Conducts* — Rossini, Dukas, Brahms, Bizet, Smetana, Sousa (RCA).

TAMAS VASARY

(pronounced: vah-*shah*-ree)

Pianist, conductor. .Born April 11, 1933, in Hungary. Studied at Franz Liszt Academy in Budapest with Kodály and Hernandi. Winner of international competitions in Warsaw and Paris, 1955; Brussels, 1956; Rio de Janeiro, 1957. Left Hungary during 1956 revolution, settling in Switzerland. A series of 1961 concerts in London established his international reputation. An animated, poetic interpreter of 19th-century Romantic and early 20th-century music.

RECOMMENDED RECORDINGS   Chopin Liszt Sonata in B minor and *Reminiscences of Don Juan* (After Mozart) (Deutsche Grammophon). Chopin Piano Concerto No. 2 and group of Nocturnes, Waltzes, Mazurkas (Deutsche Grammophon).

BRUNO WALTER

(pronounced: *vahl*-tir)

Conductor. Born September 15, 1876, in Berlin, Germany. Died February 17, 1962, in Los Angeles, California. Started conducting at age 17 in Cologne;

at 20, joined Berlin Opera's conducting staff (under his real name: Bruno Schlesinger). Became friend and protege of Gustav Mahler. Director, Munich Opera, 1913–22. During 1920s, one of Germany's most eminent conductors. Left Germany in 1933 after Nazis banned his concerts as "a threat to public order" (because he was Jewish). Settled in the U.S. Musical advisor to New York Philharmonic, 1946–50 (after declining its music directorship because of age). Widely admired for his warm, supple, sometimes introspective, often profound interpretations of Classical and Romantic works, especially Mahler.

RECOMMENDED RECORDINGS   Mahler *The Song of the Earth*, with Ferrier (London). Bruckner Symphony No. 9 (CBS).

ANDRÉ WATTS

Pianist. Born June 20, 1946, in Nürnberg, Germany, of an American G.I. father and a Hungarian mother living in Germany as a displaced person after World War II. Made debut in 1955 at a Philadelphia Orchestra children's concert. After further studies, made a highly acclaimed, last-minute substitution for Glenn Gould (who was ill) at a New York Philharmonic concert under Bernstein in 1963. One of the most popular of today's American pianists — much admired for the extroverted brilliance of his technique and the probing qualities of his interpretations, particularly with Liszt, Brahms and other 19th-century composers.

RECOMMENDED RECORDINGS   Liszt Piano Concerto No. 1 and Chopin Piano Concerto No. 2 (CBS). Liszt Piano Music (including *Un Sospiro, Transcendental Etude* No. 10, Sonata in B-minor.

ALEXIS WEISSENBERG

(pronounced: *vy*-sehn-berg)

Pianist. Born July 26, 1929, in Sofia, Bulgaria. As a teenager, spent nine months in a concentration camp following Nazi takeover of Bulgaria, escaping in 1944 to Turkey and then coming to U.S. Studied at Juilliard School in New York. Won Leventritt Award and made a much-acclaimed concert debut with the New York Philharmonic under Szell in 1947. During the early 1950s, settled in Paris, where he still lives. One of the most popular pianists of his generation, widely admired for his broadly perceptive performances, and for an incredibly fast, clean finger stroke that gives him a distinctive sound.

RECOMMENDED RECORDINGS Rachmaninoff Preludes (RCA). Ravel Piano Concerto in G and Prokofiev Third Piano Concerto (Angel).

EARL WILD

Pianist. Born November 26, 1918, in Pittsburgh, Pennsylvania. As a teenager, was engaged by Toscanini to play Gershwin's *Rhapsody in Blue* with NBC Symphony. For many years in the 1940s, house pianist at NBC in New York, participating in many radio and television shows. In the 1960s, in the forefront of the revival of Romantic piano music, performing long-neglected works by Liszt, Scharwenka, Paderewski, others. Also the soloist for premieres of piano concertos by Paul Creston and Marvin David Levy. Noted for a fantastic technique, capable of enormous velocity and virtuosity. Also has composed ballet, orchestral music, and an Easter oratorio, *Revelations*.

RECOMMENDED RECORDINGS Liszt Hungarian Rhapsodies Nos. 2, 4, 12, Transcendental Etudes, and Sonata in B minor (Etcetera). Gershwin Concerto in F, *Rhapsody in Blue*, and *"I Got Rhythm" Variations* (RCA).

DAVID ZINMAN

Conductor. Born July 9, 1936, in New York City. Studied at Oberlin Conservatory and University of Minnesota. Assistant to Pierre Monteux, 1961–64. Conductor, Netherlands Chamber Orchestra, 1964–77. Music director, Rochester Philharmonic, 1974–1985. Principal conductor, Rotterdam Philharmonic, 1979–82. Music director, Baltimore Symphony, since 1985. A generally tasteful, thoughtful conductor of a wide repertory.

RECOMMENDED RECORDINGS Beethoven *Prometheus* ballet music (Vox). Rimsky-Korsakov *Coq d'Or* Suite and *Tsar Sultan* Suite (Philips).

PINCHAS ZUKERMAN

(pronounced: zoo-ker-mahn)

Violinist, violist, conductor. Born July 16, 1948, in Tel Aviv, Israel. At age 12, won scholarship from American-Israeli Foundation for special studies. Came to the U.S., on recommendation of Pablo Casals and Isaac Stern, to study at Juilliard. Won Leventritt International Competition, 1967. Substituted for Stern in a 1968–69 series of concerts in U.S. and Europe, and quickly became one of the most popular violinists of his generation. Highly regarded as a technically brilliant, interpretively expressive violinist with a natural feeling for the big sweeping line of a composition. Since mid-1970s, has combined solo career with conducting. Music director, South Bank Festival, London, 1978–80; Saint Paul Chamber Orchestra, 1980–87. Also sometimes performs as a violist.

RECOMMENDED RECORDINGS   Mendelssohn Violin Concerto (violinist and conductor) (Deutsche Grammophon). Berg Violin Concerto (CBS).

THE TOP ORCHESTRAS

The United States has more than half of the world's two thousand professional symphony orchestras—and nearly twice as many as all of Europe's nations combined. Yet numbers are one thing, quality another. And when a person buys a recording, he or she wants it played by "the best." So the great majority of recordings seem to be made by a few dozen major orchestras in both the U.S. and Europe—as they are the ones the record companies believe will sell. Which are the greatest orchestras? This is how the author sizes them up, listed alphabetically under each group.

THE TOP AMERICAN TEN AND OTHERS

BOSTON SYMPHONY ORCHESTRA   Music director, Seiji Ozawa. Former music directors include William Steinberg, Erich Leinsdorf, Charles Munch, Serge Koussevitzky, Pierre Monteux. The members of the BSO, minus so-called "first desk" players, also make up the *Boston Pops Orchestra*, which plays a Spring Series each May and June and selected additional dates throughout the year. Arthur Fiedler conducted the Boston Pops from 1930 until his death in 1979, John Williams from 1980 to 1993. The BSO is also the resident orchestra of the annual summer Berkshire Music Festival at Tanglewood in western Massachusetts.

CHICAGO SYMPHONY ORCHESTRA   Music director, Daniel Barenboim. Former music directors include Sir Georg Solti, Fritz Reiner, Jean Martinon, Rafael Kubelik, Artur Rodzinski, Frederick Stock. The members of the CSO also play for a summer series in Chicago's Ravinia Park. Present music director for Ravinia: James Levine.

CLEVELAND ORCHESTRA   Music director, Christoph von Dohnanyi. Former music directors include Lorin Maazel, George Szell, Erich Leinsdorf, Artur Rodzinski. Since 1992 Leonard Slatkin has been director of the orchestra's annual summer Blossom Music Festival in Cuyahoga Falls, Ohio.

LOS ANGELES PHILHARMONIC ORCHESTRA Music director, Esa-Pekka Salonen. Former music directors include Andre Previn, Zubin Metha, Alfred Wallenstein, Arthur Rodzinski, Otto Klemperer.

MINNESOTA ORCHESTRA Music director, Eiji Oue. Former music directors include Edo de Waart, Stanislaw Skrowaczewski, Antal Dorati, Dimitri Mitropoulos, Eugene Ormandy. Known as the Minneapolis Symphony Orchestra until 1968, when its name was changed to reflect broader base of its support and activities. Orchestra members also play in a Sommerfest in Minneapolis each summer.

NEW YORK PHILHARMONIC ORCHESTRA Music director, Kurt Masur. Former music directors include Zubin Mehta, Pierre Boulez, Leonard Bernstein, Dimitri Mitropoulos, Arthur Rodzinski, John Barbirolli, Arturo Toscanini, Gustav Mahler. The first American orchestra to broadcast nationwide on a weekly basis, beginning in 1930 (with an Erich Kleiber concert).

PHILADELPHIA ORCHESTRA Music director, Wolfgang Sawallisch. Former music directors (since 1912) include only Riccardo Muti, Eugene Ormandy and Leopold Stokowski. The orchestra is resident at the Saratoga Festival in Saratoga Springs, New York, for the month of August. Music director for Saratoga concerts: Charles Dutoit.

PITTSBURGH SYMPHONY ORCHESTRA Artistic director, Lorin Maazel, through 1996. Former music directors include Andre Previn, William Steinberg, Fritz Reiner.

SAINT LOUIS SYMPHONY ORCHESTRA Music director, Leonard Slatkin, through 1995. Former music directors include Walter Susskind, Georgy Semkov, Vladimir Golschmann.

SAN FRANCISCO SYMPHONY ORCHESTRA Music director, Michael Tilson Thomas, from 1994. Former music directors include Herbert Blomstedt, Edo de Waart, Seiji Ozawa, Josef Krips, Enrique Jorda, Pierre Monteux.

Also ranking with the top U.S. ten are two Canadian orchestras:

MONTREAL SYMPHONY ORCHESTRA (Orchestre Symphonique de Montreal) Music director, Charles Dutoit. Former music directors include Zubin Metha, Wilfred Pelletier.

TORONTO SYMPHONY ORCHESTRA Former music directors include Gunther Herbig, Andrew Davis, Seiji Ozawa, Karel Ancerl, Sir Ernest MacMillan.

There are, of course, many other good orchestras throughout the U.S. which also make recordings. Among them:

AMERICAN COMPOSERS ORCHESTRA Music director, Dennis Russell Davies. Headquartered in New York.

AMERICAN SYMPHONY ORCHESTRA Music director, Leon Botstein, since 1992. Former music directors include Catherine Comet, Kazuyoshi Akiyama, and founder Leopold Stokowski. Headquartered in New York.

ATLANTA SYMPHONY ORCHESTRA Music director, Yoel Levi. Former music directors include Robert Shaw.

BALTIMORE SYMPHONY ORCHESTRA Music director, David Zinman. Former music directors include Sergiu Comissiona, Brian Priestman.

BUFFALO PHILHARMONIC ORCHESTRA Music director, Maximiano Valdes. Former music directors include Semyon Bychkov, Michael Tilson Thomas, Julius Rudel, Josef Krips, William Steinberg.

CINCINNATI SYMPHONY ORCHESTRA Music director, Jesús López-Cobos. Former music directors include Michael Gielen, Max Rudolf, Thomas Schippers, Thor Johnson.

DALLAS SYMPHONY ORCHESTRA Music director, Andrew Litton. Former music directors include Eduardo Mata, Donald Johanos.

DETROIT SYMPHONY ORCHESTRA Music director, Neeme Jarvi. Former music directors include Gunther Herbig, Antal Dorati, Gary Bertini.

HOLLYWOOD BOWL SYMPHONY ORCHESTRA Music director, John Mauceri. Founded 1991.

HOUSTON SYMPHONY ORCHESTRA Music director, Christoph Eschenbach. Former music directors include Sergiu Comissiona, Lawrence Foster, Andre Previn, Leopold Stokowski, Sir John Barbirolli.

INDIANAPOLIS SYMPHONY ORCHESTRA Music director, Raymond Leppard. Former music directors include John Nelson, Izler Solomon.

LOUISVILLE ORCHESTRA Music director, Lawrence Leighton Smith. Former music directors include Jorge Mester, Robert Whitney.

MILWAUKEE SYMPHONY ORCHESTRA Music director, Zdenek Macal. Former music directors include Lukas Foss, Kenneth Schermerhorn.

NATIONAL SYMPHONY ORCHESTRA Music director, Leonard Slatkin. Former music directors include Mstislav Rostropovich, Antal Dorati, Howard Mitchell. Headquartered in Washington, D.C.

NEW JERSEY SYMPHONY ORCHESTRA Music director, Zdenek Macal. Former directors include Hugh Woolf, Henry Lewis.

NEW WORLD SYMPHONY ORCHESTRA Music director, Michael Tilson Thomas. Miami Beach–based orchestra for young professionals.

ROCHESTER PHILHARMONIC ORCHESTRA Music director, Mark Elder. Former music directors include David Zinman, Theodore Bloomfield, Erich Leinsdorf, Leonard Bernstein, Jose Iturbi.

SAINT PAUL CHAMBER ORCHESTRA Music director Hugh Woolf. Former music directors include Christopher Hogwood, Pinchas Zukerman, Dennis Russell Davies.

SEATTLE SYMPHONY ORCHESTRA Music director, Gerard Schwarz. Former music directors include Milton Katims.

UTAH SYMPHONY ORCHESTRA Music director, Joseph Silverstein. Former longtime music director, Maurice Abravanel.

THE TOP EUROPEAN TEN AND OTHERS

AMSTERDAM CONCERTGEBOUW ORCHESTRA Music director, Riccardo Chailly. Former music directors include Bernard Haitink, Eduard van Beinum, Willem Mengelberg. (*Concertgebouw* means Concert House in Dutch.)

BAVARIAN RADIO SYMPHONY (MUNICH) (Bayerische Rundfunk) Music director, Lorin Maazel. Former music directors include Sir Colin Davis, Rafael Kubelik, George Solti.

BERLIN PHILHARMONIC ORCHESTRA Music director, Claudio Abbado. Former music directors include Herbert von Karajan, Wilhelm Furtwangler, Arthur Nikisch. Headquartered in former West Berlin.

CZECH PHILHARMONIC ORCHESTRA Principal conductor, Gerd Albrecht. Former music directors include Jiri Belohlavek, Vaclav Neumann, Karel Ancerl, Rafael Kubelik, Vaclav Talich. Headquartered in Prague.

PHILHARMONIA ORCHESTRA (LONDON) Music director, Giuseppe Sinopoli. Former music directors or principal conductors include Riccardo Muti, Otto Klemperer, Herbert von Karajan. For a brief period in the 1960s following a reorganization was known on recordings as the New Philharmonia.

LONDON PHILHARMONIC ORCHESTRA Music director, Franz Welser-Möst. Former music directors include Klaus Tennstedt, Bernard Haitink, Sir Georg Solti, Sir Adrian Boult, and founder Sir Thomas Beecham.

LONDON SYMPHONY ORCHESTRA Principal conductor, Sir Colin Davis. Former principal conductors include Michael Tilson Thomas, Claudio Abbado, André Previn, Istvan Kertesz, Pierre Monteux, Josef Krips.

ORCHESTRE DE PARIS Music director, Semyon Bychkov. Former music directors or principal conductors include Daniel Barenboim, Sir George Solti, Herbert von Karajan, Charles Munch.

ST. PETERSBURG PHILHARMONIC (formerly Leningrad Philharmonic) Music director, Yuri Temirkhanov. Former music directors or principal conductors include Mariss Jansons, Yevgeny Mravinsky, Kurt Sanderling.

VIENNA PHILHARMONIC ORCHESTRA Principal conductor, Riccardo Muti. Former principal conductors include Claudio Abbado, Lorin Maazel, Herbert von Karajan, Karl Bohm, Felix Weingartner, Bruno Walter.

Among the many other leading European orchestras which can also be found on recordings are:

ACADEMY OF ST. MARTIN-IN-THE-FIELDS (LONDON) Music director, Iona Brown. Founded by Neville Marriner.

BBC SYMPHONY ORCHESTRA (LONDON) Music director, Andrew Davis. Former music directors include Pierre Boulez, Malcolm Sargent.

BERLIN SYMPHONY ORCHESTRA Principal conductor, Claus Peter Flor. Former music directors include Gunther Herbig, Kurt Sanderling. Formerly the principal orchestra of East Berlin.

BERLIN RADIO SYMPHONY ORCHESTRA Music director, Vladimir Ashkenazy. Former directors include Riccardo Chailly, Lorin Maazel, Ferenc Fricsay. Originally RIAS Symphony Orchestra (Radio in the American Sector).

CITY OF BIRMINGHAM SYMPHONY ORCHESTRA (England) Music director, Simon Rattle. Former principal conductor, Louis Fremaux.

DANISH NATIONAL RADIO ORCHESTRA (COPENHAGEN) Music director, Leif Segerstam. Former music directors include Erik Tuxen.

DRESDEN STAATSKAPELLE ORCHESTRA Music director, Giuseppe Sinopoli. Former directors include Hans Vonk, Herbert Blomstedt, Rudolf Kempe, Karl Bohm, Fritz Busch, Fritz Reiner. (Once known as Saxon State Orchestra).

HALLE ORCHESTRA (MANCHESTER) Artistic director, Kent Nagano. Former directors include Stanislaw Skrowaczewski, Sir John Barbirolli.

LEIPZIG GEWANDHAUS ORCHESTRA Music director, Kurt Masur. Former directors include Franz Konwitschny, Felix Mendelssohn.

MOSCOW STATE SYMPHONY ORCHESTRA Principal conductor, Yevgeny Svetlanov. Former principal conductors include Kiril Kondrashin.

ORCHESTRE DE LA SUISSE ROMANDE (GENEVA) Music director, Armin Jordan. Former music directors include Wolfgang Sawallisch, Horst Stein, Paul Kletski, and founder Ernest Ansermet (for 49 years).

ORCHESTRE NATIONAL DE FRANCE Music director, Charles Dutoit. Former music directors include Lorin Maazel, Jean Martinon, Charles Munch.

ORQUESTRA NACIONAL DE ESPANA (MADRID) (Spanish National Orchestra) Principal conductor, Aldo Ceccato. Former principal conductors include Rafael Fruhbeck de Burgos, Jesus Lopez-Cobos, Ataulfo Argenta.

ROTTERDAM PHILHARMONIC ORCHESTRA Music director, Jeffrey Tate. Former music directors include James Conlon, Edo de Waart.

ROYAL PHILHARMONIC ORCHESTRA (LONDON) Music director, Vladimir Ashkenazy. Former music directors include André Previn, Lawrence Foster, Rudolf Kempe, founder Sir Thomas Beecham.

STOCKHOLM PHILHARMONIC ORCHESTRA Principal conductor, Gennady Rozhdestvensky. Former directors include Hans Schmidt-Isserstedt.

WARSAW PHILHARMONIC ORCHESTRA Music director, Kazimierz Kord. Former directors include Witold Rowicki, Stanislaw Skrowaczewski.

ZURICH TONHALLE ORCHESTRA Music director, Claus Peter Flor. Former music directors include Christoph Eschenbach, Paul Sacher.

Outside of Europe, there are other world-class orchestras whose recordings are also available in the U.S. Among them:

ISRAEL PHILHARMONIC ORCHESTRA Music director, Zubin Mehta. Founded by William Steinberg, Arturo Toscanini, and Bronislav Huberman as the Palestine Symphony Orchestra in 1936. Headquartered in Tel Aviv.

SYDNEY SYMPHONY ORCHESTRA (AUSTRALIA) Principal conductor, Stuart Challender. Former music directors include Sir Charles Mackerras, Louis Fremaux, Nicolai Malko, Eugene Goosens.

GLOSSARY

absolute music Usually instrumental music which is free from extra-musical implications, in distinction from *program music*.

abstract music Same as absolute music.

a cappella (Italian) Choral music performed without instrumental accompaniment.

accelerando (Italian) A speeding up of the tempo.

accompaniment The musical background, especially for a soloist. For example, a solo singer or instrumentalist may be accompanied by a pianist or orchestra. However, in piano music the left hand often plays chords which provide an accompaniment to the principal melody being played by the right hand.

acoustic In audio usage, a musical instrument whose sound is not electronically produced or reproduced.

adagietto (Italian) A tempo slightly faster than *adagio*. Also a brief *adagio*.

adagio (Italian) A slow and easy tempo, between *andante* and *largo*. In most traditional symphonies and sonatas, it is the second movement.

agitato (Italian) Agitated, restless, excited.

air In Baroque music, a song or movement of an essentially melodic character, in contrast to the dancelike style of other movements.

allegretto (Italian) A moderately lively tempo between *allegro* and *andante*.

allegro (Italian) A fast tempo, but not as fast as *presto*.

analog The pre-digital method of recording sound in the form of a continuous electrical signal.

andante (Italian) Usually considered a moderately slow tempo. Literally, the word means "walking" or "going" at a moderate speed. Some composers (including Brahms) have interpreted the word, however, as meaning considerably faster than *adagio* but not so fast as *allegretto*.

aria (Italian) An elaborate song for voice (usually solo voice). In opera, arias are frequently designed to show off the virtuosity of a singer.

arrangement The adaptation of a piece of music into a form or medium different from the one for which it was originally written. See also *transcription*.

assai (Italian) Very. For example, *allegro assai* means very fast.

atonal Music in which a tonal center or key is purposely avoided. Usually used in connection with a certain type of 20th-century music originating with Schoenberg, although he objected to the term and preferred to call his music *pan-tonal*.

ballad   A narrative song, usually telling of a romantic or adventurous occurrence.

ballade   (French) An instrumental work based on a specific or implied narrative. As used by Chopin, Brahms, and some others, a dramatic piano piece. Although the word is strictly the French word for *ballad*, the word *ballad* is commonly used in English only for a vocal work whereas *ballade* is used for an instrumental piece of the same type.

band   On recorded discs, a section of the record separated from other sections. In popular music an instrumental combo of ten or more players is called a band. An orchestra without strings is also called a band.

baritone   (Greek) Literally, low sound. A male voice between *tenor* and *bass*.

Baroque   In music, the period from about 1600 to 1750. Usually it is used to describe elegantly controlled yet twistingly fashioned music, with an interplay of formal structure and more spontaneous, virtuoso flights of fancy (as in the free *cadenza* of an aria, or the embellished repeats of an instrumental movement).

bass   The lowest male voice. Also the colloquial name for the *double bass*, largest of an orchestra's string instruments.

baton   (French) The thin, white stick used by a conductor in leading an orchestra or instrumental ensemble.

bel canto   (Italian) Literally, beautiful song. An Italian vocal style developed during the 18th century, characterized by beauty of sound and the ease and brilliance of performance rather than by dramatic or emotional expression.

bitonal   The simultaneous use of two different keys in a musical work.

blues   A style of vocal and instrumental jazz, deriving from Negro American work songs and *spirituals* of the early 20th century. Usually (but not always) slow and basically sad in mood. The name is related to the so-called blue notes of the piece which are either deliberately flatted or played out of tune.

bravo   (Italian) A term used to express approval of a musical performance. When the performer is female, the feminine form *brava* is usually used.

bravura   (Italian) A florid, brilliant style.

brio   (Italian) Spirit, dash.

buffa, buffo   (Italian) Comic. Usually used to refer to a comic character (most often sung by a bass) in Italian opera. *Opera buffa* is a comic opera.

cacophony   A discordant mixture of different sounds.

cadenza   (Italian) A solo vocal or instrumental section of a piece, usually intended to display the soloist's technical mastery. Originally, cadenzas were improvised by the performer. But in the 19th century it became customary for the composer to write out the cadenza and make it an integral part of the style of the piece.

cantata (Italian) An extended choral work, with or without solo parts, and usually with orchestral accompaniment. The *Baroque* cantata normally consisted of a number of movements and included *arias, recitatives, duets*, and *choruses*.

cappella See *a cappella*.

capriccio (Italian) A composition of a basically capricious or amusing character.

cavatina (Italian) A simple or short solo song, lacking the elaborate form or development found in an *aria*. Usually found in 18th- or 19th-century oratorios or operas.

chamber music Instrumental music in which there is usually only one player for each instrumental part, in contrast to orchestral music in which many players play the same instrumental part. A *chamber orchestra* normally consists of about 25 members, in contrast to the 80 or more players of a symphony orchestra.

choral Relating to a chorus or choir.

chord The simultaneous sounding of three or more notes or tones.

chorus Usually a large group of singers. Also the colloquial term for the *refrain* of a popular song.

chromatic (from the Greek *chroma*, color) In music, a style identified with some 20th-century composers, and involving the use of half tones and notes outside the normal degrees of the traditional scale. However, use of the term goes back to *Baroque* music, where it involved the use of altered chords to produce "color modification" in a piece.

Classical In everyday usage, the term usually means most music outside the fields of popular music or jazz. Among musicians, however, it is more strictly applied to music written in the 18th century, especially by the Viennese Classicists (Haydn, Mozart, and early Beethoven), and marked by a compactness of form and emotional restraint (in contrast to the Romanticism of the 19th century).

clavichord The earliest type of stringed keyboard instrument, originating in the 13th century and commonly used until the 18th as a solo instrument. The sound of the clavichord was very soft and delicate, in contrast to the sharper sound of the harpsichord and the more brilliant sound of later pianos.

clavier The keyboard of a harpsichord, clavichord, or piano.

coda A section or passage at the end of a composition, usually falling outside the basic structure of the composition, designed to heighten the feeling of finality.

coloratura Usually applied to a light, agile, florid style of singing.

Concertgebouw (Dutch) Literally, concert hall. Most commonly known as the name of an Amsterdam concert hall opened in 1888, and of its world-famous resident orchestra.

concertmaster The first violinist of an orchestra. In England, he is called the *leader*.

concerto Usually a piece for a solo instrument accompanied by an orchestra.

concerto grosso A type of work popular in the 17th and 18th centuries, usually (but not always) marked by an interplay between a large group of instruments and a smaller group.

counterpoint The combination of two or more melodies sounding simultaneously and in a specific relationship to each other.

countertenor An adult male voice higher than a tenor.

coupling On a disc or cassette, a selection that is included in addition to the principal work, usually on the other side of the disc or cassette if the principal work fills just one side.

crescendo (Italian) Increasing in loudness.

decibel A unit for measuring the loudness of sounds.

digital In audio terms, sound that is represented by computer digits.

diminuendo (Italian) Diminishing or decreasing in loudness.

divertimento (Italian) A work for a small instrumental group combining features of a suite and symphony, popular in Haydn's and Mozart's time.

dodecaphonic (from the Greek *dodeka*, twelve) The 12-tone technique of composition.

double bass The largest of the string instruments of the orchestra. Also sometimes called the bass viol.

duet A vocal or instrumental composition for two performers.

dynamic range In audio, the difference (in sound decibels) between the quietest and the loudest recorded signal levels that a recording or a piece of audio equipment can produce or reproduce.

exposition The initial presentation of thematic material in a composition, particularly in a *sonata* or *symphony*.

Expressionism A term applied to a certain type of musical composition of the early 20th century, particularly by German and Austrian composers. Like *Impressionism*, it took its name from the graphic arts and represented a reaction against the refined Impressionistic style. Instead, Expressionism was marked by fervent emotionalism and self-expression.

fioritura The embellishment of a melody, particularly in vocal music of the 17th and 18th centuries.

forte (Italian) Loud.

fortissimo (Italian) Very loud.

fugue (from the Latin *fuga*, flight) A type of composition in which a theme (subject) is stated at the beginning in one voice part, and then is imitated by other voices in close succession according to strict compositional rules.

Gregorian chant The liturgical music (plainsong) of the Roman Catholic Church, named after Pope Gregory I (590–604).

harpsichord The most common type of stringed keyboard instrument of the 16th to 18th centuries, similar in shape to a piano but less brilliant and varied in sound.

heldentenor (German) A male tenor voice of great strength and brilliance, appropriate for the heroic roles of Wagnerian opera.

Impressionism A term applied to a certain type of musical composition of the early 20th century, represented mainly by French composers (especially Debussy). It took its name from the graphic arts, particularly the paintings of Monet, Manet, and Renoir, and represented a reaction against 19th-century Romanticism. Musically, it is a style that hints and implies rather than explicitly describing.

improvisation The spontaneous creation of music while performing, rather than playing a composition already written.

key The classification of the notes of the musical scale. Also, in tonal music, the main note or tonal center of a composition.

ländler A triple-time folk dance common in 19th-century Austria. Used often by Mahler.

largo (Italian) Very slow. Slower than *adagio*. A *larghetto* is slightly faster than largo.

leader In British usage, the equivalent of *concertmaster* of an orchestra.

leitmotiv (German) In Wagnerian opera, a short theme identified with a specific character, place, object, or situation throughout the opera.

libretto (Italian) The text of an opera or oratorio.

lied, lieder (German) A form of German art song, particularly the 19th century songs of Schubert, Schumann, Brahms, Strauss, etc.

madrigal A type of vocal composition prevalent in the 16th century, of Italian origin but also popular in England, and secular in content.

maestro (Italian) Literally, master. An unofficial name used for the most distinguished and most respected conductors, composers, and music teachers.

major, minor Terms used for the two basic scales of music.

Mass The principal service of the Roman Catholic Church. In music, the musical setting of that service.

mastering In recording, the step in the recording production in which the final, edited stereo "mix" is converted to the proper format for manufacturing.

mazurka A Polish dance of moderate speed.

melody A succession of musical notes forming a line of expressive significance.

meter The basic grouping of beats and accents in a musical composition or section of a composition. Sometimes called *time*. For example, the meter (or time) of a piece may be ¾, ¼, ⅜, ⅝, etc., indicating the number of beats in each measure or time signature.

mezzo soprano (from the Italian *mezzo*, half) A type of female voice halfway between soprano and contralto.

microtone A fractional tone, used by some 20th-century composers.

minimalism A style of contemporary music that emphasizes the repetition of rhythmic pulses or musical patterns, often in steady, undulating phrases that pass through different regions of colors and moods. Sometimes also called neo-primitivist.

minor See *major*.

moderato (Italian) At a moderate speed. For example, *allegro moderato* is somewhat less fast than *allegro*.

modulation The change of *key* within a composition.

monaural Commonly used to describe the type of record or tape in which a single sound signal is printed on the record or tape to be reproduced through the sound system, in contrast to a *stereophonic* or *quadrasonic* recording. Nicknamed *mono*.

monophonic The oldest type of music, basically music of a single melodic line without accompanying chords. In recent years, the term has also been used to describe phonograph systems made before the 1950s, in which a single sound signal reproduces the music (in contrast to a *stereophonic* system).

movement The term for the single pieces which make up a composite musical work such as a *symphony, concerto*, or *sonata*.

mute A device used for softening the sound of a musical instrument.

nationalism In music, the movement of the 19th century which emphasized the development of strong national elements (especially folk elements) in composition, or the use of national history or legends in operas, songs, etc.

Neo-Classical A type of music written in the 20th century in reaction against Romanticism. It is basically characterized by an emphasis on musical forms derived from the pre-Romantic period, but is frequently more rhythmically and harmonically complex.

New Age A contemporary style of music that combines electronic and/or acoustic instrumental sounds, most often in a way that is conducive to relaxation and meditation, and which often concerns itself with ecology and mysticism. Its name derives from the astrological premise that Earth is entering a new age of worldwide peace and harmony.

nocturne A type of piece of lyrical mood, designed to reflect the feelings of night. First used by Irish composer John Field (1782–1837), but most closely identified with works of that name by Chopin.

nonet A composition for nine instruments or nine voices.

note A musical sound of a specific pitch and duration.

note-cluster A group of adjacent notes played or sounded together, used in some 20th-century compositions, particularly by Ives.

obbligato (Italian) Literally, a part that is obligatory and cannot be omitted in the performance of a piece. However, the term has somehow come to mean just the opposite in everyday usage — in other words, it usually refers to an optional part, *not* an obligatory one.

octave The range of musical sounds divided into eight (octo in Latin) steps. Notes that are an octave apart from each other have the same letter-names.

octet A composition for eight instruments or voices.

Ondes Martenot (French) An electronic keyboard instrument invented in 1928 by Maurice Martenot, and used in compositions by Messiaen, Honegger, Jolivet, and some other contemporary composers.

opera A type of play or drama in which all or most of the characters sing to the accompaniment of an orchestra.

opus (Latin) A term used to signify the compositional number of a work by a composer. Usually abbreviated *op*.

oratorio A type of musical composition for solo voices, chorus, and orchestra, usually based on a religious text and performed on a concert stage without costumes or scenery.

orchestra A large body of instrumentalists. The modern symphony orchestra consists of 80 to 100 players, divided into four basic sections: strings, winds, brass, and percussion. Chamber orchestras usually consist of about 25 players.

orchestration The writing or scoring of a work for orchestra.

overture Instrumental music composed as an introduction to an opera, oratorio, or other work.

pan-tonal See *atonal*.

paraphrase In music, a free modification or adaptation of a composition, as in Liszt's paraphrases for piano of music from Wagner's operas.

partita A type of *suite*, particularly of the 18th century.

passacaglia A type of composition (originally a dance) involving continuous variations of a short theme, particularly in Baroque music.

Passion A musical setting of the story of the Crucifixion as told by St. Matthew, St. Mark, St. Luke, or St. John.

percussion The collective name for those instruments whose sound is made by having a resonating surface struck by the player. Examples: drums, xylophone, triangle, tambourine.

pianissimo (Italian) Very soft.

piano (Italian) Soft. Also commonly used instead of *pianforte*, the correct name for the popular keyboard instrument first built in the early 18th century and which eventually displaced the harpsichord.

pizzicato (Italian) The plucking of the strings of an instrument rather than bowing them.

plainchant or **plainsong** A type of early church music consisting of a single vocal line, usually without accompaniment. See also *Gregorian chant*.

poco   (Latin) Slightly. For example, *poco adagio* means slightly slow.

polka   A dance in quick meter originating in Bohemia (not Poland, as commonly misunderstood).

polonaise   A stately Polish dance dating from the 16th century.

polyphonic   Literally, the simultaneous sounding of different notes. Music is considered polyphonic if it consists of two or more parts having individual melodic significance. Accordingly, in general usage, music is considered polyphonic if it has *counterpoint*.

polyrhythm   The simultaneous use of different rhythms in a passage or piece.

polytonality   The simultaneous sounding of different tonalities or keys in a passage or piece. Where only two keys are used simultaneously, the correct term is *bitonal*; much of the 20th-century music that is called polytonal is really bitonal.

postlude   A piece played at the conclusion of a church service or program. The opposite of *prelude*, but much less commonly used.

potpourri   (French) A loosely strung together collection of pieces with little formal relationship between them. In general usage, it refers to a collection of light, entertaining pieces.

prelude   Literally, a piece preceding something—as the prelude (or introduction) to an opera.

presto   (Italian) Very fast. A variation, *prestissimo*, means as fast as possible.

prima donna   (Italian) Originally, the singer of the leading female role in 18th-century Italian opera. In general usage, it also means any leading female opera star.

Prix de Rome   (French) A famous prize awarded annually by the French Academy of Fine Arts (of Paris) on the basis of a music competition. The prize entitles the winner to study in Rome. Among the winners have been Berlioz (1830), Bizet (1857), and Debussy (1884).

program music   A piece of music interpreting a specific story or extramusical idea. The *program* may be based on literature (example: Liszt's *Faust Symphony*), on history (Tchaikovsky's *1812 Overture*), or the composer's own imagination (Berlioz's *Symphonie Fantastique*).

progressive tonality   The beginning of a movement in one key and moving it systematically to an ending in another key, particularly as used by Mahler.

quadrasonic   The term used to describe the four-channel system of sound reproduction (in contrast to *monaural* or *stereophonic*) developed in the early 1970s. The system involves the use of four loudspeakers to "stretch" the sound in a 360-degree relationship around the listener.

quartet   A composition for four instruments or voices.

quasi   (Italian) Almost or approximating. For example, *allegro quasi presto* means "allegro almost presto."

quintet   A composition for five instruments or voices.

ragtime A type of early jazz of the late 19th and early 20th centuries, characterized by the constant syncopation ("ragging") of a tune.

recorder A type of reedless woodwind instrument much used from the 16th to 18th century.

recital A public performance by a soloist, in contrast to that given by an orchestra or ensemble which is called a concert.

recitative A type of speechlike singing, usually to a simple accompaniment, used for some narrative episodes in operas, oratorios, and cantatas.

refrain The part of a song that recurs at the end of each stanza, usually using the same words as well as the same tune.

Renaissance (French) The period of history roughly from 1400 to 1600, or between the Middle Ages and the Baroque period.

Requiem The mass for the dead in the Roman Catholic Church, which begins with the Latin words "Requiem aeternam dona eis, Domine" ("Give them eternal rest, O Lord").

rhapsody A musical work freely adapted from or inspired by an existing theme, as in Liszt's *Hungarian Rhapsodies* (freely based on Hungarian gypsy music), or a freely formed, improvisationlike work, as in Gershwin's *Rhapsody in Blue*.

rhythm The time value of a sequence of notes.

ripieno (Italian) In Baroque music, an indication for the full orchestra as distinct from the solo group (marked *concertino*).

ritardando (Italian) A gradual slackening of speed.

Romantic, Romanticism In common usage, the type of music developed in the 19th century characterized by the development of more emotional and subjective elements than the preceding *Classical* style.

rondo (Italian) A type of movement in a sonata or symphony, common in the time of Mozart and Beethoven, in which the principal theme recurs at least three times, with contrasting themes (called episodes) in between.

saraband A slow, stately dance originating in Spain in the 16th century.

scale A progression or succession of musical notes arranged in ascending or descending order, usually a whole tone or half tone apart.

scherzo (Italian, literally *joke*) A type of lively movement in a symphony, sonata, string quartet, etc., usually the third movement, sometimes humorous or playful in mood but not necessarily so.

score The printed manuscript of a musical work.

septet A composition for seven instruments or voices.

serial music A style of composition used by some 20th-century composers, originating with Schoenberg, in which the composition is based on a so-called series or tone-row in which the notes are placed in a particular order as the basis of the work, with no note repeated in the row. See also *dodecaphonic*.

sextet A composition for six instruments or voices.

---

signature   In music, a sign placed at the beginning of a piece indicating the *key* (key signature) and the *meter* (time signature).

sinfonietta   A short *symphony*, usually for a chamber orchestra.

solo   A piece or passage performed by one performer (soloist), with or without accompaniment. For example, in a *concerto* a soloist plays the solo part (for piano, violin, or other instrument) while the orchestra plays the accompaniment.

sonata   (Italian) A form of instrumental music, usually in three or four *movements*, following certain conventions of structure (called sonata form), and originating in the *Baroque* period. A *symphony* is a development of the sonata for orchestra.

song cycle   A group of songs connected by one general idea and designed to be performed as a unit.

soprano   (Italian for *upper*) The highest female voice. Sopranos are usually classified as dramatic, lyric, or *coloratura*, depending on tone quality and range. In children's choruses, a *boy soprano* is one with a high voice approximating the highest female voice.

spiritual   A type of religious folk song among black Americans.

sprechstimme   (German) A vocal line that is half sung, half spoken, particularly as used in some 20th-century works by Schoenberg, Berg, and others.

suite   A form of instrumental music, originating with the Baroque, involving a number of different movements based on dance rhythms and not written in *sonata* form. In modern usage, suites are most often excerpts from ballets or other stage music arranged for concert performance.

symphonic poem   A term introduced by Liszt to describe an orchestral work in which an extramusical idea (for example, a literary idea) provides the basis for the composition and the form of its development.

symphony   (From the Greek for *sounding together*) One of the major forms of orchestral music. Essentially a *sonata* for orchestra. Originally, a symphony was an overture to an opera. But since Haydn's time it has indicated a serious orchestral work of substantial length, usually with three or four contrasting movements. A *symphony orchestra* is an orchestra large enough (usually 80 or more members) to play major symphonies.

tempo   (Italian for *time*) The pace of a piece, or rate of speed at which it is to be played.

theme   A grouping of notes or musical subject which forms an important and often recurring element in a piece of music.

tone poem   A variation of *symphonic poem*.

tone row   See *serial music*.

track   On records and tapes, a continuous audio segment containing a complete section of the recorded material. On tape, the tracks are parallel; on disc, they are concentric.

transcription Essentially the same as an *arrangement*, but often with extensive changes of the original material.

trio A composition for three instruments or voices.

tune In common usage, a simple and easily remembered melody. Also a term referring to the singing or playing of a piece in the proper pitch, as "in tune" or "out of tune."

twelve-tone music See *dodecaphonic* and *serial music*.

variations A musical form in which a *theme* is presented and then altered and developed in a series of varied versions (variations).

verismo (Italian) A type of opera developed in Italy in the late 19th century, particularly by Puccini and Mascagni, with emphasis on realistic drama from everyday life, rather than on heroic, mythological, or romantic librettos.

vibrato In violin or string playing, the minute, rapid fluctuation of pitch produced by a kind of shaking motion on the part of the player's hand. In singing, the slight wavering of pitch sometimes cultivated by singers for dramatic effect, or sometimes caused by lack of full vocal control (in which case it is often deridingly termed a wobble).

virginal A type of 16th-century harpsichord, used mainly in England.

virtuoso Excelling in technical ability (when used with a performer) or in technical demands (when used with a piece of music).

vivace (Italian) Quick, lively.

zarzuela A type of Spanish opera, usually containing spoken dialogue as well as musical *arias*.

RECORDING COMPANIES
AND THEIR ADDRESSES

Angel, 810 Seventh Ave., New York, NY 10036.

Antilles/New Direction, c/o Island Records, 400 Lafayette St., New York, NY 10003.

Arabesque, 10 W. 37th St., New York, NY 10018.

Argo, c/o Polygram, 825 Eighth Ave., New York, NY 10019.

Audiofon, 44 West Flagler St., Miami, FL 33130.

BIS, c/o Qualiton, 24–02 40th Ave., Long Island City, NY 11101.

BMG Classics, 1540 Broadway, New York, NY 10036.

Book-of the-Month Records, BOMR Retail Division, 1225 S. Market St., Mechanicsburg, PA 17055.

Capitol, 1750 N. Vine St., Hollywood, CA 90028.

Capriccio, 2275 S. Carmelina Ave., Los Angeles, CA 90064.

Caprice, c/o Harmonia Mundi USA, 2037 Granville Ave., Los Angeles, CA 90025.

CBC Enterprises, Box 500, Station A, Toronto, Ontario M5W-1E6.

CBS (Sony Classical), 550 Madison Ave., New York, NY 10022.

Chalfont, c/o Varese/Sarabande, 13006 Saticoy St., N. Hollywood, CA 91605.

Chandos, c/o Koch International, 177 Cantiague Rock Rd., Westbury, NY 11590.

Composers Recording Inc. (CRI), 73 Spring St., New York, NY 10012.

Delos, 1032 N. Sycamore Ave., Hollywood, CA 90038.

Denon, 135 West 50th St., New York, NY 10020.

Deutsche Grammophon, 825 Eighth Ave., New York, NY 10019.

Discover International, P.O. Box 874, New York, NY 10023.

ECM, c/o Polygram, 810 Seventh Ave., New York, NY 10019.

Elektra, 75 Rockefeller Plaza, New York, NY 10019.

EMI/Angel, 1750 N. Vine St., Hollywood, CA 90028.

EMI/Pathé, c/o International Book & Record Distributors, 40–11 24th St., Long Island City, NY 11101.

Erato, c/o Elektra, 75 Rockefeller Plaza, New York, NY 10019.

Eurodisc, c/o BMG Records, 1540 Broadway, New York, NY 10036.

GRP, 555 West 57th St., New York, NY 10019.

Harmonia Mundi, 2037 Granville Ave., Los Angeles, CA 90025.

Hungaroton, 24–02 40th Ave., Long Island City, NY 10019.

In Sync, 2211 Broadway, New York, NY 10024.

Laser Light, 2275 S. Carmelina Ave., Los Angeles, CA 90064.

Living Music, P.O. Box 72, Litchfield, CT 06759.

London, 825 Eighth Ave., New York, NY 10019.

Louisville, c/o First Edition Records, 609 W. Main St., Louisville, KY 40202.

MCA, 70 Universal City Plaza, Universal City, CA 91608.

Melodiya, c/o Koch International, 177 Cantiague Rock Rd., Westbury, NY 11590.

Mobile Fidelity, 105 Morris St., Sebastopol, CA 95472.

Musicmasters, 1710 Highway 35, Ocean, NJ 07712.

Naxos, c/o PPI Entertainment Group, 88 St. Francis St., Newark, NJ 07105.

New World, 701 Seventh Ave., New York, NY 10036.

New York Philharmonic Radiothon, Avery Fisher Hall, Broadway at 65th St. New York, NY 10023.

Nimbus, P.O. Box 7746, Charlottesville, VA 22906.

Nonesuch, c/o Elektra, 75 Rockefeller Plaza, New York, NY 10019.

Pathé-Marconi, c/o International Book & Record Distributors, 40–11 24th St., Long Island City, NY 11101.

Philips, 825 Eighth Ave., New York, NY 10019.

Polygram Classics, 825 Eighth Ave., New York, NY 10019.

Pro Arte, c/o Intersound, 1180 Wills Rd., Roswell, GA 30077.

Qualiton, 24–02 40th Ave., Long Island City, NY 11101.

RCA/BMG Classics and *RCA/Victrola*, 1540 Broadway, New York, NY 10036.

Reference, Box 77225X, San Francisco, CA 94107.

Rizzoli, 31 W. 57th St., New York, NY 10019.

RPO, c/o Allegro Imports, 12630 NE Marx St., Portland, OR 97230.

Sony Classical, 550 Madison Ave., New York, NY 10022.

Supraphon, c/o Koch International, 177 Cantiague Rock Rd., Westbury, NY 11590.

Telarc, 23307 Commerce Park Rd., Beachwood, OH 44122.

Teldec, c/o Elektra, 75 Rockefeller Plaza, New York, NY 10019.

Turnabout, c/o Moss Music Group, c/o Essex Entertainment, 75 Essex St., Hackensack, NJ 07601.

Vanguard, c/o Omega Record Group, 27 W. 72nd St., New York, NY 10023.

Varese/Sarabande, 13006 Saticoy St., No. Hollywood, CA 91605.

Virgin Classics, c/o CEMA, 21700 Oxford St., Woodard Hills, CA 91367.

Vox Cum Laude, c/o Moss Music Group, c/o Essex Entertainment, 560 Sylvan Ave., Edgewood Cliffs, NJ 07632.

Wergo, c/o Harmonia Mundi USA, 2037 Granville Ave., Los Angeles, CA 90025.

INDEX

Performing Arts Books from Newmarket Press

AUDITIONING FOR THE MUSICAL THEATRE
How to Prepare to Get the Parts You Want
Fred Silver. Foreword by Charles Strouse.
Includes tips on acting a song, choosing material, handling a callback, selecting a vocal coach, and 130 audition songs for all types of situations. 200 pages. 5 1/2" x 8 1/4". Appendix. Index. $17.95, hardcover.

THE BLACKSTONE BOOK OF MAGIC & ILLUSION
Harry Blackstone. With Charles and Regina Reynolds.
Foreword by Ray Bradbury.
Examines the history, science, and art of illusion. Includes the Blackstone story, profiles of magic's greatest performers, instructions for 20 routines, the method behind 10 magic effects, listings of magic organizations, and more than 250 illustrations. 248 pages. 8 1/4" x 10 3/4". 250 illustrations. Appendices. Bibliography. Index. $16.95 paperback. $35.00, hardcover.

DISCOVERING GREAT JAZZ
A New Listener's Guide to the Sounds and Styles of the Top Musicians and Their Recordings on CDs, LPs, and Cassettes
Stephen M. Stroff
Describes eight distinctive periods of jazz history, discusses 125 musicians, and identifies the 60 most essential jazz albums. "This thought-provoking guide covers jazz from its 19th-century beginnings to its bop-revival present, with a glossary and specific recommendations." (*The Washington Post*) 192 pages. 6" x 9". 30 black-and-white photographs. Bibliography. Glossary. Index. Reference buying guides. $10.95, paperback. $19.95, hardcover.

DISCOVERING GREAT MUSIC
A New Listener's Guide to the Top Classical Composers and Their Masterworks—Second Edition
Roy Hemming
"The 75 best composers from Baroque to New Age and examples of their finest compositions...an excellent guide." (*ALA Booklist*) Includes a Who's Who of more than 150 recording artists and their best performances, a glossary of musical terms, and a listing of symphony orchestras. 336 pages. 6 1/8" x 9 1/4". Index. Glossary. $15.00, paperback.

DISCOVERING GREAT SINGERS OF CLASSIC POP
A New Listener's Guide to the Sounds and Lives of the Top Performers and Their Recordings, Movies, and Videos
Roy Hemming & David Hajdu
Fifty-two crooners are "written about with loving expertise by two writers who can make singers and their songs live on paper." (Clive Barnes) Features biographies, critical assessments, discographies, and videographies. 320 pages. 6" x 9". 38 photographs. Bibliography. Discography. Index. Videography. $14.95, paperback. $22.95, hardcover.

THE MELODY LINGERS ON
The Great Songwriters and Their Movie Musicals
Roy Hemming
Illustrated with 162 photos, the 16 songwriters include: Arlen, Berlin, Gershwin, Kern, Porter, Rodgers, Whiting, Nacio Brown, Carmichael, Loesser, Schwartz, Styne, and Van Heusen. Includes complete filmographies with listings of 800 movies and 200 songs. 400 pages. 8 1/4" x 10 3/4". 162 photographs. Bibliography. Discography. Filmography. Index. $16.95, paperback. $29.95, hardcover.

SHOPTALK
Conversations about Theater and Film with Twelve Writers, One Producer, and Tennessee Williams' Mother
Dennis Brown. Foreword by Kevin Kline.
Fourteen influential figures of stage and screen, collectively winners of 11 Pulitzer Prizes and 8 Academy Awards, discuss their successes and failures, and the pain behind both in these perceptive interviews. 224 pages. 5 1/2" x 8 1/4". 14 photographs. Index. $10.95, paperback. $19.95, hardcover.

Ask for these titles at your local bookstore or order today.
Send this coupon to: Newmarket Press, 18 East 48th St., NY, NY 10017.

Auditioning for the Musical Theatre
_____ $17.95 hc (0-937858-49-8)
Blackstone Book of Magic & Illusion
_____ $16.95 pb (1-55704-177-6)
_____ $35.00 hc (1-55704-182-2)
Discovering Great Jazz
_____ $10.95 pb (1-55704-169-5)
_____ $19.95 hc (1-55704-103-2)
Discovering Great Music
_____ $15.00 pb (1-55704-210-1)

Discovering Great Singers of Classic Pop
_____ $14.95 pb (1-55704-48-2)
_____ $22.95 hc (1-55704-072-9)
The Melody Lingers On
_____ $16.95 pb (1-55704-017-6)
_____ $29.95 hc (0-937858-57-9)
Shoptalk
_____ $10.95 pb (1-55704-70-9)
_____ $19.95 hc (1-55704-128-8)

For postage and handling, please add $2.50 for the first book, plus $1.00 for each additional book. For orders of five or more copies, please add 5% for shipping and handling. Prices and availability are subject to change.

I enclose a check or money order payable to Newmarket Press in the amount of $_____.

Name_____

Address_____

City/State/Zip_____

For discounts on orders of five or more copies, contact Newmarket Press, Special Sales Department, 18 East 48th Street, NY, NY 10017; Tel.: 212-832-3575 or 800-669-3903; Fax: 212-832-3629. DGM\BOB694.QXD